The Madness
OF KINGS

Personal Trauma and the Fate of Nations

The Madness
OF KINGS

Personal Trauma and the Fate of Nations

V I V I A N   G R E E N

St. Martin's Press • New York

First published in the United States of America in 1993

All rights reserved. For information write:
Scholarly and Reference Division,
St. Martin's Press Inc. 175 Fifth Avenue,
New York, NY 10010

ISBN 0–312–12043–5

Library of Congress Cataloging-in-Publication Data applied for

Jacket illustrations: front: detail from Nebuchadnezzar *by William Blake (Tate Gallery, London; photograph: The Bridgeman Art Library); back: above left: Henry VIII in later life, engraving by Cornelius Matsys (photograph: Bibliothèque Nationale, Paris); above right: Adolf Hitler at Berchtesgaden, Germany, 1937 (James Kyle); below: Richard II, painted by an unknown artist (photograph: Dean and Chapter of Westminster)*

Typeset in 10/14pt Times.
Typesetting and origination by
Alan Sutton Publishing Limited.
Printed and bound in Great Britain by
The Bath Press Ltd, Bath, Avon.

Contents

Preface

This book originated in a paper which I have given many times over past years to historical societies in Britain and America. It formed the basis of the inaugural lecture that I delivered as a visiting professor at the University of South Carolina in 1982. The paper sought to investigate the impact which health, and mental health in particular, made on personal and political history. Attention was focused in the main on kings and queens, but there was an underlying thesis that there is not merely a fundamental connection between health and politics but that political behaviour may be an externalization of private problems and personality disorders. The interest evoked by the paper was sufficient to make me think that it was worth trying to delve further into the subject.

What follows, if in some sense a pioneer study, is in the main more an informal discussion of the interaction of personality and the historical process rather than a clinical disquisition, for which I lack a specialized knowledge. It can only claim to be in part a work of original research, for it depends largely on a wide range of printed and secondary authorities to which, I hope, due credit has been given in the selective bibliographical notes. But the consequential argument is not without relevance for modern society.

In the course of teaching and writing over many years I have learned much from my colleagues and pupils. I must thank Dr Susan Wormell (Brigden) for reading the chapter on King Henry VIII, and Dr Christine Stevenson and Professor J. Schioldann-Nielsen for helping to unravel the medical history of King Christian VII of Denmark. I am especially grateful to Dr Anthony Storr for reading the first draft of the manuscript and for making many valuable suggestions, and to my friend William Scoular for his constructive and helpful criticisms.

Vivian H. Green
Burford, Oxon
1993

Introduction

For the majority of historians the forces which shape the moving stream of history, signified by the rise and fall of world civilizations, are largely economic and social, religious and political, in both character and content. In this historical process questions relating to health, whether of peoples or individuals, play a minimal part. But the more we investigate the past, the clearer it becomes that epidemics have significantly shaped the course of political, economic and social developments as well as the distribution of population, and that health, corporately and individually, has been an important and sometimes a determinant element in the making of history.[1]

It was, for instance, as the Book of Kings and the Greek historian Herodotus

A priest celebrating mass for plague victims, from an illuminated manuscript of the mid-fourteenth century (Bodleian MS Douce 313 f. 394v; The Bodleian Library, Oxford)

suggest, some form of plague that foiled the Assyrian king Sennacherib's invasion of Israel in the seventh century BC.[2] Then, at a critical moment in the Peloponnesian War, in 430–428 BC, as Thucydides described it, plague – whether typhus, smallpox, glanders, leptospirosis, tularaemia or some unknown disease remains uncertain[3] – struck Athens, causing devastating depopulation. Thucydides related that of some four thousand hoplites in the army which Hagnon led to Potidaea, one thousand and fifty died, a death rate of 26 per cent.[4] Bubonic plague was to decimate Byzantium in AD 542–3, delaying the emperor Justinian's plans for the reconquest of Italy,[5] and an epidemic of some sort, *pestis*, depopulated the British Isles in 664, jeopardizing the future of the infant Anglo-Saxon Christian Church.[6] The Black Death of 1348–9, bubonic in type, septicaemic or pneumonic in form, devastated Europe, reducing the population in some places by as much as a third, with grave social, political and economic consequences, causing, among other things, a labour shortage, a fall in landowners' revenues, some alleviation of the system of serfdom and a consequent social backlash. Until the late seventeenth century – the last outbreak in Europe occurred at Marseilles in 1720–1 – plague was an endemic and often an annual feature of city life, causing death and disruption, more especially in the warmth of summer.[7]

As malignant in its effects on the population, particularly from the sixteenth century onwards, was smallpox, which had a high mortality rate and struck equally at high and low until inoculation and vaccination became common.[8] The disease was historically significant because it was transmitted by the settlers in Central and South America and by slaves imported from West Africa to the indigenous and hitherto unexposed natives of the Spanish and Portuguese colonies with an appalling outcome, resulting in severe depopulation and the disruption of economic life.[9] In the nineteenth century cholera, of which there were some six major and two lesser epidemics between 1817 and 1902, swept through Europe causing great mortality.[10]

But such epidemics did not merely bring about depopulation and promote economic and social change. For contemporaries they formed a lesson in morality. The outbreaks of plague signified the wrath of God at work in the world of sinful men; they were a form of divine retribution for man's defiance of the divine and natural order. As a consequence there was, for instance, a powerful moral as well as social reaction to the spread of the skin disease, leprosy, so widespread in the Middle Ages.[11] The leper was treated as an outcast from society, obliged to live segregated from his fellow men and women in special lazar houses, to wear a special costume and to ring a bell, or shake a rattle or castanet to warn people of his approach. These precautions did not rest merely on the belief that leprosy was contagious, but on the supposition, rooted in scripture and Jewish tradition, that leprosy was a divine punishment for sin, contemporaries assuming that lepers were likely to be carnally minded men and women whose illness had been incurred as a result of sinful sexual incontinence.

In the sixteenth century there was a similar attitude to the spread of syphilis, which as a strain of treponematosis had probably been prevalent in the later Middle Ages but which became more especially virulent from the early sixteenth century onwards, supposedly believed to have been imported from the New World.[12] Syphilis was despatched 'into the world by the Disposition of Providence, either to restrain, as with a Bridle, the unruly Passions of a Sensual Appetite, or as a Scourge to correct the Gratification of them.'[13] In some quarters there has been an equally strong reaction to the spread of AIDS, the full significance of which for world history has yet to be registered;[14] 'nature in retribution', so Patrick Buchanan of the 'moral majority' judged it, 'God's will, the wages of sin, paying the piper'.

If physical disease can so dramatically and catastrophically affect the world's history, what of mental illness? Mental illness is not, of course, contagious or infectious. It is a rare but not wholly unknown phenomenon for groups of people to fall victim to mental or psychological disturbance. The medieval Flagellants who sought to placate the wrath of God by scourging themselves with leather thongs tipped

Scene of the Piazza Mercatello in Naples during the plague of 1656, from a painting by Micco Spadaro (Museo Nationale, Naples; photograph: The Wellcome Institute Library, London, © The Trustee of the Wellcome Trust, 1993)

Habit des Medecins, et autres personnes qui visitent les Pestiferés, Il est de marroquin de leuant, le masque a les yeux de cristal, et un long néz rempli de parfums

A doctor's costume for visiting plague victims (from *Traité de la Peste* by Maurice of Toulon-sur-mer; photograph: The Wellcome Institute Library, London, © The Trustee of the Wellcome Trust, 1993)

with iron spikes until the blood ran were conceivably mass victims of a religious frenzy which bordered on the psychotic and presented, at the very least, a case of mass hysteria.[15] Another similar medieval group suffered from the dancing mania. As men and women danced from place to place, they screamed, begging to be freed from the torments of the demons who beset them and the hallucinations which they endured. Contemporaries described them as mad, believing them to be possessed by the devil. More probably they were the victims of ergotism or ergot poisoning, caused by eating bread made from rye infected with a mould or fungus, ergot, which contains the clinical compound, lysergic acid or LSD, giving rise to manic hallucinations.[16] There was an outbreak of ergotism with similar mind-boggling delusions at Pont-Saint-Esprit in France in 1951.[17] Another example of mass psychological disturbance occurred in the 1930s among a Ugandan tribe, the Ik, who became, so it was reported, a 'group of cold, relatively isolated, selfish psychopaths' as a result of the stress they experienced after the land where they had habitually hunted animals was turned into a game reserve.[18] Some bizarre religious sects have been in the past, and still are, prone to what can only be described as a corporate psychological disorder,[19] sometimes with disastrous social effects, as the mass suicide of some 900 members of the small religious sect The Temple of the People at Jonestown in Guyana in 1978, and what happened to David Koresh and his followers of the Branch Davidian Sect at Waco in Texas in 1993 demonstrate.

The scope of this study is narrower: to examine past rulers who have been described as 'mad', the nature of their madness, and its effect on the history of their countries. Were the leaders under consideration really insane or was the adjective 'mad' bestowed on them by their enemies to explain some major blemish in their rule or character? If they were in fact mad was their madness lifelong, sporadic or progressive? How did the disease express itself in patterns of thought and action? Is it possible, given the limitations, the dubious nature of the available evidence and the long lapse of time, to explain and trace the onset of the illness and to make an acceptable diagnosis? How far have the judgements and decisions of such sovereigns, politicians and dictators been affected significantly by physical and mental ill-health? Finally how far were their public policies shaped by, and to some extent an externalization of, their private traumas?

I

The Wilderness of the Mind

'Prithee, Nuncle,' the fool asks King Lear, 'tell me whether a madman be a gentleman or a yeoman?' 'A king,' Lear replies, 'a king.'[1] Made distraught by the stress brought on by the ingratitude of his daughters, Goneril and Regan, in the agony of his disturbed mind, garlanded by the wild flowers of fantasy rather than a golden crown, 'cut to the brains' as Lear describes his illness, Lear yet still remains the king:

> Ay, every inch a king:
> When I do stare, see how the subject quakes.

Lear is confronted by the paradox which faces every mad king: how is it possible to reconcile the madness which is upsetting the balance of his mind with the act of governance, for which, by the very nature of kingship, he is responsible.

There have, of course, been kings so mentally unbalanced that they have been obliged to surrender their responsibilities and to acquiesce in the appointment of a regent or vicegerent to rule on their behalf. Among such rulers were Frederick William IV of Prussia after his health collapsed in 1858, King Otto of Bavaria, the brother of Ludwig II, who in a reign of nearly thirty years was kept in complete seclusion, the Empress Zawditu or Judith of Ethiopia for whom the future Emperor Haile Selassie acted as regent, and in his latter years the father of the Emperor Hirohito, the Emperor Taisho (Yoshihito) of Japan.

But most of the kings who have been called mentally deranged either only suffered from sporadic attacks of madness or were not so obviously insane that they were unable to exercise authority. Even those kings whose mental faculties had been permanently impaired continued, at least nominally, to act as head of their state, as, for instance, Charles VI of France and Christian VII of Denmark were to do. George III's attacks of so-called insanity were very intermittent and between such attacks he appeared to act normally. Although Henry VI of England experienced some degree of mental weakness, more specifically in the latter years of his reign, he was only critically ill for less than two years in a reign of thirty-nine years. Eric XIV of Sweden similarly had an acute and violent but comparatively short attack of schizophrenia from which he apparently recovered.

But what of those kings who were not clinically insane but who suffered from some

1

imbalance of the mind and some degree of abnormality in their personalities which led contemporaries to describe them as mad? Plainly we are at once confronted with a problem which any discussion of madness inevitably raises and which needs resolution before we investigate the madness of kings. What, simply, does madness mean? Is madness less an illness than a breach of the conventional way of thinking and behaving, a piece of social engineering? Could it be that the mad are those who have chosen to look at the world and its problems in ways different from those of the mass of their contemporaries, dropping out of society or even protesting at the nature of the milieu in which they live? 'What the mad say', Roy Porter has written in a very perceptive book, 'is illuminating because it presents a world through a looking-glass, or indeed holds up the mirror to the logic (and psychologic) of sane society. It focuses and puts to the test the nature and limits of the rationality, humanity and 'understanding' of the normal.' 'Labelling insanity', he adds, 'is primarily a social act, a cultural construct . . . a badge we pin on people displaying a rather subjectively defined bundle of sympathies and traits, but who at bottom are just mildly or severely "different" or "odd".[2]

Such a view is not to be dismissed lightly, if only because the borderline between sanity and madness is thin and blurred. Robert Burton, writing in 1621, in *The Anatomy of Melancholy*, was aware that this was the case:

> But see the Madman rage distraught
> With furious looks, ghastly sight
> Naked to chains doth he lie,
> And roars amain, he knows not why.
> Observe him: for as in a glass
> Thine angry portraiture it was
> His picture. Keep still in thy presence;
> Twixt him and thee there's no difference.

All of us have the aptitude to enter into the world of madness, if only to linger shortly on its fringes, as, for instance, when we momentarily give way to an explosion of anger; for though it is possible to use electric currents to stimulate anger in the brain, what actually induces feelings of rage in the brain remains mysterious. No wonder that the Angevin kings of England, much given to fury, were sometimes called 'possessed'. 'He is', the seventeenth-century Bishop Hall observed, 'a rare man that hath not some kind of madness reigning in him.' 'My father', Charles Darwin once remarked, 'says there is a perfect gradation between sound people and insane, that everybody is insane at some time.'[3] 'In this sense,' Raskolnikov's doctor comments in Dostoevsky's novel, 'we all, in fact, very often act like madmen, with the slight difference that the people who are "mental" are a little madder than we are. A normal person, it's true, hardly exists at all.'

Yet it would be quixotic to deny that madness is not a fact. It may be very differently interpreted but there can be no doubt that madness exists. Whether it is an illness, what causes it and whether it is curable may be matters of debate, but madness is a condition that has been with us as long as society itself. As a descriptive term it covers a very broad spectrum of behaviour, ranging from the madman or mad woman who is so completely incapable of looking after him or herself that he or she has to be confined and, if given to unprovoked violence, even kept under restraint, to the persons who suffer from so comparatively innocuous a psychosis or neurosis that to all intents and purposes they appear as normal. There is still disagreement, for instance, as to whether the psychopath or sociopath can properly be called mad. Although the psychopath may not be classified as psychotic, either legally or according to psychiatric criteria, there can be hardly any doubt that he has an aberrant personality.

Madness in general represents a departure from the norm expressed by behaviour which in ideas, attitudes and activity is aberrant. Yet its constituents vary immensely, not merely because it is difficult to establish what constitutes normality but because of the very wide range of abnormal behaviour. The madman's most obvious feature might be described as his irrationality. In thirteenth-century England the jurist Henry Bracton described the madman as one who could be likened to a wild beast. Madmen were brutes who lacked the power of human reason. A lunatic, so Sir Edward Coke wrote, in the reign of James I, was a man 'that hath sometimes his understanding, and sometimes not . . . is called *non compos mentis*, so long as he hath not understanding'. 'To have stronger and more vehement passions for anything, than is ordinarily seen in others', the seventeenth-century philosopher Thomas Hobbes wrote in *Leviathan*, 'is that which men call Madnesse.' The pioneer psychiatrist Kraepelin concluded that irrationality and passion were the mark of the insane. Yet it may be too simplistic to suppose that irrationality is the most obvious or even necessary ingredient in madness. Roy Porter's discussion of autobiographical writings of mad persons indicates that mad people are capable of communicating their feelings and ideas, occasionally showing genuine insight into their condition, and into the world in which they live.

There is, we may say, a method in their madness but they tend to argue from a false or distorted premiss, if in a pseudological way. An early textbook describes the case of the man who thought that his legs and buttock were made of glass and feared that he might break, a delusion from which King Charles VI of France and many another was to suffer. Another case spoke of a man who thought that he was made of butter and in danger of melting. A third, a citizen of Siena, would not urinate because he was afraid that he might drown the town; to cure him the doctor set fire to his house 'whereupon

Rotary machines for treating the insane, designed by Hallaran (from *Traité sur l'Alienation Mentale et sur les Hospices des Aliénes* by Joseph Guilain, Vol. I, pl. 5; photograph: The Wellcome Institute Library, London, © The Trustee of the Wellcome Trust, 1993)

he pissed and was by that means preserved'.[4] Madmen can act and speak rationally and show consciousness of their problems, yet there is a residue of irrationality with which the normal mind finds it difficult to cope or to argue.

In practice madness seems like a foreign country and its inhabitants aliens, either permanent residents or temporary visitors, and as a consequence treated in more recent centuries as social outcasts. It is perhaps most true of the madman that his grip on reality is fluctuating and transient, and that he easily crosses the border from reality into fantasy. He looks at the world in a topsy-turvy way as through a kaleidoscope of coloured spectacles. His imagination and thought patterns appear to be disordered. He is emotionally labile, moving from extreme excitability to apathetic immobility, and sometimes given to unprovoked violence. As early as the thirteenth century the physician, Gilbertus Anglicus, described his characteristic symptoms as depression, lack of appetite, insomnia, headaches, irrational fears (such as the belief that the sky might fall) and hallucinations. Though with the advent of psychiatry some attempt has been made to systematize and rationalize the madman's behaviour and thought-patterns, a strange and alien life-style, often irrational, still seems the basic symptom of madness, for peasant as for king.

But what caused madness puzzled early physicians as indeed it still does. Was it an illness, like a physical sickness, caused by an organic disease? Was it supernatural in its causation, something like lightning sent from the gods or a dispensation of divine providence? Or was it simply a moral trauma, produced by inner conflicts of the mind? It remains a question which even modern experts have been unable fully to resolve.

Those who looked for a semi-physical explanation found it in the so-called humoural pathology which, from the time of Hippocrates in the latter half of the fifth century BC, of Galen and Rufus of Ephesus in the second century AD to the Renaissance and beyond held more or less undisputed sway. Madness, like physical ill-health, resulted from an imbalance of the humours which conditioned man's temperament and explained the illnesses, mental and physical, by which he was afflicted.

'Man's body', so wrote the seventh-century Spanish encyclopaedist, Isidore of Seville,

is divided among the four elements. There is the quality of earth in the flesh, of moisture in the blood, of air in the breath, of fire in the vital heat. Moreover, the four-fold division of the human body represents the four elements. For the head is related to the heavens, and in it are two eyes, as it were the luminaries of the sun and moon. The breast is akin to the air, because the breathings are emitted from it as the breath of the winds from the air. The belly is likened to the sea, because of the collection of all the humours, the gathering of the waters as it were. The feet, finally, are compared to the earth, because they are dry like the earth. Further, the mind is placed in the citadel of the head like God in the heavens, to look upon and govern all from a high place.[5]

The four elements did not merely prescribe the nature of man's complexion but accounted for the vicissitudes of his temperament. An excess of any one humour was thought to explain the onset of physical or mental sickness; but mental trouble was specifically put down to an excess of black bile, which generated the melancholy temperament, and so caused madness. It was believed that the vapours rose to the brain, affecting its activity, the fore part of the brain being the source of sense and sensory perception, the central part, of the reasoning power and the posterior, of the memory. Any imbalance between these functions produced the conditions for mental disturbance as the brain became overheated.

Even with the growth of a more scientific approach to mental and medical problems, the explanation of human ills preferred by humoural pathology was slow to die. 'Melancholy or blacke choler is a natural humor cold and dry, thicke, grosse, black and sharpe', Valentinus wrote in his *Epitome of the whole course of physicke* in 1612, 'when melancholy is burned, it becometh vicious and causeth madnesse.'[6]

There were, however, always those who were convinced, whether or not the explanation for man's madness lay in his temperamental make-up, that the onset of madness could not be explained in purely physical terms, but only in supernatural and extra-terrestrial language. Madness resulted from a conjunction of the stars or was in the lap of the gods. The madman was made mad by forces external to himself; he became a man 'possessed', and was a victim of powers which took over or muddled his mind. *Quem Jupiter vult perdere dementat prius*. 'Whom God would destroy He first sends mad', as the seventeenth-century poet and dean of Peterborough, James Duport, put it. Madness was seen by some as a divine punishment. The tyrannical Babylonian king, Nebuchadnezzar, was reduced to a condition of bestial madness, depicted by medieval illuminators as naked and hairy and in his madness reduced to subsisting on herbs and grass.[7] King John was said by some contemporary chroniclers to be 'possessed', *plenus daemonio*. Both Charles VI of France and Henry VI of England were said to have been 'bewitched'. The bestowal of the nickname *el hechizado* on Charles II of Spain screened a bizarre scenario in which the physically decrepit king played a central part. Yet, contrariwise, madness might even be a sign of divine grace. The voices which the madman heard could be the voices of God. In an age of faith the madman might appear as the messenger of God. The history of the Christian saints as well as that of holy men of other religions is replete with the cases of men and women who suffered from deep psychological problems but who were revered as holy fools speaking with the voice of God.[8] They were seers and prophets, their discordant and even incomprehensible incantations – speaking with tongues – bewildering their hearers and yet evoking admiration and even adulation.

The early physicians could only treat madness as they treated physical illness, with the limited range of prescriptions with which they were familiar, with blood-letting, by the application of clysters, with purges, in the hope that somehow they might be able to restore the true balance of the humours. 'To purge choler and melancholy after a nightmare', Chaucer advised, 'for Goddes love, take thou some laxatyf', such as 'lauriol, century, and fumitory or elles of elderbery.'[9] Since the seat of madness was in the brain, surgeons made incisions in the head in the hope of relieving the pressure on the brain, so draining the poisonous fluids and vapours which were corrupting it. Charles VI of France had a cautery made at the occiput and Henry VI may have been similarly treated. An operation of a similar character was performed on Don Carlos of Spain. In his *Livre de Seyntz Medicines* (1354) Henry, duke of Lancaster, advised that a red cock recently killed should be applied to the head of a man suffering from frenzy in the belief that the warm blood of the dead bird would settle in the brain and rid it of

Surgeons making incisions in the head, from a painting by Pieter Brueghel the Elder (photograph: The Wellcome Institute Library, London, © The Trustee of the Wellcome Institute, 1993)

the dangerous vapours by which it was afflicted.[10] Treatment of a similar kind, in these cases of recently slaughtered pigeons, was given in the seventeenth century to help improve the mental and physical health of the grand duke of Tuscany, Ferdinando dei Medici, and of Charles II of Spain.

Since in the Middle Ages many thought that madness might be supernatural in origin, more trust was placed in remedies that were more specifically psychological and spiritual than in those that were physical: in the offering of the Mass, in the application of relics to the afflicted and in the use of exorcism to drive away the evil spirits. Jesus Christ had himself expelled devils. St Cuthbert cured people 'from the troubling of foul spirits' by prayer, touching and exorcism.[11] A woman suffering from *calamitas insaniae*, who was possessed of a devil, who moaned, ground her teeth and wept, was cured when she touched the reins of Cuthbert's horse. Cuthbert's contemporary St Guthlac treated a young man who, under the stress of *immensa dementia*, had murdered a man with an axe and then mutilated himself. Guthlac 'breathed the spirit of health into his face' after prayer, fasting and washing him, so driving out the evil spirit which had possessed him.[12] Exorcism was used too on kings. Charles VI of France submitted to a series of strange rites involving exorcism which proved unavailing. Charles II of Spain was exorcised with apparently some temporary benefit to his health.

The use of holy relics in trying to cure the mentally afflicted was widespread throughout the Middle Ages. The early history of the shrine of St Bartholomew in London, as recorded in its *Liber Fundationis*, lists a large number of cases from the late twelfth or early thirteenth century.[13] A London prostitute went out of her mind, rolling her eyes, talking obscenely, tearing her clothes, so that she had to be put in bonds from which she wrenched herself free, but after she was brought to the shrine of St Bartholomew she was cured. Similar cures are recorded of mad men and women brought to the shrines of Archbishop Thomas Becket at Canterbury[14] and of King Henry VI at Windsor.[15]

In general, unless he or she were violent, the lunatic in the Middle Ages continued to live in the community, cared for by his family and friends.[16] In the medieval play *Le Jeu de la Feuillee* the madman appears as a violent and indecent man but after being treated by the priest with relics he returns to rest quietly at home. Even the patients at Bedlam were allowed to wander abroad unless they were positively dangerous.

It was natural that sooner or later hospitals should be set up to care for those who were incapable as a result of mental illness of looking after themselves. One of the first to be established in western Europe was set up at Gheel in Belgium at the shrine of St Dympna, an Irish woman who had been murdered by her father in a fit of rage and who became the patron saint of the mentally unbalanced. In the fourteenth century Robert Denton founded an institution at All Hallows, Barking, for priests and others 'who suddenly fell into a frenzy and lost their memories'. Before the close of the fourteenth century the hospital of St Mary, Bethlehem, Bishopsgate, better known as Bedlam, came into being.[17] While the treatment of the mentally sick was never entirely free of harshness, the mad remained within the confines of the local community and in the care of their own homes and families.

From the late sixteenth century onwards, for social rather than medical reasons, there was a slow change in the treatment of the insane, leading to what Michael Foucault called the 'period of confinement'.[18] The mad were to be separated from the community and housed in special institutions. Private madhouses were set up, often run by clergy to augment their incomes, although the treatment provided was sometimes benevolent and sensible.[19] But the belief was growing that the mad had to be 'managed' and kept under restraint for their own good. 'The first indication, viz. *Curatory*,' Dr Thomas Willis wrote in 1684, 'requires thretnings, bonds, or strokes, as well as Physick. . . . And indeed for the curing of Mad people, there is nothing more effectual or necessary than their reverence of standing in awe of such as they think their Tormentors . . . Furious Madmen are sooner, and more certainly cured by punishment, and hard usage, in a strait room, than by Physick or Medicine.'[20] It was of such notions that King George III was to be the victim in the late eighteenth century.

Although the treatment of lunatics became in general more humane and sympathetic, institutionalization and management were its keywords from the late eighteenth century onwards. Like the prison and workhouse, the asylum was where the community housed its deviant members. The asylums served as centres of a social and gender control where the mad could be segregated from the outside world behind high walls. 'Whereas for [Robert] Burton in 1621', Roy Porter has written, 'the madhouse was essentially a metaphor, by the time of the 1815 House of Commons Committee (which set up a public enquiry into madhouses; an act of 1815 had first instituted public lunatic asylums) it had become a literal matter of nuts and bolts.'[21]

By the closing years of the nineteenth century with the advent of psychiatry[22] there began to be new insights into the understanding of mental illness, even if in the late twentieth century madness still remains alien corn. In the 1890s Emil Kraepelin first analysed mental illness by differentiating between affective or manic depressive psychosis, in which a patient's condition was marked by changing emotional disturbance from which he or she would probably recover, and a more serious and incurable disorder which he called dementia praecox, actually an inadequate description since the disease was not dementia in the sense of progressive brain damage, nor did it always appear in adolescence as the word praecox might suggest, but Kraepelin was right to emphasize its serious nature. Characterized to a greater or lesser degree by delusions, hallucinations and thought disorder, it was renamed schizophrenia by Professor Eugen Bleuler of Zurich. The classification and diagnosis of mental illness have made great progress since Kraepelin's day, as the long catalogue of personality disorders, listed in the most recent issue of the American Diagnostic and Statistical Manual (1980), clearly demonstrates.

Such is the background against which the madness of kings has to be set. The historian is placed at an acute disadvantage by the sparse and sometimes distorted evidence of the distant past. The knowledge with which the modern specialist is equipped – the molecular and functional structure of the brain, brain wave activity, the role of neuro hormones, changes in enzyme activity and cell metabolism, skin responses, eye movement and so forth – do not exist for mad monarchs. The evidence for their madness is often tenuous, if not positively ambiguous, the sources biased and the information scanty. There must, therefore, be an element of speculation and guess work in seeking to cut a swathe through such unpromising terrain.

In practice mad kings and queens were the likely victims of the ordinary run of mental illnesses. Mental illness can be caused by a brain dysfunction, usually resulting from damage done to the brain at birth or from injuries sustained later in life. If a man develops a degenerative disorder of the brain that damages the cerebral cortex, then he may become disinhibited and prone to aggressive behaviour.[23] The injury to the head which Philip II's heir Don Carlos sustained in 1562 may very likely explain the progressive nature of his mental illness, more especially if, as seems probable, he also suffered brain damage at birth.

There are physical illnesses that can precipitate mental sickness. Encephalitis lethargica, an acute infectious disease of the central nervous system, can cause prolonged mental change, involving visual, tactile and acoustic hallucinations, accompanied by headaches, irritability and insomnia, symptoms very similar to those of schizophrenia.[24] In the 1920s after an outbreak of encephalitis children infected by it became destructive and aggressive. It is possible that encephalitis explains the insanity of the Roman Emperor Caligula and the mental imbalance of President Woodrow Wilson. Similar in its effects is temporal lobe epilepsy. Serious illness, the exact nature of which it is now impossible to ascertain, preceded signs of mental imbalance in the Russian tsars Ivan the Terrible and Peter the Great.

Syphilis in its tertiary stages can lead to paralytic dementia, bringing about the degeneration of bodily and mental powers.[25] Syphilitic infection is said to have been at work, but without corroborative evidence, in the apparent mental imbalance of Ivan and Peter as also in the madness of Ludwig II of Bavaria. It has been mentioned, but without adequate supporting evidence, with reference to Benito Mussolini and Adolf Hitler.

The madness of George III is now thought by some experts to be organic in origin, a symptom of the metabolic disorder, variegate porphyria, which has, so it has been alleged, afflicted many of his ancestors and descendants.

Where there is an absence of direct physical causation, a mental breakdown originates in the central nervous system. Varieties in brain organization, genetically determined, moulding differences of temperament and personality, may well underlie the predisposition to mental disorder. A mental breakdown never comes like a bolt from the blue but represents a pre-existing tendency in the individual's nervous system. How far this is the result of genetic factors remains still unclear, for it has as yet proved impossible to locate the gene or chromosomes responsible for schizophrenia or manic depressive insanity, though there can be no doubt that genetic factors are operative, as this study of mad rulers suggests, in many psychiatric syndromes.[26] It may be that the predisposition to mental illness represents the interaction of multiple genes rather than that of a single gene. What part, if any, the hemispheric divisions of the brain play in the onset of mental disorder is equally difficult to determine.[27] It has been argued that hallucinatory voices, such as those, for instance, which Joan of Arc said she heard, originate in the right hemisphere of the brain.[28] It is important to stress that the onset of insanity reflects a pre-existing tendency, dating from birth or even conception. Madness is never a totally new development but normally an accentuation or distortion of normal human responses. 'Traits of temperament', Gordon Claridge writes, 'are synonyms with predisposition to differing forms of mental illness. People develop the kind of psychiatric disorder or form of aberration to which their basic temperament makes them susceptible.'[29] It is for this reason that childhood and adolescence are of crucial importance. If we knew more about the relationships of mad kings with their parents and the nature of their upbringing we might find important clues to their subsequent lack of balance. The personal problems confronting Edward II and his great-grandson Richard II become more comprehensible in the light of their inheritance and education.

But if the onset of insanity reflects a nervous predisposition to mental illness, it has to be triggered by environmental and external factors. Stress was perhaps the single most important component in bringing about a breakdown, as the illnesses of Henry VI and Eric XIV of Sweden may demonstrate. In some cases psycho-neurotic disorders represent an escape from the traumas and difficulties of every day existence, and may even, as Sir George Pickering showed,[30] give rise to creativity. Ludwig II of Bavaria escaped from political crises by soaking himself in Wagner's music and by building fanciful castles. Contrariwise, madness may be activated by a desire to call attention to some inner need, real or imagined, or to hide an intolerable inner conflict. Whatever its type, whether a crippling breakdown or a comparatively mild nervous illness, it requires an occasion to come into the open.

The principal mental illnesses from which mad kings and queens seem to have suffered were schizophrenia[31] and manic-depressive ailments, which have very similar symptoms. Schizophrenia is a portmanteau term with a very broad spectrum of

A bishop exorcising a man and woman possessed by evil spirits, from an illuminated manuscript of the fifteenth century (Bibliothèque Nationale MS 424 f. 26r; photograph: The Wellcome Institute Library, London, © The Trustee of the Wellcome Institute, 1993)

degrees of severity. As its name implies it means the splitting of certain fundamental basic mental faculties, such as speaking, moving and feeling, the 'splitting of psychic functions with the fragmentations of the personality', not to be confused with a split or multiple pesonality. Its onset is marked by significant changes in patterns of thought, speech and behaviour, what Gordon Claridge describes as a 'chaotic interaction between the person and his environment, manifest in swings of physiological arousal, fluctuating attention, disordered mood, distorted perceptions of reality and patterns of thought and language that disrupt social communication.'[32] In its most pronounced form schizophrenia can generate hallucinations, bizarre delusions, incoherent or illogical speech and inappropriate emotional reactions. Schizophrenic paranoia can lead to acts of violence, as was evidently the case with Charles VI of France, Eric XIV of Sweden and Christian VII of Denmark.

In its moderate form schizophrenia is not necessarily a permanent condition, though even after a recovery there is likely to be a legacy of residual impairment, mentally and emotionally. Charles VI had periods of lucidity in which he took up the reins of government, but his mental powers had evidently been enfeebled. Eric XIV made a recovery but died insane. Christian VII had his lucid periods, but for the greater part of his long reign of over forty years was never fully normal. Schizophrenia may come and go over a period of years or make a once and for all attack. It may ultimately change to a chronic state, leading to a virtual disintegration of the personality. Vulnerability to the illness evidently springs from a genetic and temperamental disposition of the nervous system, interacting with environmental and familial surroundings. Except in the most extreme cases schizophrenics do not lose complete touch with reality but tend to have a distorted or partial view of it; nor, by and large, are they unaware of their aberrant behaviour.

Other mad kings were seemingly the victims of manic-depressive insanity,[33] though the degree of its severity varied. Depression, *melancholia*, derived originally from the Greek *'melaina chole'*, was long held to originate in the black bile, the *atra bilis*, of the humours. It was not until 1899 that Emil Kraepelin first used the term manic-depressive insanity to describe the more severe forms of the depressive state, though there had been a long line of depressives, among them Samuel Johnson. Depression does in fact vary greatly in its severity, ranging from a comparatively short-lived and shallow mood or a superficial emotional upset to a condition so deeply rooted in the constitution as to require treatment and to be hardly distinguishable in its outward signs from schizophrenia. Depression may originate as a mild form of mental sluggishness, with fluctuations of mood described clinically as cyclothymia, an inability to reach a decision, a defective memory and a general lack of interest, but in its more acute form it can escalate into clouded consciousness, incoherence, strong feelings of fear and sadness, sometimes accompanied by gastro-intestinal problems.

In his later years Richard II was surely a moderate depressive. Queen Juana of Castile became a victim of manic-depressive insanity. In its severe form it can sometimes give rise, as it did with Juana, to delusions and hallucinations. Religious feelings, accompanied by a strong sense of guilt and fear of divine punishment for wrongdoing, may be a cause or a sequel to depression, as the experience of Philip V of Spain was to demonstrate. The manic-depressive may alternate between a wild state of excitability and elation followed by deep depression, expressed in complete immobility and passivity, such as distinguished Henry VI's illness.

Less severe in their impact are a group of psycho-neuroses or personality disorders, which extend from the near normal to the psychotic. They may not come within the full scope of insanity, but they can have disturbing and fatal consequences for their victims. The brain may be malfunctioning, but it is like a flickering light rather than a spent bulb. Such borderline syndromes may manifest themselves in irrational fears or in inexplicable anxieties, in phobias and neuroses which are almost indistinguishable in their effects from insanity. Such, for instance, is the so-called borderline personality[34] of which it has been said, though inconclusively, that Adolf Hitler was a victim. Though the sufferers' hold on reality is tenuous, it is never wholly obliterated. Such disorders are often precipitated by some unresolvable conflict between an inner overweening desire and its fulfilment. Personality disorders have an incapacitating effect on those who hold positions of authority and responsibility, for conditions which may well be tolerable for a common citizen may prove to be disastrous in a ruler or statesman.

There remains a further grey and difficult area where the victim shows signs of an aberrant personality but does not seem to be suffering from a mental illness. The psychopath or sociopath may seem to fall outside the range of clinical insanity, but as Lady Caroline Lamb said of Byron, he is 'mad, bad and dangerous to know'.[35] Although he may not suffer from any specific mental disease, and appears outwardly able, alert and intelligent, fundamentally he is a deeply disturbed person whose brain appears not to be functioning normally. The psychopath is wholly egocentric, living according to his own rules or inclinations without concern or compassion for other people. He is in some sense insulated from the outside world, lacking affection and feeling, often as a result of deprivation in childhood and adolescence, for parental rejection is a primary aetiological factor in the making of the psychopath. His feelings for other people are shallow and he is rarely able to form an integrated sexual relationship. He will be flexible in his behaviour, suiting his actions to what he conceives to be his basic objectives. He will use plausible words but his words are divorced from his feelings. He is a master at manipulating other people, convincing them of his good intentions. He has failed to respond to the process of socialization and his feelings are internalized. He lacks any sense of remorse or guilt, is thoroughly untrustworthy and can be prone to abnormally aggressive or seriously irresponsible conduct of an anti-social nature.

The psychopath may well be ambitious, brutal, pitiless and violent, but his sphere is not confined to the realm of the criminal delinquents. He is to be found at all levels of society. There have been princes who seemed to display psychopathic qualities, even if they were not in fact psychopaths, among them the Emperor Tiberius, Don Carlos of Spain, Tsar Peter the Great and his long-time successor the Russian dictator Joseph Stalin. But it is not easy to identify the mind of the psychopath, more especially with respect to characters in the past. 'Like a cancer', it has been said of psychopathic disorder, 'it grows in the dark. It grows in the inner recesses of the mind, its roots embedded in early childhood. It is the AIDS of the mental health world.'[36]

What constituted the 'madness of kings' and how such madness affected the peoples

Tom Rakewell in Bedlam, from an engraving in the last episode of *The Rake's Progress* by William Hogarth (photograph: The Wellcome Institute Library, London, © The Trustee of the Wellcome Institute, 1993)

over whom they reigned is the subject of what follows. It forms a study in personality which, among other things, demonstrates how the atmosphere of a royal court, threaded by suspicion and intrigue, can provide an appropriate setting for a mental breakdown, more especially when the ruler is young, immature and impressionable. It shows how political stress can create the conditions for the onset of madness and how even an apparent return to normal health might well conceal a continuing impairment of the mental faculties.

The effect of their rulers' aberrant characters on the history of their peoples is more difficult to define. It takes outstanding characters, an Alexander the Great, a Napoleon, to change the course of history, but political crises may be affected significantly by the leading personalities in any one country. A Caligula or a Nero affected the destiny of the Roman Empire. The character of King John was one ingredient in the troubles which were eventually to overwhelm him. The disorders of Edward II's reign bore the imprint of the king's personality. Richard II might have escaped deposition, imprisonment and murder had he been a different sort of person. Henry VI's mental debility was a prime ingredient in the civil strife which we know as the Wars of the Roses. Similarly the madness of his grandfather, Charles VI of France, has to be related directly to the chaotic divisions which for long wrought havoc in his kingdom. The madness of Eric XIV of Sweden was critical not merely for his own future but for his country. The illnesses of Queen Juana of Castile and Don Carlos of Spain had a long-term significance for the Spanish Empire, as did the ill-health of later Spanish kings, Charles II and Philip V. George III's madness precipitated a dangerous political crisis. The course of Danish history in the late eighteenth century was plainly affected by the prolonged insanity of the Danish King Christian VII.

On the other hand the aberrant natures of other kings may have had only a superficial effect on their countries. It is arguable as to whether the personality disorder of Gian Gastone, the last Medici Grand Duke of Tuscany, or that of Ludwig II of Bavaria were politically of great significance. It is even more difficult to decide how far the possible health problems affected the Russian tsars, Ivan the Terrible and Peter the Great, though there cannot be the least doubt that their grandiose policies were of fundamental importance in Russian history. In a sense we have to wait for the era of the modern dictators to see how millions of people, indeed the whole world, may be brutally affected by the mental illness or decay of a great leader, the psychopathic Stalin, the deranged Adolf Hitler and the senile Mao-tse-tung. It is even arguable that a manic disposition is a necessary ingredient in the making of a successful ruler or politician. The personality of the ruler still remains one of the most important influences in history. '*Le plus importante ressource de la royauté*,' as the French historian Charles Petit-Dutaillis observed, '*c'est le génie personnel du roi*.' ('The most important of the resources of the monarchy is the personal ability of the king.')[37]

II

Roman Orgies

The Roman emperors ruled over a vast territory, stretching from the inhospitable island of Britain and the dangerous frontiers of the Rhine and Danube to the hot shores of North Africa and the deserts of the Near East. Whatever lip service they paid to the maxims of so-called constitutional government, their word was ultimately law. They assumed a dignity that had a sacred character; many of them were deified after death, and some even in their lifetime claimed a semi-divine status. The consequences of an unbalanced head of state could therefore be far-reaching and momentous.

Fortunately, though the empire was often the prey of power-seeking generals, there were relatively few deranged emperors. Yet, in the first half of the first century, and at the close of the second, the Roman Empire was at the mercy of men who were abnormal personalities, who could indeed be loosely described as mad. The Julio-Claudian emperors, of whom Nero was the last representative, bore the imprint of their genetic inheritance, both on their temperaments and their health, which the stress placed upon them by the absolute power they wielded was further to accentuate. The founders of the line, Julius Caesar and his great-nephew Octavian (or Augustus as he became), were not in any significant respects abnormal, but Augustus's step-son and successor Tiberius may have been a psychopath or at least had psychopathic qualities. Of his successors Gaius or Caligula, as he is more usually called, had periods of insanity after a serious illness in AD 37, Claudius was certainly neurotic and Nero was very likely mentally unbalanced. The second group of emperors, Commodus, Caracalla and Elagabalus, who reigned in the later second and early third centuries, were nearly all young men with limited political experience whose talents were clearly unequal to the tasks of government, and whose heads were almost literally turned by the vast powers at their disposal. They found release from their responsibilities in self-indulgence, dissipation and oppression which brought them to the brink, and possibly over the brink, of madness and to a violent end. The governance of these emperors illustrates admirably the different if converging features which may precipitate mental imbalance, with disastrous effects at least for some of their subjects.

To understand the setting we have to go back a generation or so to watch the rejection of the republican tradition which had for so many centuries determined the character of Roman government and which for long remained the cherished ideal of Rome's intellectuals, and the subsequent gestation of the Roman Empire. At the heart

17

of its inception there stood the formidable figure of Julius Caesar, the great general who had swept his rival Pompey from power at the battle of Pharsalus, who had subjugated Gaul and invaded Britain. While he attained princely power, he was never accorded the princely title which the senatorial order, suspicious of his ambition, was reluctant to give him. He was dead before constitutional changes could be made in the government of the state, but the title of 'dictator' which was eventually conferred upon him for life, was in fact a screen for a form of authoritarian monarchy.

To whom should his immense power and possessions pass? Caesar was a lusty man, a womanizer who frequently deserted his marriage couch, and who had fallen victim to the wiles or charm of the beautiful Egyptian queen, Cleopatra, by whom he had a son, Caesarion. He was sufficiently wide-ranging in his sexual tastes to court the warrior king of Bithynia, Nicomedes, whose 'queen', the Roman wits said, Caesar had become. 'Caesar conquered Gaul; Nicomedes Caesar.' 'He was', as Curio the Elder put it, 'every man's wife and every woman's husband.'[1] Caesar had only a legitimate daughter, and as his heir adopted his great-nephew Octavian who was eventually to emerge as the beneficiary of his power. At the great sea battle of Actium in 31 BC Octavian's forces wrought Mark Antony's and Cleopatra's defeat and death (by suicide). Within four years Octavian assumed the principate as Augustus, the first in the long line of emperors that lasted in the west to 476 and in the east until Constantinople fell to the Turks in 1453.

Although the outward trappings of constitutional power were retained, and the Roman senate enjoyed a nominal authority, for the state was described as a dyarchy, in practice the empire was a military despotism. Augustus was *Imperator Caesar Divi Filius*, the son of the deified Caesar, inaugurating by his title alone a power that was sacral in its nature and which in a mentally unbalanced occupant of the imperial throne could become obsessive and extravagant.

Augustus was himself a shrewd, solid statesman, immensely successful in peace and war, a brilliant administrator and, though amorous by habit and nature, a loving husband. Augustus' wife, Livia, was beautiful and ruthless, 'Ulysses in skirts' as the future emperor Caligula called her, '*genetrix orbis*', 'a woman implacable in her ambition, frigid and tenacious, a cat or a panther as it might suit her'. She was above all concerned to foster the fortunes of her own family and in particular to ensure that Tiberius, her son by her previous husband, might succeed her husband as the next emperor. Tiberius' character was powerfully affected by his ambiguous relationship with his powerful, dominating mother. If she loved him, it seems doubtful whether he loved her or indeed was capable of deep affection. He was to remain much under her thumb until she died in her eighty-sixth year, but resentful of her unrelenting influence, he had his revenge by refusing her the honour of deification after her death.

Tiberius may well have wished for a private rather than a public existence, pursuing his military career without the political responsibilities of empire,[2] but he could not escape the imperious ambitions of his mother, even though his step-father, the Emperor Augustus, regarded him with half-concealed dislike. If we knew more in detail of Tiberius' early life before his mother married the emperor, part of which was apparently spent in exile, we might well discover the roots of resentment and suspicion which were to fructify in the later stages of his life.

The question of the succession to the Roman Empire was as much in Augustus' mind as in that of his wife Livia. Augustus wished the empire to pass to members of his own immediate family, the sons of his daughter Julia, rather than to his step-children, Livia's brood. Julia's husband, Marcus Agrippa, who would have been a suitable successor to Augustus, had died in 12 BC. Julia was too significant a pawn to be left a widow for long. Livia realized that if Julia could be married to her son Tiberius this would be likely to enhance his chance of becoming emperor. At the command of Augustus Tiberius agreed, if reluctantly, to divorce his wife, Vipsania, and to marry Julia. That Tiberius and Julia were incompatible was soon plain. Tiberius was a cold egocentric, neither affectionate nor warm-hearted. Julia was over-sexed, a pathologically erotic nymphomaniac for whom the sexually timid Tiberius was no match.[3] Julia's private life was so scandalous that it brought about her own ruin and momentarily foiled Livia's plans for Tiberius. Seneca wrote:

> the divine Augustus exiled his daughter, who had surpassed in impudicity every infamous meaning of the word, thus covering the imperial house with scandal: lovers admitted in droves: nightly orgies throughout the city; the forum and the Tribune, whence her father had proclaimed laws against adultery, chosen by his daughter as a place of disorder; daily meetings beside the statue of Marsyas, where, worse than an adultress, a mere prostitute, she claimed her right to every shamelessness in the arms of the first passer by.[4]

When the emperor, long kept in the dark, heard of his daughter's life-style, he sent her in harsh exile to the island of Pandateria. Her husband, Tiberius, may not have regretted Julia's passing from his life but he suffered deep humiliation as a result of the scandal. When he became emperor he withdrew her allowance and, so it was alleged, had her starved to death. Tiberius had been manipulated into a loveless and disastrous marriage. He was now to be pushed by his mother into position as Augustus' successor. No wonder that one of his modern biographers called his life 'a study in resentment'.

The fates served Livia's purposes well in frustrating her husband's plans for the succession to the empire. Augustus' grandchildren and immediate heirs, Gaius and Lucius, educated so that they might later inherit the imperial mantle, died young. The emperor then felt that he had to associate his surviving grandson Agrippa Postumus with his son-in-law Tiberius as his probable successors. But, young as he was, Agrippa had no better reputation than his mother: 'a brutal and violent temper', 'extremely depraved in mind and character', 'grossly ignorant and stupidly proud of his physical strength'. He 'grew', Suetonius wrote, 'no more manageable but on the contrary became madder from day to day'.[5] His unsuitability for rule was so painfully apparent that he was banished to the island of Planesia where he was probably put to death on the orders of his dying grandfather, with the connivance of Tiberius, now the only candidate for the succession.

Reluctantly but inevitably Augustus accepted Tiberius as his heir. 'Since cruelty of fortune has robbed me of my sons,' Augustus was reported as saying, 'let Tiberius Caesar be my heir.' 'This wording', Suetonius wrote, 'confirmed the suspicion of those who thought that Augustus had chosen his successor not so much through affection as through necessity.'[6]

Tiberius was already fifty-six years old when he became emperor and he had twenty-two years in front of him. Although his face was scarred by ulcers, which he tried to conceal with plasters, suggesting a skin infection, he was physically a healthy man. He was so strong that he could break open a green apple with his hands. He evidently suffered from hemeralopia, for his sight was poor in daylight though, as Pliny reported, he could see in the dark like an owl. In many respects he was frugal, almost austere in his tastes, his favourite food, asparagus, cucumbers and fruit. But at least in his early days he was so addicted to drinking that his soldiers gave him the nickname 'Biberius'. His heavy drinking may have contributed to his personal problems; alcoholism has not infrequently been an ingredient in government.

Tiberius may not have wanted to be emperor. Cold and impersonal, he seems to have made no effort to win the affections of the Romans, failing to provide them with the bread and circuses which they regarded as their due, so earning their hostility. But, in the early years of his principate, he appears to have ruled conscientiously and efficiently, seeking to uphold Augustan law and order and repressing tribal trouble on the frontiers.

But there were signs of cracks in the façade which betrayed not merely a growing sense of insecurity, increasingly paranoic in its intensity, but also other features, for example eccentricity, lack of feeling, untrustworthiness, vengeance on foes and friends alike, which seemed psychopathic in their nature. There was a canker in Tiberius' personality which became steadily most pronounced. This developing angst was demonstrated in his relations with his own nephew Germanicus, the son of his elder brother Drusus, who had been married to Agrippina, the ruthless and energetic daughter of Julia, Tiberius' former wife. Germanicus' close kinship to the imperial house was such that, should Tiberius die, he would have better claims to the imperial diadem than Tiberius' own son, Drusus.

Tiberius was jealous of Germanicus who seemed to be exploiting his position to win favour and saw his growing reputation as a threat to his own power. Germanicus was an attractive young warrior, the darling of the people upon whom the good fairy had poured all her gifts, save one, that of good health, for Germanicus suffered from epilepsy, a disease which he was to pass on, possibly with ultimately fateful results, to his son, the future emperor Caligula. Fate eventually conspired to bring down the popular Germanicus, for he fell seriously ill. Rumours that he had been poisoned may have been true, given Tiberius' hatred for him. Tiberius reacted characteristically. He was fearful that fingers might point to him as the author of the deed and decided that the best way out would be to find a scapegoat, no less a person than his own legate, Calpurnius Piso. The legate returned home and in the best Roman tradition cut his throat, leading Tiberius to complain that by taking his life Calpurnius Piso was trying to shift the blame onto himself. It was characteristic of Tiberius' psychopathic habit that he readily sacrificed those who served him to save himself.

Germanicus' removal did not settle the problem of the succession, for his two elder children, Nero and Drusus were accepted as heirs rather than Tiberius' own son, Drusus. If Germanicus was dead, the claims of his family were represented by his widow, Agrippina, a woman after the model of Livia, with, as Tacitus commented, an 'insatiable desire to dominate', so much so that her 'virile passions diverted her from the vices of her feminine sex'.[7] Suspicious of her motives, apprehensive of her popularity, Tiberius regarded her with hostility.

He had meanwhile allowed more and more authority to pass to the prefect of the Praetorian Guard, Sejanus. The emperor himself was increasingly neglectful of the details of administration and his interest in government, always lukewarm, was slackening. He believed that he had a faithful servant in Sejanus, but Sejanus was to use his position to advance his own fortunes, with an eye to the imperial throne itself. He managed to procure the elimination of Germanicus' widow, Agrippina, and two of her sons. Her youngest surviving son, Gaius or Caligula, together with the emperor's young grandson, Tiberius Gemellus, constituted the only close heirs to the ageing emperor. Tiberius had, however, foiled Sejanus' desire to marry his own son's widow. Sejanus could only wait and hope.

Tiberius, having largely withdrawn from active government, had retreated to the beautiful island of Capri. It was ideally situated as a fortress and a refuge where he was free from fears of conspiracy and assassination which haunted him. It was at Capri that the septuagenarian emperor felt at liberty to indulge in the perverse pleasures which were to blemish his reputation. Tacitus wrote:

In that place he gave rein to his inordinate appetites. . . . With the pride of eastern despotism, he seized young men of ingenuous birth and forced them to yield to his brutal gratifications. . . . New modes of sensuality were invented, and new terms for scandalous refinements in lascivious pleasure.[8]

Suetonius was more explicit. In the presence of the emperor young men and women would copulate in groups of three 'to excite his waning passions'. Little boys whom he called his 'minnows' were trained to chase him when he went swimming 'and get between his legs to lick and nibble him'. He tricked men into drinking huge draughts of wine 'and then suddenly knotted a cord tightly around their genitals, which not only cut into the flesh but prevented them from urinating'. He perpetrated acts of torture and sadistic cruelty. 'In Capri they still shew the place at the cliff tops where Tiberius used to watch his victims being thrown into the sea after prolonged and exquisite tortures.'[9]

Whether these scenes actually occurred we cannot be absolutely certain. In the context of the emperor's lonely life they do not seem entirely implausible, for after years of apparently sedate chastity, in the private paradise of Capri, Tiberius could take a voyeuristic pleasure in a sensual recall to the youthful past. He was an old, unhappy man, *tristissimus hominum* as Pliny calls him, who found temporary oblivion in visual sensation and who may have experienced sadistic, perhaps sado-erotic, satisfaction in acts of torture and death, perhaps as a measure of compensation for the humiliations which, as he saw it, he had been forced to endure. Although it is possible that such pleasures may have been the result of growing senility, there is insufficient evidence to suggest that the emperor was in the grip of senile dementia.

The trust which he had once placed in Sejanus had already proved to be unfounded. After Germanicus' mother, Antonia, managed to send a secret message to Tiberius informing him of Sejanus' seditious ambition, he acted promptly to rid himself of his treacherous minister. For three days Sejanus' body suffered the insults of the mob before his soiled remains were thrown into the River Tiber.

But Sejanus' death did not make the emperor any more popular. He had suffered the last, perhaps, to him the greatest betrayal: Julia, Germanicus, Sejanus. He had outlived them all but stood alone, in his old age paranoid, ready to strike out at the real or imaginary enemies who threatened him. He acquiesced in, if he did not initiate, innumerable acts of cruelty and of injustice which made him feared and reviled. When Agrippina took her life, the emperor grimly informed the senate that she was fortunate that she had not been strangled and exposed on the Germoniae for her supposed adultery with Asinius Gallus. The senate, servile men in awe of their prince, thanked the emperor for his clemency and in celebration voted an offering to Jupiter. Condemnations, executions, forced suicides, occurring at the slightest whisper of imperial displeasure, punctuated the closing years of the emperor's reign.

At Capri Germanicus' son, Gaius, the emperor's eighteen-year-old great nephew kept him company. As he was the sole survivor of the Julio-Claudian clan who had escaped the decimation of his family, with Tiberius Gemellus he could look forward to being Tiberius' successor. So he flattered the old emperor and perhaps encouraged him in his perverse pleasures. Tiberius was, however, still shrewd enough to size him up. He did not love him, nor anyone else. When Gaius mentioned the famous republican politician Sulla, the emperor commented sharply that Gaius had all Sulla's vices and none of his virtues. He predicted that Gaius would soon rid himself of Tiberius Gemellus: 'You will kill him and another will kill you.'

In March 37 Tiberius fell ill at Misenum. When he collapsed in a coma, it was supposed that he had died but just as the court officials began to congratulate Gaius on his accession to the principate, Tiberius stirred and even apparently asked for a drink. Gaius' chamberlain, Macro, went into the bed chamber and smothered the emperor with the bed clothes. The detail of Tiberius' death varies in other accounts, but the dying man may well have been hurried to his fathers. No one regretted his passing. The Romans, by whom he had been so rarely seen in recent years, execrated him: '*Tiberius in Tiberim*', they shouted, 'Tiberius into the Tiber.' Macro read the emperor's will to the senate in which he decreed that Gaius and Tiberius Gemellus were to be jointly his heirs: but Gaius wished for no rival, even though only a boy. The senate obligingly declared that Tiberius had been of unsound mind when he made his will. Many of the emperor's other bequests were implemented but before the year was out Gemellus was dead and Gaius reigned supreme.

The senate's decision that Tiberius was of 'unsound mind' has been dismissed by historians as a political ploy instigated by his successor to ensure the removal of Tiberius Gemellus. That this was the case is not indeed impossible, but Tiberius' mental balance may have been in question in his later years, even if there seems insufficient evidence to support the conclusion of a modern German historian that Tiberius was a schizophrenic. It seems more likely that Tiberius may have been a psychopath, though the Spanish historian and psychologist Gregorio Marañón found the root of his troubles in a cumulative resentment at the personal and political rebuffs he had encountered. In his formative years he experienced the uncertain climate of exile before his family was restored to favour. Although he was said to have been fond of his first wife, he appeared a lonely, introspective man, incapable of giving or receiving affection. His step-father Augustus disliked him; he grew to resent his dominating mother. He had been acutely jealous of Germanicus and acquiesced without remorse in the decimation of his family, Gaius alone excepted. He may have wished his son Drusus to succeed him but he seemed to be unmoved by his death. Sejanus in whom he had placed so great a trust betrayed him. No wonder if to escape the humiliations and fears of the real world he found a temporary escape in the perverse voyeurism of Capri. In human relations he lacked warmth and sacrificed friends and enemies alike to suit his convenience. He was an embittered and unhappy man. He was abnormal, on the brink, experiencing what may be described as a 'borderline syndrome', not mad 'yet . . . not entirely in his right mind'.[10] While there may be insufficient evidence to describe Tiberius definitely as a psychopath, there were undoubtedly psychopathic qualities in his make-up.

The jeers which greeted his corpse contrasted with the enthusiastic reception accorded to his successor, the Emperor Gaius, better known as Caligula, so called from the military bootees (*caligae*) which he had worn when a child in his father's camp. The old emperor had been an aged recluse of seventy-eight. Caligula, unlike his father, Germanicus, was not physically attractive. He was tall and pale with spindly legs, prematurely bald and so sensitive about his lack of hair that sometimes he ordered those with a fine head of hair to be shaved. He made up for lack of hair on his head by an abundance of body-hair. About this too he could be equally sensitive; even the mention of 'hairy goats' in conversation might have dangerous consequences. But if Caligula was not the acme of good looks, he was young and energetic. That at least to the Romans promised better things.

To do the Emperor Caligula justice his reign was not void of achievement. He began well, relaxing some of the more unpopular features of Tiberius' rule. His policies and his performance in many respects showed good sense and some political judgement. At the hands of modern historians, he has, like Tiberius, undergone some measure of rehabilitation. His English biographer, Dacre Balsdon, found that there was much to be said on his behalf, and following the German writers H. Willrich (1903) and M. Gelzer (1918) refuted the charge of madness, suggesting that the features of his life which were thought to indicate signs of his insanity were simply 'certain undeveloped (and unpleasant) traits in his own character'.[11] Since it is often the overdevelopment of traits in character that constitutes madness, the conclusion is not a happy one.

The Roman historians, if writing some time after his death, had no doubt that he was either bad or mad, and probably both. 'Nature', Seneca commented, 'seemed to have created him in order to demonstrate what the most repulsive vices in the highest in the land could achieve. You had only to look at him to see that he was mad.'[12] He was, Tacitus wrote, *'commotus ingenio'*. Suetonius called him a monster made so by lunacy.[13]

What were the features of his personality that seemed to suggest mania? He was plainly bisexual. Possibly guilty of incest with his sisters, he was married four times, and had a number of homosexual affairs, with an actor Mnester whom he was accustomed to kiss in public, as with Marcus Lepidus and Valerius Catullus. Suetonius claimed that Caligula had exhibited his wife in a state of nudity; and that he had actually opened a brothel in the palace where matrons and free-born youths could be hired for money. Such activities suggest that Caligula was lecherous and licentious, and may hint at a measure of mental instability.

The real trouble with Caligula was that he took his divine nature so seriously that he entered a world of fantasy with bizarre manifestations. It was his self-indulgence in this fantastic world which was the root of his insanity. He believed that he was divine. Deification, oriental in its origins, was to become a part of the Roman imperial tradition though it was not an honour bestowed on all (Julius Caesar and Augustus were described after death as gods but Tiberius was not accorded the honour). On his death-bed the Emperor Vespasian chuckled wryly 'Methinks I am becoming a god.'

Caligula did not doubt that in his own lifetime he was divine and entitled to behave as a god and to receive the honours suitable to his position. Addressed by one of his eastern cities as the 'New Sun', he believed implicitly in his divinity and threatened those who did not accept him with condign punishment. Philo wrote:

He no longer consented to remain within the bounds of human nature, but began to stretch beyond them in his aspiration to be thought to be a god. They say that at the beginning of this lunacy he reasoned as follows: just as the keepers of animals, goatherds, cowherds and shepherds are not oxen or goats or sheep, but men, possessing a more powerful estate and resources than their charges, so I too, who am the herdsman of the best of herds, mankind, shall be considered different, and not upon the human plane, but the fortunate possessor of a mightier, a more divine estate. With this notion stamped upon his mind, the fool carried about as infallible truth what was in reality only the invention of his fancy.[14]

He may have been a 'fool' but his folly was masterful and dangerous. He dressed and lived the role of a god. By his extravagant expenditure he was soon to exhaust the imperial treasury. He was clothed in rich silk, ornamented with precious stones, wore jewels on his shoes and dissolved pearls in vinegar which he then drank. He was called '*princeps avidissimi auri*' who even provided golden bread for his guests and golden barley for his horses.

He claimed fellowship with the gods as his equals, identifying himself in particular with Jupiter.[15] Dressed for the part, brandishing a supposed thunderbolt, he issued a challenge to the god intimating that the god was really an imposter and that he, Caligula, was the real Jupiter. To support these pretensions he had a piece of machinery designed which produced a passable imitation of thunder and lightning. When Jupiter spoke through the medium of a thunderstorm, Caligula repeated Ajax's challenge to Odysseus in the *Iliad*, 'Destroy me or I'll destroy you.'

Yet on other occasions he called Jupiter his brother and even claimed to talk with him. 'Styling himself Jupiter Latiaris, he attached to his service as priests his wife

A bust of the emperor Caligula (The Mansell Collection/Fratelli Alinari)

Caesonia and other persons who were wealthy, receiving ten million sesterces from each of them in return for this honour.' Claudius' entrance fee was so prodigious that he fell into debt. There was perhaps after all a method in Caligula's madness.

'He set up', so Suetonius states, 'a special temple to his own godhead, with priests and victims of the choicest kind. In this temple was a life-sized statue of the Emperor in gold, which was dressed each day in clothing such as he wore himself. The richest citizens used all their influence to secure the priesthoods of his cult and bid high for the honour. The victims were flamingoes, peacocks, guinea-fowls and pheasants, offered day by day each after its own kind.'[16] When the emperor asked the actor Apelles which of the two, Jupiter or himself, was the greater, the actor's natural hesitation in making an immediate response led to his being put to the torture.

Caligula had married his wife Caesonia when she was already pregnant and held that their daughter Drusilla was in fact the child of Jupiter; the infant was placed on the knees of the god's statue in the Capitol and the goddess Minerva was employed to suckle her.

But the emperor was nothing if not logical. If earth-wise he was married to Caesonia, as a sun god he was married to the moon or at least he talked to her and courted her embraces, chilly as these must have been. Once he enquired of the courtier Vitellius if he had seen the moon goddess in his company, to which he replied with some presence of mind, 'No, sir, only you gods can see one another.'

Divine family relationships were as complex, indeed far more so, than human ones. Caligula did not confine himself to one divinity but explored the gamut of heaven. He 'would pose as Neptune because he had bridged so great an expanse of sea; he also impersonated Hercules, Bacchus, Apollo, and all the other divinities, not merely males, but also females, often taking the role of Juno, Diana or Venus. . . . Now he would be seen as a woman, holding a wine bowl and thyrsus, and again he would appear as a man equipped with a club and a lion's shield and a lion's skin. . . . He would be seen at one time with a smooth skin and later with a full beard.' To add to his other problems the emperor certainly suffered from gender confusion.

It was in his role as Neptune that shortly after his accession he decided to proclaim his mastery of the sea. He had a bridge of boats constructed across the northern part of the bay of Naples, from Puteoli to Baiae, making a sort of roadway along which the emperor, having made a sacrifice to Neptune, rode on horseback, garbed in a cloak of purple silk studded with gems which sparkled in the sunlight. He wore the breastplate which had supposedly belonged to Alexander the Great. The infantry and cavalry followed. After spending the night in Puteoli, he returned in triumph the next day in a chariot drawn by two racehorses. He spoke of the building of the bridge as a work of genius and praised the soldiers for their achievement in crossing the sea on foot.[17]

That the sea had remained calm showed that even Neptune feared the emperor. In the junketing which followed, Caligula, inflamed by drink, 'hurled many of his companions off the bridge into the sea, and sank many of the others by sailing about, and attacking them in boats equipped with beaks'.

Another triumph, again more imaginary than real, awaited him when in 39–40 he masterminded expeditions to Germany and Gaul with the ostensible object of invading Britain (which though Caesar had invaded it in 55 BC was not under Roman control). Modern historians have suggested that the emperor's expedition was more serious and sensible than the Roman chroniclers suggest. It was intended primarily to pacify the Rhine frontier and to abort a serious conspiracy against the emperor in which the legate of upper Germany, Gaetulianus, was involved. Yet the expedition had also elements of the pantomime in which the emperor loved to indulge. Across the Rhine there was no conflict, a few woebegone prisoners were taken and seven times Caligula was hailed as the imperator. In northern Gaul he embarked on a trireme, then disembarked and ordered the soldiers to collect sea shells from the shore.[18]

There were those who knew how to curry favour with the emperor who responded to their flattery with gestures which revealed his mental instability. When his sister, Drusilla, whom he had named as his heir, died suddenly, he had a temple erected in her honour. A senator, Livius Germinus, flatteringly told the emperor that he had seen a vision of Drusilla ascending into the heavens and being received by the gods, and was rewarded richly for his sycophantic vision. He lavished gifts on his lover, the actor Mnester, and if anyone interrupted his performance he was likely to be scourged. Eutyches, the leader of the green faction in the charioteers of the circus, whose cause the emperor championed enthusiastically, received some two million sesterces in gifts. Highest of all in Caligula's estimation was his favourite horse, Incitatus, whose health he drank in a golden goblet. He had, we are told, though the story may be *ben trovato*, 'a stall of marble, a manger of ivory, purple blankets and a collar of precious stones, he even gave this horse a house, a troop of slaves and furniture . . . and it is also said that he planned to make him consul'.[19]

The applause that had greeted Caligula when he became princeps had long subsided. The senatorial order was offended by the favours which he showed to men of low rank, actors, gladiators and others whose company he liked to frequent. After four years his rule was as tyrannical and cruel as that of Tiberius. His actions were often unpredictable as well as unjust. When Caligula was ill a loyal citizen, Afranius Potitus, swore that if the emperor recovered he would give up his own life. When Caligula recovered his health, he took Afranius at his word, had him wreathed as for sacrifice, driven by the imperial slaves through the city and flung to his death from the Tarpeian rock. He suffered from a *folie de grandeur* which had no compensations for his people who suffered from the grinding taxation which his extravagance promoted. His life-style was as capricious as it was bizarre. He would summon staid senators to see him at midnight so that they might watch him dance 'dressed in a cloak and a tunic reaching to his heels' to the sound of flutes.

When his end came he was celebrating the Palatine games. As he walked forward to greet the young Greeks who were to perform the Pyrrhic dance, a group of conspirators led by the prefect of the Praetorian Guard, Cassius Chaerea, himself a victim of the emperor's mockery, stabbed him to death. 'Gaius', as Dio Cassius put it succinctly, 'learnt in fact that he was not a god.'

The conspirators' watchword had been *libertas* but *libertas* in a constitutional sense was a remote dream. All was confusion. The senate was as impotent as ever. But a soldier wandering through the imperial palace found the prince Claudius crouching behind a curtain in fear of his life. He was dragged reluctantly to the Praetorian camp and proclaimed emperor.

What was the nature of Caligula's mental trouble, for even if he had periods of lucidity when he showed some political gifts, he was not wholly sane? His madness was said to have been a sequel to a serious illness which he had suffered soon after his accession in 37. If this was encephalitis, then it could very likely have been a contributory factor to the bizarre features of his life-style, for post-encephalitic disabilities can involve a marked change in character and give rise to impulsive, aggressive and intemperate activity, similar in its symptoms to those of schizophrenia. There is another possible or additional explanation, which gives added force to the assumption that Caligula's madness was organic in its origin. Caligula had inherited epilepsy from his father, Germanicus. 'He was sound neither of body nor of mind. As a boy he was troubled with the falling sickness, and while in his youth he had some endurance, yet at times because of sudden faintness he was hardly able to walk, to stand up, to collect his thoughts or to hold up his head.' He suffered severely from insomnia, never sleeping for more than three hours a night, 'and even for that length of time he did not sleep quietly, but was terrified by strange apparitions, once for example dreaming that the spirit of the ocean talked with him.' In his restless state he would leave his bed to sit on the couch or wander through the corridors and colonnades of the palace, longing for the dawn. Even before his illness in 37 Caligula may have been a victim of temporal lobe epilepsy, which has symptoms similar to those of schizophrenia, and to the post-encephalitic syndrome. A chronic brain syndrome could well have caused Caligula's mental impairment. While on the existing evidence it is impossible to come to an absolutely firm decision about Caligula's madness, there seems good reason to suppose that the emperor's derangement was a sequel to organic disease.[20]

Although his successor Claudius was very far from being mentally unbalanced, he too may have been a sufferer from encephalitis which left him physically frail and neurotic by disposition. Claudius was a man whom the imperial family had never taken very seriously, considering him to be sickly and half-witted to the point of imbecility.[21] He found standing so fatiguing that he habitually sat when addressing the senate, and was always carried in a litter through the streets of Rome. His head and his hands shook; his voice faltered. Understandably he was fearful of assassination and conspiracy; he had had his predecessor's murderer put to death because of his temerity in slaying an emperor. All who approached him were searched for weapons.

But if Claudius might in modern times have been a candidate for the psychologist's couch, he was no gormless pedant. Even his supposed stupidity may have been a protective cover in the hothouse atmosphere of the imperial court. He was to prove a shrewd and sensible ruler, showing moderation and good sense, for he reversed many of Caligula's unpopular measures, actually abolishing the charge of *maiestas* or treason which had been used so often in the past to bring both the guilty and the innocent to death. He ended some of the much-hated taxes, recalled the exiles and promoted more harmonious relations with the senate. In spite of his physical disabilities he made the tough journey to Britain after Aulus Plautius' invasion and conquest in 43.

Claudius' weakness arose less from his public policy than from his personal relationships, most especially with his wives. His third wife, Messalina, by whom he had had a son, Britannicus, was a promiscuous woman who flaunted her affairs with the consul-elect, C. Silvius. But when Claudius learned of this, Silvius was put to death and Messalina committed suicide. She was replaced in the emperor's bed by her rival, Agrippina, a sister of the former emperor Caligula, who was above all ambitious to ensure that her son by her first husband, Nero, might succeed to the imperial throne.

When Claudius himself conveniently died while watching a pantomime in 54, Britannicus was naturally pushed aside and displaced by Agrippina's son, Nero, who had been married the previous year to Claudius' daughter Octavia. Nero was to be the last emperor of the Julio-Claudian house and the most notorious,[22] 'the destroyer of the human race', 'the poison of the world' according to the elder Pliny. He was to be the first emperor whom the senate would declare to be a public enemy. Future generations were to see in Nero the prototype of wickedness, even of anti-Christ. He became in literature, as in Shakespeare's *Hamlet* and Racine's *Brittanique*, a synonym for matricide and unnatural cruelty. He was a hero to the marquis de Sade. Of him, even more appropriately than of Caligula, it may be said that he was a 'tainted hereditary degenerate corrupted by absolute power'.

Among historians there has been a reaction in his favour and with a more judicial, less highly coloured approach Nero's rule becomes more understandable and the emperor himself a more sympathetic figure. Yet from the very start of his reign there were indications not merely of vicious propensities but of mental instability. He roamed the streets of Rome with a gang of like-minded toughs, robbing passers-by and committing acts of violence. Tacitus supposes that it was the death of his adviser Burrus and the ending of the influence exerted over him by the intellectual Seneca and their replacement by the evil prefect Tigellinus which really marked the change in the nature of his governance.

He now determined to rid himself of his ambitious and scheming mother Agrippina. She may well have supposed that, like Livia, she could continue to exercise influence over her pleasure-loving son, but Nero was passionate and self-willed and resented her attempts to dominate him, more especially to order his private life. Nero did not love his wife Octavia and took a freedwoman, Acte, as his mistress. Agrippina, jealous of Acte's influence over her son, threatened to resurrect the claim of Claudius' son, the four-year-old Britannicus. Nero was not to be blackmailed by his mother. Britannicus died, poisoned as he sat at the children's table in the palace. Acte's influence soon faded as she was replaced by the love of Nero's life, Poppaea.

Meanwhile the emperor arranged for his mother Agrippina to travel in a collapsible boat when she sailed across the bay of Naples where she had been with her son at the celebrations of the feast of Quinquatria at Baiae. The boat sank, but the indomitable Agrippina swam ashore. She realized, however, that it was her own son who had treacherously engineered the shipwreck. Confronted by the naval officer whom Nero had sent to kill her, she ordered him bluntly to pierce the womb which bore her killer with his sword.

Three years later Nero decided to discard his wife and marry Poppaea. Octavia was charged with adultery with a slave, divorced and sent to the island of Pandateria, so full of ominous memories, where under duress she opened her veins. Poppaea, beautiful, passionate and ambitious, became Nero's bride. The milk of 500 asses was needed for her bath. Her husband, who was a cultured man with literary aspirations, wrote a song in praise of her amber-coloured hair. But three years later when she was pregnant, in a fit of rage, he kicked out at her, and, as a result, she died. Nero's remorse and grief were intense, for self-indulgent as he was, he was not void of feeling. There was, however, a curious sequel. His eye glanced upon a young freedman, Sporus, who much resembled Poppaea in looks, so much so that the emperor had him castrated and went through a marriage ceremony with him.

Caprice and passion seemed more and more to dominate Nero's life. He made government subserve his private pleasures which themselves imposed a public obligation upon his subjects. He was a philhellene with a genuine appreciation of Greek culture; but his love of the theatre and of chariot racing became so obsessive that he allowed it to influence his public policy.

That the emperor should take part in activities thought to be more suitable for slaves and freedmen than men of noble rank helped to antagonize the senatorial order, doubtless only too aware of Caligula's similar preferences and their dire consequences. At first Nero's performances were held in semi-privacy, but the emperor was proud of his prowess and yearned for an admiring audience. Indeed, he cherished his voice with the care of a modern pop-singer, so much so that he would lie down with lead weights on his chest to strengthen his diaphragm. He paid close attention to his diet to keep his vocal chords in good shape and to ensure that he had the physique appropriate to a professional charioteer. The elder Pliny commented that on certain days Nero would only eat chives preserved in oil; and he followed the example of the professional charioteers by imbibing dried boar's dung in water, perhaps the first century's equivalent of anabolic steroids.

By themselves these fads or eccentricities might well seem innocuous if they did not reflect a basic imbalance which affected not merely his personality but his politics. His policy, a recent historian has said, was a mixture of 'exhibitionism as a means to popularity, and repression as an antidote to fear',[23] and somewhere along the line the latter was to take precedence over the former. Bread and circuses failed to win the popular favour he wanted. His personal intolerance of rivals and critics even penetrated the world of entertainment, so that he came to believe in his own innate superiority as an artist as well as a ruler. It was popularly believed that he wished to found a new city named Neropolis. He had a great bronze statue of himself erected. The great fire which swept Rome in 64, attributed if groundlessly by popular rumour to arson initiated by the emperor, added to his growing unpopularity.

More and more fantasy seemed to take over his life. His reputation for depravity was enhanced by the celebration at a public banquet of another so-called marriage to a male lover, the freedman Pythagoras. Insulated from public opinion by flattery, Nero lived increasingly in a world of illusion which was in part sustained by acts of tyranny and cruelty. A plot to murder him as he was attending the chariot races in the Circus Maximus was unearthed in 64, leading to a series of prosecutions and enhancing further the emperor's paranoic suspicions. Inflated fiscal demands added further to his unpopularity. 'Nero's expectation of wealth', Tacitus commented, 'contributed to national bankruptcy.'

Although the emperor believed that he was threatened by the hostility of the senatorial order, he decided to visit Greece where he might enjoy the fame and glory that had eluded him at Rome. Rumblings of revolt were beginning to suffuse the empire, and army generals began to defect, among them Galba, the consular governor of Hispania Tarraconensis. The movement against Nero snowballed, and the senate declared him to be a public enemy.

He took refuge in the villa of Phaon outside Rome with four of his freedmen in attendance, one of whom, Epaphroditus, helped him to stab himself to death, just as horsemen arrived from the city. '*Qualis artifex pereo*' he murmured as he expressed the wish that his grave should be adorned with marble.

It is difficult to determine to what extent Nero was mentally unbalanced. It could be argued that he was acting according to his own conception of what the Roman principate required. If he fell it was rather because of his vicious life and mistaken policies than because of lack of mental balance. But Nero's vices, his insecurity and his tyranny seemed to originate in a mental attitude which verged on the abnormal. The genetic features of the Julio-Claudian house did not make for normality. He came of a line of strong-minded, passionate women, among them his great-grandmother Livia, his grandmother the elder Agrippina, his mother the younger Agrippina. It would take a trained geneticist to measure the effect which their genes had on their offspring. His emotional life, instanced by his love for Poppaea, might suggest that he was not a psychopath, though there were aspects of his life that seem psychopathic in their nature. That he was a schizophrenic is conceivable. At the least Nero was almost certainly affected by a personality disorder which brought him to the brink of madness. Like Tiberius he may not have been mad, but he was not wholly sane.

With Nero the Julio-Claudian line of emperors came to an end. For the next hundred years, apart from the Emperor Domitian who resembled Nero in his philhellenism, exhibitionism and tyranny, the emperors were to be men of experience and ability, warriors, administrators, builders, lawgivers, even philosophers: Vespasian, Titus, Trajan, Hadrian, Antoninus Pius, Marcus Aurelius. This was truly to be, as the eighteenth-century historian Edward Gibbon commented, the golden age of the empire.

Then suddenly, at the end of the second and in the early third century, the Roman Empire succumbed to rule by a group of young emperors who became mentally unbalanced: Commodus, Caracalla and Elagabalus. The golden age had ended with Marcus Aurelius' death in 180 and in the ensuing forty years, interrupted indeed by the stable reign from 192 to 211 of the able Emperor Septimus Severus, a majority of the emperors were untried youths whose minds seemed to be literally twisted by the absolute power which they wielded. Void of real talent they found compensation in a capricious, oppressive and unbalanced use of authority and, like Caligula, by claiming to possess divinity. If they were not clinically insane, they were certainly victims of personality disorders which would in modern times have required restraint and psychiatric treatment.

Commodus exemplified the way in which the possession of great power can not merely lead to the perpetration of grave injustice but can actually warp the mind to the point of madness, for what we know of Commodus suggests that he was very likely the victim of schizoid paranoia. Apparently an athletic youth without intellectual interests Commodus became a besotted and mentally unbalanced tyrant. By nature averse to administration he was content at first to leave government in the hands of his father's experienced advisers headed by the ambitious but honest Tigidius Perennis.

After Perennis was assassinated he made a Phrygian slave M. Aurelius Cleander his chief minister until riots against Cleander's corrupt rule led the emperor to sacrifice the minister in the hope of stilling the widespread discontent, and saving himself.

After Cleander's death Commodus indulged in a life-style which was bizarre to the point of madness. Like Caligula before him, Commodus proclaimed that he was a living god. 'So superlative was his insanity', Dio Cassius, a contemporary historian, wrote, 'that he described himself as *Ducator orbis, Conditor, Invictus, Amazonianus Exsuperatorius.*'[24] He claimed to be the incarnation of Hercules and obliged the senate to make sacrifices to his divine spirit. 'Such was his state of mental derangement', Herodian commented, 'that first he refused to use the family name and gave orders that he should be called Hercules, son of Zeus, instead of Commodus, son of Marcus.'[25] In pursuit of his delusion, he had the names of the months of the year changed, calling them after his own titles most of which were in some way associated with Hercules. The lion skin and club of Hercules were carried on the imperial throne as Commodus' insignia.

Since Hercules was the embodiment of physical strength, Commodus with insane logic came to believe that the best way of proving his identity with the god was to display his prowess in the public games. 'Animated by a mythologizing imagination', he loved to lay about his rivals with the club of Hercules. He proved to be an over-enthusiastic and sadistic exponent of his role, for he had such an insatiable appetite for bloodshed and slaughter that his actions can only be seen as the fruit of a diseased mind. He commanded the devotees of the orgiastic cult of Bellona to cut their arms '*studio crudelitatis*'. The priests of Isis were ordered to beat their breasts with pine cones until the blood streamed down their bodies. It was reported that the emperor had himself killed a man in the rites of Mithras.

But it was in the Roman amphitheatre that the emperor found his real opportunity to demonstrate his Herculean skills, and his schizoid nature. From a protected box he shot arrows at his victims, exotic animals from all parts of his empire and even beyond, elephants, hippopotamuses, rhinoceroses and giraffes.[26] In the Flavian games which lasted fourteen days, he slew a hundred lions, and initiated an ostrich hunt. The ostriches were slain by arrows which had blades so shaped (like a half-moon) that at least momentarily the animals were able to walk without their heads. Grimly holding an ostrich head in one hand Commodus walked towards the boxes where the senators sat, hinting that this would be the senators' fate if they did not obey his commands.[27]

Beasts were not enough to gratify his blood lust or to provide adequate opportunity for him to show his prowess. He decided that he must 'engage in gladiatorial combat with the stoutest young men'. Dumped in the arena stripped and ready for battle, his opponents knew that they dare not win but fortunately the emperor appeared to be satisfied if he only wounded them. They did not emerge unscathed but at least they

A bust of the emperor Caracalla (The Mansell Collection/Fratelli Alinari)

escaped a worse fate. Such was Commodus' infatuation with this new role that he decided that he would move from the palace and take up residence in the gladiatorial barracks. Furthermore he decreed that henceforth he should be known personally by the name of a former hero of the gladiatorial ring, Scaeva. It was a decision which was to lead indirectly to his downfall.

For his insensate, sadistic rule, accompanied by murders, terror and rigged prosecutions could in the long run have only one conclusion. Yet the senate, so long tame, appeared remarkably supine, and the populace of Rome took some pleasure in the extravagant spectacles that the emperor provided for their entertainment. It was from within his own inner circle that the plot for his destruction materialized.

Fearful for their own lives, members of his household, headed by his mistress Marcia, prepared a bowl of poisoned drink. When the emperor subsequently began to vomit, the athlete Narcissus strangled him.[28] Commodus had almost certainly been the victim of a severe form of psychosis, schizophrenic in character, which was given open expression as a result of the powers that he had wielded as emperor.

After Commodus' death the empire enjoyed twenty years of strong, masterful rule under Septimus Severus, but his death in 211 was to be followed by anarchy as generals fought each other for the imperial diadem, epitomized by the reigns of two emperors both of whom appeared in some respects mentally unbalanced, Caracalla and Elagabalus.

Caracalla, who was Septimus Severus' son, so-called because of the military cloak, a short tunic, Celtic or German in origin, which he wore, ascended the imperial throne jointly with his brother Geta. The brothers hated each other, and Caracalla planned to eliminate Geta. Under pretence of paving the way for a reconciliation with his brother he induced Geta to meet him in the apartment of their mother, the dowager empress, where he stabbed his brother to death, justifying the action by saying that he had forestalled an attack on himself by Geta. He managed to win over the soldiery by generous donations, which ruined the imperial treasury, and had all his brother's supporters eliminated.

His short reign was a catalogue of disasters, for he was as despotic in temper and seemingly almost as mentally disturbed as Commodus. Obsessed by a desire for military glory, he considered himself an incarnation of Alexander the Great in whose footsteps he sought to tread, adopting Macedonian costume and recruiting a special phalanx of Macedonian soldiers, whose commanders were to be called by the names of Alexander's generals. At Ilium he paid a visit to the tomb of Achilles.

Restive and suspicious, haunted by the nightmare of the fratricide which he had perpetrated, fearful of assassination, he constantly sought the advice of soothsayers and seers, and rid himself of all whom he thought to be his critics, whether there were good grounds or not. He ordered a particularly brutal massacre of the young men of

Alexandria because he had got it into his head that the city had made insufficient obeisance and made a mock of him. His ill-temper and caprice may have been made worse by the constant ill health from which he suffered, the exact nature of which we do not know; but in search of a cure he visited the shrines of the Celtic deity, Apollo Grannus at Baden-Baden, then called Aurelia Aquensis, and of Aesculapius at Pergamum.[29] In the spring of 217 he was murdered at the instigation of the Praetorian Prefect Macrinus.

Caracalla's assassination was no solution to the empire's problems, and there was a touch of make-believe about Macrinus' attempt to become emperor. A lawyer by profession, Macrinus sought vainly to consolidate his position, but he had powerful enemies in the old imperial Severan family headed by the emperor's widow, Julia Domna, and after her death by her sister, Julia Moesa. She was energetic and indomitable, intent on forwarding the fortunes of her two grandsons (for she herself had only daughters), Bassianus and Alexianus.

Bassianus, soon to be known as Elagabalus after the sun god whom he served,[30] was a strikingly beautiful fourteen year old who occupied the family position of high priest, presiding over a magnificent temple at Emesa, the central object of which was a large conical black stone which, legend said, had been sent from heaven. The handsome high priest, a youthful exhibitionist, averse to wearing Roman or Greek wool, ready to wear only silk next to his skin, exulted in the gaudy vestments of his office.[31]

Although Elagabalus probably had no political ambitions, he was to be the vehicle of his grandmother's determination to mould the destinies of the Roman Empire. She viewed Macrinus with contempt, and in her determination to restore the house of Severus to its rightful position bribed the soldiery with generous sums of money, circulating the rumour that the real father of Elagabalus was none other than the Emperor Caracalla.

As the news filtered quickly through the eastern province, she and her family hatched a plot to make Elagabalus the emperor, leaving the city with her daughters for the soldiers' camp. Macrinus, who was in Antioch, did not at first take the news of a potential mutiny seriously, but as more and more troops defected, he lost heart, so that when the two armies faced each other, he shed his purple cloak and imperial insignia, shaved his beard and took flight. He hoped to make for Rome where he might find supporters, but at Chalcedon he was discovered and promptly executed.

The high priest of the sun, Elagabalus, who now became emperor, was probably the most bizarre person ever to preside over the destinies of the Roman Empire. In so cosmopolitan a world, it was unimportant that he was a Syrian; Septimus Severus had been a Libyan. But his lack of experience, his youth and his aberrant personality were to be matters of serious concern. He was a strange, sensitive youth thrust into a position for which he was totally unsuited. This did not worry his grandmother, Julia Moesa, who doubtless assumed that she would exercise real power while her grandson played a nominal role. She simply told him when the court prepared to leave Nicomedia for Rome that he should try to dress more soberly and adapt himself to western Roman customs.

Elagabalus was engrossed by his position as high priest and the combination of his priestly destiny with political power formed a deadly prescription for imperial rule, upsetting the balance of a mind which was probably never wholly normal. Like Caligula and Commodus before him, he came to believe that human and divine were fused in his person, and a high priest of the sun god, be became the embodiment of the god himself. Even if he appeased the Romans by generous largesse and the provision of lavish spectacles in the amphitheatre he soon upset the religious susceptibilities of the serious-minded senators by demoting Jupiter in favour of his own god.

One of his first actions had been to erect a magnificent temple in which the image of the god was to be installed. The god was conveyed to his new house in a chariot decorated with gold and precious stones and drawn by a team of six white horses. To the spectators it appeared as if the god was driving the chariot himself, but in practice Elagabalus ran in front of the chariot facing backwards, holding the horses' bridles. The Roman onlookers, fascinated by so unusual a spectacle, showered the procession with flowers and wreaths while dignified military prefects, dressed in long tunics in the Syrian style, were conscripted to bear the entrails of the sacrificial victims mingled with spices of wine in golden bowls. When he reached the temple the emperor climbed on to a specially constructed tower and scattered gifts, gold and silver cups, clothes, linen and even domestic animals, excepting pigs which his religion forbade the emperor to touch, among the excited throng of citizens.

Such antics, providing a spectacular pantomime for the onlookers, were in themselves harmless enough, but Elagabalus' obsession overmastered him. If he was a god, he argued that he must marry a goddess. When the statue of Pallas was brought to the temple as a possible consort, Elagabalus demurred, declaring that his intended bride was of too warlike a disposition. His choice finally alighted on the Carthaginian goddess of the moon, Urania, Tanit or Astarte as she was variously called. Indeed, what more appropriate bride for the sun god could there be than the moon goddess? More practically he demanded a large sum of money for his dowry and ordered his subjects to celebrate the marriage with festivities and banquets.

But it is one thing to marry a goddess and another to consummate the marriage. This young, handsome emperor had a very human sexual drive, perhaps even an overdrive. In human terms he married first an aristocratic Roman lady but then divorced her to wed Julia Aquila, who happened to be a Vestal Virgin, a priestess of the Roman goddess Vesta, vowed to chastity. Such a union obviously constituted a serious breach of religious decorum but the emperor confounded his critics by declaring that a marriage between two such sacred persons as he and Julia Aquila was not an impious but a particularly holy union. Although he had declared that the ties binding himself to Julia Aquila were sacred, he was soon to discard her in favour of a member of the imperial family, even though at the end of his short life he was to return to her embraces. Before that happened he had contracted a fifth marriage, all of which was not bad going in four years.

Elagabalus suffered from sexual as well as mental confusion. So much in love with finery, be began to dress as a woman. With his face rouged and painted, golden necklaces glittering on his silken tunic, he readily danced for a public audience. 'He worked with wool, sometimes wore a hair-net and painted his eyes, daubing them with white paint and alkanet. Once, indeed, he shaved his chin and held a festival to mark the occasion; but after that he had the hairs plucked out, so as to look more like a woman.'[32] At another time he considered having his genitals removed. Dio Cassius wrote that

> He used his body both for doing and allowing many strange things. . . . He would go to the taverns by night, wearing a wig, and there ply the trade of a female huckster. He frequented the notorious brothels, drove out the prostitutes and played the prostitute himself. Finally, he set aside a room in the palace and there committed his indecencies, always standing nude at the door of the room as the harlots do, and shaking the curtain which hung with gold rings, while in a soft and melting voice he solicited the passers-by.[33]

His clients had apparently to pay good money for the imperial favours.

His standing as emperor was hardly enhanced by rumours of these exploits which would have been less harmful had he not appointed as ministers and imperial officials men of like tastes. His principal favourite was a former Carian slave, Hierocles, who had attracted the emperor's attention when he fell off a chariot revealing his handsome face and fair yellow hair. Elagabalus summoned him to the palace, had him teach him the art of charioteering, and eventually went through a form of marriage with him, calling Hierocles 'his husband'. The emperor's passion for Hierocles, who came to exercise immense influence in the palace, was so ardent that he risked his grandmother's wrath by suggesting that he should be made Caesar. Yet Hierocles was not the only man whose 'nocturnal feats' entranced this imperial transvestite. Those who sought his favours were first induced to commit 'adultery' with him. The emperor was a masochist who liked nothing better than being discovered and beaten up by his lover, 'so that he had black eyes'.

Once only was Hierocles' influence put to the test. News had reached the emperor of a beautiful young man, Aurelius Zoticus, a cook's son from Smyrna, an athlete whose 'private parts . . . greatly surpassed all others'. Elagabalus made Zoticus his chamberlain and, 'finding him when stripped equal to his reputation, burned with even greater lust'. But Hierocles, jealous of a dangerous rival, managed to administer a drug to Zoticus that sapped his sexual prowess. After 'a whole night of embarrassment, being unable to secure an erection', Zoticus was driven from the palace in disgrace.[34]

Such singular goings-on at the imperial palace reacted on the imperial government and ultimately on the Roman populace, creating a wave of discontent. Elagabalus responded to criticism as his predecessors had done, by imprisoning and executing those who questioned his activities and by rewarding his minions with high office. Charioteers, freedmen, actors, a barber, a mule driver, a locksmith, all of whom had attracted the emperor's attention by their looks, were entrusted with high government office. 'The emperor', Herodian commented, 'was driven to such extremes of lunacy that he took men from the stage and the public theatres and put them in charge of the most important imperial business.'[35]

All this was not exactly what his grandmother Julia Moesa had bargained for. She wanted power and position, and as the sister-in-law of the Emperor Septimus Severus may have had a greater sense of political responsibility than her grandson. She had supposed that he would be her tool and here too she had suffered acute disappointment. Desperately worried by Elagabalus' indiscretions, she managed to persuade him to appoint his cousin, her other grandson Alexianus, who changed his name to Alexander, as Caesar, so at least managing to provide for the succession should Elagabalus disappear from the scene. As Elagabalus was still only in his early twenties, Julia Moesa was evidently contemplating the possibility of bringing her grandson's manic rule to an end. To substantiate Alexander's position she now gave out that he also was Caracalla's son, Caracalla having been passed from the embraces of one sister to the other. Alexander's mother Mamaea, fearful for her son's safety, tried to get him removed from his cousin's dissolute court, so that he could be properly instructed in academic and martial arts.

Disturbed in mind as he was, Elagabalus had sufficient grip on reality to perceive the drift of events. Angrily he banished Alexander's tutors from the palace. Mamaea warned Alexander that he must not eat or drink anything prepared in the imperial kitchen. She and her mother began secretly to distribute money to the soldiery so that if things came to a crisis they would not lack support. Elagabalus tried to abrogate the title of Caesar which he had recently conferred upon his cousin.

In late 221 discontent among the soldiery led to a mutiny which was suppressed by the Praetorian prefect, but it was an ominous indication to Elagabalus of the loathing with which the army, which held the key to his continuance in office, regarded his government. In an effort to regain their support he dismissed some of his unpopular advisers and restored his cousin Alexander, whom he had previously announced was at death's door, to the office of Caesar. To allay the soldiers' suspicions, Alexander was himself brought in a litter to the camp. But it was too late. The soldiers, won over by Julia Moesa's bounty, acclaimed Alexander and ignored the emperor. In his extremity Elagabalus spent the night at the shrine and as a desperate last resort ordered the arrest of Alexander's leading supporters.

But it was the end. The soldiers turned the tables on the emperor as they were so constantly to do in imperial history. They slew Elagabalus, his mother Soaemis and his favourites, Hierocles among them. Their bodies were dragged through the city, mutilated and thrown into the sewers which ran into the River Tiber. Alexander Severus was proclaimed emperor. His grandmother Julia Moesa and his mother Mamaea could breath again; and the sun god was banished from Rome.

In practice Elagabalus meets all the criteria of what a modern psychologist would describe as a narcissistic personality disorder.[36] He had a grandiose sense of self-importance and he was preoccupied with fantasies of finery and power to the exclusion of political realism. He expected special favours and absolute service without assuming any special responsibilities towards his subjects or those who served him. He was an exhibitionist who required constant admiration and attention. His personal relationships were disturbed, in part because of a lack of empathy, so that he gave little real affection and received little in return. To criticism he reacted with indifference or rage. He was wholly self-centred, if originally encouraged to become so by his grandmother, and his life was threaded by sexual instability and gender confusion. He ran through a gamut of wives, and it is doubtful whether he ever had a significant real relationship, except a physical one, with his male favourites. Ultimately an immature and egotistical young man, demanding adulation and even worship, he was so supremely egocentric as to be the victim of a specific narcissistic personality disorder.

The Roman emperors whom we have been considering suffered from different forms of derangement, mental and physical, but they were united by one thing, the possession of absolute power. It was this power which made it possible for Tiberius and Nero to act as tyrants, and for Caligula, Commodus and Elagabalus to claim divine status. But power is like a drug. Its addicts become its slaves, for power 'grows by what it feeds upon'. So the emperors' visions became clouded, their judgements perverted and their perceptions dulled, with detrimental effects for their subjects thoughout their wide domains; the Roman senate was cowed into submission, the treasury was constantly plundered, innocent men and women suffered torture and death.

III

Medieval Trilogy

The Roman emperors whom we have been discussing were absolute rulers, their minds distorted and disturbed by the powers at their disposal. The English medieval kings were men of a different mould, brought up in the Christian tradition, their authority limited by the responsibilities which custom imposed and by the oaths which they had taken at their coronation. They were, whatever their deficiencies and lack of native capacity, by and large aware of the duties they owed their people, to wage successful war and to administer justice. In effect, most of the medieval English kings within the context of their times coped more or less adequately with the problems with which their magnates and the economic and political uncertainties of their age brought into being.

There were, however, four kings who were far less successful, whose reigns were disturbed by civil strife and ended in disaster: John, Edward II, Richard II and Henry VI. Of the four the last three were deprived of their thrones and eventually murdered. John may have escaped deposition by dying. Of the four Richard II and Henry VI ascended the throne as minors, a factor which helped to condition the policies they followed and which may have contributed to the disastrous conclusion of their reigns. Although John and Edward II were both mature young men when they became king, their personal background and adolescence may well explain the more abrasive aspect of their personalities.

Each of these kings had what may be described as a personality problem which led some contemporaries and some modern historians to use the label abnormal, even mad. John was described by a contemporary chronicler as 'possessed' and 'sent mad by sorcery and witchcraft'. A modern French historian, Charles Petit-Dutaillis, writing in 1936, believed him to be the victim of a deep psychological disorder. John Lackland, he wrote,

> was subject to a mental disease well known today and described by modern psychiatrists as the periodical psychosis. It is surprising that modern historians have been able to estimate his character so wrongly and suggest for instance that he was a villain whose wickedness was cold and deliberate, who never allowed passion to guide him, and must, therefore, be regarded as all the more unpardonable. . . . All the symptoms we have enumerated are those of the periodic psychosis or cyclothymia. Philip Augustus (the French King, his enemy) had a madman as his rival.[1]

In his own times Edward II was regarded as perverse rather than mad, and it was left to an early twentiety-century American scholar to deduce that he was insane. The king, Dr Chalfont Robinson held, suffered from what 'medical science recognizes under the general name of degeneracy' caused by 'a diseased condition of the brain'.[2] The British historian, A.B. Steel, believed that in his later years Richard II was a schizophrenic.[3] Whatever doubts there may be about this diagnosis, Henry VI certainly suffered a severe nervous breakdown between 1454 and 1456 and may well have never fully recovered his senses. Each then of these kings was the victim of a personality disorder and may have suffered some degree of mental impairment.

But how serious were these personality disorders and what was their character? How did they affect the events of these kings' reigns? Modern historians have gone some way to rehabilitate the reputation of John, so long regarded as the worst of the English medieval kings, tyrannical, immoral and unjust.[4] He was certainly faced by intractable problems which would have tried the skill of statesmen of greater ability and resources. His reign was full of troubles for which he can hardly be blamed: growing baronial discontent, the hostility of the great French prince, Philip Augustus, the quarrel with Pope Innocent III, the inflation of the economy. He did not lack talent in trying to resolve these crises but there was a cumulative series of disasters as his plans went astray. The pope placed England under an ecclesiastical interdict, banning all church services and religious ceremonies, until John gave way and became the pope's vassal, an act which many regarded as unforgivably humiliating. His extortionate fiscal demands led to increasing complaints from the barons, so that eventually there was a general uprising which obliged the king to agree to the great charter of liberties, the Magna Carta, sealed in May 1215. Whether the king had any intention of keeping the terms may be doubted; the malcontent barons had already invited the French to help. At this juncture, having lost his baggage including the royal regalia in the rising waters of the Wellstream estuary, John became seriously ill and died on 18 October 1216 as a fierce wind whipped the waves.

To what extent did John's personality exacerbate these problems, and in what respects, if any, could he be described as mentally disturbed? That John's character was complex and enigmatic must be readily granted. Whether there is any justification for calling him a madman is more a matter of doubt. His personality has to be understood in the light of his ancestry and upbringing. For he came of a long line of able but unbalanced princes, the counts of Anjou, a small principality in central France, the territory of which by masterful manipulation they had gradually extended. John's father, Henry II, had become king of England, duke of Normandy and through an advantageous but unhappy marriage with Eleanor of Aquitaine, duke of Aquitaine, covering a substantial area of south-west France, a vast empire encompassing England and much of France which John was to inherit from his brother, Richard I in 1199.

The Angevin family, the Plantagenets, were known familiarly as the 'devil's brood'. Folk tales spoke of a weird ancestry. A count of Anjou came back with a new wife, a strange girl of extraordinary beauty but she kept very much to herself. Unusually in so religious an age she was reluctant to attend the Mass. When she did go she always hurried from the church before the consecration of the host. Her husband, who was puzzled by her behaviour, told four knights to keep watch and to try to delay her departure from the church. When she got up to go, one of them trod on the hem of her train. As the priest raised the host to consecrate it, she screamed, wrenched herself free, and still shrieking, flew out of the window, taking two of her children with her. In reality the countess was the wicked fairy, Melusine, the daughter of Satan, who cannot abide the consecration of the body of Christ in the Mass. It was from the children that she left behind that the counts of Anjou and the Angevin kings of England were said to be descended. In a superstitious age and a credulous society, such a legend might seem to explain the abnormal traits of the members of the Plantagenet family.

So 'devilish' an ancestry accounted for the demonic energy and passionate ill-temper by which these princes seemed often afflicted. 'We who came from the devil', John's brother, Richard I, was reported as saying caustically, 'must needs go back to the devil.'[5] 'Do not deprive us of our heritage: we cannot help acting like devils.' '*De diabolo venit et ad diabolum ibit*', commented St Bernard of Clairvaux, 'From the devil he came, and to the devil he will go.'[6]

John's father, Henry II, was a man of great ability and ruthless determination, habitually restless and given to outbursts of violent rage. When he was angry, his eyes flashed fire. 'He is great, indeed the greatest of monarchs', Arnulf of Lisieux told Archbishop Thomas Becket of Canterbury who was later to feel the violent impact of the royal rage, 'for he has no superior of whom he stands in awe, no subject who may resist him.'[7] Admonished by a brave bishop for a show of ill-temper, Henry said roughly that if God could be angry, there was no reason why the king should not be also. When an unfortunate counsellor, Richard du Hommet, happened to say some words in praise of his enemy, William the Lion, the king of Scotland, Henry 'flung his cap from his head, pulled off his belt, threw off his cloak and clothes, grabbed the silken coverlet off the couch, and sitting as it might be on a dung heap started chewing pieces of straw'.[8]

Such an ancestry may explain some of John's traits, more especially when it is remembered that John's mother, Eleanor of Aquitaine, was herself an imperious and turbulent woman. John was the youngest of the devil's brood, the spoilt child, a fop who seemed to prefer the luxury of the court to the martial arts, and who was immature in behaviour and outlook. It would be possible to interpret John's aberrant character in terms of his upbringing and environment. He was at the centre of a tug of war between an arbitrary father and a dominant mother. His mother tended to despise him. His father favoured and then threw him overboard. The Angevin court in which he was brought up was a school for dissimulation and treachery; and John proved a ready pupil. Passionate and self-centred, he appears as much the victim as the maker of the problems which were eventually to overwhelm him.

What, then, specifically can be said which might suggest that his mind was unbalanced? Petit-Dutaillis described him as the victim of a manic-depressive illness which accounted for the way in which his life seemed to alternate between periods of great energy and an all-pervasive lethargy. His inertia was a major ingredient in the loss of Normandy to the French in 1204.[9] The king, the chronicler commented, lived it up at night and stayed long in bed in the morning with his young wife, Isabella. On the very day that he was shipping his horses, dogs and falcons to Normady to be sure that they would be available there on his arrival, the linch-pin in the English defence of Normandy, the powerful fortress of Château-Gaillard, overlooking the River Seine, fell to the enemy. Yet a close examination of the documentary evidence does not suggest that this flagrant alternation between energy and indolence was a continuous feature of his life. John's attention to government may on occasions have been sporadic, but in general while he had fits of indolence, he was hard-working, even a conscientious king.

If this charge fails, what is left to suggest that John was mentally ill-balanced? It has been said that his furious rage and excessive cruelty were such that men thought that he acted like a madman. 'His whole person', Richard of Devizes recalled of a confrontation between John and Richard I's chancellor, William Longchamp, 'became so changed as to be hardly recognizable. Rage contorted his brow, his burning eyes glittered, bluish spots discoloured the pink of his cheeks, and I know not what would have become of the chancellor if in that moment of frenzy he had fallen like an apple into his hands as they sawed the air.'[10] Such gross ill-temper suggested certainly that he may have had a personality disorder, but ill-temper was a characteristic of the Angevin house.

He lived in a brutal age, mollified as it was by prayer and sanctity but often awash with mutilation and blood. Yet even by the standards of his age John was overly cruel, 'a very bad man, cruel towards all men and too covetous of pretty ladies' was the chronicler's comment. His cruel, sadistic nature was revealed in his treatment of his nephew, Arthur of Brittany, who might have been thought to have had a better claim to the English throne than John himself.

Arthur's mother, Catherine, fearful of an attempt on the life of her son, then a boy of twelve, sent him for safety to the court of the French king, Philip Augustus. The Bretons accepted him as their lord enthusiastically which angered their neighbours, the Normans, who declared for John. The king could not rid himself of the nagging fear that young Arthur was a dangerous rival.

Fate played into the king's hands. At length, in 1202 at Mirebeau the young prince became John's captive, and disappeared from history. The chronicler Ralph of Coggeshall said that John had ordered that Arthur should be blinded and castrated at the castle of Falaise but that his guardian, Hubert de Burgh, managed to frustrate the foul deed, a story which Shakespeare was later to incorporate in his play *King John*.[11]

A more likely tale occurs in another chronicle originating at the Cistercian abbey of Margam in Gloucestershire of which William de Briouse, who had captured Arthur at Mirebeau, was patron.

> After King John had captured Arthur and kept him alive in prison for some time, at length, in the castle of Rouen, after dinner on the Thursday before Easter [3 April 1203], when he was drunk and possessed by the devil ['*ebrius et daemonio plenus*'] he slew him with his own hand and tying a heavy stone to the body cast it into the Seine. It was discovered by a fisherman in his net and being dragged to the bank and recognized, was taken for secret burial, in fear of the tyrant, to the priory of Bec.[12]

The Briouse family were much in John's favour at this time and enriched by him with land and lordships; but relations between John and William de Briouse became strained and issued in the now familiar story of suspicion, terror and cruel death. De Briouse may have thought that he had not been rewarded generously enough. The king feared a masterful subject who possessed a deadly secret, his murder of Arthur. When John demanded of de Briouse's wife, Matilda, that she should surrender her sons as hostages, she told the king's emissaries somewhat indiscreetly that she would not dream of giving up her sons to the man who had murdered his own nephew. John was to pursue the de Briouse family with unrelenting vindictiveness.

John was a vindictive, cruel king but his cruelty, whether impulsive or calculated, was hardly so sadistic or on such a scale as to deserve the attribution of insanity; he compares favourably, for instance, with the Russian tsars, Ivan the Terrible and Peter the Great, whose sadistic treatment of their enemies bears the hallmark of mental imbalance.

Possibly the imbalance of John's mind appears most forcibly in his sense of insecurity, which gave rise to the cruel and vindictive treatment of his enemies, and the all-enveloping jealousy and suspicion with which he tended to treat friend and foe alike. He readily abandoned those who had supported him loyally, men such as Hubert de Burgh and William Marshal. He had a narrowing circle of advisers and relied on foreign mercenary soldiers like Gerard de Athies. Masterful and able as he undoubtedly was, at the last he was confronted by a situation beyond his control; a disappointed baronage made fractious by extortionate fiscal demands, an insufficient revenue to which rising costs and falling income contributed, and enmity of two of the greatest men of the age, Philip Augustus of France and the pope, Innocent III. He was unlucky rather than mad. Yet there were undoubtedly aspects of his character which puzzled and alarmed his contemporaries. He was 'possessed by the devil' the Margam chronicler said,[13] 'sent mad by sorcery and witchcraft' Roger of Wendover commented harshly.[14] If he was not mad, was he fully sane? Were those traits of temperament, some of which he inherited from his ancestors, pushing him over the brink of sanity? We must give him the benefit of the doubt, and yet remain still uneasy at the way in which he sometimes behaved. His occasional bouts of lethargy, his rage and cruelty, his obsessive suspicions may well suggest that he was the victim of an acute personality disorder.

Edward II, John's great-grandson, who became King of England in 1307, was not favoured by fortune. His reign, as Christopher Marlowe intimated in his play, was a personal tragedy. It was to be as disastrous as that of King John and for not dissimilar reasons. If the flaws in John's character exacerbated the crises by which he was faced, no less, indeed to an even greater extent, the nature of Edward II's personality was a contributory factor in his downfall. There can be no doubt that private animosities

Detail of the tomb of Edward II, Gloucester Cathedral (by courtesy of the Dean and Chapter of Gloucester Cathedral)

47

became entangled with public policy. But was Edward's personality disordered, as an American writer thought some eighty years ago, to the point of insanity?[15] While his personality had abnormal traits and to many of his contemporaries seemed unfitting for a king, Edward II was not a madman.

As with so many other princes, his personality was shaped significantly by his upbringing. The son of Edward I who had named him Prince of Wales in 1301, he found the royal court an uncongenial environment. His mother, Eleanor of Castile, had died when he was thirteen. His father, Edward I, was a terrific warrior, hard-headed and energetic, with the characteristic Angevin ill-temper. The wardrobe accounts, for instance, tell of a payment made in 1297 to Adam the royal goldsmith to replace a 'great ruby and a great emerald bought to set in a certain coronet of the countess of Holland, the king's daughter', which Edward in a fit of rage had thrown into the fire.[16]

His young son reacted against the warlike atmosphere of the court and his harsh, tempestuous father. Edward II was no namby-pamby, for he grew into a strong, handsome man, who delighted in horsemanship. He was more cultured than most of the magnates at the court, for he had an eye for poetry and a taste for theatricals. It was rumoured that his chancellor and archbishop of Canterbury, Walter Reynolds, originally caught his attention because of his talent as a producer of drama. As king Edward kept a small orchestra in his employ.

As Edward grew up, so his recreations seemed less and less those expected of a knight, let alone of a royal prince: boating, swimming and even menial pursuits like hedging and ditching, all activities which, innocuous in themselves, were thought unnatural in a future king. The royal accounts, for instance, mention a payment which was made to Robert 'his fool' when Edward accidentally injured him in a frolic in the water in February,[17] a strange time of year surely to go swimming, not in any case an activity in which medieval men and women indulged for pleasure. He apparently found greater satisfaction in the company of sturdy young labourers than in the well-heeled knights of the court. 'Undervaluing the society of the magnates', so wrote the chronicler, 'he fraternized with buffoons, singers, actors, carters, ditchers, oarsmen, sailors and others who practised mechanical arts.'[18] After the disastrous defeat which his army received at the hands of the Scots on the battlefield of Bannockburn in 1314, one of the king's servants Robert le Messager gossiping with Saer Keym, the sub-bailiff of Newington in Kent, speculated that Edward could hardly expect to win battles if he spent so much of his time in 'idling and applying himself to making ditches and other improper occupations'.[19] 'Had he devoted as much time to arms', another chronicler commented, 'as he gave to rustic arts, England would have prospered and his name rung through the whole earth.'

What seemed even more unnatural and shocking was his obsessive affection for a young squire at his father's court, Piers Gaveston, whose father, the Bearnese knight

Arnold de Gaveston had come to England in 1296 and received royal patronage. Piers was a handsome, witty, flamboyant young man whose close companionship freed Edward from his icy isolation within the royal household and perhaps gave him a measure of self-confidence which he had lacked. But though Piers and his father had been befriended originally by the king himself, his blood was thought to be insufficiently noble for him to become the prince's boon companion, more especially when Edward and Gaveston paraded their intimacy before the court. Edward, Sir Thomas Gray reported, 'was too familiar with his intimates, shy with strangers and loved too exclusively a single individual'.[20] 'And when the king's son saw him, he fell so much in love that he entered upon an enduring compact with him, and chose and determined to knit an indissoluble bond of affection with him, before all mortals.'[21]

The relationship between his heir and the young knight puzzled and worried the king. Deep friendship beween men was a recognized feature of medieval society. A contemporary compared Edward's friendship with Gaveston to that of David and Jonathan, the authentic scriptural justification of male intimacy. But such intimacy, which, as the Anglo-Norman poem *Amis and Amiloun* declared, might even take precedence of loyalty to a wife, was based on mutual reciprocity and had to be devoid of any physical relationship.[22] If there was a physical relationship in which one partner was active and the other passive, this constituted an unnatural act and a clear breach of the moral law. Whatever contemporaries suspected, they hardly dared voice their suspicions in Edward's lifetime. It was only after his death that the author of the Chronicle of Melsa could state categorically that Edward '*delectabat invitio sodomitico nimium*, delighted inordinately in the vice of sodomy, and seemed to lack fortune and grace throughout his life'.[23]

Whatever Edward I's suspicions, he wished to be shot of Gaveston, more especially as he was negotiating for his son's marriage to a French princess. When in the spring of 1307 his son, greatly daring, asked his father to confer the county of Ponthieu upon his friend, the king responded violently. 'Whoreson, misbegotten boy, wilt thou give away lands who has never gained any? As God liveth, if it were not for fear of breaking up the kingdom, thou shouldst never enjoy thy heritage.' He turned on his son, seized him by the head, tearing out his hair by the roots.[24] On 26 February he issued a decree, expelling Gaveston from the kingdom and ordering his son never again to make contact with his favourite. A few months later, on 7 July 1307, the ill-tempered warrior king died on his last expedition against the turbulent Scots.

Edward II at once reversed his father's edict, *qui statim revocavit amasium suum Petrum de Gaveston*,[25] summoning Gaveston back to court, creating him earl of Cornwall (on 6 August 1307), and endowing him with substantial estates, among them property in the ownership of his father's minister, Walter Langton, bishop of Coventry, who had once administered a sharp rebuke to Edward for his unseemly life-style.

For reasons of convenience both men entered into marriage arrangements. Gaveston married the king's niece, Margaret de Clare, a sister of the young earl of Gloucester and a substantial heiress in her own right, by whom he had a daughter. Edward was married, as his father had already arranged, to the twelve-year-old daughter of the French king, Isabella. Edward was in fact bisexual, for he was to have two sons and two daughters by his wife as well as an illegitimate son, Adam. It was, however, upon Gaveston that Edward lavished his affection, so much so that some wondered whether he was the victim of the black arts.[26] Gaveston, flamboyant and insensitive to the magnates' disapproval, revelled in his new position.

Fundamentally the majority of the magnates were less concerned with Gaveston and his influence over the king, though they much resented the way in which he controlled the king's powers of patronage, than with their own political rights of which they believed Edward II's father had deprived them and which they wished now to retrieve, but Gaveston formed a scapegoat at whom they could direct their hostility. They managed to get a new clause inserted into the oath which the king took at his coronation to the effect that Edward promised to observe the 'rightful laws and customs which the community of the realm shall have chosen', obliging the king, as they saw it, to make concessions to the 'community of the realm', which they had no difficulty in identifying with their own elitest interests. As a prelude to forcing the king's hand the council demanded Gaveston's banishment on 28 April 1309.

Edward was placed on the horns of a dilemma. If he defied the barons, he might be faced with a civil war which he could not win. He was emotionally bound to Gaveston but hoped that if he agreed to banish him a way might be found of getting him back. He was banished from court on 18 May but on 28 June appointed lieutenant of Ireland, a post in which he was to acquit himself well. In desperation at losing his companion Edward accompanied him to Bristol from where he was to sail for Ireland, and later even besought the French king's help to bring about his return to court. The pope Clement V absolved Gaveston from the threat of excommunication and he returned to court.

Neither Gaveston nor Edward knew how to be politically discreet. Gaveston behaved as insolently and arrogantly as before. He had enraged the magnates by devising appropriate nicknames for them. 'Here comes the black dog of Arden,' he would say as the powerful earl of Warwick approached; the earl of Lincoln was called 'broste bely', the earl of Lancaster the fiddler or play actor, the earl of Gloucester the whoreson, the earl of Pembroke, Joseph the Jew. 'Let him', Warwick growled, 'call me hound; one day the hound will bite him.'[27] The hound was indeed to have the last word or rather the last bite.

After Gaveston's return the situation deteriorated rapidly. Edward was in such financial difficulties, which some attributed to Gaveston's greed, that he was obliged to agree to a new scheme for the limitation of his power, the appointment of twenty-one barons as ordainers to draw up a scheme for the reform of government, which included not surprisingly a renewed demand for the banishment of Gaveston.

Once more Edward was faced with the difficulty of choosing between his favourite and the magnates without whose support he could not govern. Fearful for his safety, Edward sent him to the massive fortress of Bamburgh, towering over the North Sea and then agreed unwillingly that he should seek refuge at Bruges in Flanders. But he could not really live long without him; Gaveston soon returned to favour and new riches.

To the barons Gaveston represented the royal defiance of their wishes. The archbishop of Canterbury excommunicated him and his followers. Edward, without adequate military resources, fled with Gaveston first to Tynemouth and then to Scarborough where the favourite remained while the king withdrew to York. Hot in pursuit the earls of Warenne and Pembroke prepared to besiege Scarborough. Gaveston, hoping against hope that he might be granted a safe conduct, decided, misguidedly, to surrender. He was sentenced to death after a mockery of a trial and executed at Blacklow Hill on 19 June 1312. His death was naturally a horrific experience from which Edward never properly recovered. 'I do not remember', as a contemporary put it, 'to have heard that one man so loved another.' The Dominican friars took his body which was eventually given sumptuous burial by the king's orders at King's Langley, the chantry there being in effect transformed into a memorial shrine. Edward was never to forget or to forgive the earls who had hounded his favourite to death. His affection for Gaveston had been the one constant thing in his life and it was to condition all that was to happen in his remaining fifteen years. Henceforth there was to be 'perpetual hatred . . . between the king and the earls'.

Gaveston's death was a watershed in Edward's life. Did it foreshadow a deterioration in his mental grasp and political capacity? If *prima facie* there is little evidence for this, more and more people plainly thought that Edward was by nature so unsuited to be king that they even questioned his royal birth. Men and women were far less ready to avail themselves of the custom of being touched for the king's evil by Edward, the royal touch supposedly affording a cure to the tuberculous eye disease, scrofula. Where his father had sometimes touched as many as 1,700 in a single year, his son apparently never touched more than 214.[28] Rumour spread that Edward was a changeling, substituted by a nurse soon after birth to replace the royal prince who had been savagely mauled by a wild boar. 'A certain writer named John, who had a cat as his familiar spirit', appeared at Oxford, claiming to be the genuine king. 'The rumour ran through all the land and troubled the queen beyond measure.'[29] After a period of reconciliation his relations with the queen had sunk to a new low. Edward, it was reported, 'carried a knife in his hose to kill Queen Isabella, and had said that if he had no other weapon he would crush her with his teeth'.[30] There was some reason for thinking that his judgement was unbalanced and that his mind might be unhinged.

Yet set against this his governance was firmer and stronger in the last years of his reign than it had been in earlier years. After a period of semi-baronial rule, Edward had recovered his royal powers, in part through the instrumentality of two magnates, Hugh Despenser and his son. It is possible that the younger Despenser may have taken Gaveston's place in his affections. But their role was primarily political. The royal army defeated the baronial leader, the king's cousin, the earl of Lancaster at the battle of Boroughbridge in Yorkshire in 1322.[31] After a summary trial, Lancaster was led out to his execution. His fate, seemingly curiously and appropriately reminiscent of Gaveston's execution ten years earlier, must have afforded the king much personal satisfaction.

Although some attempts were made to introduce administrative reforms and so promote the effectiveness of government, Edward's rule was ruthless and even tyrannical.[32] He tried to win over a band of loyal supporters but failed to do so, even though he had the money and patronage to buy support. He determined to consolidate his position by building up a royal treasure, by extortionate fiscal measures and the confiscation of estates from barons of suspected loyalty, all of which would make him independent of baronial control. Unwisely he placed too much trust in the Despensers. Even more insatiable in their greed than Gaveston they set about acquiring a vast estate in South Wales as well as a massive treasure, some of which they sent abroad to Italian bankers. In spite of his own success in filling the royal treasury, Edward seems to have lost his political grip.

There was smouldering discontent among all classes. At Coventry in 1323 some citizens of the town, angered by the prior of Coventry, a protégé of the Despensers, hired a local magician, John of Nottingham, to kill the king, the Despensers and the prior.[33] Their bizarre experiment failed, but it was symptomatic of the generalized desperation.

Discontent was burgeoning. The rising resentment was felt especially in London where the treasurer, Walter Stapledon, the bishop of Exeter, was dragged off his horse near St Paul's and had his head hacked off with a butcher's knife. In September 1326, Edward's wife, Isabella, who had been sent on a mission to France, escorted by her lover Roger Mortimer (who had recently escaped from the Tower of London by drugging his jailers), landed in Suffolk, and so unpopular was the king that the shire levies and the barons who should have withstood her flocked to her arms.

Desperate and disillusioned Edward II fled with the Despensers to Wales, but the elder Despenser was apprehended at Bristol and summarily executed. The king and the younger Despenser took ship at Chepstow but contrary winds drove them ashore in Glamorgan where Lancaster's brother, Henry, took them both captive. It was Edward's last glimpse of his loved favourite. Ironically one of his last acts had been an order to give Hugh his copy of the romances of Tristan and Iseult, 'the most famous of all the tales of infatuated and doomed love'.[34]

After his arrest Hugh refused to eat or drink. Outside Hereford he was taken from his horse, stripped and dressed in reversed arms. A crown of nettles was placed on his head. Biblical graffiti denouncing arrogance and evil were daubed on his skin. To the sound of trumpets and the jeers of the crowd he was drawn by four horses and hanged from a gallows 50 feet high. He was still alive when his genitals were sliced off and burned before his eyes, a grim reminder of what some believed to be his unnatural relations with the king. Later his head was sent to be affixed on London Bridge and his quarters were distributed to four other towns.

Edward was himself sent to Kenilworth Castle. In the catastrophic collapse of all his hopes and loves, Edward appeared a confused, broken man. 'Unless he resigned', he was told, 'the people would withdraw their homage and fealty from him.' It was a form of words. In fact they had already done so. When he was confronted by the bishop of Hereford, he fell to the ground in a dead faint. He was taken to Berkeley Castle in Gloucestershire where in all probability he was brutally murdered. It was said that a red-hot plumber's iron was inserted in his arse, 'a hoote broche putte thru the secret place posterialle', a gesture symbolical, if it really took place, of his unnatural life-style.[35] There is a circumstantial story which was told by Manuel Fieschi, a Genoese priest, which had a happier ending.[36] According to this the king managed to escape from the castle and fled first to Ireland and then to France, but it seems a most unlikely conclusion.

The king was buried in St Peter's Abbey, Gloucester, where, as had happened earlier with his hated rival Lancaster's tomb at St Paul's, his tomb became the centre of a minor cult. The king's heart was removed, placed in a silver urn and interred with his queen in the Franciscan church at Newgate in London when she died twenty years later, in 1358. By a subtle historical irony she was buried in her wedding dress.

Edward II was surely neither mad nor degenerate but the complexities of his private life found a public expression. If we would find a personal reason for his attempt to strengthen the powers of the crown and assert the regality, we may well find its roots in his unhappy childhood and his desire to avenge himself on the enemies who had killed his close friend. He craved for affection but seemed by and large unable to evoke it or to give it. Introspective and insecure, under stress he was in danger of losing his personal balance. His life was tragic and his personality more than ordinarily interesting, for there was seemingly an abnormal streak in it, but it would be too crude to find a reason for the complexities of his life, however enigmatic it was, in a mental disease.

Richard II in his coronation seat, from a painting in Westminster Abbey (by courtesy of the Dean and Chapter of Westminster Abbey)

Richard II succeeded his grandfather, Edward III, as king of England in 1377.[37] Like his great-grandfather, Edward II, whom he greatly admired and whose canonization as a saint he sought vainly to procure, his reign was disturbed by bouts of violent civil war, and ended with his deposition and murder. There seems little doubt that in the latter years of his reign his judgement was often capricious and ill-balanced, and that his personality underwent something of a change. He became increasingly introspective and his grip on reality seemed to weaken. His modern biographer, A.B. Steel, believed that Richard was the victim of a mental illness, schizophrenia, and that this accounted for the enigmatic decisions which he made and the disastrous policy he followed, with its fatal dénouement. In the last stages of his illness, A.B. Steel wrote, 'the regality had grown until it had swallowed the entire world and as Richard looked around him he saw nothing but the mirror of his royal personality, inhabited by flickering shades whose movements could be governed by a glance.' At the end, in Steel's opinion, he was 'a mumbling neurotic, sinking rapidly into a state of acute melancholia'.[38]

What grounds were there for reaching such a verdict? Was the verdict likely to be true? And if it is unacceptable, is there any alternative explanation? Undoubtedly, as with other royal princes his upbringing had some bearing on the development of his character. He was in his eleventh year when he became king. His grandfather, Edward III, had been a great warrior prince whose fame even the follies of senility in the latter years of his life could not entirely dim. His father, the Black Prince who had died the year before his accession, had an outstanding reputation as a knight and soldier. His image must have been presented constantly and even tediously to his young son. But Richard seems to have had no ambition to follow in his father's footsteps. Although he paid conventional lip-service to chivalric pursuits, like Edward II, he reacted against the military atmosphere of a court where warfare, jousting and military games seemed to take precedence over all else. He was essentially his mother's son, for he was devoted to the beautiful dowager princess of Wales.

Far then from growing up in the conventional pattern as a young warrior prince, Richard II, like Edward at an earlier date, was a young man of aesthetic rather than military pursuits. He had had a sympathetic tutor in Sir Simon Burley to whom he may have owed the concept of regality which was to play so large a part in his life, and to shape his attitude towards his magnates. He never had any doubt about his regal powers. There formed in his mind a semi-mystical conception of divine right to which he was to cling to the very end.

He was self-centred to the point of narcissism. Elaborately and carefully dressed, he was very careful of his appearance and coiffure. He appears in his portraits as handsome and elegant, not far short of six feet tall with a head of thick dark yellow hair. He took baths regularly, an unusual habit in his time, and was the inventor of the pocket handkerchief.

He was probably the most cultured king of his line. His library suggests that he read books as well as listened to others reading to him. He was the patron of painters, artists and writers. He was fascinated by exotic and refined cooking, as the court cookery book *The Forme of Cury*, with its elaborate recipes, its spices and other rich ingredients shows.

Passionate and sensitive, he could at times be devious and calculating and, like so many other members of his family, was liable to fits of violent ill-temper, but he was generous to his friends. He loved his mother and became intensely devoted to his wife, Anne of Bohemia. Her death was a traumatic blow from which he never seems to have recovered fully. He had Sheen Palace where she died demolished. Yet there was a bisexual element in his personality. He had an intimate friend in the flamboyant Robert de Vere, whom he raised to great power and influence and who was never to be replaced after Robert's death. When Robert's body was brought back after three years of exile to be buried at King's Colne, Richard ordered the lid of the coffin to be raised so that he might look once more on the face and touch the hand of the man he had loved.

This was the young man upon whom at so early an age were thrust the responsibilities of kingship; devoted to his mother, in awe of his father's memory but not by nature a warrior, and brought up in the seamy, not to say steamy, atmosphere of a court pervaded by faction and suspicion. It was dominated by his uncles, his father's brothers, rich, magnificent, politically ambitious and grasping men, supported by bands of liveried knights, John of Gaunt, duke of Lancaster, who became the virtual regent, Edmund of Langley, earl of Cambridge, later duke of York, Thomas of Woodstock, earl of Buckingham, later duke of Gloucester, an avuncular brood whom Richard came to detest. For the young and impotent boy king the royal household must at times have seemed a cage in which he was imprisoned while the magnates eyed each other with distrust, seeking to feather their own nests by patronage and power. An impressionable spirit such as his could not easily withstand the ambiguities and intrigues of court life. The desire to liberate himself from his confines was to be early a feature of his life.

Once indeed as a young boy he showed his mettle. During the Peasants' Revolt, an uprising occasioned by the ill-judged imposition of a poll tax, and after the rebels had given violent expression to their grievances, Richard had insisted personally on going to parley with the rebels. His courage paid off and the tide was stemmed, even tamed. Richard told the rebel Kentishmen after their leader Wat Tyler had been stabbed to death that he would henceforth be their leader. It was, of course, a meaningless gesture but such was the charisma of royalty that the peasants believed what their king told them and were soon to disperse and to meet their savage deserts as the forces of law and order re-established themselves.

For Richard it must have been a traumatic moment. He had no real concern for the peasants and such promises as had been made to remedy their grievances were soon forgotten. But the fourteen-year-old boy had taken the centre of the stage. He had shown that, like his father, he was a *preux chevalier*, a true knight. He had won his spurs not on a battlefield in distant France but in his own capital city. And how? By the royal will he had been king in deed as well as in name, at least for a day.

He was soon back in leading strings, shackled to the magnates; but while his formidable uncle, John of Gaunt, was attempting to forward his claims to the throne in distant Castile, Richard was forming his own faction. He had found an intimate friend whom he could trust, Robert de Vere, the ninth earl of Oxford, a man whose wealth, however, was not proportionate to his ancient lineage. Richard fell for his flamboyant, rather flashy charm, lavished favours on him and may have been shortly his lover. He was made a marquess, the first title of the kind, and duke of Ireland. Unfortunately de Vere was incompetent and arrogant. The magnates were offended by the social misalliance which his marriage to one of the queen's ladies-in-waiting, Agnes Launcekron, caused. The rebellious magnates, the Appellants as they came to be called, summoned their men to arms and at Radcot Bridge by the Thames near Oxford they defeated the royal forces.

Richard was terribly humiliated. De Vere was in exile; his other ministers were judicially murdered or fled abroad. He found himself isolated with his own powers severely circumscribed. The effect of his failure must have been psychologically traumatic. If the attempt to assert his regal powers had failed disastrously, the experience only made him the more determined to revenge himself on his enemies. Indeed, baronial government was to turn out to be even less competent than that of the king. Richard took advantage of the internecine rivalry between the different factions among the magnates and by manipulation and patronage began to build up a party of his own and to create an armed force of men loyal to the crown, their personal loyalty to the king symbolized by the badge of the white hart, Richard's personal emblem, which they wore.

The wheel of fortune had turned in the king's favour but whether he could consolidate his victory was more doubtful. His mind became more and more focused on the furtherance of the royal power and the sanctification of the royal position. His adversaries were disgraced, executed, imprisoned or exiled. Like Edward II, he realized that a strong king must be a rich and solvent one and readily used illegal and unaccustomed methods to fill the royal treasury, but he did little to win popular favour and much that further alienated the magnates. In an idiosyncratic judgement at the tournament of Coventry he banished his cousin, Gaunt's son and heir, Henry Bolingbroke, as well as his adversary, the king's one-time friend, the powerful magnate, Thomas Mowbray, duke of Norfolk.

More and more his mind appeared warped, twisted by the humiliations he had suffered, into an unnatural exaltation of majesty, which moved easily enough into the realm of fantasy. He spoke of the laws being in his own heart. In his powerful image of the king Shakespeare with some justice had him exclaim:

> Not all the water in the rough rude sea
> Can wash the balm from an anointed king.[39]

He would sometimes sit on his throne wearing a crown, his court standing around him, for hours on end, the silence only broken as the king nodded and the courtiers with a rustle of robes bowed their knees to him.[40] If he was only doing what kings of his age often did,[41] there was about this ceremony an eerie sense of make-belief. He played, how realistically it is difficult to know, with the notion of becoming Holy Roman Emperor. The death of his wife, Anne of Bohemia, to whom he had been so devoted, plunged him into melancholy. 'After her death', Steel commented, his 'neuroses deepened rapidly and the outer world came to reflect for him more and more a mere mechanical extension of his own favourite dream . . . the sacred mystery and unfettered nature of the royal power.'[42] His neurotic propensities were to prove a hostage to fortune.

From the moment that Gaunt's son, Henry Bolingbroke, landed at Ravenspur in early July 1399, Richard's cause was lost. Just as the shire levies and the magnates had flocked to Queen Isabella's standard seventy-two years earlier, so history repeated itself. Bolingbroke claimed that he came simply to take over his father's estates of which the king had wrongfully deprived him, but the real prize was the crown itself. Richard, returning from an expedition to Ireland, found himself friendless and collapsed in hopeless melancholy.

The spiritual indelibility of his royal office was no help in his hapless position, for it could not sustain him or insulate him against the castle walls of Leeds in Kent or of Pontefract in Yorkshire. Yet he could not easily put aside the spectre of power which had so long enchanted him. He was to tell the chief justice, Sir William Thirning, that there existed no power on earth which could take away from him the spiritual authority with which he had been invested at his coronation.

When Adam of Usk saw him on 21 September 1399 he found him 'very melancholy'.[43] Richard spoke to him of the ingratitude of a land that had betrayed so many kings. The author of the *Dieulacres Chronicle* told how Richard placed his crown on the ground and resigned his powers to God.[44] On St Michael's Day he submitted to the demands made upon him, how willingly we do not know, for one story suggests that in a characteristic flash of anger he threatened to 'flay some of these men alive'. But he handed his royal signet ring to Henry, and on 30 September 1399 parliament or rather more properly a parliamentary assembly accepted his abdication and confirmed Henry's claim to the throne.

Richard disappeared into the shadows, finally to Pontefract Castle where, according to Adam of Usk, his jailer Sir Thomas Swinford starved him to death. The St Alban's Chronicle states, however, that Richard starved himself to death, perhaps not so unlikely a story, given the depth of his despair. When his body was later exhumed, it showed no signs of the murderous blows which Sir Piers Exton in Shakespeare's play struck at him. He was dead before February 1400 and brought for honourable burial at Westminster; his death mask showed a face tinged by sadness and prematurely aged, for at the time of his death Richard was only thirty-four years old.

Was then Richard II mentally unbalanced and was his lack of mental balance an ingredient in his downfall? There is in fact very little evidence to sustain Steel's assertion that he was suffering from schizophrenia. If we compare Richard II with his contemporary, Charles VI of France, who was undoubtedly schizophrenic, the two cases are completely different. If Richard's sense of political reality seemed to fluctuate, he did not suffer from delusions nor was his personality unhinged. It has been suggested that he was the victim of an acute inferiority complex dating back to his childhood which the humiliations he suffered in later life accentuated. Yet his convictions about the nature of regality should not be interpreted simply in terms of a psychological neurosis.

It seems most probable that Richard II suffered from a moderate, even possibly an acute, depression which bordered at times on manic-depressive insanity. The chroniclers mention the deep melancholy which overwhelmed him in the closing stages of his life. It impaired his judgement and warped his personal relations; his following became increasingly constricted. He could only restore his self-esteem by withdrawing more and more into himself. In the course of less than three decades he had experienced a series of personal setbacks, his soured relations with his uncle John of Gaunt and the royal dukes, the execution and exile of his friends and supporters, the death of Queen Anne, his growing isolation and finally his abandonment by all but a few of his supporters. He became the victim of a moderately deep depression which the events of the last year of his life deepened. Richard was not mad but his judgement became unbalanced and fantasy intruded more and more into his existence.

What seemed to be signs of incipient madness in John, Edward II and Richard II were in fact pronounced personality traits, in part inherited, in part a result of upbringing, in part an effect of the personal and political stress they experienced as kings. John's relations with his father had been strained, so that affection changed to hatred. Edward II had feared and disliked his father. Richard II could not have helped feeling that he compared unfavourably with his warrior father the Black Prince. Their personalities acting in combination with the policies they sought to follow were to arouse the hostility of their greater subjects, resulting in the depositions and deaths of Edward II and Richard II, a fate which John may have conceivably avoided by dying of natural causes.

Moreover the policies which all these kings followed were to some extent conditioned by their temperaments and by their private and possibly compulsive propensities. King John's high temper and suspicious nature had been a prime ingredient in his deteriorating relations with his barons; Edward II's hostility to the magnates was in part coloured by the treatment which they had meted out to his lover, Gaveston; Richard II's temperament likewise increasingly brought him into collision with his subjects.

Nor were the crises which overwhelmed them purely personal tragedies. They were to affect the future shape of English history. John's monument was the Magna Carta which he had accepted so reluctantly and which became, whatever interpretation was placed upon it at the time, the cornerstone of English liberties. The crises which brought the downfall of Edward II and Richard II proved to be landmarks in the growth of the English parliament. So the private distemper of these three kings had public consequences which significantly affected the future of English history.

It seems likely that neither John nor Edward II nor Richard II was strictly speaking mad, even if under stress the balance of their personalities seemed occasionally to be in question. Although the personality disorders that afflicted them affected English history, they were the victims of neurotic rather than psychotic derangement. If, however, the attribution of madness to John, Edward II and Richard II does not hold water, there can be no doubt that at least for a critical period in the history of his reign their fifteenth-century successor King Henry VI was insane.

IV

The Royal Saint

King Henry VI may have had an innate disposition to mental weakness, inherited from his grandfather, Charles VI of France, but it was the political pressures to which he was subjected during his reign which eventually brought about his acute nervous breakdown. The story of the political strife, which culminated in the Wars of the Roses, forms the core of Shakespeare's history plays, which tell of the rise and fall of the House of Lancaster from the accession of Henry IV to the deposition of Henry VI. After the deposition of Richard II and his murder, to which Henry IV may have been privy, Henry IV reigned as king until ill-health left him in the latter years of his reign a secluded figure, whose physical and mental deterioration raised the hopes and ambitions of his young, vigorous son, the future Henry V.[1]

Henry V's short reign witnessed the conquest of France. As a sequel to Henry's triumph, the imbecilic French king, Charles VI, gave him the succession to the French throne as well as the hand of his daughter Catherine in marriage. But Henry died young, leaving the crown to his infant son, Henry VI. After the king's death there was a slow but unmistakable period of anti-climax, leading to eventual defeat in France, the revival of factionalism and civil strife in England and the deposition of the king. Shakespeare's plays may be an oversimplification of events but in showing how the legacy of the past came to fruition in the anarchy and bloodshed of Henry VI's reign he was surely not far wrong.[2]

There were, however, not many signs of what the future portended in Henry's early life. After his birth his mother returned to France to join her husband, leaving the baby boy in the care of one of her ladies-in-waiting, Elizabeth Ryman. Before he was a year old Henry had assumed the crowns of both England and France.

Naturally Henry was only a cipher. His father had intended that in the event of his death his brother, John, duke of Bedford, should become regent of France and his younger brother Humphrey, duke of Gloucester, regent of England, but the royal council, suspicious of concentrating too much power in Gloucester's hands, made him only Protector and Defender of England (and only that when Bedford was out of the kingdom).[3] Until Henry came of age, the royal council was itself to be the principal agent of government, trying to cope with the continuous dissension which raged between the late king's half-brother, the wealthy and influential churchman, Henry Beaufort, bishop of Winchester (Gaunt's son by his mistress and later wife, Katherine Swinford)[4] and the ambitious and fiery Gloucester.

Of such matters the boy king can have been hardly conscious, but the responsibilities of kingship were kept in front of him from an early age. When he was only three years of age he was brought from Windsor on 13 November 1423 so that, in the words of the Speaker to the House of Commons, his subjects might see 'your high and royal person to sit and occupy your own rightful seat and place in your parliament to whom our recourse of right must be to have every wrong reformed.'[5] At Staines the young child had a tantrum, 'shrieked and cried and sprang would not be carried further', but the following Wednesday 18 November he was presented to parliament and was given a loyal address. Such things must have meant little to him but who can say what impact such events may conceivably have had on his unconscious mind? He was four years old when he went to service at St Paul's, and rode from Cheapside to Kennington.[6]

At eight he endured the long, tiring, if splendid, ceremonial of his coronation at Westminster Abbey; and in December 1431, just ten, his uncle Cardinal Beaufort crowned him king of France. From the start of his life the responsibilities of his position were brought home to him. He must early have realized their implicit dangers, aware of the internecine rivalries and intrigues of his own royal relatives and their retainers. He was himself the centre of the bitter struggle between his two uncles, Humphrey of Gloucester and Cardinal Beaufort, both of whom wished to bring the king under their immediate supervision. When, in 1425, Gloucester momentarily triumphed over the cardinal, Henry accompanied his uncle on a ceremonial ride through London.[7]

When he was sixteen years old he attained his majority. It is difficult to penetrate behind the formal portrait of Henry VI. Tudor propaganda, more especially the hagiographical reportage of John Blacman, created a picture of an innocent, highly moral, well-intentioned monarch, the victim of political feuding, a saint in the making.[8] In practice he was a precocious, even a determined young man who made some attempt to reassert the royal authority, for so long during his minority exercised by the royal council, but his political grasp was less than realistic. He did not realize the nature of the grave problems which confronted the country and became the tool of a political faction led by the Beauforts.

The situation facing Henry VI became more and more intractable. English fortunes in France (still nominally under English rule) were fast beginning to fail; within little more than a dozen years so disastrous a retreat had occurred that England was only left in possession of the port and staple of Calais. The English parliament criticized the royal government for its failure to conduct the war effectively but was reluctant to vote enough money to fight it. Fiscal exactions caused by near bankruptcy led to a bubbling tide of discontent. Rising crime and lack of justice, often perpetrated by the great nobles and landowners who were supposedly responsible for suppressing disorder, became endemic. By 1450 royal government was suffering from a mortal paralysis.

Henry cannot escape responsibility for these troubles. The more he tried to cope with the problem confronting the country the deeper the morass into which he fell. He had given too much power to the incompetent Beaufort clan, the nominal head of which was John, duke of Somerset, but whose real leader was William de la Pole, duke of Suffolk. But there was an opposition party among the magnates led by Richard, duke of York, who could have been argued to have had a stronger claim to the throne than the spineless king.

So the ship of the state juddered as it ploughed its way under an incompetent helmsman into stormy waters. The kingdom was descending rapidly into chaos. Henry's leading adviser, Suffolk, was impeached, banished and beheaded as he tried to leave the country. Two bishops, Adam Moleyns of Chichester and William Ayscough of Salisbury, were murdered. There was an armed rising under Jack Cade calling for reforms. Many people held Henry responsible for the misgovernance of the realm. Thomas Carver, bailiff to the abbot of Reading, was imprisoned for questioning the king's capacity to govern.[9] The keeper of Guildford Gaol said that the king should be hanged and his wife drowned. A Dutchman living at Ely christened his fighting cocks Henry of England and Philip of Burgundy, and was delighted when the latter won.[10]

More particularly people were beginning to question Henry's mental capacity. The king was, as Abbot Whetehampstead of St Albans put it, 'half-witted in affairs of state'.[11] A London draper asserted that Henry 'was not in his person as his noble progenitors had been, for his visage was not favoured, for he had not unto a child's face and is not steadfast of wit as other kings have been'. A Dutchman said bluntly that Henry looked like a child, and it would be more appropriate to have a sheep than a ship engraved on the coins of his realm. A husbandman at Cley in Norfolk called the king a fool. In 1450 two commoners from Brightling in Sussex declared that 'the king was a natural fool and would oftimes hold a staff in his hands with a bird at the end, playing therewith as a fool, and that another king must be ordained to rule the land, saying that the king was no person able to rule the land.' Some eight years earlier a yeoman from Farningham in Kent had been indicted but had sought the king's pardon for stating 'the king is lunatic, as his father was';[12] did he mean Henry's grandfather, Charles VI?

Such comments reflected a current of opinion and perhaps were the more interesting for their repeated suggestion that the king's mind was unbalanced. Perhaps the breakdown in 1453 was less a bolt from the blue than it was made out to be.

With rising discontent, military failure abroad and the threat of bankruptcy, the strain of government must have been beginning to tell on Henry's impressionable mind. In some sense he sought to escape from the turmoil of government by following up his other interests. He managed to implement his passionate desire to erect a monumental memorial for posterity by founding the colleges at Eton and Cambridge, in their design pushing even William of Wykeham's magnificent earlier foundations of Winchester and New College into the shade. Reading and prayer, and even acts of ostentatious piety, could, however, only form a momentary way of retreat from the realities and burdens of public life.

Nothing could screen the dismal record of his government or arrest the feuding among his magnates. Cade's rebellion had been suppressed but the French were punishing the English armies. Henry's wife, Margaret of Anjou, was now pregnant but the prospect of the birth of an heir would raise new problems since it would have the effect of barring the claims of the heir-apparent, Richard, duke of York, to the throne.

Henry was under cumulative stress. He was not a man of strong mind, and was easily influenced. He must have been only too aware of his inability to resolve the problems which confronted his government and to still the rising chorus of complaint. Under the strain, the balance of his mind, for genetic and temperamental reasons disposed to nervous trouble, would be upset, and he would descend into a state of severe melancholia and a depressive illness.

This happened in the summer of 1453. He was apparently well enough to receive the kiss of homage from Sir William Stourton on 7 August at the royal hunting lodge at Clarendon, near Salisbury. Then blackness descended.[13] The onset of his illness was marked by a 'ffransy' or 'a rash and sudden terror' but he soon relapsed into a state of passive withdrawal. 'His wit and his resoun [were] withdrawn.' He had 'no natural sense nor reasoning power', and was wholly indifferent to what went on around him, nor would he wash or dress of his own accord.[14]

Naturally, as in other cases, it was rumoured that he had been bewitched. A felon who had turned king's evidence reported that a group of Bristol merchants had used sorcery to destroy the king on 12 July 1453. Another declared that at the instigation of Lord Cobham (who was himself in prison) a spell had been cast over a cloak which belonged to the king.[15]

The royal physicians busied themselves with a series of prescriptions, drugs, purgatives, gargles, baths, poultices and bleedings but the patient remained impassive. Henry's son and heir, Edward, had been born on 31 October 1453 but the father was completely unmoved. 'At the prince's coming to Windsor', John Stodely wrote on 19 January 1454:

the duke of Buckingham took him in his arms and presented him to the king in godly wise, beseeching the king to bless him; and the king gave no manner answer. Nevertheless the duke abode still with the prince by the king; and when he could no manner answer have, the queen came in, and took the prince in her arms and presented him in like form as the duke had done; but all their labour was in vain, for they departing thence without any answer or countenance saving only that once he looked on the prince and cast down his eyes again without any move.[16]

Henry remained physically and mentally immobile like a frozen statue.

Coming at a time when the English were being chased out of France and the magnates were dangerously divided, the king's breakdown created a political crisis. Richard duke of York was declared on 27 March 1454 to be Protector and Defender of the kingdom.[17] The birth of Prince Edward had removed his immediate hope of the throne but for the moment he accepted the situation with a seemingly good grace. The death of the chancellor, Archbishop Kemp, on 22 March 1454, presented the government with a serious problem, since it was the king himself who had to approve the appointments of a chancellor and archbishop of Canterbury. Moreover Kemp's death made invalid the great seal by which he exercised his authority.

It was therefore a matter of some urgency that Henry should be persuaded to act. In spite of the king's condition, the ministers made an effort to penetrate the dark screen of his mind. A delegation of lords spiritual and temporal came to Windsor on Lady Day 1454. After the king had finished his dinner, the bishop of Chester addressed him, requesting him to nominate a new chancellor and archbishop, but he stayed silent and unmoved. After an embarrassing pause the bishop of Winchester suggested that the delegates should go to dine in the hope that Henry might be more responsive later. But when they returned to the audience chamber Henry still remained silent. The king got up and went to his bedchamber. 'They could have no answer, word or sign; and therefore with sorrowful hearts they went their way.'[18] Henry appeared to have no memory, found difficulty in moving about without assistance and had to be watched constantly by grooms and pages day and night.

The royal doctors were at their wits' end. The council had set up a medical commission which did what it could. The list of treatments included electuaries, potions, syrups, confections, unguents, laxatives, clysters and suppositaries, head shaving and head purges (based on the belief that the waste products of the brain could be excreted through the scalp), gargles to remove catarrhal fluid, fomentations and blood-letting.[19] The doctors were acting in accordance with current humoral theory to rid the brain of its black bile and so restore the balance of the humours.

Whether any of the treatment was effective it is impossible to know but slowly the king began to show signs of returning normality. He was apparently well enough to receive the kiss of homage from the new archbishop of Canterbury and to give him his cross on 22 August 1454. On 27 December he ordered his almoner to take a horse to Canterbury and his secretary to go to Westminster that they might give thankofferings for his recovery at the shrines of Thomas Becket (at Canterbury) and King Edward the Confessor (at Westminster).

When three days later Henry was told the name of his now fourteen-month-old son, he enquired as to the names of the child's godparents. He was told that they had been Archbishop Kemp, who had died, and the duke of Somerset. Although the king had actually installed Kemp's successor the previous April he revealed that he had not known that Kemp was dead.

Edward Clare wrote to John Paston:

The Kyng is well amended and hath been since Christmas Day and St John's Day when he commanded his almoner to ride to Canterbury with his offering. And on Monday afternoon the Queen came to him, and brought my Lord Prince with her and he asked what the Prince's name was and the Queen told him Edward; and then he held up his hands and thanked God thereof. And he said that he never knew till that time, nor wist what was said to him, nor wist not where he had been while he hath been sick till now. And he asked who was godfathers . . . and she told him that the Cardinal [Kemp] was dead, and he said he knew never thereof till that tyme . . . And my Lord of Winchester and My Lord of Saint John's [Priory] were with him on the morrow after Twelfth Day and he spoke joy. And he seith he is now in charity with all the world, and he would all the Lords were. And now he saith matins of our Lady and evensong, and heareth his Mass decently.[20]

By the early months of 1455 the king had apparently recovered his health as well as his memory. The duke of Somerset was restored to favour and the duke of York was once again relegated to the sidelines of power. Yet how far Henry's recovery was complete or permanent was in doubt. When, in June 1455, Gilbert Kymer, now dean of Salisbury, was summoned to Windsor, it was 'for as much as we be occupied and laboured as ye know weel with sickness and infirmities'.[21] On 15 July special payments were ordered to be given to the surgeons 'for what they had done for the king: *pro diversis magnis laboribus et diligenciis et per ipsos factis circa personam domini Regis*'.[22] What function had the surgeons performed? It would seem very likely that they had made an incision in the king's head to relieve the pressure on the brain. And when had they so acted, in 1454 or 1455?

Whether or not Henry had had a relapse he was present when parliament met on 9 July 1455. Yet by 28 October John Gresham was writing somewhat enigmatically to John Paston that 'so much rumour is here. What it meaneth I wot not. God turn it. Some men are afraid that he is sick again.'[23] There may well have been some truth in this rumour for in November the duke of York was again appointed Protector nor was Henry present at parliament *'ob certas justas et racionabiles causas in persona nostra*

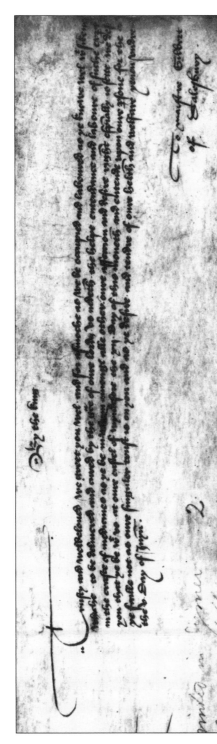

Letter of June 1455 to Gilbert Kymer, Dean of Salisbury and royal physician, summoning him to treat King Henry VI for a probable collapse into mental illness.
The text reads:

Henry the King

Trusty and wellbeloved we greet you wel and for asmoche as we be occupied and laboured as ye knowe wel w^t sikeness [and infirmities of the] whiche to be delivered and cured by the grace of oure lord us nedeth the helpe entendance and labour of such expert [notable and proved men] in the crafte of medicines as ye be in whom amongst alle other oure affection and desire right especially is sette we desire [wille and hertily pray] you that ye be w^t us at oure castel of wyndesore the XII day of this moneth and entende upon oure persone for the [cause aforesaid and that] ye faille not as oure singular trust is on you and as ye desire and tendre of oure helth and welfare yeuen undre [oure Prive Seel at Westminster] the V Day of Juyn.

(PRO SC 1 43; text transcribed from a complete eighteenth-century copy from T. Rymer, *Foedera*, London, 1704–1735, Vol. 2, p. 366) *non poterimus interesse'.*[24] All these somewhat oblique references to the king's illness, together with a lack of royal signatures on official documents between 12 December 1455 and 2 March 1456 suggest that there is good reason for thinking that Henry had had a recurrence of his mental trouble.

What was the nature of the mental illness which took him out of circulation for nearly two years? There can be little doubt that it was brought on by stress, by his inability to solve the problems dogging his government and by the failure of English arms in France. It seems that the arrival of bad news from France may have been the last straw. We have seen that after initial excitement Henry had lapsed into a state of monumental stupor, completely indifferent to his own needs or the needs of his family or country. On his recovery he did not remember anything of his illness; amnesia had mercifully blocked out all that had happened. The illness from which he suffered must surely have been either catatonic schizophrenia or a manic-depressive stupor. Henry was a grandson of Charles VI of France who certainly was schizophrenic. Since schizophrenia is often inherited, the possibility that this was the source of the mental disease from which he suffered cannot be wholly dismissed. But it seems more likely that Henry was the victim of a manic-depressive stupor rather than of catatonic schizophrenia.[25] There was none of the signs of frenzy, except possibly at the first onset of his illness, hallucinations and paranoia evident in the case of his grandfather and while his mental faculties may have been permanently impaired, his recovery was relatively swift.

Yet for the remainder of his reign the king's 'inanity' was a major ingredient in government in spite of his apparent recovery. The mental trouble which had overwhelmed him in 1453–5 had come home to roost. After 1455 Henry's government plunged further and further into debt and proved completely unable to ensure the maintenance of justice, law or order. The king lacked the will or the capacity to suppress or control the faction feuds between the magnates which were fast to deteriorate into bloody civil war, the so-called Wars of the Roses. When the king's army was routed by the Yorkist forces, Henry fled over the border into Scotland, while Edward, now duke of York, for his father Richard had been killed at the battle of Wakefield, claimed the throne and was crowned as Edward IV.

The bedraggled Lancastrian king was captured and placed in the Tower of London. At the end of September 1470 there was a brief Lancastrian recovery, engineered by the earl of Warwick, the 'king-maker', but for Henry it was a meaningless charade. He was pushed into a triumphant procession but appeared 'not so worshipfully arrayed nor so cleanly kept as befitted such a prince'. With the collapse of the so-called readaptation he returned to the Tower. On 4 May 1471 the remnants of the Lancastrian forces were defeated at Tewkesbury, and his heir, Prince Edward, was struck down and killed as he fled from the field. His death sealed his father's fate. He too was murdered. When his remains were exhumed in 1911 the hair daubed with blood on the skull showed that he had met with a violent death.

There was to be a strange sequel after the Lancastrian Henry VII, his mother's grandson, was victorious. Henry VI had been buried at Chertsey Abbey and then had been removed to Windsor by Richard III. Henry VII tried to get his remains transferred to Westminster Abbey and sought to persuade the pope to canonize him. Although he was unsuccessful in both these objectives, Henry became the centre of an unofficial cult, for sufferers flocked to his tomb at Windsor for succour; a list of 172 miracles survives out of nearly 500 attributed to his prayers.[26] Even Henry VIII once, in June 1529, made an offering at his altar.

Yet the king's claim to sanctity was largely based on myth. He was certainly not a vindictive nor a cruel king and in his own way he was devout. But he had a congenital mental weakness which made him an inept ruler in hard times. The nervous strain was such that he was completely laid low in 1453–4 and possibly again in 1455–6, his illness coinciding with acute political crises. Even in apparent good health he was an ineffective king. 'The intermittent fighting commonly called the Wars of the Roses', so a recent biographer sums up his reign, 'had originated from the gross misgovernment and mismanagement of the nation's affairs at home and abroad by Henry VI in which aristocratic enmities and struggles for power were generated and fostered. . . . He was both an incompetent and a partisan king. . . . In 1461 Henry VI was at last deposed, primarily because of his own failings.'[27] Yet surely those failings were rooted in a mind never fully balanced and racked at the most critical period of his reign by a mental illness for which he can take no blame.

V

Happy Families

Whether or not Henry VI owed his mental weakness to his grandfather, Charles VI of France, it is unquestionable that Charles was for over thirty years the victim of severe attacks of madness, which had the most appalling effects for his people. His symptoms suggest that Charles was afflicted by schizophrenia which in its more acute attacks gave rise to hallucinations and even acts of violence. Although the intervals between a supposed recovery and a return of his illness were of diminishing duration, there were periods when the king seemed sane enough to take up the reins of government. But there were also occasions of varying length when his illness made it impossible for him to govern responsibly or even to go through the motions of government at all. Nor can there be any doubt that even in periods of apparent normality the king's mind was still impaired by the traumas of his illness.

The effects of Charles VI's ill-health were widespread and prolonged. It transformed his personality. It had the most grievous effects on the royal family, already bitterly divided by the selfish ambitions and deep jealousy of its leading members. France, which required strong, firm government, was to be crippled and bloodied by internecine rivalries between the great princes, and to suffer renewed devastation at the hands of the English armies led by Henry V. If the effects of Henry VI's comparatively short illness on the political strife in England were momentous, the consequences of Charles VI's relapses proved to be even more disastrous for his country.

Charles VI came in 1380 to the throne of a country which was only recovering slowly from the immense devastation wrought by invading English armies and their savage mercenary allies. The French countryside had been plundered; French towns were sacked and the royal treasury was impoverished. Charles VI's father, Charles V, not unjustifiably nicknamed 'the wise' (*le sage*), took advantage of the lull in the fighting which had occurred during the reign of Richard II of England, to pursue a policy of reconstruction and retrenchment. To some, notably the French poetess, Christine de Pisan, Charles V seemed to be the very paragon of Christian virtue and wisdom. Neither Charles V nor his father the chivalric mediocrity John II nor his grandfather, Philip VI, a vigorous, intelligent and moderately successful king, betrayed any signs of mental weakness, albeit Philip VI's wife, Jeanne of Burgundy, had had a bad press, a 'she-devil' so Robert of Artois called her, 'the wicked lame queen . . . who behaved as king and had those who threatened her will destroyed'.

Charles V's wife, Jeanne de Bourbon, however, had had a severe nervous breakdown in 1373, losing *'son bon sens et son bone memore'*.[1] Since she had recently given birth to her seventh child it is possible that she was simply suffering from a post-natal depression, but the Bourbon family had had a history of mental infirmity. Her brother, Louis II de Bourbon, for instance, suffered from an acute depression. Queen Jeanne may then have passed on a congenital mental weakness, or at least a temperamental predisposition to mental trouble, to her son, the future Charles VI. Her husband who greatly loved her went on a pilgrimage to seek his wife's recovery. She did recover, but she was to die five years later of a puerperal infection.

Charles VI had the great disadvantage of succeeding his father when he was only a boy of twelve, and so like Richard II and Henry VI, he became a king at too youthful an age. Without any earlier experience, impressionable and malleable, he was likely to be the tool of his household or at least of those around him rather than the master. Indeed, like Richard II, naturally inexperienced as well as indolent, he consigned real power to his ruthless royal uncles, Louis duke of Anjou, Philip duke of Burgandy and John duke of Berry, a great patron of artists and a lover of beautiful things, and of his cousin the duke of Bourbon. Although Charles officially came of age in 1381, it was the princes of the blood who controlled the government. The duke of Berry contented himself with plundering Languedoc; the duke of Anjou busied himself with trying to acquire the kingdom of Naples. The duke of Burgundy had an eye to the county of Flanders and the possibility of creating a semi-autonomous appanage.

As for Charles, he was a pleasure-loving young man, energetic to the point of hypomania, for he was an ardent hunter and an enthusiast for the joust, riding nine courses at the tournament held to celebrate the double marriage of the duke of Burgundy's son and daughter. He was indeed much criticized for going straight to take part in a tournament immediately after he had received the holy unction at his coronation. On the other hand he was genial, generous and affable, so that his people were to nickname him *le bien aimé*, the well-beloved, an ironical title in view of his future life, but a cognomen which he was to enjoy until his death.

He was a lusty as well as an energetic young man. According to the monk of St Denis, his 'carnal appetites' were strong. His uncles had arranged what they thought would be a diplomatically advantageous marriage with a Wittlesbach princess, Isabeau, the daughter of Stephen III the Fop, the duke of Upper Bavaria-Ingolstadt, one of the more powerful of the German states; her grandfather was the duke of Milan, Bernabo Visconti. The Bavarian duke's emissary was not best pleased when he was told that the bride had to be examined in the nude to ensure that she would be able to bear children, but the wedding went ahead. Indeed, so enthusiastic was the young king that after seeing his bride he let it be known that arrangements must be made for an immediate marriage which took place in Amiens Cathedral on 17 July 1385. 'And if', Froissart commented, 'they passed that night together in great delight, one can well believe it.'[2]

In 1388 there was a major change in the government, for the royal council, disgruntled by the policies followed by the royal uncles, declared that the king was sufficiently responsible to take over the government. The uncles, demanding compensation for their services, were momentarily sent packing. The reorganized council contained some men of honest purpose and administrative gifts, a group known as the Marmosets who wanted to revive Charles V's administration and to purge the corruption which had grown up under the uncles' dispensation. But in fact real power had simply passed from one group to another, to the queen, Isabeau, a grasping and selfish woman, intent on enriching herself and her family,[3] and to the king's younger brother, Louis duke of Touraine (later of Orléans), who, it was later rumoured, possibly unjustifiably, became the queen's lover.[4]

The king seemed content to leave government to his advisers and to concentrate on his pleasures. Then, in 1392, an incident occurred which was to change his life. One of the king's favourite advisers was the constable of France, Olivier de Clisson, whose bitter enemy was John IV, duke of Brittany. A protégé of the Breton duke, Pierre de Craon, who had been recently dismissed from his post as chamberlain at the court, engineered a plot to kill Clisson by ambushing him as he made his way to his hôtel in Paris after dining with the king at the Hôtel St Pol. Clisson managed to escape the fatal thrust of his attackers, and staggered, badly wounded, into the doorway of a baker's shop where he was rescued.

Craon, who believed that the plot had been successful, escaped from the city, rode to Chartres and thence made his way to the friendly territory of the duke of Brittany. 'It is diabolic', he told the duke when he learned that Clisson was safe. 'I believe all the devils of hell to whom the Constable belongs, guarded and delivered him out of my hands, for he suffered more than sixty blows by swords or knives and I truly believed him dead.'

The king was outraged and extremely excitable when he heard of what he regarded as an unprovoked attack on a faithful royal servant, and he was determined on revenge. Charles had only recently recovered from a serious illness which had struck him down at Amiens the previous April when he was conducting negotiations for peace with the English. What the illness was we do not know but it had undoubtedly been grave, and may have been a preliminary to the subsequent attack of madness. The chronicler said that it was a 'strange and hitherto unheard of disease', in the course of which the king became prostrate with a high fever and later lost his hair and his nails.[5] It could have been typhoid, cerebral malaria, encephalitis or even syphilitic meningitis. As 'many others', including the duke of Berry, were ill at the same time, it seems most likely to have been typhoid or encephalitis.

The king had made only a slow and perhaps partial recovery before he was confronted with the crisis caused by the attempted murder of the constable. After a month in bed at Beauvais, Charles had returned to Paris determined to lead his army against the duke of Brittany who had given Clisson's assassin, Pierre de Craon, refuge. The royal physicians opposed the expedition on the grounds that the king still suffered from occasional bouts of fever, often appeared light-headed, and was over-anxious and incoherent. The after effects of his illness in the spring were evidently still with him when he left Paris to head the expedition against Brittany on 1 July 1392.[6]

The intensity of the king's anger against Craon may itself point to a basic instability of mind, for all who had assisted the unfortunate man were to suffer severe penalties: his steward, two squires and a page were executed; a canon of Chartres who had given him shelter was sentenced to imprisonment for life and deprived of his benefices. That his uncles thought the expedition impolitic and unwise may have strengthened Charles's determination to go through with it.

It is evident that the king was in poor health as the expedition made its slow way to the south-west. The doctors thought him 'feverish and unfit to ride'. That indefatigable chronicler, Michel Pintoin, the monk from St Denis, who was with the army, reported that the king did not seem himself. His words were: *'velut vir non sane mentis verbis fatuis utendo, gestis eciam majestatem regiam dedecentes exercuerat inter eos'*, which in plain English meant that Charles was talking nonsense and making rude gesticulations.[7] This suggests that, as a result of his previous illness, the king was in a state of nervous prostration even before the incident which brought about his collapse.

This was to take place on a very sultry summer's day, 5 August 1392, as the king and his entourage approached the Breton borders. Charles, who had consumed a good deal of wine, was wearing a black velvet jacket as well as a cuirass and a hat of scarlet velvet ornamented with pearls. Although his brother and uncles who had been originally opposed to the expedition were with him, the king was riding apart from the others because of the very dusty nature of the tracks along which the horses were making their way.

When the expedition was in the vicinity of the forest of Le Mans, near a leper colony, a roughly dressed man stepped from behind a tree and seized the bridle of the king's horse shouting, 'Ride no further, noble king! Turn back! You are destroyed!' *'Non progrediaris ulterius'*, in the words of the monk of St Denis, *'insigne rex, quia cito prodendus es.'*[8] *'Roy, ne cheavauche plus,'* Froissart wrote, having learned of what was happening from the lord of Coucy who was an eye-witness, *'mais retournant, car tu es trahy.'*[9] The king's attendants forced the man to release the bridle, though somewhat surprisingly he was not placed under arrest, possibly because he was thought to be a madman. But his melancholy voice of doom, calling betrayal, re-echoed in the forest. The incident clearly greatly disturbed the king.

Worse was soon to come. For when the cavalcade emerged from the forest into the hot open plain, one of the king's pages, half asleep because of the heat, dropped the king's lance which fell with a clatter on the steel helmet of his companion. Charles, startled by the sound, at once drew his sword and shouting 'Forward against the traitors! They wish to deliver me to the enemy!' struck out at everybody within reach, killing four or five of his own knights, among them a well-known Gascon, the chevalier de Polignac.[10]

'My God', the duke of Burgundy exclaimed, 'the king is out of his mind! Hold him someone!' At last Guillaume Martel came up from behind and seized the king while others took his sword which had been broken in the mêlée. Lifted from his horse, Charles lay prostrate and speechless on the ground, his eyes rolling wildly from side to side.[11] Eventually his attendants placed him in an ox-cart which took him back to Le Mans.

For two days he was in a coma. When he became conscious at first he talked gibberish and seemed to recognize no one. It was commonly believed that sorcery had been at work, though there were those who said that his illness was an act of divine judgement for his government's failure to end the schism which was dividing the church and for the imposition of heavy taxes on his people. The monk of St Denis, describing the immediate aftermath of his breakdown, said that 'during two days of unconsciousness without the use of his limbs, his body got colder, a little heat remaining in the chest, and the heart-beats were faint'.[12]

But gradually under the care of his physician, de Harcigny, the king's health seemed to improve. Guillaume de Harcigny, ninety-two years old, who was a man of great experience and good sense, at once surmised that Charles was suffering from an illness similar to that which had afflicted his mother, Jeanne de Bourbon. '*Ceste maladie est venue au roy de tourble. Il tient trop de la moistur de la mère.*'[13] Harcigny sensibly advised that the king should be given plenty to eat and drink, and should rest and sleep. Within a month he was well enough to convalesce. In the autumn of 1392 Charles went to give thanks for his recovery to the church of Notre Dame de Liesse at Laon and attended the patronal festival at St Denis.

What was the nature of the illness which had struck down the king? Froissart described it vaguely as '*un chaude maladie*' which might suggest, according to the humoral pathology of the time, the rising of heated humours to the brain. It is certainly possible that, given the exceptionally hot weather, the king could have suffered heat stroke or an attack of hyperthermia, which may damage the brain. But whatever Charles suffered it was not in some sense irreversible, for at least superficially he was to make a recovery. That there was a predisposition to mental trouble may be inferred from his mother's illness and from the nature of the malady which had struck him shortly before the expedition set out. In view of his later history we must surely

Jean Froissart offers his Chronicle to King Charles VI, from an illuminated manuscript (N. Acq. Fr. 9604 f. 1; photograph: Bibliothèque Nationale, Paris)

suppose that this was the onset of schizophrenia which was to recur to a greater or lesser extent throughout the remainder of his life, no less than thirty years.

The king's breakdown had immediate political effects. The royal uncles saw in it a good opportunity to rid themselves of his advisers the Marmosets, whose leaders Rivière and Mercier were dismissed and imprisoned, and to recover their power. Harcigny had sensibly suggested that if the king was to return to good health he should be freed from matters that were likely to worry or irritate him.[14] With such advice the king's brother Louis and his uncles were well content as was the king himself.

Neglectful of the government he could follow his own inclinations and enjoy himself. There was, however, a dreadful disaster which occurred in the New Year of 1393 which boded ill for the future. At a masque which the queen gave on 28 January to celebrate the third marriage of a lady-in-waiting, there was a charade, 'contrary to all decency', in the course of which six young men were to appear dressed as wild savages, wearing costumes made of linen cloth which had been soaked in resinous wax or pitch 'so that they appeared shaggy and hairy from head to foot'.[15]

They wore masks to conceal their identity but among them was Charles himself. Because of the combustible nature of the material, torches were forbidden to be carried while the 'savages' capered, making obscene gestures. While the king was talking to the young duchess of Berry, his younger brother, Louis, accompanied by attendants bearing torches entered the hall. A spark from a torch fell on to a dancer. With frightening rapidity it spread from one to another. The queen, who knew that her husband was among the dancers, screamed and fainted. The king was himself saved by the swift action of the duchess of Berry who threw her skirt over him. Panic set in as those present tried to cut the burning costumes from their writhing victims. The comte de Joigny was burned to death. Yvain de Foix and Aimery Poitier died of their burns two days later. Huguet de Guisay, who had devised the spectacle and was reputed as one who 'corrupted and schooled the young' died the day after.

While there is no particular reason to suppose that this tragic and dramatic incident affected the king's mind, it must have been a traumatic experience which could have had delayed after-effects. All those associated with it expressed expiation for their sins and went to offer thanks for their preservation, but within six months Charles had a relapse. When he was at Abbeville in June 1393 he was 'covered by such heavy shadows' that it was plain that he was in the grip of another serious attack of insanity. He not only seemed unable to recognize people or places but often acted violently and made improper gestures. He suffered delusions, declaring that 'he was not married and had never had children; he forgot likewise his own person and his title of King of France, maintaining that he was not called Charles and did not have the Fleurs de Lys as arms. When he saw his arms or those of his wife engraved on his gold plate or elsewhere he furiously effaced them.'[16] Although he had brief snatches of lucidity, it was over six months before he made a pilgrimage to Mont St Michel to offer thanks for his recovery and to found and endow a chapel there.

After eighteen months, in November 1395, he suffered a further relapse. Strangely enough it occurred shortly after the dismissal and banishment of his doctor Renaud Frèron. The reason for Frèron's dismissal is not known nor in what way he had aroused the king's displeasure. At the time Charles appears to have been suffering from a delusional persecution neurosis which was a symptom of his schizophrenic condition. It was his custom to run shrieking through the Hôtel St Pol, exclaiming that he was escaping from his enemies, until he collapsed from very exhaustion. To prevent scandal his attendants had the doors walled up. It is possible that Frèron was a victim of the king's delusions.

These again involved the problem of his identity. He declared that he was not a king and that his name was Charles but that his real name was Georges and that he had neither a wife nor children. Whenever he came across his arms or his wife's he again tried to erase them, jumping about and making 'obscene capers' (*'inhoneste et displiceter saltando'*) as he did so.[17] His real coat of arms, he said, was a lion with a sword thrust through it. He was perhaps seeking to identify the lion with himself, suffering the agony of his illness, an image which was connected in a vague way with his calling himself George, perhaps St George, which R.C. Famiglietti has described as a 'good example of the kind of logic used in schizophrenic thought'.[18] By early 1396 this attack had subsided, for on 6 February 1396 he went to offer thanks for his recovery at the church of Notre Dame and began in earnest to negotiate for the marriage of his young daughter Isabella to the widowed English king Richard II.

But it was not long before he had a further relapse, and with the passage of time the intervals between apparent sanity and the onset of lunacy became shorter as chronic schizophrenia tightened its hold on the unhappy king. Sometimes he was feverish and excitable, running about wildly and behaving grotesquely, at others he was prostrate and listless. There is ample evidence of his lunatic behaviour. The royal accounts record his numerous breakages and other damage. He cast clothes and other objects into the fire. He urinated on a gown (*houppelande*) which subsequently had to be cleaned.

The future pope Pius II reported that 'he sometimes believed that he was glass and could not be touched, he inserted iron rods in his clothes, and in many ways protected himself lest he broke in falling'.[19] The future pope's report was confirmed by Juvenal des Ursins who mentioned that in 1405 a small piece of metal had been found attached to his skin.[20] For some months that year he had apparently refused to change his linen, to bathe or to be shaved, and as a consequence had been afflicted by skin trouble as well as by lice. In desperation the physicians decided that the king could only be cured by shock treatment, so in November a group of ten men with blackened faces were secretly introduced into the royal apartments to frighten him. The ruse worked. Charles agreed to be washed, shaved and dressed.[21] By Christmas he had recovered sufficiently to go on a visit to his daughter Marie to dissuade her from the idea of entering a nunnery, so that she might be free to marry the duke of Bar.

His attitude to the queen, Isabeau of Bavaria, had the ambivalence characteristic of the schizophrenic. Charles was evidently strongly sexed and uxorious; by Isabeau he had twelve children in twenty-one years, the last a boy who died immediately after birth in 1407. But his attitude towards his wife underwent a radical change. She became the prime target of his resentment. 'Who is that woman?' he said of her, 'the sight of whom torments me? Find out what she wants and free me from her demands if you can, that she may follow me no more.' His aversion to Isabeau became so strong that she was apparently ready to withdraw from his bed and tolerate in her place 'a very beautiful and agreeable and pleasing young woman', a horse-dealer's daughter, Odette de Champdivers, who was known as the 'little queen'. By Odette he had a daughter, Marguerite de Valois, who was married later to Jean de Harpedene and whom his son Charles VII was to legitimize in 1427.[22]

While it may appear unjustifiable to speculate on the king's relations with his wife, where there is so little evidence, there can be little doubt that it played some part in the progress of his disease. Juvenal des Ursins reported that the night of 9 March 1408 'the king went to sleep with the queen, and it was said that this was the reason he was afterwards more ill than he had been in the last ten years'.[23] If it was symptomatic of his illness that he regarded his wife with hostility and even disowned her, it was natural that Isabeau herself should have found her half-witted husband a trial and have looked for compensation elsewhere. It was rumoured that Louis of Orléans had become her lover, but the assumption rests on later innuendo and was not supported by contemporary evidence.[24] Moreover, later assertions that the dauphin Charles was a bastard appear to have been derived from his disinheritance by the king at the close of his reign rather than from any early doubt about his legitimacy. Yet the queen's court at her own palace, the Hôtel Barbette, had an undoubted reputation for gaiety, extravagance and promiscuity. That the king was offended by the queen's behaviour, and that this may have exacerbated his mental trouble is not improbable.

But the real break in their relations came in one of the king's saner moments when in 1417 he ordered his wife to disband her court, separated her from her daughter Catherine and banished her. The official reason for the queen's banishment was the supposedly dissolute behaviour of the queen's ladies-in-waiting, but it is likely that it was at the queen herself that Charles was directing his wrath. The chief victim of the king's displeasure was the queen's grand maître d'hôtel, Louis de Bosredon, who had previously been chamberlain to the duke of Orléans, with whom he had fought at

Agincourt. He was rumoured to be the queen's lover. On the king's orders de Bosredon had been arrested, imprisoned and kept in chains at Montlhèry before he was drowned secretly at night in the River Seine. The leather sack which contained his body bore the words '*Laissiez passer la justice du roy*'.[25] Whether or not Louis de Bosredon had been the queen's lover must remain speculative, but if he was it would at least account for the drastic action which the king took against him in 1417.[26]

After Harcigny died, the royal physicians were at a loss as to how best to deal with their difficult patient. They made use of the normal methods for dealing with madness but without avail. In 1393, at the suggestion of the duke of Bourbon, a surgeon from Lyon performed a '*purgacion par le teste*', evidently a trepanning, which was intended to relieve pressure on the brain. While the king felt some momentary relief after the operation, he soon suffered a relapse.

In desperation recourse was to be made to less orthodox practitioners. So a sorcerer, Arnaud Guillaume, who was said to own a book which God had given to Adam containing the remedies for original sin, was brought to court to treat the king. But, in spite of his qualifications, he was no more successful than the royal physicians and was ignominiously expelled, still declaring that the king's illness was an effect of diabolic possession.[27]

Many (among them churchmen and doctors of the university) had certainly come to believe that Charles had been bewitched and was the victim of sorcery. It was hardly surprising that in 1397–9 an attempt had been made to exorcize the king. Two Augustinian friars used magic incantations and a potion made of powdered pearls to ward off the demonic influences, but failing in this task they accused the king's brother, Louis d'Orléans himself, of '*malefica extrinseca*', and for their affrontary were tortured and beheaded.[28] In a wood near Dijon two sorcerers, Poncet du Solier and Jean Flandrin, even tried to raise the devil in a magic circle and also failing were themselves burned at the stake.[29] In 1408 a Lombard monk, Maître Helye, asserted that Charles had been bewitched by a silver 'image' which had been made by the command of the duke of Milan.

All the time processions and prayers were invoked in the hope of helping to bring about a cure. In 1399 the king spent a week in prayer before a '*sudarium*' brought especially to Paris by the monks of Citeaux; but the news of the fate of his son-in-law Richard II so affected him that he had a relapse. Although Charles suffered from delusions, he was in general only too bitterly aware of his affliction. When in 1397 he felt the onset of madness, he requested that his dagger should be removed, and told the duke of Burgundy to take away their knives from all the courtiers. 'In the name of Jesus Christ,' the unfortunate monarch cried, 'if there is any one of you who is an accomplice in this evil I suffer, I beg him to torture me no longer but let me die!'

But between his attacks the king had periods of lucidity, sometimes long, sometimes

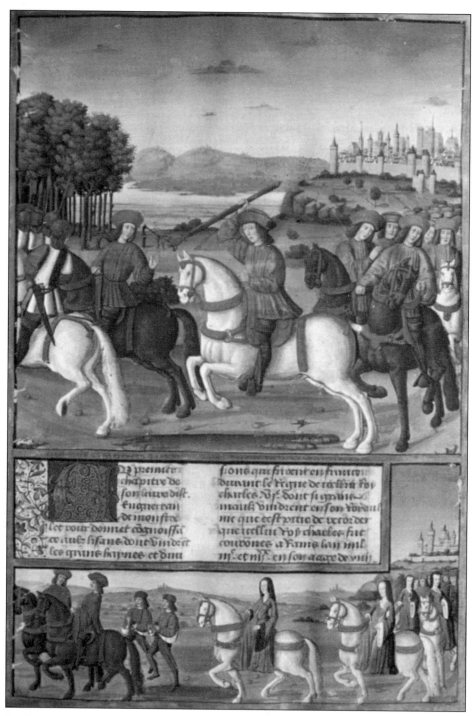

The folly of Charles VI: in the onset of madness the king attacks his own knights, from the Chronicles of Enguerrand de Monstrelet, MS 875/321 book 1 f. 1 (Musée Conde, Chantilly; photograph: The Bridgeman Art Library, London)

short, in which he went through the motions of government, presiding over the royal council and negotiating with foreign powers. In 1398, for instance, he was at Rheims to discuss the possible ending of the great schism, which was splitting the church, with the Emperor Wenceslas, a fitting foil for France's neurotic king, for Wenceslas, who was more often drunk than sober, was himself violent and unstable. It was said that he had had a cook who had failed to provide an appropriate meal turned and roasted on the spit. He had shot a monk while he was out hunting, remarking casually that monks should not wander about in the woods but set their minds on higher things. In 1400 the German princes, angered by the emperor's incompetence, his insobriety and cruelty, were to depose him, a fate which Charles VI avoided, though Pierre Salmon wondered whether he might not, like Richard II of England, be deprived of his throne.[30] In his lucid periods Charles even spoke of himself as the 'chief of Christian kings' who might lead a crusade against the Turks 'in defence of the faith, Hungary and the emperor of Constantinople'.

But each successive relapse into mental ineptitude seemed to impair his powers. He lacked the capacity to concentrate and his judgement was often poor. Competing politicians made unscrupulous use of his infirm will and clouded memory. Even in his lucid moments he was little more than a figurehead. 'We've got enough to do to put up with all this taxation', a citizen wrote in 1398, 'the king is mad and off his head and monsieur le duc d'Orléans is young and likes playing dice and whoring.'[31]

France was to reap the whirlwind as a result of Charles's prolonged mental instability and weak rule in the shape of civil strife, divided counsels and foreign invasion. In the political vacuum which the king's illness created, faction fights developed in the royal family between competing candidates for political power, more especially the king's brother, Louis of Orléans and his uncle Philip duke of Burgundy. The queen showed no political good sense, for she was more interested in pillaging the royal treasury to enrich herself and her Bavarian relatives, once despatching six horses laden with treasure to Bavaria, than in trying to remedy the ills of her adopted country. The king's brother, Louis of Orléans, who was married to an Italian, Valentina Visconti, one of the few people who seemed able to soothe the king in his more distracted moments, had political ambitions in Italy, and to finance his plans squandered money from the royal treasury. Abroad and in France he and the duke of Burgundy pursued different and incompatible policies. From 1401, if not before, affairs of state were dominated by the escalating conflict between Orléans and Burgundy and their followers.

The dénouement was violent. Duke Philip of Burgundy died in 1404 but his son and successor, John the Fearless, was ambitious and ruthless. He managed to win control over Paris and diminished Orléans's power in the royal council. But Orléans's days were numbered for as he left the queen's residence, the Hôtel Barbette, on the evening of 23 November 1407, he was set upon by a gang of armed men and murdered in the Vielle Rue du Temple.

There was little doubt in the people's minds that Duke John was responsible for Orléans's death, and it was greatly to exacerbate the family feuding. When the duke returned to Paris in 1408 a Norman theologian, Jean Petit, justified the murder in a scholastic disputation.[32] The weak, confused king seemed not to know where he stood in the matter. On the day on which he was due to give audience to the duke, he was too ill to do so and his place was taken by his son, the duke of Guyenne. At first persuaded by Burgundy that Orléans had been killed because he was plotting against him and his heirs, the king agreed to pardon the duke but then when he was at Melun revoked the pardon. Eventually a reconciliation was patched up between the interested parties when they met together at Chartres on 9 March 1409. The duke's representative Jean de Nielles sought pardon for the killing, even though, he stressed, it had been done for the good of the kingdom. Charles agreed to this request and besought Orléans's sons, who were both in tears, to respond which they promised to do. This peace, so Charles' official letter stated, was to last for ever.

Of that there was not the slightest hope. For the next quarter of a century France was to be racked by internecine struggles which the impotent king was powerless to control. Orléans's cause was henceforth championed by his son Charles and his father-in-law, Bernard VII, count of Armagnac, later constable of France, who gave his name of Armagnac to the Orléanist party. Violent conflicts broke out in 1411 but the situation continued so fluid that it changed from day to day, and war alternated with an endless series of negotiated and short-lived peaces. Political power shifted as one or other of the rival groups got a powerbase at court. The duke of Burgundy at first managed to win control over Paris and then lost it, his opponents, the Orléanist party and the Armagncs condemning him as a rebel.

While these divisive events were taking place, a new danger to France appeared on the horizon in the shape of a revival of English claims to the French throne. The ambitious young English king, Henry V, by virtue of the treaty of Brétigny which had been signed in 1369 by his great-grandfather Edward III, renewed his claim to the surrender of territories agreed in the treaty and to the crown of France.

An English army landed on 14 August 1415 and captured Harfleur, but as the army was decimated by a severe outbreak of dysentery Henry decided to return to England by pushing up through Normandy and embarking at Calais. On 24 October 1415 the small bedraggled English army faced the much more numerous French force on the rain-soaked battlefield near the village of Agincourt. The English threat had at least persuaded the bickering French princes to agree to a temporary reconciliation but the French knights were undisciplined and no match for the English longbowmen. At comparatively little cost to themselves, the English had slain 7,000 men and taken many notables, including the duke of Orléans, prisoners.

The English victory at Agincourt left the French both leaderless and divided. The scenario became increasingly complex and tragic. The king's health remained precarious. The duke of Burgundy pursued his own interests. The king's heir, the duke of Guyenne, who had shown signs of resourcefulness, suddenly died and was followed to the grave by his brother, John duke of Touraine, leaving his fourteen-year-old third brother, Charles, as dauphin. His mother, Queen Isabeau, alienated from her husband, came to terms with the duke of Burgundy. Temporarily the English threat brought the French princes together. The dauphin and the duke of Burgundy agreed to meet at Montereau-sur-Yonne on 10 September 1419; but as the duke of Burgundy walked on to the bridge where the meeting was to take place, he was set on and murdered. It was widely thought that he was struck down deliberately to rid the dauphin (who was believed to be privy to the act) and the Armagnacs of a dangerous rival, and in retaliation for the previous murder of Louis d'Orléans.[33]

Burgundy's murder did not, however, greatly help his opponents. It naturally gave great comfort to the English who were pushing all before them and had recently taken the Norman town of Gisors. The queen herself wrote to the English king condemning Burgundy's murder and expressing her goodwill. The hapless king, once more at loggerheads with his son, empowered the new duke of Burgundy, Philip, who was married to his daughter Michelle and whom he had appointed lieutenant-general of the kingdom, so displacing the dauphin, to begin negotiations for a truce with Henry V.

In the hopelessly divided country the English emerged triumphant. A treaty was arranged, confirmed in the cathedral of Troyes on 21 May 1420, by which Henry was to act as regent for the French king while he lived and to succeed him as king when he died. The treaty was to be cemented by Henry V's marriage to Charles's daughter Catherine which took place on 2 June following; their children were to be kings of both France and England as the unfortunate Henry VI was soon to be. In agreeing to the treaty the French king disinherited his own son who had 'rendered himself unworthy' to succeed the throne.

Time was to prove too short to see whether the treaty of Troyes could be properly implemented. Nor is it possible to deduce the state of Charles's mind, though outwardly he was enjoying one of his more lucid periods, playing tennis with the English king and actually accompanying him on military sorties and hunting expeditions. Then, in the spring of 1422, Henry fell sick and on 31 August he died, leaving his ten-month-old son, Henry VI, as his successor. Charles VI had himself been taken ill with fever in July 1421 but, fed with enormous quantities of fruit, some 200 to 300 oranges (so rich in Vitamin C) as well as pomegranates, he had recovered. In the autumn of 1422 he fell ill again with quartan fever and died on 21 October. At his obsequies at St Denis the King-of-Arms shouted 'God grant long life to Henry, by the grace of God King of France and England, our sovereign lord.' But Henry VI's inheritance, in mind as in territory, was to bring him at long last to a fatal end.

There can be little doubt that the schizophrenia which for so long afflicted the French king had been an important ingredient, perhaps the most significant one, in the disorder, division and misgovernment which characterized thirty years of his governance. It was to be many generations before the insidious impact of Charles's lunacy would be eliminated. It was perhaps even more ironical that as France recovered its strength under Charles VI's two successors, his son Charles VII and his grandson Louis XI, England under Henry VI was to succumb to the internecine aristocratic faction fights which the English king was powerless to control and to the continuance of which his own mental breakdown contributed.

But was there a genetic inheritance so far as Charles VII and Louis XI were concerned? Although the lawyers had no difficulty in showing that Charles' father had not been entitled to disinherit him, he inherited a divided and occupied kingdom nor in the first instance did he show much capacity or consistency in trying to cope with his problems. Yet through some shrewd political manipulation and a surge of patriotic feeling associated with the strange enigmatic figure of Joan of Arc, half mystic, half patriot, possibly a transvestite, assisted by the defection of the duke of Burgundy from the English alliance, English power in France slowly crumbled, allowing Charles VII to recover his authority and to reconstruct his administration.

Yet though in many respects Charles VII was a successful king, there were in the complexities of his personality some indications that he may have inherited some of the nervous weakness of his father.[34] The French commentator Etienne Pasquier, writing in 1621, hazarded that he might have been mad. His nineteenth-century biographer, Fresne de Beaucourt, said that he was 'many men within one man'. 'The small, hooded, rodent-like eyes, the long bulbous nose, the thick sensual lips, and the unhealthy colouring', so Malcolm Vale describes his portrait in the Louvre, 'exclude the sitter from consideration among the finer types of royal physiognomy.' His character seems in part to have been a reflection of his portrait, for he was unattractive, inconsistent, fickle, irresponsible, suspicious, resentful and sensual. His sensuality was said to be of such proportions as to verge on priapism. His court had a poor reputation. The chronicler Chastellain alleged that Charles's mistress, Agnes Sorel, was herself the author of 'all that can lead to *ribaudise* and dissoluteness in the matter of costume', a charge which Jean Juvenal des Ursins was to elaborate in 1445 when he commented 'you can see women's nipples and breasts and the great furred trains, girdles and other things'.

But what really suggests a mind not fully balanced was his phobic insecurity. Like James I of England, he was fearful of attempts at assassination, a fear not perhaps without some reason in the treacherous and violent court in which he had been brought up. He cannot ever have forgotten the brutal murder of the duke of Burgundy on the bridge of Montereau to which he was probably privy. Charles had himself a phobia about bridges. 'He did not dare to lodge on a floor, nor cross a wooden bridge', Chastellain commented, 'unless it was sound.' In October 1422 a floor had actually collapsed while he was holding court at La Rochelle; subsequently he instituted a special Mass at the Ste-Chapelle at Bourges to commemorate the occasion 'when God saved us from the danger that we were in at La Rochelle, when we fell from an upper to a lower room'. Some of his attendants, including the lord of Preaulx, died and the king was severely bruised.

If Charles VII suffered from a hereditary disorder of the nervous system, his health seemed generally good, apart from his neurotic anthrophobia, until the last decade of his reign. But by the late 1450s he was ailing, his legs painfully swollen and oozing pus, his mouth and jaw affected by a septic infection, by sores, abcesses, possibly osteomyelitis, probably the secondary symptoms of venereal disease, even conceivably syphilis.

Charles VII had been disinherited by his father in January 1421. His own relations with his son and heir, Louis XI, were severely strained. There seemed indeed to be few royal families less happy than the Valois princes of France. There were some indications that Louis XI may himself have inherited some nervous disorders.[35] In spite of his competence as king and the success with which he followed in his father's footsteps in restoring the authority of the crown, Louis XI was neurotic, the victim of phobias, in part perhaps as a reaction to the Kremlin-like atmosphere of the royal court, but possibly a part of his genetic inheritance. Louis was an intelligent, shrewd and masterful man, but he was highly suspicious, very untrustworthy and very superstitious. Physically he was poorly endowed, suffering from a skin disease, conceivably erysipelas, which made him fear that he might be a leper. There were hints that he had epileptic tendencies. He was, the French historian, Charles Petit-Dutaillis, held,

[a] neuropath, his nervous disorder found expession in idle chatter which spared nobody and often cost him dear, or, again in a craving for movement, which sometimes landed him on long hunting expeditions, most exhausting for his entourage, and sometimes caused him to undertake at top speed a journey across his kingdom. He was on edge, suspicious, wished to manage everything, and interfered in even the most trifling matters.[36]

As much as his father, Louis was 'many men in one man', for he was a fusion of contradictions, informal yet distant, cruel yet capable of friendship, fearful yet courageous. His quirks of character, his liking for deception which earned him the title of the universal spider, his unreadiness to dress like a king or enjoy the trappings of regality, his moodiness suggest that he may have been a victim of a mild neurosis which he may have inherited from his father and grandfather. The argument must not be overstressed but it is at least possible that the genes of Charles VI may explain some of the personal idiosyncrasies of his son and grandson. With the death of Louis XI's son Charles VIII in 1498 the Valois line came to an end. Their Bourbon successors were to be largely (though not entirely) free from significant neurotic tendencies.

VI

Spanish Madness

In the grim and gloomy palace of Tordesillas the torches flickered on the walls of the room where in the tapestried bed an old woman lay dying on Good Friday 1555. She was Juana, the queen of Castile, who had been incarcerated there as a mad woman for forty-six years. Some thirteen years after her death, her young great-grandson Don Carlos tossed and turned as he too lay dying in the castle where he had been confined by the orders of his father, Philip II, because of his mental incapacity. The castle of Arévalo where he had been held happened also to be the lodging where Queen Juana's own grandmother, the second wife of King Juan II of Castile, had much earlier spent a long widowhood as a demented madwoman. In such episodes there seemed to be rooted symbolically the nervous and psychotic disorders which to a greater or lesser extent were to haunt so many members of Spain's royal family in the centuries that followed.

With the possible exception of Henry VIII, whose personality was in some respects aberrant, the English royal house was to be free from mental imbalance until George III's attacks of seeming insanity. The Valois and Bourbon kings of France, apart from depression which affected some of the Bourbon princes, were free from madness. In northern Europe the Swedish king Eric XIV experienced an attack of insanity, and the mental balance of the Russian tsars, Ivan the Terrible and Peter the Great, was in question. But it was the Spanish Habsburgs and their successors the Spanish Bourbons who were to be most afflicted by ill-health, whether mental or physical in its nature, which had undoubted consequences for the vast empire over which they presided.

Juana of Castile was the third child of Ferdinand of Aragon and Isabella of Castile who had brought the union of the Spanish kingdoms into what was to be a single state. Juana was not a Habsburg princess but she was to marry a Habsburg prince. From the start of her life she was a pawn which her parents played in the game of European politics, the object of which was to win greater power and influence for the Spanish sovereigns. In 1495 her elder brother Juan had been married to Margaret, the daughter of the Holy Roman Emperor, Maximilian I, and sixteen-year-old Juana was herself married to Maximilian's son and heir, the Habsburg archduke Philip. Juana's elder sister, Isabella, had been married to the Portuguese king and had a son Miguel. It so happened that Juan, who had been heir to the Spanish dominions, died six months after his marriage and his wife was delivered of a stillborn child. Isabella of Portugal died in 1498 and her infant son, Miguel, two years later, so leaving Juana heiress to the vast and growing Spanish Empire in Europe and America while her husband, Philip, already ruler of Flanders and the duchy of Burgundy, was his father's probable successor as emperor. The richest inheritance in the world lay before Juana and Philip.

For this neither Juana nor Philip were well fitted. Philip was a handsome, flaxen-haired young man, but he was in many respects a playboy, devious, selfish and a philanderer. 'Nothing', as a contemporary observed, 'seemed to him better than women's pretty faces.' 'They take him', Fuensalida reported in February 1505, 'from banquet to banquet and from one lady to the next.' His wife, Juana, soon gave signs of a neurotic disposition which may have been inherited but which her personal and political experience was to intensify, and which was ultimately to make her a manic depressive. In 1499 a priest had commented that she seemed to him 'so frightened that she could not hold up her head'. She respected her parents, standing much in awe of her powerful and ambitious father, King Ferdinand, but she concentrated her affection upon her husband, Philip, by whom she was to have five children, the second of whom, Charles, was eventually to become king of Spain and Holy Roman Emperor.

From the very start of the marriage Juana showed herself obsessively jealous of her husband and could not bear to be separated from him. Philip had come to Castile, of which as Juana's husband he was likely on the death of Juana's mother, Isabella, to

A triptych by the 'Master of Affligham', featuring Philip the Fair and Juana of Spain on each side in the park of the Palais de Coudenberg (Musées Royaux des Beaux Arts, Brussels)

become king-consort, but, disliking Spanish customs as well as the people, he hurried home, leaving his wife in Spain. Separated from her husband she became distraught, fretted, suffered from insomnia and lost her appetite. She would spend her days staring dejectedly at the ground, deeply resentful of her inability to join Philip. When her mother, Queen Isabella, forbade her to sail to Flanders because of the danger of the winter storms her actions showed how precarious was the balance of her mind, for she fled from the Castel de la Motta, near Medina del Campo where she had been living, and even after she had been induced to return, she spent a night and half the next day sitting sullenly by the portcullis in the open courtyard. It was only after her ailing mother, Isabella, promised her that she would be allowed to sail to Flanders to be united with her husband that her deep melancholy seemed to lift.

Yet in Flanders her conduct was such that even her husband suspected that she might be mentally unbalanced. His own behaviour had undoubtedly helped to bring this about. 'Donna Juana', the chronicler recounted, 'felt the change which had taken place in the Prince's love. His manner to her was very different from what it had been; and as a woman who loved him beyond measure, she sought to discover what the cause of the alteration might be. She was told that the archduke had a mistress, an exceedingly handsome noblewoman, with whom he was passionately in love.' When Juana saw the prince's reputed mistress hide a missive in her corsage, it was reported that she snatched it from her; but the other woman seized it back and swallowed it. In her fury Juana attacked her rival, cutting at her tresses with a pair of scissors. When the woman tried to defend herself, Juana stabbed her in the face. 'So infuriated was the Princess that, like a raging lioness, she sought out her enemy and, it is said, injured and misused her, and then commanded that her hair should be cropped to the roots.' Not unnaturally relations between husband and wife became increasingly sour. Juana was 'so much affected at being thus treated by her husband . . . she took to her bed and almost went out of her mind.' Philip, fearful that Juana might be losing her senses, instructed her treasurer, Martin de Moxaca, to keep a diary of his wife's seemingly mad behaviour.

To personal stress there had to be added the political crisis caused by the death of her mother, Isabella of Castile, on 23 November 1504 which left Juana at least in name queen of the kingdom of Castile with all its wealth and extensive resources, for it was the Castilians who were colonizing and exploiting the newly discovered lands of America. By her will Isabella had recognized Juana as her 'heiress and lawful successor', with the qualification that if she should absent herself from the kingdom or 'if being here she should lack the desire or ability to rule or to administer it', her father Ferdinand of Aragon should 'rule, govern and administer the kingdom in her name'. The clause suggested that Isabella had had doubts about her daughter's capacity, and it formed an open invitation to Ferdinand to take over in Juana's name.

Juana was now to be so pressurized both by her husband, who had himself designs on her Castilian inheritance, and by her father, who was intent on retaining his power over a united Spain, that her mind became increasingly unbalanced, and she sank deeper into a depression from which she was never to be able effectually to free herself. Ferdinand paid lip service to his daughter's rights, claiming only to act as regent on her behalf. Philip pushed his wife's claims so that he might act as king consort, but to justify his right to act on his wife's behalf he used the information which Moxaca had compiled to question her sanity. 'In Spain', as she wrote pathetically on 3 May 1505, 'it is being declared that I am out of my mind. . . . I know that the King, my lord and husband, wrote to Spain, complaining of me in some sort, in order to justify himself. But that matter ought not to go beyond us parents and children . . . the only cause was jealousy.' But all Juana could do to protect her inheritance was to protest as her husband and her father tried to come to an agreement about the future governance of her own kingdom. Both Philip and Ferdinand blew alternately hot and cold, but neither of them showed any compassion, let alone understanding, for the unfortunate queen. 'You know', Philip wrote testily, 'that when she is with child she is apt to grow angry without cause.'

Philip decided that he must travel to Spain to support his own and his wife's claims. With their arrival there seemed a real danger of civil war, even though Ferdinand and Philip reached a seemingly amicable agreement at Villa Fafila on 27 June 1506 by which they divided the spoils of power between themselves, declaring that Juana was mentally incapable of government. 'Should she wish to participate this would lead to the utter destruction and annihilation of our kingdom, owing to the maladies and passions which it would be indecorous to describe.'

Juana was no doubt a neurotic, highly strung woman, but her neurotic propensities were to be given ever fuller rein by the treatment to which she was being subjected by her manipulative and power-hungry father and her unfaithful and uncaring husband.

Confused as she was, she still claimed the right to rule her mother's kingdom, but she fluctuated as to whether to associate her husband or her father with her in her governance. The two men, who were still insisting that Juana was insane, were falling out between themselves. Juana, fearful that her husband might place her under restraint, at the town of Cogeces, 'dismounted and flung herself on the ground. . . . She refused to enter the town and spent the night on the back of a mule, riding hither and thither.' Then, at Burgos, Philip was taken seriously ill, either with smallpox or measles, and on 25 September 1506 he died. Juana, who had been most assiduous in her attendance on her sick husband, 'never leaving him by day or night', was grief stricken. She left Burgos at the end of December intending to take her husband's body for burial in distant Granada where her mother Isabella had been entombed. On the way she made two visits to the Carthusian monastery of Miraflores, ordering his coffin to be opened in her presence. 'She looked at and touched the body without any sign of emotion and shed no tears.' She may well have ordered the coffin to be opened because of her fears that the Flemings might secretly have taken Philip's body to the Netherlands, for his heart had been already embalmed and transferred there. Juana's bleak journey never reached its destination, for at Torquemada she felt the pains of childbirth upon her and had to stop; her daughter Catherine was born on 14 January 1507.

Her father, Ferdinand, had been in his Italian territories when he heard without regret of his son-in-law's death. He ordered the Castilians to obey Juana, but plainly he had no intention of allowing her to govern. When he returned to Spain he persuaded her reluctantly to accompany him to the fortress palace of Tordesillas, some 24 miles from Valladolid, which was to be her home, if such it could be called, for the next forty-six years. When she realized that she was to be incarcerated by her father's orders she became intensely depressed. Her husband had been at last buried in the cloister of the neighbouring monastery of Santa Clara at which the queen could gaze sadly from her window. Steadily she sank into ever deeper melancholy. 'The Queen', it was reported in November 1510, 'would neither eat nor sleep nor dress herself properly, was exceeding weak and disordered. . . . Because her life was of such a kind, because her clothing was so pitiful and unbecoming her dignity, and because she had been so greatly reduced by her way of living, there seemed little hope that she could survive many days.'

But survive she was to do in a mental time capsule. Her father, Ferdinand, governed Castile in her name. He had married as his second wife a French princess, Germaine de Foix, in the hope of siring an heir; but their son, born in 1509, did not survive, and the love filtre, concocted from various herbs and bull's testicles, which was prescribed, instead of strengthening his diminished potency only made him ill. He and his wife visited Juana in January 1513. Three years later he died, leaving his lands to Juana's eldest son, Charles. 'I alone am Queen and my son Charles is nothing more than the Prince', Juana protested but it was in vain, for Charles had no intention of surrendering his authority. Charles had not seen his mother since he was a boy and when at last he paid her a visit he was shocked by her emaciated appearance and shabby clothing. But he found the atmosphere of Tordesillas depressing. When he suggested that his sister, Catherine, who had been with her mother since birth, should leave the palace, his mother became hysterical.

Isolated from the outside world, Juana was kept deliberately misinformed of what was happening. She was kept under continuous observation and was not even allowed to attend Mass at Santa Clara. 'In one way or another', her governor, the marquis of Denia, wrote, 'I shall prevent her going out and even though excuses may be difficult to find, I shall devise something to keep within the forms of decency.' The fading woman lost her appetite, neglected her dress, would not go to bed regularly and what seemed to Denia the most alarming symptom of all, was reluctant even to attend Mass.

Then, for one astonishing if brief period the mad, neglected queen came into the limelight. Her son's government had proved so unpopular that it provoked an armed rising against Charles and his hated Flemish advisers. What better justification could there be for the rebels than to press the claims of the Queen, Donna Juana, and to seek to set her free to exercise her sovereign powers. The rebels captured Tordesillas and the poor, confused queen seemed at first to respond to the rebels' demands. 'For sixteen years', it was reported she had said, 'I have been deceived and ill-treated. For nearly twelve I have been penned up here in Tordesillas.' The regent, Cardinal Adrian, told Charles:

> The worst of it is that in all they do the rebels claim the authority of the Queen, our Sovereign Lady, as a person in her right mind and fully competent to rule, whereby they deprive Your Majesty of his authority. Indeed it is hardly proper to call them rebels, since they obey her royal commands. . . . Almost all the officials and servants of the Queen . . . insist that wrong has been done to Her Highness by keeping her under restraint for fourteen years on the pretext that she was insane, whereas throughout she had been as perfectly sane as she was at the time of her marriage.

Yet Juana was obviously so dazzled and confused by the unexpected turn of events that she hardly knew how to deal with them. If at first she had shown sympathy towards the rebels, ultimately she was to disown them.

After the rebels had been defeated at Villalar on 23 April 1521, Juana returned to the living tomb of Tordesillas, where she was to exist for another thirty-four years, forbidden even to leave the palace. 'Having been made so arrogant by the respect paid to her during my absence', Denia reported, 'everyone here has had a great deal of trouble with her.' She continued to be indifferent to her surroundings and neglectful of her person. Her daughter, Catherine, had at last left her, apparently none the worse for having been cooped up with her mother, to marry her cousin King John III of Portugal. More and more Juana relapsed into the fantasy world of the manic depressive. Even the consolations of religion were no longer able to still or soothe her unquiet spirit. 'On Christmas Eve', Denia reported, 'when divine service was being held in the chapel, she came in to fetch the Infanta (Catherine), who was hearing Mass, and screamed that the altar and everything on it must be taken away.' Her indifference, even her hostility to religion, led to the suspicion that she might be the victim of demonic possession. She said herself that she was besieged by evil spirits. She pictured a spectral cat which devoured her mother's soul, tore her father's body into

Juana of Spain, a detail from the triptych by the 'Master of Affligham' (see p. 88)

pieces and was only lying in wait to dismember her own body. The saintly Jesuit, Francisco Borja, found her in a very confused state of mind when he visited her in her closing years.

The exact nature of her illness has caused problems for historians. There are those who have argued that she was never mad but simply the defenceless victim of maltreatment by her husband, her father and even her son. Others have suggested that she suffered from attacks of schizophrenia but it seems most probable that she was subject to depression which left her at the last a chronic manic depressive.

She died on Good Friday 1555 in her seventy-sixth year. After her death Charles told his brother Ferdinand that as his mother lay dying the cloud on her mind had lifted and that she had called on her Saviour. Although Juana never exercised the power that was properly hers as queen of Castile, her madness had had an incalculable effect on the history of the world, since it was this which had made possible the accession and long reign of her son Charles. If Juana had been queen of Castile until her death in 1555, the year in which Charles surrendered his imperial title and only the year before he abdicated the Spanish throne, European history might have followed a very different course. Charles' younger brother might have become king of Aragon, and the precarious Hispanic union might have been sundered. Moreover, Spanish or rather Castilian resources might not have been squandered in a series of imperial wars which only peripherally served the country's interests, for whereas Aragon looked towards Italy and the Mediterranean, Castile's interests were more focused on the rich, expanding and still partly unexplored lands of America. Such suppositions must remain purely speculative. The reality was the dying woman at Tordesillas who had never enjoyed the power which was hers by right because of her mental incapacity.

In different circumstances but for similar reasons Juana's great-grandson, Don Carlos, too was eventually deprived of the powers which he might as heir-apparent to the Spanish Empire have expected to wield. But the story of Don Carlos was to be very different from that of his great-grandmother, for it was to attract attention both in his own time and in later generations. It was to be an ingredient in the black legend, the *leyenda nigra*, by which his enemies sought to denigrate the reputation of Don Carlos's father, King Philip II, spreading the rumour that the king was a tyrant and persecutor whose son had fallen victim to his intolerance and anger. Novelists and dramatists were drawn to the theme. In his drama *Philip II* Alfieri used the conflict between father and son, Don Philip and Don Carlos, to depict a struggle between good and evil, darkness and light, between the liberalism which he saw, albeit mistakenly, embodied in Don Carlos and the despotism represented by Philip II. Schiller's *Don Carlos*, deeper in its tragic undertones, showed Carlos as a friend of liberal

Don Carlos as a child, from a painting by Antonio Mors (photograph: © Staatliche Museen Kassel)

Protestantism and hopelessly in love with his beautiful and high-minded stepmother, Elisabeth of Valois, the third wife of Philip II. Their sacrifice, for in the play they are put to death at the cruel king's orders, was portrayed as a sacrifice made for love and liberty.

The reality was far more prosaic and yet no less dramatic, for the short life of Don Carlos seemed to epitomize how the richest and most powerful princes could be haunted by personal tragedy which had political and public implications. Queen Juana had never been in a position to exercise her royal powers. Don Carlos never became king, but for all his life he was the heir to the greatest and wealthiest empire in the world. If Juana was placed under restraint at Tordesillas to ensure that she might not be queen, it was because Don Carlos might one day become king that his life culminated in tragedy.

Don Carlos may never have been completely insane, but he evidently suffered from a severe personality disorder from birth; this disorder was to be further accentuated by an accident which damaged his head in 1562. There can be no certainty but it is not wholly impossible that he may have inherited his temperamental disposition from his great-grandmother, Juana, though her son, the emperor Charles V and her grandson, Don Carlos's father, Philip II, showed no sign of such incipient insanity; but inheritance is not entirely out of the question. His mother and his grandmother were Portuguese princesses in whose family there seems occasionally to have been a streak of madness. More arguably, his mental weakness may have been organic in its origin. It is possible, though unlikely, that Carlos was an autistic child. It seems much more probable, though again the evidence is extremely tenuous, that he may even have suffered a brain dysfunction at birth. His delivery was difficult and supervised by an inexperienced midwife (the queen's ladies-in-waiting were absent at an *auto da fé*). His mother, Maria of Portugal, died four days after Carlos's birth. While there is no direct evidence of brain dysfunction, the pattern of his behaviour as a young child and adult fits very exactly the symptoms of those who have suffered brain damage, usually as a result of loss of oxygen and blood sugar. In such cases the limbic brain takes over, causing, if circumstances call it forth, mindless violence and irrationality; the child displays 'impulsive hyperactivity resistant to social control', is 'indiscriminately aggressive and impulsively violent', averse to book learning and reckless in his behaviour. While such a hypothesis is purely speculative, it goes some way to explain the vagaries of Don Carlos's personality, pronounced even in his earliest years. In Don Carlos, physical frailty and mental imbalance went hand in hand to create a tragic young man whose personality and activities constituted problems for his father and for the empire over which he ruled.

Although Don Carlos lacked a mother's care from the very start of his life, his governess Dona Leonor de Mascareñas, a pious lady who had once been Philip's own governess and who had recently wondered whether she should not enter a convent, was told by the king 'to treat him as if you were his mother'. Carlos seems to have developed some affection for her, leaving her some holy relics in his will. 'What is going to become of me, without father or mother', the boy complained when she left his household, 'my grandfather in Germany, my father in Monzon?' When he was seven years old, he was removed from female tutelage and placed under Don Antonio de Rojas, to whom in his will he bequeathed a relic from the crown of thorns. The general supervisor of his studies was Honorato Juan, a member of a noble Spanish family who had studied under his compatriot the Renaissance scholar Vives before joining the court. Juan de Muñatones instructed him in religious matters.

He can have seen relatively little of his father, for Philip II was seldom in Spain until he assumed the crown. In 1554 he had married the English queen, Mary Tudor, the stepmother whom Don Carlos was never to see. According to the marriage treaty if children were born to Mary and Philip, as Mary so devoutly hoped, the eldest son was to inherit England, the Netherlands and the Franche Comté, but Spain and its dependencies would fall to Don Carlos. If the marriage proved to be childless, then Philip's rights in England lapsed.

There was every indication from the very start of his life that Don Carlos was a difficult, temperamental child, which again suggests that he may have suffered a brain dysfunction at birth. The Venetian ambassador gravely informed his government that Carlos had been born with teeth and that he bit and even tried to chew the breasts of his nurses, causing three of them painful injuries. He was very slow to talk, stammering badly until early manhood. It was commented later that although he had a good voice, he had considerable difficulty in enunciating his words, more especially in pronouncing the letters 'r' and 'l'. Tiepolo commented that the first word he had ever uttered was 'no'.[1]

He was self-willed and obstinate, and averse to book-learning. 'When', so the Venetian ambassador, Paolo Tiepolo reported in 1563, 'he passed from infancy to puberty, he took no pleasure in study nor in arms nor in horsemanship nor in any virtuous things, honest and pleasant, but only in doing harm to others. . . . In everything he shows a great repugnance to being useful and a very great inclination to do harm. He speaks with difficulty.'[2] 'It grieves me', Honorato Juan reported, 'that he does not make as much progress as I would wish.' 'With respect to his studies', Don Garcia de Toledo wrote, 'he makes little progress because he studies with an ill grace. He is the same with gymnastic exercises and fencing.'[3] 'Curious in his demands, and of a good wit,' the English ambassador declared in 1563, 'but otherwise utterly unbookish.'[4]

He greatly admired his grandfather the emperor because of his military achievements and expressed a desire to see him. Charles V had abdicated the empire and retired to the Jeronomite monastery at Yuste in Spain. Don Carlos was so eager to see his grandfather that his new governor, Don Garcia de Toledo had great difficulty in preventing him from mounting his horse there and then and riding to see his illustrious ancestor.

Eventually an interview was arranged at Valladolid in October 1556. Don Carlos, full of martial ardour, followed the emperor's account of his campaigns with the greatest interest. But when the emperor confessed that on one occasion he had been obliged to retreat, Carlos became angry, vowing that he would never flee. In certain circumstances, his grandfather repeated, it might be the reasonable thing to do. Don Carlos fumed. 'It seems to me,' Charles told his sister, Eleanor of France, that he 'is a very turbulent young man; his manners and his humor do not please me: I do not know what one day he will become.'

Carlos was physically unattractive, indeed to the point of deformity. His head was abnormally large, one shoulder higher than the other, his legs spindly, one slightly longer than the other, his right hand apparently withered, his complexion pallid. He had been so sickly as a young child that it was rumoured that his chances of survival into adult life were slim. 'The prince', the Venetian ambassador wrote, 'is small in height. His figure is ugly and unpleasing. His complexion is melancholy, this because from the age of three he has suffered, almost without interruption, from the quartan fever, to the alienation of his spirit.'[5] Originally 'short and thin' he began to put on weight as he grew towards manhood; 'it is not to be marvelled at', the English envoy Thomas Chaloner commented on 21 November 1562, 'as he is a great eater.' Everyone commented on his ravenous appetite. 'He eats greedily', the imperial ambassador, Baron Dietrichstein, reported, 'and hardly has he finished before he is ready to begin again. This gluttony is the cause of his illness and many think that if he continues in this way he will not live long.'[6]

Even more worrying was his hasty and furious temper, which revealed that he had a strongly sadistic streak in his nature. For his enjoyment he had young girls whipped in his presence. 'The paleness of his complexion', another Venetian envoy, Badoaro, reported, 'suggests a cruel character. . . . When rabbits are taken in the hunt, or other animals are brought to him, his pleasure is to see them roasted alive . . . he has a pride without parallel, for he cannot suffer to remain a long time in the presence of either his father or his grandfather, holding his cap in his hand. He is angry more often than a young man should be.'[7] 'When people appear to give him less consideration than he thinks fit', his fellow Venetian Tiepolo wrote, 'he orders them to be whipped or bastinadoed, and not so very long ago he wished someone to be castrated. He loves no one but there are many he hates.'[8] He threatened to kill Cardinal Espinosa, drawing a dagger from his cloak, for preventing the actor Cisneros from presenting a comedy in his presence. He told his treasurer, Juan Estevaz de Lobon, that he would have him thrown out of the window, a fate with which he also menaced the son of the marquis of Las Navas.[9] His accounts included payments made by way of indemnity to people whose children had been beaten by his orders. He treated animals in a similar fashion, maiming horses which had displeased him with such fury – twenty-three were mentioned – that they had subsequently to be destroyed.

The stories of his misbehaviour were legend, and even if their reliability may be sometimes in doubt they suffice to demonstrate his pathological ill-nature. He had boots made, so it was said, as was then fashionable for young men to wear, of a very large size so that small pistols could be pushed inside them. When his father heard of his son's request, he ordered the bootmaker to disregard his son's instructions. But Don Carlos was furious when the bootmaker delivered boots of a less 'kinky' character than those he had ordered, commanding that the boots be cut up in small pieces, *'fricasser comme tripes de boeuf'*, and obliged the unfortunate cobbler to consume the uninviting dish. On another occasion, when some water was thrown inadvertently from the balcony of a house, splashing down near him, he ordered that the offenders should be executed, adding that of his clemency he would allow them to receive the last rites before their execution. The French gossip, Pierre de la Bourdeille, lord of Brantôme, who was in Spain in 1564, related that the prince roamed the streets with other wild young men, causing mayhem and kissing the girls.[10] But, as the French ambassador put it, *'le plus souvent il est si fou et si furieux, qu'il n'y a celui qui ne juge mal fortunée la femme qui aura a vivre avec luy'* ('he is often so mad and furious that there is no one who does not judge the woman who will have to live with him very unfortunate').

Fundamentally Don Carlos lacked affection. Affection was perhaps hard to come by in a sixteenth-century court, but Carlos lacked grace and charm; to all intents and purposes he seemed a young psychopath. His aunt Juana tried to help him but he repelled the attempts which she made to win him over. With his father his relations seemed always to be distant. The only person whom he seemed to appreciate was his young step-mother, Elisabeth of Valois, who showed him sympathy. Among the documents found after his death there was a paper in his hand entitled 'a list of my friends'. These included Queen Elisabeth 'who was always good to me' and Don Juan of Austria (the handsome and attractive illegitimate son of the emperor, his uncle). But another list which was headed 'a list of my enemies' began ominously: 'The king my father, *El rey, mi padre*; Ruis Gomez de Silva, the Princess of Eboli; the duke of Alva.'

A difficult child, a disturbed adolescent, Don Carlos's condition was seemingly aggravated by a serious accident which he sustained in 1562. On Sunday 19 April he was at Alcalá de Henares, 20 miles from Madrid, where he had been sent to convalesce after a bout of quartan fever. As he was descending the palace staircase he spied a pretty girl, Mariana de Garcetas, the daughter of the palace's concierge, whom he may already have known,* walking in the garden. He rushed down the stairs, 'in the hasty following of a wench' as the English ambassador, Sir Thomas Chaloner, informed Queen Elizabeth, lost his footing five steps from the bottom, turned completely over and fell head first, striking his head against the garden door (which as it was locked would in any case have frustrated his plan), sustaining damage to the posterior part of the head on the left of the skull.[11]

For a time it seemed as if the prince might die. Philip II sent his personal physician, Juan Gutiérrez together with two royal surgeons, Pedro de Torres and Dr Portugués to join the two other doctors in charge of the case, one of whom, Daza Chacón, was later to write a full description of Don Carlos's illness.[12] He had a wound 'about the size of a thumbnail, the edges well contused and the pericranium laid bare, and also appearing to be somewhat contused'. Don Carlos recovered consciousness, was blooded (eight ounces of blood the first day and six ounces on the two subsequent days) and was even allowed to eat some prunes, broth, and a chicken leg, which he finished off with marmalade. But several days later the wound began to fester and the prince developed a fever as well as swollen glands in his neck.

The physicians feared that there might have been an internal lesion and a highly reputed surgeon, the Bachelor Torres, was brought from Valladolid to make an incision in the scalp, 'lest', as Chaloner told his mistress, the queen of England, 'the scalp should be crazed'. The incision was made 'in the form of a T' but it was 'impossible to see if there was damage to the cranium because of the great flow of blood; we could do no more than stop it and apply a dressing'.

Don Carlos's condition deteriorated further, so alarming his father that he came post haste from Madrid, bringing with him the highly respected anatomist, Andreas Vesalius.[13] Vesalius, who was regarded with suspicion by his Spanish colleagues, was actually physician to the Netherlanders at Philip's court and not his personal doctor. 'The King', Chaloner wrote home, 'brought Dr Vesalius (not unknown for his excellent skill) from Madrid with him, whose better learning the Spanish make not account of according to his worthiness, *quia figulus odit figulum*.'[14] Vesalius was acquainted with Daza Chacón as they had both been present when Henry II of France received a mortal brain injury during a joust in 1559.

Philip II was personally present when the physicians dressed his son's wound with a curious concoction, of powdered iris and birthwort, followed by an unguent of turpentine and egg yolk, topped by honey of rose and a plaster of betony; but Don Carlos remained very ill. Chaloner told Queen Elizabeth:

---

*In his will, dated 19 May 1564, he bequeathed Mariana, described as at present in the monastery of San Juan de la Penitencia at Alcala, 4000 ducats if she married and 2000 if she entered religion ('*para ayuda a su casamienda o entrar en religion*'). His accounts show that he presented her with a mantilla on 9 April 1566.

Next day being Ascension Day, because his face began to swell his doctor gave him an easy purgation, which wrought upon him fourteen times, overmuch by the half in his constitution to bear it out. The same afternoon the swelling increased, with small fiery pimples called erysipelas, which redoubled the doubts of the doctors and heaviness of the King. On Friday 8 May his state improved, the wound of his head waxing dry. The Saturday [9 May] the swelling so increased that his eyes were closed up, so that when the King came to visit him he was obliged to lift up his eyelids.[15] . . . The swelling extended first through the left side, the ear and the eye, and then the right, so that the abcess covered the whole face, and extended to the neck, chest and arms.

The doctors decided that the prince was too weak to be blooded but he was cupped and purged. Vesalius believed that there was probably an internal lesion and recommended trepanning, but as some of the others disagreed, he accepted a compromise, to ruginate or scrape the skull, so as to release the suppurating matter.

Don Carlos was still very dangerously ill, so much so that a Moorish doctor from Valencia, Pintarete, was introduced into the sickroom and applied unguents to the wound; but the wound 'went from bad to worse because the black unguent had burned it so that the skull became as black as ink'. Pintarete was sent packing. Prayers for the prince's recovery were offered, relics in the churches were exposed and, as Sir Thomas Chaloner reported, 'there have been solemn processions of all the religious orders, with images of our Lady and saints'. As a final gesture the desiccated corpse of a holy friar, Fra Diego, highly reputed for his sanctity – he had won a great reputation as a preacher in the Canary Islands – was brought to the Prince and laid all night in bed by him'.[16]

Don Carlos's death was expected daily. The pallor of his complexion, the pope's nephew, Count Annibale d'Emps told the Florentine ambassador, could only betoken the approach of death. The king betrayed every sign of genuine sorrow, his eyes filled with tears; and the duke of Alva did not leave the bed chamber, even to take off his clothes. 'For though', Chaloner reported realistically, 'the appearance of the prince's manners and disposition seemed to denote him to be of a sullen, cruel mode, much misliked and feared, yet considering he is the only legitimate son of his father, it maketh them to tender his loss the more.'[17]

Sorrow-stricken the king left for the monastery of St Jeronimo, 'intending (if the prince dies) to remove to some other more retired', having ordered mourning clothes and deposited instructions for the prince's funeral with Alva and the count of Feria.

But there followed as striking an improvement in the prince's health as to appear to contemporaries to be a miracle. On 16 May, probably Vesalius, though Daza Chacón gave the credit to Dr Pedro de Torres, made a further incision to drain the pus, 'thick white matter' which had accumulated behind his left eye (and extended towards the right). The operation was repeated at intervals and the prince began to show real signs of improvement. By 22 May the fever had gone and the English ambassador could report on 1 June that 'the prince of Spain is well recovered and now the former sorrow turns into feasts'. On 14 June he got up, heard Mass and received the Sacrament. His head was treated with powder of the bark of the pomegranate tree; but the scar was slow to heal. On 5 July he paid his respects to the body of the blessed Diego, and then attended a bull fight in the public square and a 'performance of the game of spears'. By 17 July he was back with the royal family in Madrid.

'I believe', the English ambassador wrote sensibly, 'that God's minister, nature, hath in despite of the surgeons' inconsiderate dealing, done more for the Prince than they are aware of.' But, in any case, it was Fra Diego rather than the doctors to whom credit for his recovery was given. 'On that same occasion', Don Carlos said in his testament of May 1564,

> at the prey of that malady, abandoned by the doctors, left for dead by the king, my father and lord, and preparations being made for my burial, they brought me the corpse of the aforesaid holy Fray Diego; and from the moment when it had approached me and when I had touched it, I felt the improvement that God our Lord designed to give me – such were the merits of Fray Diego and the intercession he made for me from the Divine Majesty, so judged all who were present; that it became my intention to secure his canonization and I pray my father to undertake this.[18]

Don Carlos's wish for Fra Diego's canonization was one that his father was to respect. In spite of lack of cooperation from successive popes, Philip at last obtained Fra Diego's canonization at the hands of Pope Sixtus V on 12 July 1588, the year of the Armada when the king himself surely required divine aid.[19] Sir Thomas Chaloner had at long last been proved right in telling Cecil, 'If God send the Prince to escape, the friar is not unlike to be canonized for his labor.'

Although 'Vesalius by his skill preserved Don Carlos from evident death', as Charles de Tisnacq told the duchess of Parma,[20] Don Carlos's mind henceforth seemed to be more severely damaged, his character more depraved, his judgement more capricious. Baron Dietrichstein, the imperial ambassador, said that though Carlos talked sensibly enough on occasions, his behaviour sometimes resembled that of a seven-year-old child. Aware of his immaturity, his father told the duke of Alva in 1564 that his son lagged 'far behind what is normal at his age' in 'intelligence and personality as well as in judgement'. It seems most likely that the head wound and the subsequent treatment to which he had been submitted had exacerbated further Don

Carlos's condition. He became even more violent, making at least six homicidal attacks on men who had in some way or another offended him. Mentally retarded and psychopathic, Don Carlos's head wound had damaged further an already malfunctioning brain.

What might have been merely tragic in a family of commoners had wider repercussions, since Don Carlos was the heir to the throne, and the virtual ruler of what was in area and resources the greatest empire in the world, stretching from the Mediterranean to south and central America. In the hope that he might measure up to his future responsibilities he had been entrusted with high office. When he was nineteen, in 1564, he was made a member of the council of state, and seems to have made some attempt to carry out his duties. 'We are advised', the regent of the Netherlands, Margaret of Parma, wrote, 'that Monseigneur the prince grows ever more stronger and already frequents the Council of State, to the great satisfaction of everyone, for the great hope that it gives of his person and spirit.'[21] He was even made president of the councils of state and of war. His income was increased and he was promised that he should accompany his father to the Low Countries, something which Don Carlos had set his heart on doing.

It was understandable that Don Carlos should wish to visit the Low Countries, for they had become the centre of a crisis which was to form a constant strain on Spain's resources in men and materials. The Low Countries had become wealthy through trade, were passionately attached to the preservation of their traditional liberties and were increasingly infiltrated by the reformed religion which Philip, a devout Catholic, vowed to suppress. The Low Countries deeply resented his policy of centralization and were already in the first stages of revolt against Spanish rule.

To seek to secure himself against this growing trouble, Philip needed to win friends and to neutralize his would-be enemies. Hostilities between France and Spain had been ended by the treaty of Câteau-Cambrésis in 1559, and a good relationship with France was fostered further by Philip's third marriage to Elisabeth, the charming daughter of the French king, Henry II, for whom Don Carlos was himself to develop some affection.

But Philip was averse to allowing Don Carlos to interfere in the heady troubles of the Low Countries. He was too inexperienced, too headstrong, too unreliable to be of any use. Where, however, Don Carlos might be useful to his father was in any marriage that he might contract. Of dubious value as a suitor, he was nonetheless a valuable pawn in the diplomatic marriage stakes. The possibility of marriage with the recently widowed Mary Queen of Scots was discussed. It made some appeal to Don Carlos but Philip was cautious, for he feared that such a marriage might ultimately alienate both France and England. Another possible candidate was his young aunt, Juana, the widowed queen of Portugal, a charming and intelligent woman, but the proposal was not to Don Carlos's liking. The bishop of Limoges reported that he treated his aunt with such disdain that '*la pauvre dame maigrit à vue d'oeil*'. He viewed with greater favour a possible marriage with his cousin, a princess of the Austrian Habsburg house, Anne, a granddaughter of the Emperor Ferdinand II, Don Carlos's great uncle.

When he was walking with his step-mother, Queen Elisabeth, in the woods of the park of the castle of Valsain near Segovia, she asked the prince who seemed, as he so often was, taciturn and moody, what was on his mind. He replied that his thoughts were far away. 'And how far away?', the queen asked him. 'At my cousin's home,' he replied.

But the negotiations hung fire. When Anne's father, Maximilian, became emperor himself in 1564 he again pressed his cousin to agree to the marriage. King Philip sent secret instructions to his envoy in Vienna, stating again that 'my son is not physically fit for marriage, and . . . I am still obliged, not without real grief to repeat this again; although my son is 19 years old and one sees other young people retarded. But God has willed that he should be more than most of them. . . . We must exercise patience and adjourn this business until the moment when the marriage takes place.'[22]

It is not plain why Philip hesitated but it is very probable that he was worried by rumours of his son's impotence. Don Carlos was not indifferent to sex as his roaming the streets looking for girls showed. He had shown positive interest in the plans for his marriage. But if the marriage was to serve its purpose in the procreation of children Carlos's impotence could be a real barrier to its fulfilment. The imperial ambassador, Dietrichstein, observed that Don Carlos had no 'leaning for women, whence we may infer that he is likely to be impotent'. 'According to others,' Dietrichstein continued, 'he has said that he wishes that the wife whom he marries will find him a virgin. According to others he said that he has become so chaste because his father will give him no authority and this makes him despair.' 'The general opinion', he wrote later, 'is that he has not had a woman until now. It is rumoured that his father has been advised to make a test. When they talk to him of 'rapports avec les femmes', he replies that he does not wish to know any other than the one who will become his wife, must they therefore treat him as a eunuch and make up jokes on his account?'[23] The French ambassador, De Fourquevaulx, summed up the situation by describing Don Carlos as 'un demi-homme naturel'.

It was doubtless in the light of these considerations that a test of Don Carlos's virility was devised, operated by three doctors, his barber Ruy Diaz de Quintanilla and his apothecary. They procured the services of a young girl, who was rewarded with a gift of a house for herself and her mother and 1,200 ducats. She was introduced into the prince's bedchamber but the results appear to have been inconclusive. The French ambassador informed his master, Charles IX, that it seemed very likely that if the prince married he would have no children. '*Tutta la notte va in bordello con poca dignita et molta arroganza*,' was the Venetian ambassador's comment.[24] There, for the moment, the question of Carlos's future marriage stayed.

There were more urgent matters on Philip's mind for his son was still demanding that he should go to the Low Countries, a prospect which greatly alarmed Philip. He became increasingly critical of his father for delaying his proposed journey there, and wrote angrily of Philip's own seeming unwillingness to leave Spain. According to Brantôme he headed a sheet of paper '*Los grandes viajos del rey don Felipe*' ('The great journeys of King Philip') and below it wrote '*El viaje de Madrid al Pardo, del Pardo al Escorial, del Escorial a Aranjuez*' ('the journey from Madrid to the Pardo, from the Pardo to the Escorial, from the Escorial to Aranjuez', all royal palaces within easy reach of Madrid').[25]

Don Carlos smouldered with irritation. He was impressionistic and unreliable as his father well knew. Inexperienced and naive, it was not outside the realms of possibility that he had been led into even more treacherous currents by making personal contacts with some rebellious Dutch nobles, led by Berghes and Montigny, who had visited Spain on a supposed conciliatory mission in 1565. It was alleged later but without proof that they had promised to assist the prince to go to the Netherlands where they would obey and serve him. It is impossible to know whether there was any truth in such rumours, but that they existed at all must have terrified the king and have made him even more suspicious of his son.

Yet he was not in a position to disown him. Don Carlos was a member of the council of state and heir to the throne. Philip gave out that it was his intention to visit the Low Countries in person accompanied by his son. This at least would reassure those who were upholding the Spanish cause there; but the Castilian Cortes reacted by stating that if the king went to Flanders, then it would be in the interests of Spain for his heir to remain in Spain. Don Carlos flatly refused this suggestion. 'You must know', he told the delegates, 'that my father plans to go to Flanders and that I have every intention of going there myself. At an earlier Cortes, you had the temerity to pray my father that he should marry me to the princess my aunt. I find it very singular indeed that you should interfere in my marriage which does not concern you. I would not wish that the fancy now comes to you to commit a new rashness in urging my father to leave me in Spain.'[26]

All this in a sense was now play-acting for events in the Low Countries had reached such a climax that there seemed no possibility of pacifying the insurgents, short of a policy of violent repression. The king appointed the duke of Alva to carry out this mission. Don Carlos was furious at the apparent collapse of his plans, threatening at one moment to kill Alva when he came to take his leave. Alva tried to pacify him by reminding him that the life of the heir to the Spanish throne was too precious to be exposed to such danger. Once the Low Countries had been pacified, then surely the prince could accompany his father there. But the prince's response was simply to draw his sword, shouting, 'You shall not go to Flanders, or I will kill you.' Alva seized him roughly by the arm and took the sword away.

News of this incident must have reinforced Philip's growing conviction that his son was unsuitable for any office of responsibility, let alone as his successor. It is easy to sympathize with his predicament. In spite of his later reputation, which owed much to propaganda, more especially to the diatribes of his enemies William the Silent and Antonio Pérez, Philip was no monster, even if the demands of the state made him on occasion countenance acts of calculated deception and even cruelty. Privately he was an affectionate man, as his correspondence with his daughters shows,[27] but he subordinated private affection to his faith and to the state, tending indeed to identify one with the other.

He was coming to the decision that Carlos must not succeed him as king of Spain. As always he moved slowly if deliberately. His decision may have been facilitated by his learning that Carlos like his mad great-grandmother, showed signs of irreligion, and was reluctant to go to confession. 'What', Suárez wrote to the prince, 'will people say when people learn that he [the prince] does not go to Confession and when they discover, what is more, certain things so terrible that the Holy Office [the Inquisition] might feel called to intervene?'[28]

Don Carlos's attitude to his father was becoming pathological. It is not improbable that his reluctance to go to confession was rooted in his realization that he might have to reveal to his confessor his unfilial feelings towards his father. 'There is marvellous indignation and ill-satisfaction between the Catholic king and the prince his son', the French ambassador informed Catherine de Medici on 12 September 1567, 'if the father hates him, the son does no less; from all of which, if God affords no remedy, only great misfortune can come.'[29]

There was no sign that God was likely to afford a remedy, rather the reverse. Don Carlos still put his hopes on the proposed journey to Flanders. Philip still asserted that he was about to embark at Corunna and go by sea; alternatively letters were written to Charles IX seeking his permission for his men and horses to travel overland through French territory. Don Carlos himself sought similar permission for fifty horses to cross French soil.

But the king dallied. It would be unwise, he told the French ambassador Fourquevaulx, to begin such a journey in September in the worsening weather. He informed the papal nuncio that he was simply delaying his journey to the following spring. All this reacted on the unstable mind of the prince badly nor did he seek to hide his bitter disappointment. He spoke of leaving Spain without his father's permission, travelling to Portugal, Italy or even the Low Countries. Fearful of what his father might do, he kept arms by his bedside and in the garde-robe. He would allow none of his gentlemen to sleep in his room and he employed a French engineer, Louis de Foix, to construct a device which enabled him to open and shut his door from his bed. A weight was placed on the top of the door so that it could crush a man to death if he tried to make a forced entry.

Such plans had an obvious element of fantasy, even if his fears did not lack foundation. It was hopeless to suppose that he could leave Spain without assistance in men and money. He tried to arrange a loan of 600,000 ducats from the merchant bankers. He sent letters to various nobles inviting them to accompany him on an important voyage. But he had no real friends. The king hardly needed spies to tell him of his son's hazardous and potentially treasonable plans. The admiral of Castile forwarded a compromising letter from Don Carlos to the king.

Don Carlos's lack of secrecy underlined his mental instability He complained to everybody that his father would not forward his marriage because he hated the thought of his crown passing to the children of a detested son. He reminded the nobles of the oath of loyalty that they had taken to him in the cathedral of Toledo seven years earlier. He promised them recompense for such service as they might give him, but the reversionary interest was of no account in Spain where the king held all the cards in his hand, and the representative of that interest was a sickly, unbalanced youth.

He placed his greatest hopes in his young uncle, Don Juan of Austria, whom he had always admired. As the commander of the fleet his cooperation was essential, for it was Don Carlos's intention to sail from Cartagena for Italy. On the 23 or 24 December 1567 he summoned Don Juan to the palace and requested his help. 'What do you expect from the king,' he asked him bluntly. 'See how he treats his own son. He will always leave you poor. But if you support me I will give you the kingdom of Naples or the duchy of Milan.' Don Juan had treated the young prince kindly but he had no wish to be compromised in the king's eyes by taking part in a hair-brained scheme which would lead to certain ruin. He tried to discourage Carlos, pointing out the difficulties and dangers of the projected journey. He knew how angry Don Carlos could be, so he compromised by asking him to give him twenty-four hours before he replied. Next day he wrote to Don Carlos to tell him that he had been called to the Escorial on duty.

In fact he told the king of his son's schemes. Philip was celebrating the aftermath of the Christmas festival, concerned with winning the papal indulgence, and at first appeared more irritated than surprised by what he had learned. There was, however, worse news to come. Don Carlos had made his Christmas confession to a monk at the monastery of San Jeronimo at Madrid, telling the monk that he had murder and hatred in his heart. The monk refused to give him absolution. The prince responded by saying that if he were not absolved he could surely be given a non-consecrated host, so that to the people he might appear to take communion. When the prior of Atocha questioned him further, he at last confessed that it was his own father whom he hated. The news reached the king.

Philip could hardly avoid taking the action which must have been gradually taking shape in his mind for many years. He prolonged his own retreat at the Escorial. He sought the prayers of the principal convents of Madrid. He consulted doctors and the council of state. Only one reply has survived, that of the lawyer Navarro Martin Dazpilacueta. He recalled the case of Louis XI of France who as dauphin had rebelled against his father Charles VII, and he stressed that Spain would be placed in the greatest danger if Don Carlos fled abroad. The rebels in the Low Countries might make him a figurehead, and the cause of religion would be itself imperilled.

The die was cast. When Don Carlos learned that Philip had returned from the Escorial to Madrid, he was uneasy, wondering how much he had heard. He was told that the king was indeed very dissatisfied with his conduct, though when father and son actually came face to face a few days later each of them dissembled. Don Carlos had a further interview with his uncle Don Juan of which two different accounts survive. According to one account Don Carlos reiterated his decision to embark at midnight at Cartagena, asking for Don Juan's help. Once again Don Juan prevaricated. According to the other account Don Carlos asked his uncle what had taken place at the Escorial and when his answers were evasive seized his sword. When Don Juan went to the door, he found it bolted, and had to shout to the prince's attendants to open it.

It was at 11.00 p.m. on the night of 18 January 1568 after Don Carlos had retired to bed that Philip, attended by some of his gentlemen, the duke of Feria, prior Don Antonio de Toledo, Luis de Quijada and Ruy Gomez, prince of Eboli, who had been the governor of the prince's household, entered the prince's apartment, with two aides carrying hammers and nails. The duke of Feria headed the procession, carrying a lantern; the king wore armour under his robe.

In spite of Don Carlos's precautions they opened his door without difficulty, for the machinery had been put out of order, and took hold of the prince's arms. He called 'Who is it?' 'The council of state' was the response. As he saw his father, he cried 'Does your Majesty wish to kill me?' The king, self-controlled as ever, promised that he would meet with no harm. 'What I wish is only for your good.' The aides nailed up the windows; the arms, even the fire-drop, were taken away as were all the prince's papers. Don Carlos dropped on his knees before his father. 'Your Majesty – kill me and do not arrest me – for this will be a great scandal for your kingdom. If your Majesty does not kill me, I will kill myself.' He moved towards the fireplace as if to throw himself into the burning logs. Don Antonio grappled with him while the king said coldly, 'If you kill yourself, that will be the act of a madman.' 'I am not mad,' the prince murmured, 'I am in despair at the bad treatment your Majesty has shewn towards me.' Sobbing desperately he continued to reproach his father for his harshness. 'I shall not treat you as a father henceforth' was Philip's only comment. He ordered those who had accompanied him never to leave the prince unattended by night or day. 'I count on the fidelity and loyalty that you have shown to me.' He was confined in the tower of Arévalo Castle where his grandmother, Juana's own mad grandmother, Isabella of Portugal, had spent her declining years, and he had as his keeper the son of his grandmother's brutal jailer.

The news of Philip's action resounded through the courts of Europe, causing consternation to his friends and joy to his enemies. Don Carlos's step-mother and his aunt Juana appear to have interceded on his behalf. The French ambassador reported that Elisabeth had wept for two days and could not speak of what had happened without pain and would have counted it no less unfortunate had Carlos been her real son. But in talking to the ambassador she implicitly admitted his disability when she said, 'God has willed his nature to be made public.'

Secretive as ever, Philip remained silent and implacable. 'The king', Don Juan de Zuñiga, the Spanish ambassador in Rome, wrote, 'did not give any special reason to his Holiness for his action, but I do not think that was anything more than what we all know of the prince's action.' Later, in May, Philip gave as full an explanation to the pope for what he had done as he was ever to give. It was not, he told Pope Pius V,

the passion or the fault of the prince, nor any intention on my part to chastise or correct him, for if this had been my motive I would have taken other measures, without going to this extreme. . . . But since, for my sins, it has been God's will that the prince should have such great and numerous defects, partly mental, partly due to his physical condition, utterly lacking as he is in the qualifications necessary for ruling, I saw the grave risks that would arise were he to be given the succession and the obvious danger that would accrue; and therefore, after long and careful consideration, and having tried every alternative in vain, it was clear that there was little or no prospect of his condition improving in time to prevent the evils which could reasonably be foreseen. In short my decision was necessary.[30]

To all intents and purposes Don Carlos was dead. 'They speak of the prince as if he were dead,' commented a foreign ambassador. 'The prince of Spain', said the Florentine envoy, 'is so forgotten that he appears truly never to have been in the world.' Philip placed all his hopes in the pregnancy of his wife Elisabeth, for the birth of a son would enable him to proceed with disinheriting Don Carlos. The king's lawyers found a convenient precedent: Prince Charles of Viana had been disinherited by his father Juan II of Aragon in 1461. The king told his wife to cease to weep. The grandees were ordered to refrain from talking about Don Carlos or even from mentioning him in their prayers 'because the poor young man is becoming more deranged every day'. 'He was', the French ambassador commented, 'rapidly passing into oblivion, and is spoken of scarcely more often than if he had never been born.'

But Don Carlos was still alive, sometimes lucid, sometimes deranged. He was kept in close confinement, not allowed to leave his room or to show himself at any window. The only light came from a window high in the wall and even the fireplace was covered by a grill to prevent his trying to throw himself into the fire. At first he was not allowed to hear Mass, but later a window with a wooden trellis was made which enabled him to follow the service.

Although there were times when he hoped that he might be restored to favour, he became utterly depressed and contemplated suicide. Having heard that a diamond introduced into the stomach was poisonous, he tried to swallow a ring. He went on hunger strike and had to be fed forcibly. 'When he is really hungry,' Philip commented, 'he will eat.' At Easter he made his confession to the king's own confessor Fra Diego de Chaves, in the hope that he might be pardoned. It was rumoured that he was quieter, less furious than he had once been. Philip wrote to his sister Maria so that she could pass on the information to the emperor:

Your highnesses know that there are moments when the spirit is saner than in others, and that the imperfections of his character must be envisaged in a different manner to what concerns government and public actions than the personal acts of private life . . . for it can very well be that one is perfectly capable of the second and entirely incapable of the first. Your highnesses must understand that the prince's fault lies not in a particular act but in defect of understanding which, for my sins, God has permitted in my son.'[31]

There was no glimmer of light at the end of the tunnel. The accounts of his death vary but it is said that tossing in the heat of the Madrid summer, he lay naked on his bed, on which he ordered ice brought from the Sierras to be laid. He then consumed paté made from four partridges which he washed down with large quantities of iced water. Physically weak, he became ill with fever and at dawn on 24 July 1568 he died. It was said that he was perfectly lucid at the end and made his peace with his Maker, but a similar report had been made at his grandmother's death.

Few can have mourned the death of so unquiet a spirit. 'His removal to heaven', the duke of Alva's agent reported, 'was a great boon to all of Christendom because certainly had he lived he would have destroyed Christendom. His mental state and his habits were entirely disordered. He is very well up there; all of us who knew him thank God for his death.' Philip decreed that there should be general mourning for nine days and of the court for a year. Don Carlos's step-mother, Elisabeth of Valois, seemed to grieve even more than Philip. 'I assure you I feel the misfortune no less than if he were my own son.' Her health was soon to deteriorate and she died on 3 October 1568, not yet twenty-three, giving birth to a girl who died shortly afterwards. For the remainder of his long life, except on state occasions, Philip would always wear black. But the Spanish Empire still lacked an heir until in the fulness of time he married the princess Anne to whom his son had so nearly been affianced.

Naturally tongues began to wag, more espcially among Philip's many enemies. 'The prince of Spayne dyed, not without great suspytion,' the English envoy Dr Man told Cecil.[32] In his *Apology*, dated 1581, the Dutch leader, William the Silent, declared that Don Carlos was a victim of his father's hatred and of the Spanish Inquisition: 'The father unnaturally murdering his own child and heir, to the end that by that means, the Pope might have a gap, to give a dispensation, for so execrable an incest', a reference to Philip's later marriage to Anne, his own niece.[33] Philip's former secretary, Antonio Pérez, who sought refuge in France in 1593, alleged that for four months poison had been intermingled with the prince's food.

The longer the lapse of time, the more rumours mushroomed. Don Carlos was suffocated by a pillow said one; he was executed, wrote the French historian, Mathieu, writing in the reign of Henry IV, by four slaves; he drank poisoned broth was de Thou's comment. In his *Memoirs* the duc de Saint-Simon, the French gossip writer, noted that he had been told by the diplomat Louville that the Spanish king, Philip V, had ordered Don Carlos's sepulchre in the Escorial to be opened.[34] The head was found separate from the body, lying between the legs, suggesting that he had been executed.

Amidst such a mass of legendary material it is easy to lose one's way. Philip II had added a codicil to his will on 24 August 1587 ordering that his private papers should be burned at his death. It was said that documents relating to the case had been deposited in a green chest in the castle of Simancas where the Spanish archives were housed, but that when during the Peninsular War Napoleon's general, Kellerman, ordered the chest to be opened it was discovered that the supposed papers related to the reign of Philip V, not Philip II. Tragic as was the life and death of Don Carlos, his father may well have been right in supposing that had he lived it would have been even more tragic for Spain.

VII

Great Harry

Henry VIII overshadowed sixteenth-century England like a Colossus. If he sent spasms of fear into the hearts of many of his subjects, he also earned their respect and, curious as it may seem, at least at first, their love. In the ostentatious pageantry of his life, in the colourful splendour of his court, in his grave learning which enabled him to write discerningly on theological matters, in his love of music which he both played and composed, in the grandeur of his buildings, at Whitehall, Hampton Court and Nonsuch, in his skill as a dancer, jouster and hunter he seemed to be the Renaissance prince *par excellence*. His positive achievements were such that few English kings have made a greater mark on their country. He played a prominent, if not always a successful, part in European politics, astutely treading a careful path between the conflicting rivalries of Habsburg and Valois. From being *Defensor Fidei*, he became Supreme Head of the English church, breaking with the pope and creating a national church completely under his control, in so doing paving the way for a vernacular scripture and the protestantization of the liturgy and the dissolution of the monastic houses. The administrative machinery of government became more effective as a result of the efforts of Thomas Cromwell; and parliament emerged as the vehicle for an immense quantity of legislation which was to bring the reformed Church of England into existence. In some sense he was a founder of English naval power, the very names of his ships *Great Harry* and *Harry Imperial*, conveying the pretensions of their imperious master. Even if Harry relied for the details of his policy and government on the initiative and advice of superlatively able counsellors, Thomas Wolsey and Thomas Cromwell, he remains a great king or at least left the impression of being a great king. 'He ruled', as Elton said, 'as well as reigned', and always retained the last word. Through the medium of art and ceremonial, he orchestrated a theory of kingship.

But if Henry was built on a scale larger than life, that building was flawed, streaked by an all-absorbing and abounding egocentricity, by impulsiveness and suspicion, permeating every aspect of his private life and running through his court like an electric current, ultimately affecting the governance of his country. Great king that he was, he had the ingredients of a tyrant, with features in his character which verge on the abnormal. The eyes which stare at us from his portraits are cold, cunning and callous. In one of his last portraits by Cornelis Matsys, he looks very much the monster that he had become.

Henry was the great-great-grandson of the schizophrenic Charles VI of France. His great-grandmother, Catherine of Valois, wife of Henry V, had married as her second husband, Owain ap Tudor, and was the grandmother of Henry VII. While it would be obviously absurd to claim that in Henry VIII's personality there lurked the disturbed genes of France's mad king, Henry's personality showed signs of mental and emotional disturbance. Henry's mother, Elizabeth of York, had died in childbirth when he was twelve years old. His relations with his father, Henry VII, were distant, for he was Henry's second son, intended, so gossip said later without secure foundation, for a career in the church. The figure of his elder brother, Arthur, Henry's heir, cast a long shadow over his life. In a speculative essay an American psychologist sought to explain Henry's marital troubles in terms of an Oedipus complex.[1] His argument, though by no means void of interest, is naturally incapable of proof, but the figures of his father and elder brother were certainly in the background of the youthful Henry's mind.

His father provided a pattern of monarchy which he had to emulate and surpass; he succeeded his brother not simply as heir to the throne but as the husband of his brother's wife. The fifteen-year-old prince of Wales, Arthur, had died of tuberculosis in April 1502. Immediately, Henry was betrothed to his brother's widow, Catherine of Aragon. Seven years later, shortly after his father's death, on 11 June 1509, Henry was married to Catherine. Catherine was the daughter of the Spanish sovereigns, Ferdinand and Isabella, and the sister of the 'mad' queen Juana, with both of whom Henry's own father had at one time contemplated marriage. Although the marriage was delayed until 1509 and at one stage seemed likely to be put off altogether as a result of Henry VII's disillusion with the foreign policy of the Spanish sovereigns, Prince Henry, writing in April 1506, described Catherine as 'my most dear and well-beloved consort, the princess my wife'. Because Catherine had been married to his brother, a papal dispensation had to be sought from an impediment of affinity in the first degree collateral (even though Arthur had boasted lewdly that he had been 'in the midst of Spain all night' Catherine always insisted strongly that her first marriage had never been consummated) which was granted in 1505.

In his early years as king Henry was a charismatic figure, strikingly handsome, wondrously energetic, acclaimed as a great hope of the humanists, a brilliant games player and a gifted musician, content by and large to leave the conduct of public policy to his able and devoted servant, Cardinal Wolsey;[2] though even as early as 1513 More suspected elements of tyranny in his rule. By his side, Catherine, five years older than her husband, appeared a dowdy, dull woman, devout and humane but increasingly not a fitting helpmate, more especially as the tally of her miscarriages mounted. Henry, prince of Wales, born in 1511, lived seven weeks. Only a daughter, Mary, born in 1516, survived. Four other children were apparently stillborn. One such premature birth was attributed by Peter Martyr to the shock and apprehension caused to her by the deteriorating relations between Henry and her father, Ferdinand of Aragon. Her husband was upbraiding the innocent queen with her father's desertion, 'and spat out his complaints against her' (*'et conquestus suos in eam expectorabat'*).[3]

By 1524 Henry had ceased to sleep regularly with his wife, though they were for long to maintain a charade of living together. Amorous by nature, he had within five or six years of his marriage become involved with one of his wife's ladies-in-waiting, Elizabeth Blount, by whom in 1518 he had a son, later the duke of Richmond. She was followed by Mary Boleyn, and then by her sister Anne, a sophisticated and well-read young lady, 'radiating sex'.[4] He wanted her to become his mistress, but she resisted, more surely from calculated ambition than moral principle for she was desirous of replacing Catherine who was now beyond child-bearing as his wife. 'I am resolved', she was once reported as saying 'to have him whatsoever might become of his wife.'

To understand the situation Henry's own complex character has to be taken into consideration. Belief in the sacral character of kingship as an expression of divine authority and concurrently the obligation of unconditional obedience to the monarch, however excessive or tendentious his demands, was a widespread feature of the Tudor age. In Henry it became an obsession, Byzantine in quality, perhaps a necessary response to his underlying feeling of personal inadequacy. It was a belief in which he had been indoctrinated from an early age and which he soaked up; it was buttressed by a growing pamphlet literature. With a sublime capacity for self-deception he never questioned the rightness of his actions or his objectives, irrespective of their outcome. What he wanted he would seek to procure because it was his royal will to do so. The pope's unwillingness to annul his marriage to Catherine was itself a challenge to Henry's sovereignty. He had to marry Anne Boleyn, not merely because he thought he loved her, but because it became increasingly necessary to his self-esteem as an assertion and authentication of his divinely given monarchical power. 'The drive to marry Anne', so Eric Ives comments, 'was thus not only an attempt to satisfy his emotions and desires; it was a way to vindicate his kingship.' He wished to rid himself of Catherine, even at the cost of bastardizing his daughter Mary, and to marry Anne, and to bring this about everything had to be swept aside to ensure that his will should ultimately prevail.

There was, however, another aspect of what came to be called the king's 'Great Matter'. He was seriously and sincerely worried by the sterility of his marriage, concluding that it must have been a breach of divine law, contravening, as the much-quoted texts from Leviticus demonstrated, the teaching of scripture, a law from which even the pope had no power to dispense him. Once more the figure of his elder brother, Arthur, overshadowed him; and the sin of incest raised a sinister spectre. For an amateur Henry had a remarkable knowledge of theology which he had shown already in his tract in refutation of Lutheranism which had led the pope to bestow upon him the title of Defender of the Faith. In such circumstances the course seemed to Henry plain enough. The pope should release him from his irregular union to Catherine, so enabling him to marry Anne, and allow him to have by her a legitimate heir to the English throne.

Anne became virtually betrothed to Henry, for they both expected that the pope would agree to an annulment of his marriage to Catherine. Yet five or six years were to pass before the hoped-for denouement occurred. In the process Anne stiffened the king's will when he showed signs of nervousness, and after Wolsey failed to deliver the goods worked for his disgrace.

What followed provides an excellent illustration of the thesis that public policy may often be an externalization of personal traumas, for in the ensuing decade to seek the fulfilment of his personal and private desires, frustrated as they were to be by the intricacies of papal and imperial policy, Henry readily humiliated his wife, destroyed a faithful minister, trampled upon the liberties of the church and repudiated the authority of the pope and the Church of Rome. While it would be absurdly simplistic to argue that the English Reformation was a bastard child of Henry's desires, yet without his personal appetites, it would surely have taken a different path. Henry may have justified to himself the course which he was taking as being in some way for the ultimate good of his kingdom, even of his own soul, but what he did was an expression of an exceptionally self-centred will.

Henry's life appears indeed as a manifestation of ruthless egocentricity wrapped up in a strong conviction that he possessed God-given powers. The ending of his marriage to Catherine of Aragon and the break with Rome were to open new vistas into some of the more malign tendencies in Henry's personality, which became the more pronounced as he grew older. On these too his marriage to Anne Boleyn casts a sombre light.

For many years Anne resisted his more intimate embraces and did not sleep with him until she was convinced in her own mind that the divorce from Catherine would go through. Archbishop Warham of Canterbury died in August 1532. In October Anne, recently ennobled as marchioness of Pembroke, accompanied Henry to France. By the end of the year she was pregnant. The king, made aware of the agreeable prospect of a child, with the rising stars of Thomas Cranmer and Thomas Cromwell as his willing accomplices, hastened on the procedure for divorce, with or without papal approval. On 25 January 1533, Anne was married secretly to the king and Cranmer, raised to the see of Canterbury partly at the behest of the Boleyns, gave judgement on 23 May 1533 that Henry's marriage to Catherine was null and void.

The break with Rome, managed largely by Thomas Cromwell, based on the supposition that the pope's claims were themselves unscriptural, had radical implications for England and the English church which Anne herself was to promote, influencing appointments to bishoprics and in other ways forwarding reformed ideas. But Henry's overriding concerns remained predominantly personal. A daughter Elizabeth, was born on 7 September 1533.

There was a further ingredient in the situation that again throws light on Henry's nature. Once Anne had become wife and mother, she had, as it were, lost status, for while before marriage Henry had been a suppliant for her favours, after marriage as a wife she became, according to contemporary ideas, simply his obedient and subservient subject. Henry obviously saw nothing out of the way in indulging, as he had done with Catherine, in passing dalliances with the ladies of his court. He soon became unfaithful to Anne.[5] That Anne, independent and self-willed, resented her husband's behaviour cannot be doubted, if only because it made her apprehensive of her position as wife and queen. She could not take kindly to the king's infidelities which he himself may have regarded as part of his prerogative. For Henry, as his future marriages showed, marriage implied subordination to the royal will. What seemed to challenge the king he would not tolerate. Yet the possibility of the birth of an heir to the throne momentarily papered over the cracks in their deteriorating relationship as Henry's ardour cooled.

At the end of 1535 Anne was pregnant once more. If she bore Henry a son, it was possible that his new infatuation, for Jane Seymour, might well recede, even if for Henry the chase seemed more important than its sequel. It was this which gratified his self-esteem. By the latter months of 1535 Anne's fate was in the balance.

At this juncture he suffered a serious accident. On 17 January 1536 when 'the King being mounted on a great horse to run at the lists [at Greenwich], both fell so heavily', so the imperial envoy Chapuys told Granville on 29 January, 'that everyone thought it a miracle he was not killed, but he sustained no injury.'[6] Dr Ortiz, writing to the empress from Rome on 6 March, added more cautiously, 'The French king said that the king of England had fallen from his horse, and been for two hours without speaking. 'La Ana' was so upset that she miscarried of a son . . . although the king has not improved in consequence of his fall, it is a great mercy that his paramour miscarried of a son.'[7]

This was the second accident that Henry had experienced at the jousts, for on 10 March 1524 he had charged his opponent, the duke of Suffolk with his visor still open.[8] Although the king came within an ace of being killed, he seemed not seriously shaken by what had happened and continued with the tournament. It is fair, however, to recall that in the late 1520s Henry was a victim of persistent headaches. Heneage told Wolsey on 21 July 1528 that the king 'complains of his head';[9] 'The king cannot write because of his head. As the plague is at Grafton the king will not go there.' 'His head is not the best,' he added next day. In August Henry himself explained the shortness of his love letter to Anne 'by cause of some pain in my head. Wishing myself specially an evening in my sweetheart's arms, whose pretty dubbys, I trust shortly to cusse.'[10]

In general Henry's health appeared to be singularly robust. He had escaped the tuberculosis which had killed his father and his brother, and which was to find further victims in his sons, the duke of Richmond and Edward VI. He was, however, from time to time laid low by various illnesses, an attack of smallpox or measles in the early spring of 1514, and of malaria and fever in 1521 and subsequent years. He was much in dread of the serious attack of the sweating sickness in 1528 but escaped its onslaught.[11] In 1528 there appears the first reference to trouble with his legs, for Thomas Vicary, who became in 1530 serjeant surgeon, was called in 'to cure the king of a sorre legge'.[12]

The fall which Henry suffered in the joust in 1536 may have been a crucial event in his life. By the standards of his day he was already a middle-aged man at forty-four and very overweight. He was heavily built and a prodigious eater, six feet in height with a massive frame. In 1514 at the age of twenty-three his waist measured 35 in and his chest 42 in. By 1536 his waist was probably 37 in and his chest 45 in. By 1541 his waist measurement had gone up to 54 in and his chest to 57 in. In January 1536 he had lain in his heavy armour on the ground, the mailed horse on top of him, and apparently remained unconscious for two hours, so foreign envoys contended. Although he was never again to be an active protagonist in a tournament, he recovered, so that by 4 February 1536 Cromwell informed Gardiner that the king was merry and in good health. It is, however, difficult not to believe that this accident, apart from concussion and bruising, may have had long-term deleterious effects on his general health and behaviour. The likelihood that, apart from its possible effect on the trouble with his legs, Henry had sustained cerebral damage cannot be lightly dismissed, and may be supported by his subsequent actions, more especially the ruthless and rapid arrest and execution of Anne Boleyn who was dead by 19 May 1536.

On 29 January 1536, twelve days after the king's fall, Anne miscarried a male child. It has been suggested that the foetus was probably deformed and that this convinced Henry that he had been seduced into marrying Anne by witchcraft,[13] but Anne herself explicitly attributed her miscarriage to the shock she had experienced on learning from the duke of Norfolk of Henry's fall at the tournament. Chapuys claimed that others put down her miscarriage to her defective constitution and her 'utter inability to bear male children', or to her fear that Jane Seymour was replacing her in the king's affection.[14] It is not unreasonable to assume that the news of the king's fall may well have contributed to the miscarriage, for if the fall put the king's life in danger, then Anne herself, surrounded by enemies, would also be in danger. Her miscarriage was to have even more disturbing effects.

'I see', the king commented, 'that God will never give me male children', and within months a plan had been drawn up, in which Cromwell's hand can be seen, which was to bring about her doom and destruction. It had taken six years to bring Anne to the king's bed. She had been his wife for three years. It took only four months to destroy her. She was accused of adultery with several men, some of loose reputation, among them her own brother, Lord Rochford, so renewing in the king's mind the theme of incest. Dr Ortiz informed the empress on 23 May 1536 'that in order to have a son who might be attributed to the king, she committed adultery with a singer who taught her to play on instruments'.[15] Passionate as Anne was by nature it seems unlikely that she had been guilty of much more than minor indiscretions. She and those who were executed with her were probably the victims of a deliberate set-up. If the design was Cromwell's, the will was Henry's.

Although characteristically Henry indulged in crocodile tears, he showed himself hard and heartless, marrying Jane Seymour within days of Anne's death. Yet could his response have been affected by brain damage which he had sustained at the January tournament? There is obviously no real answer to the question, but circumstantially there are surprising features in Henry's attitude. He had once loved Anne, but that love was turning to hate. He wished to replace her by Jane Seymour, pushed forward by the predatory Seymour family, but Jane was pliable and subservient where Anne had been ambitious and self-assertive. Henry commented that he came to heaven from hell when he married Jane. But does this satisfactorily explain the king's ruthless determination, his readiness to indulge in a judicial farce which in a close examination of the evidence would itself have shown to be ill-founded? With a total lack of compassion, he had sacrificed the woman he had once loved and men who had served him faithfully to his own inordinate egocentricity. Yet his attitude seemed senseless as well as cruel. At one and the same time he had virtually bastardized his two heirs, the princesses Mary and Elizabeth, without any guarantee that Jane Seymour would have a son.

If he believed the charges against Anne it was because he wanted to believe them. It is not easy to follow his mental process. Rumour even asserted that Anne had been involved in poisoning Catherine, whose death at Kimbolton Castle from cancer on 7 January 1536 had led the king to indulge in a characteristic and unfeeling act of celebration; dressed in yellow silk he danced the night away on hearing of her death. Ironically as the day of her burial at the abbey of Peterborough had coincided with Anne's miscarriage, it was almost as if Henry had lost two wives on the same day. 'When', Chapuys reported on 19 May 1536, 'the Duke of Richmond went to say good night to his father, and ask his blessing after the English custom, the king began to weep, saying that he and his sister, meaning the Princess (Mary) were greatly bound to God for having escaped the hands of that accursed whore, who had determined to poison them.'[16] He complained bitterly that he was the victim of witchcraft, and that the 'witch' Anne had had unslaked sexual capacity. He may even have convinced himself that Anne was a witch. He showed a morbid, nauseating interest in the details of his wife's execution, even arranging for a special executioner to be brought over from Calais to carry it out. 'The king', Chapuys told Granville on 19 May, 1536, the day of Anne's execution, 'believed that more than an hundred had criminal relations with Anne Boleyn. The new bishops . . . persuaded her that according to the said sect . . . it was lawful to seek aid elsewhere, even from her own relations, when her husband was incapable of satisfying her'.[17]

Chapuys's comments point by innuendo to an important aspect of Henry's life which is all-important for a consideration of his personality. It seems that in spite of six wives and at least two mistresses sex may have been a sphere in which Henry underachieved. In his own day and later he had something of the reputation of a Don Juan. The duke of Norfolk averred that he 'was continually inclined to be amorous'. 'Our sovereign lord', Counsell, a porter at Syon, told John Hale, the vicar of Isleworth, 'had a short (stock) of maidens at one of his chambers at Farnham while he was with the old lord of Winchester'.[18]

There are, however, hints that Henry was better in the prologue than in the act. His potency may have been impaired, as Anne's brother, Lord Rochford, seemed to be suggesting at the trial when he was reported as saying that 'le Roy nestoit habile en cas de soy copular avec femme, et quil navoit ne vertue ne puissance.'[19] 'According to the account of him by the concubine [Anne Boleyn],' Chapuys reported on 18 May 1536, 'he had neither vigour nor competence.'[20] When, in April 1533, Chapuys expressed doubt as to whether replacing Catherine by a new wife would result in children, Henry responded excitedly, 'Am I not a man like other men? Am I not? Am I not?' adding 'I need not give proofs of the contrary, or let you into my secrets.'[21]

Jane Seymour at least fulfilled his expectations by giving birth to a son, the future Edward VI, but she died of puerperal fever twelve days later. It is impossible to say what would have happened to Jane had she lived, given the king's impulsive and changeable nature. Chapuys even cast some doubt on Jane's virtue. 'I leave you to judge', he wrote to Antoine Perronet on 18 May, the day before Anne's execution, of the future queen, 'whether, being English and long having frequented the Court, "*si elle ne tiendroit pas a conscience de navoir pourveu et prevenu de savoir que c'est de faire nopces*" ' ('if she would not in fact supply and have knowledge of what marriage means'). 'When', he added, 'he had a mind to divorce her he will find enough witnesses.'[22]

He slept with his fourth wife, Anne of Cleves whom he had married in January 1539 but because of her physical unattractiveness, so Henry alleged, he lacked 'the will and power to consummate the marriage'. He thought, so his doctor, Dr Chambers,

Henry VIII in later life, from an engraving by Cornelius Matsys (photograph: Bibliothèque Nationale, Paris)

argued, that he was 'able to do the act with other but not with her'. Boastingly he told his other physician Dr Butts that he still had wet dreams (*'duas pollutiones nocturnas in somno'*). It is surprising that he should have found it necessary to insist still upon his ability. Anne was divorced on 10 July 1540.[23]

Did he try to do the act with the young Catherine Howard whom he wed on 28 July 1540?[24] He certainly seems to have hoped that she would bear him a child. Although she was proclaimed queen of England, she was never crowned. In April 1541 the French ambassador reported that Catherine was 'thought to be with child, which would be very great joy to this king, who, it seems, believes it and intends, if it be found true, to have her crowned at Whitsuntide'.[25] One of the charges which was to be brought against her was that the 'physicians say she cannot bear children'.[26]

The marriage with Catherine proved to be an unmitigated disaster. Flighty and silly, a pliable instrument in the hands of the Howard family, Catherine had had affairs before the king married her. Her lover Henry Madox was charged that he had 'commonly used to feel the secret and other parts of the Queen's body'. Francis Dereham, so Catherine herself confessed, had laid 'upon my bed with his doublet and hose and after within the bed and finally he lay with me naked, and used me in such sort as man doth his wife many and sundry times'. They had 'kissed after a wonderful manner and hang by their bellies as they were two sparrows'. 'Yours', a surviving letter of Catherine to Dereham ends, 'as long as life endures.' But life was not long to endure. With astonishing indiscretion, after her marriage to the king she had taken another lover, Thomas Culpeper who 'intended and meant to do ill with the queen and that in likewise the queen so minded to do with him'.

When Henry was informed by Archbishop Cranmer of his wife's infidelity, for though the whole court knew what was happening only Cranmer would tell him, he refused at first to believe it until the evidence, so much more convincing than in the case of Anne Boleyn, showed that it was likely to be true. Convinced of Catherine's betrayal, he was dreadfully shocked, hardly surprisingly for Catherine's affair showed that whatever Henry had been like ten years earlier, he had by now lost his virility and was a grey and festering man, no longer physically attractive and emotionally labile. Catherine's repulsion is at least fully understandable. But to the king it was an act of treachery, judicially designated treason, a blow at his self-esteem, a dagger plunged into the most sensitive part of Henry's anatomy. Marillac told Francis I on 7 December 1541:

The king has changed his love for the queen into hatred, and taken such grief at being deceived that of late it was thought he had gone mad, for he called for a sword to slay her he had loved. Sitting in Council he suddenly called for horses without saying where he would go. Sometimes he said irrelevantly ['*hors de propose*'] that that wicked woman had never such delight in her continency as she should have torture in her death. And finally he took to tears regretting his ill-luck in meeting such ill-conditioned wives and blaming the Council for this last mischief.[27]

Catherine was beheaded on 13 February 1542.

Marillac reported to his master, Francis I, on 3 March 1541, 'he said he had an unhappy people to govern whom he would shortly make so poor that they would not have the power to oppose him.'[28] 'He seems very old and grey', he added, 'since the *malheur* of this last queen, and will not hear of taking another, although he is ordinarily in company of ladies, and his ministers beg and urge him to marry again.'[29] Eight months later Chapuys confirmed that the king was 'still sad and disinclined to feasting and ladies'.[30]

But he appeared to recover his spirits and on 12 July 1543 he made his last marital experiment by marrying the twice-widowed Catherine Parr. She had married her first husband, Sir Edward Burgh, grandson of the second Lord Burgh who had gone mad, when she was only sixteen or seventeen. Left a widow she then became the third wife of John Neville, Lord Latimer, some twenty years older than his wife. He had been partly compromised by involvement in the rebellious Pilgrimage of Grace, but managed to wriggle out of any complicity. Neither this nor his wife's convinced Protestantism deterred Henry from making overtures shortly after Latimer's death in March 1543. Apparently no better-looking than Anne of Cleves, she was a good-natured woman and proved to be an affectionate and caring wife, nursing Henry in his illness and kindly disposed towards his children. She obviously had a penchant for ailing and ageing husbands but may have thought that she had found compensation by marrying shortly after Henry's death her fourth husband, the raffish Thomas Seymour, Lord Seymour of Sudeley, Edward VI's uncle. Death, however, seemed to linger in the wings of Catherine's domestic life; she herself died in 1548 of puerperal fever, after having given birth to a daughter, Margaret, which at least saved her from witnessing the execution of her husband for treason on 20 March 1549.

Although Catherine Parr was capable of bearing a child, there seems no evidence that Henry attempted to give her one. The evidence may indeed by circumstantial and speculative but there are reasons for questioning Henry's sexual prowess, for suggesting that he was sexually inadequate, and that some of the brutal and cruel things that he did were a response to a subconscious realization that he was unable to fulfil as effectively as he wished the function of lover and husband, and as king to provide heirs to the throne.

Less circumstantial, much more positive, is the evidence of the king's declining health after 1536 which made a significant impact on the king's character. Within less than a year after his jousting accident he was suffering from problems caused by the progressive ulceration of his leg. 'I dreamed that the king was dead', Henry Pole, Lord Montague, said at his trial on 24 March 1537, 'but he will die suddenly, his leg will kill him.' A month later, on 30 April 1537, Husee told his master, Lord Lisle, that the 'King goeth seldom abroad, by reason his leg is something sore.'[31] On 12 June Henry himself told Norfolk that he was unable to travel to York ('which you must keep to yourself') because a 'humour has fallen into our legs, and our physicians advise us not to go far in the heat of the year'.[32] Subsequently both his legs became infected, causing a serious crisis in May 1538 when Castillon reported to Montmorency that 'the king has had stopped one of the fistulas of his legs, and for ten or twelve days the humours which had no outlet were like to have stifled him, so that he was sometime without speaking, black in the face, and in great danger.'[33]

If the trouble was sporadic, it would not go away. Lord Montague's brother, Sir Geoffrey Pole, who was likewise condemned to death but actually reprieved, commented in November 1538 that Henry had a 'sore leg that no pore man would be glad of', adding perhaps in a moment of wishful thinking that Henry was not expected to live long.[34] In March 1541 his legs again gave him serious trouble. As Marillac told the French king, the legs, 'formerly opened and kept open to maintain his health, suddenly closed, to his great alarm, for, five or six years ago, in like case, he thought to have died. This time prompt remedy was applied, and he is now well and the fever gone.'[35] 'He is so weak on his legs', the imperial ambassador told the queen of Hungary in May 1544, 'that he can hardly stand.' He has, he told the emperor on 18 May 1544, 'the worst legs in the world, such as those who have seen them are astonished that he does not stay continually in bed and judge that he will not be able to endure the very least exertion without danger of his life.'[36] Latterly he had to be carried upstairs in a specially constructed tram or sedan chair. Mrs Elizabeth Holland 'confessed . . . that the King was much grown of his Body, and that he could not go up and down stairs, and was let up and down by a device'.[37]

Apart from the psychological effects which this painful and persistent complaint had on Henry's mind, the state of Henry's legs constitutes a medical problem. It was once thought that his illness was the result of a syphilitic infection which explained the miscarriages suffered by his wives. Apart from the ulceration of his legs, which could have been a sequel to syphilis, the malformation of his nose, evident in his later portraits, might suggest syphilitic gummata. Yet neither he nor his children showed any real signs of syphilitic infection nor is there any mention in the records, as there would surely have been, of the application of any of the contemporary remedies for syphilis, such as doses of mercury. That Henry was the victim of syphilis seems most improbable.[38]

More recently Henry's health problems have been attributed to his ill-balanced diet which gave rise to scurvy or scorbutic disease.[39] He ate too much meat, often spiced or pickled in the winter months, took too little fruit or fresh vegetables and so suffered from an acute lack of ascorbic acid or Vitamin C. The features of his ill-health seem to fit well with the characteristic symptoms of a severe attack of scurvy or scorbutic disease: ulceration of the foot and leg with consequent fungoid growths, pain and sores, bad breath, fatigue, difficulty in walking, shortness of breath, oedematous swellings, a reddish complexion, irritability and depression. Yet Henry can surely have only been one among his contemporaries who suffered from similar dietary deficiencies. While the suggestion is an interesting one, like other theories, such as that which maintained that Henry suffered from diffused gout,[40] it remains speculative.

What seems significant is that although there was a reference to a 'sore leg' in 1528, the real trouble followed closely upon his serious accident on the jousting field in 1536. It appears most likely that this helped to give rise to a varicose ulcer, causing, if not adequately treated, thrombosis of the leg and a chronic ulcer on the thigh. Alternatively he might have been afflicted by osteomyelitis, a chronic septic infection of the thigh bone to which the accident he experienced in 1536 could have contributed.

After 1536 physical pain and discomfort could have caused enhanced irritability, impulsive judgement and consequently an apparent deterioration of character. Henry's authoritative biographer, Professor Scarisbrick, has, however, found no great difference in Henry before and after 1536. 'Henry', he wrote, 'was not notably more cruel afterwards than he had been before, nor more aggressive or appetitive.' Elton agrees in part with this verdict, but adds that 'unquestionably, his physical grossness, suspicious arrogance and political dexterity grew more marked as self-indulgence and the effects of adulation worked on one of the most egotistic temperaments known to history.'[41] Certainly, his earlier history had already underlined both his caprice and hardness of heart, in bringing about the fall of Wolsey whom he had sought to make a tool in his 'Great Matter', in his unfeeling treatment of his first wife and daughter, and in the execution of Sir Thomas More with whom he had been apparently on terms of intimate friendship. Yet after 1536 there appears a heightening of tension at Henry's court while the king himself becomes more suspicious and capricious. He took a macabre pleasure in playing with his victims, as a cat with a mouse, one moment sentencing them to death, the next reprieving them but leaving them uncertain of their fate to the last moment. When, in 1543, it seemed likely that Archbishop Cranmer was about to fall from favour, even when the king decided to save him from disgrace, he kept him deliberately on tenterhooks, leaving him waiting for some time before he was told of his reprieve.[42]

Throughout his reign his inordinate egocentricity predominates, becoming more pronounced, more liable to changes of mood and temper as his physical health deteriorated. It was more than a personal caprice and seemed to represent a basic inadequacy which was expressed in his personal relationships and in his role as king. Constantly he needed to recover his self-esteem both as king and lover. Emotionally the king seemed like a small child, behaving as a spoiled brat, grasping at what he wanted irrespective of the consequences, and when he was frustrated giving way to savage tantrums. 'The king beknaveth him twice a week', so it was said of his treatment of the all-powerful minister Thomas Cromwell, 'and sometimes knocketh him well about the pate, and yet, when he hath been well pummelled about the head, and shaken up, as it were a dog, he will come out into the great chamber shaking of the bush with as merry a countenance as though he might rule all the roost.'[43] 'Everything', so Chapuys said, 'must go as the king wishes it.' 'Such a prince', as Cranmer's secretary Ralph Morice put it, 'as would not be bridled nor be against-said in any of his requests.'[44]

He tolerated no obstruction to his will. 'It is no new thing to see men hanged, quartered or beheaded, for one thing and another', a visitor to London in 1541 commented, 'sometimes for trifling expressions construed as against the king.'[45] 'I do not recall', the French ambassador Marillac wrote of the atmosphere of Henry's court that self-same year, 'having ever seen these people so morose as they are at present, for they do not know whom to trust, and the king himself having offended so many people, mistrusts everyone.' 'I may add,' Marillac told his master, Francis I, on 29 May 1541, 'that yesterday all the heads which were fixed upon [London] bridge were taken down, in order that the people may forget those whose heads kept their memory fresh, if it were not that this will people the place with new . . . for . . . before St John's tide, they reckon to occupy the Tower of the prisoners now there.'[46]

Terror had become an instrument of policy. 'I think,' Castillon told the French king, 'few Lords in this country are safe.' State trials were initiated of which the conclusion was foreknown. The Pole family, who might be thought to bear some claim to the crown, was decimated.[47]

No fewer than fifty-three people were attainted in 1539–40, many of whom were subsequently executed. If the responsibility rested in part with the king's advisers, it was the king himself who willed what happened. Death stalked the land in Henry's shadow. 'In England death has snatched everyone of worth away, or fear has struck them.'[48] The king was, in the German reformer Melanchthon's words, an 'English Nero'.[49] Henry, Castillon commented on 26 January 1538, had become 'the most dangerous and cruel man in the world'.[50] 'He is', he added, 'in a fury and has neither reason nor understanding left.' 'Diseased and frightened, Henry became', one of his recent biographers states, 'the most dangerous kind of tyrant, secretive, neurotic and unpredictable.'[51]

The process was a cumulative one. If the accident which he experienced in 1536 and the subsequent osteomyelitis and ulcerations of his legs were landmarks on the road, bringing into the open streaks of personality which had always been there, his subsequent adventures in matrimony were traumatic in their effects, at least until he married Catherine Parr. Yet if Foxe is to be believed, even Catherine Parr seemed once about to fall in favour.[52] She had apparently disagreed with the king over a theological matter. The king was so affronted by her temerity that, advised by Stephen Gardiner, he had articles drawn up charging her with heresy and approved an order for her arrest. 'A good hearing it is', Henry commented angrily, 'when women become such clerks; and a thing much to my comfort, to come in mine old days to be taught by my wife.' By good fortune Catherine learned what was afoot and told the king that it would be quite wrong of her to express opinions on religious matters which differed from her husband. Henry was mollified. 'And is it even so, sweetheart, and tended your argument to no worse end? Then perfect friends we are now again as ever at any time heretofore.' His egocentricity was such that in a modern historian's view he 'suffered from a disease of the mind, from megalomania brought on by a society that viewed its sovereign as the only possible bulwark against a renewal of civil war, and that was determined to worship both as a paragon of a man and as the symbol of public peace and security.'[53]

Was such megalomania a screen for a deep feeling of personal inadequacy? To assert that Henry suffered from a basic inferiority complex which stretched from his personal to his public life may seem to go against all contemporary judgements and against the verdict of most modern historians. He was regarded by contemporaries as one of the most talented men of his time, and modern historians who may differ about his personal responsibility nonetheless pay tribute to his astute statesmanship. Yet behind the bluff and bluster a small spoiled child peeps out. He was beset continuously by fears and anxieties of plots and conspiracies designed to bring about his overthrow. He was fearful of sickness and death, even compiling himself a compendium of salves and medicines, and was much under the influence of his physicians, especially Dr Chambers and Sir William Butts. He was a hypochondriac who went scurrying for safety at the outbreak of sweating sickness, a comparatively novel and mortal disease, which seemed to find its victims most especially among the well-born. 'The name of the sweat', Gardiner reported, 'is so terrible and fearful to his highness' ears that he dare in no wise approach unto the place where it is noised to have been.'[54] When there was an epidemic of the sweating sickness in 1528,[55] which laid both Anne Boleyn and her brother George low, Henry kept to his own chamber, isolating himself as far as possible from company. The king, the French ambassador commented, was 'the most timid person in such matters you could meet with'.

Henry's father, if unpopular in the closing years of his reign, had been a conscientious and efficient monarch who had balanced the budget and refrained from expensive foreign ventures. Henry, remote from his prematurely aged father, abandoned his father's policies, spending money extravagantly and reviving the traditional enmity with France; he spent wildly on building, dissipating the moneys he had acquired from the dissolution of the monasteries, and initiating the 'Great Debasement' of the English economy. Throughout his reign he had depended on loyal and able ministers who articulated and rationalized the policies which he sought to follow. Henry was extraordinarily vulnerable to psychological attack and in many respects intellectually impressionable, accepting policies drawn up by others which he believed to be his own. Equally he was also capricious, reversing or changing policies which he had once enthusiastically embraced, and destroying those upon whom he had become dependent. Fickle and volatile, he was, Scarisbrick commented, 'consistent only in the fulfilment of his own imperious and impulsive will'. Left to his own resources he blundered, as the years of governance following the fall of Thomas Cromwell showed only too well. While he had, as Eric Ives suggests, 'a terrifying fixity of purpose, which was the fundamental activating quality in the king's character', the purpose could change according to the king's mood. His claim to be a great king seems to be based on a series of historical accidents rather than on a chain of real achievement.

'Great Harry' was very likely a victim of a severe personality disorder to which the circumstances of his life and reign gave full expression. There was an astonishing moral chasm between his professions and his performance. If he did not deceive himself, as he may well have done, believing what he said when the facts showed the contrary, he was the greatest of hypocrites. If was characteristic of Henry that on his death-bed he requested by his will that an altar should be erected by his tomb at Windsor for the 'saying of daily masses while the world shall endure', so endowing thousands of masses for himself, while, by the Chantries Act, he denied them to his subjects. He placed his soul in the hands of 'the holy company of Heaven', recalling his 'own good deeds and charitable works' which he had performed for the 'honour and pleasure of the Lord'. It was a singular commentary on his disturbed personality. His constant violent changes of mood, his overt suspicion, his capricious judgement, were rooted in a massive egocentricity promoted further by bouts of severe ill-health. 'For', as Sir Thomas More observed, 'syth the soule and the body be so knytte and joined together, that they bothe make betweene them one persone, the dystemperance of both twayne.' The many who endured death and imprisonment at Henry's command may surely have been less the victims of any rational policy than of the disordered nuances of the King's personality.

VIII

Swedish Saga

Although the madness of Juana of Castile and of Don Carlos may well have constituted a threat to the stability of the nation, neither of them had possessed direct or effective authority over their peoples. In practice there were only two among the so-called deranged medieval monarchs who actually presided over their governments and made a significant impact on the history of their countries: Charles VI of France and Henry VI of England. Although Charles's attacks of insanity had been, as we have seen, intermittent, they occurred over a long period of years, destabilizing the government and contributing to the unhappy and chaotic state of a nation at war with the English. Henry VI's attacks of madness were comparatively short-lived, but coming as they did at a time of acute political crisis they had been crucial in their adverse effects. So too was to be the madness of the Swedish king, Eric XIV. His reign only lasted eight years and ended with his deposition in 1568, but the effects on the Swedish monarchy and nation of the breakdown in mental health, evidently schizophrenia, which he experienced towards the close of his reign, were disastrous and long-lasting.

The nation of which Eric was to become king in 1560, ancient as was its history, had only been moulded comparatively recently into a modern state. Since the Union of Calmar in 1397, for a century and a half, Sweden had been united with Norway and Denmark in a joint kingdom ruled by the Danish king. Then in 1520 after a massacre of the Swedish leaders at Stockholm – some eighty had been summarily executed on a single day, 8 November 1520 – perpetrated by the pathological Danish monarch Christian II, who was himself a victim of madness,[1] the Swedes had risen against their Danish masters under the lead of the noble Gustav Vasa who had himself lost his immediate relatives in the 'bloodbath'.

Gustav Vasa was to fashion a new Sweden. He promoted its economy, broke the authority of the ancient Roman church and championed a Protestant reformation which was to be very much, as in England, under the control of the crown. He won over the fractious Swedish nobility, in part by browbeating them and in part by bribing them, more especially by granting them property confiscated from the church. He created a strong, effective monarchy, and made Sweden the dominant power in the Baltic.

The first king of this newly independent Sweden was a man of immense ability and shrewdness, but there were some dark patches in his personality, suggesting traits of mental instability. 'A tyrant and a bloodhound', his enemies called him. If roused, his temper could be frightening. When once his daughter Cecilia made him angry, he clutched her hair and tore it out by the roots. A goldsmith who had taken a holiday without leave was so mangled by the king that he died; a terrified secretary who had annoyed him was chased by Gustav, dagger in hand, round and round the castle courtyard. His temper was so violent that in his rages he acted like a madman. One son, duke Magnus of Ostergotland, became insane. Another son, Eric's successor, John III, if better able to control his feelings, was far from well balanced. He kept an iron hammer available which he did not hesitate to use on those who angered him.

No dark shadows seemed at first to hover over his eldest son and successor, Eric XIV. In many respects he seemed a paragon of all the virtues, the exemplar of what a Renaissance prince should be. He was skilled in Latin, knowledgeable in French, Spanish, German, Italian and Finnish; he had books in Greek and Hebrew on his shelves. He read deeply, in geography, in history and in political thought, including the works of Machiavelli whom he took as his mentor in politics and war. He showed an interest in contemporary technology, in architecture, for he could draw and etch, and in the military arts in which he was an important innovator, though better as a theorist than as a practitioner. He played the lute, was an apiarist and was passionately interested in astrology, allowing himself on occasions, with fatal results, to be guided by the stars. He had all the makings of a great prince, and was esteemed a fit suitor for Elizabeth of England.

All the makings? Eric seemed more adept at abstract thought than at practical politics. Aware that the Vasas were of no more illustrious ancestry than other Swedish nobles, he developed a grandiose conception of his position as a king. That he should have called himself Eric XIV – Eric XIII had died in 1440 – was itself symbolic of his desire to stress the continuity of the Swedish monarchy and to point backwards to earlier ancestral kingships. He was fascinated by Sweden's glorious and 'Gothic' past, and in prison was later to translate Johannes Magnus's imaginary history of the Goths into Swedish.

The cult of monarchy was, of course, a commonplace in the sixteenth-century world, but in his concern to magnify his position, to distance himself from his great nobles of whose political aspirations he was suspicious, there was a megalomaniacal strain. Fundamentally, perhaps, he was an insecure man, fearful of any seeming challenge to his regality. He was the first Swedish king to insist on being called 'His Majesty'. He was obsessively distrustful, mercurial by temperament, on the look out for conspiracy in every nook and cranny of the court. What may have been at first a character defect of minimal significance became in time an overmastering obsession. In Michael Roberts' words, 'The gem was flawed from the beginning; and under a sharp blow was always liable to disintegrate.'[2]

Before his father died, negotiations were opened for Eric's marriage. Eric's choice fell upon the young English princess, Elizabeth, then half-sister and heiress to Queen Mary Tudor. At first sight she might not have seemed too good a bargain, for as a Protestant her relations with her Catholic sister Mary were strained (and indeed by Catholic teaching she had been born in bastardy), nor was it yet plain that Mary's supposed pregnancy was in vain. Eric's father, Gustav Vasa, was less enthusiastic than his son but if Elizabeth became queen the marriage would be immensely prestigious and help to consolidate Swedish power in northern Europe. In any case, marriage with a Swedish noble family appeared politically undesirable and the number of Protestant princesses was limited. Elizabeth might then prove an excellent catch.

Eric's tutor, Dionysius Beurreus, was despatched to London to survey the situation and, if necessary, to open negotiations. Beurreus, described as *legatus perpetuus*, argued that Eric's marriage to Elizabeth would promote English trade with the Baltic. He stressed Eric's royal ancestry; he was no mere scion of a 'clown who had stolen the throne from the crown of Denmark'. But Queen Mary Tudor as a Catholic had little time for a prince from the Protestant north and resented that the Swedish envoy made his addresses first to her sister whom she regarded with scant affection, so she rejected the approaches made by Beurreus on Elizabeth's behalf.

Within a year of Beurreus's arrival the scene had, however, changed out of all knowledge for Elizabeth had succeeded her sister as queen. She informed Eric's father, Gustav Vasa, that the friendship which he had shown her, more especially in the dark days of her sister's rule, was something she greatly valued, but 'she cannot entertain marriage [with Eric] since God has inbred her mind with such a love of celibacy that she will not willingly suffer herself to be diverted from it'. She felt bound as a consequence to refuse Eric's 'beautiful and kingly present', but she would do whatever she could to further Eric's suit to marry any other princess, being 'willing to oblige him in any point except this of matrimony'.[3]

None of this deterred Eric from pressing his suit. Once he became obsessed with an idea he would not readily give it up. He wrote to the queen with egocentric ebullience of his love '*ut omnino confidam et amare ne prosequi*'. He was, he told her, bound to her by an eternal love, had loved hitherto faithfully and constantly, and had been encouraged by her 'great tokens of favour and affection', whatever these may have been.[4]

Elizabeth had made herself plain, even if no one believed her. 'Hearing', she had told the Swedish ambassador on 6 May 1559, 'that the Prince contemplates a marriage with her, she regrets that she is unable to enter into such an arrangement.'[5] In spite of this an imposing Swedish mission headed by Eric's brother, Duke John, arrived in England to press Eric's suit. The queen apologized for the poor accommodation which they had been given but reiterated on 23 July 1559 that she had no wish to 'change this kind of solitary life. . . . She cannot be persuaded to decide upon matrimony, or listen to any solicitation thereupon.'[6]

Eric decided that the only way to induce the queen to change her mind was to present himself personally to Elizabeth. His father gave his consent, the Swedish Riksdag voted money for his journey but before he could depart Gustav died (on 29 September 1560) and Eric became king. Surely Elizabeth would not turn down the offer of the hand of a reigning and powerful prince. Shortly after his coronation, without a safe-conduct from the English queen, he set sail, but the elements were against him. There was so strong a storm in the Skaggerak that his ship had to run for safety; one of the ships was wrecked and another in which his younger brothers Karl and Magnus were travelling was temporarily lost. Eric wrote deploring the failure of his voyage, but all was not lost if it showed the serious nature of his intentions. 'He will not grudge all this toil and trouble if it will only induce her to consider his proposal of matrimony. . . . He loves her better than herself. No-one is so stupid as to continue to love without being loved. . . . His fortune has been hitherto harder than steel and more cruel than Mars.'[7]

There was no getting away from this importunate lover who promised to sail for England the following spring. From his envoy in London, Nils Gyllenstierna, he received glowing reports of Elizabeth's charm and intellect and somewhat less credibly of the great enthusiasm with which she awaited the king's arrival. In response the king sent romantic letters composed in courtly Latin, signing himself '*VM frater et consanguineus amantissimus, Ericus*'.

> The king was persuaded by the shifty English agent in Stockholm, to buy jewels for presentation to the queen. In view of the king's anticipated arrival the London hucksters were selling woodcuts to gullible passers-by which shewed Elizabeth and Eric side by side on separate thrones. The burghers of Newcastle had agreed to place the Queen's House at Eric's disposal and procured special tapestries to adorn it. The town spent 10s 'for whyting the great haull in the Queen's Majestie's Manor agaynste the cumyng of the king of Swethyn' and Robert Horsbroke was to be paid £2 for a 'tonne of beer' to entertain the royal guest.[8]

While Elizabeth might deny that she had any thought of marriage, European courts continued to take the matter seriously as Spelt told Cecil on 22 April 1560.

It is difficult to know whether this charade had any foundation in reality, but a charade it evidently was. While some English councillors, among them Cecil, would not have objected to such an alliance, there was little enthusiasm. Eric was himself much disturbed, as were also some of those much nearer to the queen, at the undue favour which she seemed to bestow on Robert Dudley, the earl of Leicester, so that some even suspected that he might be the queen's lover. In his anxiety the Swedish king played with the possibility of having Dudley removed from the scene by assassination and wondered whether it would be appropriate to challenge him to a duel. This greatly alarmed his envoy in London, for Gyllenstierna saw himself standing proxy for his king, but he managed to persuade Eric that it would be unseemly for so sacred a person as a king to place himself on the same footing as a mere English noble. That the Swedish king could so view the situation suggested a lack of balance in his mental make-up.

Yet Eric progressed to the extent of having marriage contracts drawn up, which carefully safeguarded Swedish independence and his own rights. He continued to state his intention of visiting the English court to offer Elizabeth his hand. 'News from London', John Cuerton told Sir Thomas Chaloner as late as May 1562, 'states that ten of the queen's ships are ready to receive the king of Sweden at his coming'.[9]

Elizabeth herself was reported as saying that 'if the king be such a one as is reported, he is not to be refused of any woman'.

The negotiations had in fact reached a climax. Although the marriage compact was not given up, it was to be effectively grounded. Eric's envoy, Gyllenstierna, heavily in debt, returned home while Eric actually opened negotiations for the hand of Elizabeth's cousin, Mary, Queen of Scots – hardly the best way to win Elizabeth's approval. His matrimonial projects were now more dictated by Sweden's political needs than, whatever Eric might write to the queen in his courtly Latin, by feelings of the heart. So he turned from England to Scotland, that failing, to the German prince Philip of Hesse, the hand of whose daughter Christina he now sought in marriage.

He was justifiably worried how Elizabeth would react if he seemed to be spurning her, and to placate his intended bride he wrote a letter to explain his position. He had, he reassured her in October 1562, 'never sought the Queen of Scots for himself but for his brother', Duke John. His attempt to woo Christina of Hesse was simply to test Queen Elizabeth's own constancy, though he admitted his jealousy of Dudley had something to do with it. He 'would never have thought that any woman would have lived single for so long on his account, especially when urged so strongly to marry as she is'.[10] He still entertained high hopes that Elizabeth would agree to marry him. Unfortunately, the letter misfired in more ways than one, for its bearer was captured by the king's enemies, the Danes, who promptly sent it, via the elector of Saxony, to Philip of Hesse. In high dudgeon he married Christina off to Adolf of Holstein, promising to 'wipe the Swedish noses in the dust'.

Elizabeth's own feelings for Eric became increasingly dilute. Once again he wrote that his love for her was unabated and that he would readily lay down his wealth, his kingdom and his life; but he did not forget to suggest that it would be appropriate for Swedish merchants to be given privileges in England similar to those enjoyed by the

Eric XIV, King of Sweden, from a painting by S. van der Meulen (The National Swedish Art Museums)

Hanseatic traders.[11] Whatever Elizabeth may have thought of the king's flattering letters, she was clearly beginning to find the Swedish king capricious and tiresome. She remonstrated with him for his harsh treatment of his brother Duke John, whom she had found to be a faithful servant during his visit to London. When he sought English help in his fight against the Danes Elizabeth made only a half-hearted offer to mediate.

Eric had indeed weightier matters on his hands, both foreign and domestic. Determined to assert his authority, with the support of the Swedish Riksdag or parliament, he sought to reduce the semi-autonomous powers enjoyed by his brothers, the dukes John, Magnus and Karl. Naturally enough they took umbrage. John defied his brother by wedding Katarina, the sister of the Polish king whom Eric regarded as an enemy of Sweden. He declared that John had forfeited his constitutional rights to the succession and had him imprisoned in the castle of Gripsholm.

Eric was confronted by a ring of enemies, the Danes, the rich Lubecker merchants as well as by the Poles and the Russians now governed by the ambitious tsar, Ivan the Terrible. If Sweden's enemies won, Sweden's dominance in the Baltic would evaporate. But Eric showed skill and determination, acquiring the port of Reval which gave Sweden a foothold on both sides of the Gulf of Finland and making a successful invasion of Norway. That Sweden escaped at the end of his reign without undue damage was a tribute to his vigour and insight.

The domestic situation was in some sense as dangerous as foreign hostility. At home Eric was from the start suspicious of the aspirations of the great nobles. By seeking to win the support of the lesser gentry he replaced the native-born aristocracy with those of humbler birth whom he felt more able to trust.

His right-hand man was Joran Persson, a highly intelligent but ambitious and greedy man who became his secretary of state. Under his guidance a recently established High Court meted out summary, savage punishments on noble offenders who were alleged critics of the crown. The number and nature of the offences, some trivial in their nature such as that of the man charged with painting the royal arms upside down, showed how increasingly suspicious the king was becoming of his own subjects, and his constant fear that his greater subjects were conspiring against him. He sensed, in the long run obsessively, that the nobles aimed to retrieve their ancient rights and to weaken the power of the crown.

Suspicion and fear were directed more especially at the powerful Sture family. The king had come to believe that his marriage plans had been foiled because of aristocratic plots designed ultimately to ensure that he had no legitimate heirs; he had mistresses and bastards enough. But his policy was neither consistent nor indeed comprehensible. He subjected Nils Sture to ignominious humiliation, for he had been told by astrologers that the Swedish crown might be conferred on a 'light haired man' which seemed to fit Nils's appearance (though in fact his hair was gingerish rather than flaxen). Then he promised Nils the hand of his bastard daughter Virginia in marriage and appointed him as his ambassador in his latest marital plans to wed Christina of Lorraine. The project was impossible and Sture's failure in the negotiations was bound to fuel the king's suspicions that he was himself once more the victim of an aristocratic plot.

There could be no doubt that the king's mind was becoming unhinged. He stalked restlessly through the corridors of the royal castle, intent on finding offences, often where there was none. If he saw that the royal pages were too elegantly dressed, it was, he supposed, because they wanted to seduce the women of his court. His royal chamberlain was brought before the High Court because the royal sceptre had been found damaged in his room. It could be dangerous to whisper to one's neighbour, even to clear one's throat lest it screened a plot against the king. Two guards were sentenced to death on the grounds that they had placed a jug, a cloak and a halter in the royal privy 'to annoy the king'. If the king passed haystacks covered with fir branches, he flew into a violent rage because inverted fir trees reminded him of Nils Sture's triumphal arch.

To crown all this Eric's personal life had reached a crisis point, for he had decided to marry his mistress Karin Mansdotter, a girl of humble origin, a gaoler's daughter who had been a servant in a tavern. It seems as if he may have been genuinely in love with her, and a child by her would guarantee the succession. But to marry her would bring all the accumulated wrath of the Swedish nobility, into whose ranks he had not deigned to wed and who would be deeply offended by such a social misalliance, upon him.

Personal and political stress proved too much. Momentarily Eric's brain snapped in an attack of schizophrenia. The king, who was still convinced that there was a noble conspiracy against him, ordered the arrest of a number of nobles, had them brought before the High Court which condemned them to death. Nils Sture, who had just returned from his abortive mission to the court of Lorraine, was sent to join his father in prison. Eric's mind was clearly in a state of disordered ferment. He believed that he was the victim of betrayal and treason and that his own servants were untrustworthy. He had summoned the Swedish estates to meet at Upsala but lost the notes of the speech which he intended to make; it was, he alleged, his wicked servants who had stolen his speech on purpose to discredit him.

His behaviour became increasingly paranoic. He could not decide whether to seek a reconciliation with the Sture party or to eradicate it. On 24 May 1566 he visited Nils's father Svante Sture in Upsala Castle. At first it seemed as if there was to be an effective reconciliation, but the king's mind was like a leaf whipped by the wind. A few hours after the supposed reconciliation he strode up to the castle in a fury, his hat low on his head, walking so fast that the guards found it difficult to keep pace with him, and on reaching it he stabbed Nils Sture to death.

The king then rushed headlong from the castle, having given orders that all the prisoners should be killed immediately, excepting a 'Herr Sten'. Who the king meant no one knew but his incoherent remark helped to save the lives of Sten Leijonhufvud and Sten Baner. Then he mounted his horse and left the town, unclear as to where he was going, only seeking to avoid the attackers whom he imagined were in pursuit of him. His former tutor, Dionysius Beurreus, followed him in a vain effort to calm him down, but Eric killed him. As darkness fell the deranged monarch wandered through the forest, dazed and aimless.

That Eric was the victim of a paranoid schizophrenia seems plain enough. Rather surprisingly there was no immediate attempt to depose him, itself proof that the king's fear of a noble conspiracy designed to bring this about was a delusion. Joran Persson was a convenient scapegoat, apprehended, tried and condemned. The king's mind was totally confused. On one occasion, convinced that he had actually been deposed, he thought that he was the prisoner of his brother duke John whom he had himself incarcerated in Gripsholm Castle. When John was eventually released, in a scene that had comic elements, the two men knelt to each other, Eric still deluded into believing that he was his brother's prisoner, John that Eric was his lord. Yet he had sufficient understanding of the situation to go through with his marriage to Karin Mansdotter.

By the New Year of 1568 Eric seems to have recovered something of his mental balance. Savage as the attack had been, the schizophrenia subsided. He took up the reins of command, not indeed before time, and showed vigour in repulsing the Danes who had taken advantage of the virtual collapse of the Swedish government to invade Swedish territory. On 28 January 1568 his wife gave birth to a son and the king wrote a special anthem for his official wedding which took place on 4 July following. Next day she was crowned queen of Sweden. Joran Persson, who had been condemned to death, was reprieved and even restored to his former powers. Characteristically arrogant, the king sought to justify the actions which he had taken against the so-called conspirators at Upsala.

The nobles were even more resentful of the king's actions in his apparent sanity than in his fit of madness. His brothers, dukes John and Karl, gathered their levies, captured Stockholm, put Persson to death and proclaimed Eric's brother John as King John III. Eric and his young wife and child were sent to prison. The charges made against the king were numerous and in part fabricated. His madness, it was alleged, was merely an attempt to cover his misdeeds, but there was a suspicion that he had been bewitched, possessed by a special demon who was called Koppoff.

In prison Eric continued to justify what he had done, arguing that he had been defending the rights of the crown and had acted within the law. He resisted strongly the suggestion that he had ruled tyrannically, claiming that he had always had the good of his people at heart. He requested that he should at least be allowed to go into exile: 'the world is wide enough for even fraternal hate', so he wrote, 'to be mitigated by distance'.

But while Eric remained alive, he was the obvious focal point for conspiracies against his successor, and for varied reasons plots against the new king were manifold, often with the complicity of the Danes. The most dangerous of these was headed by one of Eric's former commanders, the French noble, Charles de Mornay, assisted by Scottish mercenaries, but the plot was betrayed and the ringleaders were executed. It was apparently not merely loyalty to Eric or hatred of King John that spurred on the plotters, for it was widely believed that before his deposition Eric had buried a vast treasure with the help of his garden-master, Jean Allard, who was a refugee abroad. Even the king was himself only reluctantly dissuaded from putting Eric to the torture to get him to reveal the whereabouts of the treasure. Fearful of the former ruler, wanting to ensure that no claim could be made for his children, John ordered that Eric be separated from his family and moved round from one castle to another.

Egocentric, morbid, kept in conditions of increasing harshness, Eric seemed to have relapsed eventually into madness. From 1569 onwards his successor contemplated the possibility of having him executed, in June 1575 authorizing Eric's gaoler to carry this out in a particularly brutal fashion. At last on 24 February 1577 Eric XIV died, very probably, as a recent exhumation has indicated, from arsenical poisoning.

'Eric', Michael Roberts wrote, 'bequeathed two things to Sweden, and both were evil legacies. One was the commitment to imperial expansion, from which no Swedish government would be able to cut free for a hundred and fifty years. The other was the fear and suspicion with which monarchy and aristocracy were to regard each other for the next half-century. From Eric's morbid imaginings had been distilled a poison, fatal to himself, which would taint the blood of Swedish politics for many a day.'[12]

IX

Russian Bears

The fulcrum of Eric XIV's foreign policy was the friendship, neutrality or hostility of Sweden's Baltic neighbour, the able, ambitious, unstable Russian tsar, Ivan IV, not unjustifiably called the Terrible. As a great power sixteenth-century Russia was only impinging slowly on European history. To westerners the Russians remained for the most part a mysterious, little-known and semi-barbaric people. Russia seemed to be on the fringe of western civilization. For the Elizabethan traveller, Giles Turberville, writing in 1568, the Russians were not unlike the wild Irish:

> A people passing rude, to vices vile inclinde
> Folke fit to be of Bacchus traine, so quaffing in their kinde.
> Drink is their whole desire, the pot is all their pride,
> The sobrest head doth once a day stand needful of a guide

> Wilde Irish are as civil as the Russies in theyr kinde.
> Hard choice which is the best of both, each bloudy, rude and blinde.

The Slavonic temperament seemed particularly prone to extreme emotions: love and hate, pity and terror, themes which threaded the music of the great Slavonic composers and kindled the genius of Russian novelists. It is hardly surprising that some of the Russian rulers should also have displayed elemental qualities, larger than life. Eric's attack of schizophrenia, fundamental in the history of Sweden, pales into insignificance by comparison with the prodigal but bizarre personal qualities displayed by three of the greatest of Russia's rulers, Tsars Ivan IV the Terrible, Peter the Great and the dictator Joseph Stalin. In their governance there were features not far short of genius, in their statecraft, in their determination and in the iron control they exerted over their people. Yet their genius was flawed, if not by actual madness, at least by a lack of mental balance. Separated as Ivan and Peter were by a century, their rule, enlightened and forward looking as in many respects it undoubtedly was, was founded on a seemingly sadistic delight in terror and torture, used not simply as instruments of policy, though this may well have been the case too, but as a means of self-gratification. Power-drunk and barbaric in their cruelty they undoubtedly were, but their characters and actions seem to demand some deeper psychological explanation.

Tsar Ivan IV was three years old when he succeeded his father as the Grand Duke of Muscovy in 1533 and, as with Peter the Great, some of the excesses of his personality become to some extent explicable in the light of childhood experience. His mother, the dowager Grand Duchess Elena, advised by her lover, Prince Obolensky-Telepnov, was a capricious and unpopular regent until her death in 1538, probably by poisoning, opened the way to a power struggle in the state between two conflicting princely families, the Belskys and the Shuiskys, the latter of whom eventually gained the upper hand.

The powerful Russian boyars treated the young prince as a plaything to be tossed from one to the other. The trauma of his impotence at the hands of the great nobles remained with him all his life, helping both to condition his personality and his politics. As Ivan was supposed to have told Prince Kurbsky:

Yuri [Ivan's brother] and I remained orphans in the absolute sense of the word. . . . Our subjects saw their decrees fulfilled; they remained an empire without a master. . . . As for my brother Yuri and me, they treated us like foreigners or beggars. What privations did we not endure, lacking both food and clothing. . . . We were allowed no freedom. . . . We were not brought up as children should be.

Kept short of food and clothes, treated with ignominy, the humiliations which Ivan then experienced created a deep scar in his mind which time never completely obliterated.

But his childhood revealed too the latent cruel streak in his nature of which he was never to divest himself and which was to worsen with the passage of time. He evidently enjoyed causing pain, throwing dogs and cats from the palace roof and tearing feathers off birds while he pierced their eyes and slit open their bodies. Like other irresponsible young princes, he roamed the streets in violent fashion with youthful boyars as his companions.

Nonetheless Ivan was an intelligent boy who read widely, fascinated by the chronicles of Russia's past history. On 16 January 1547 he was crowned as tsar in a resplendent ceremonial in the profusely decorated, onion-domed Uspensky Cathedral in Moscow. The title of tsar had itself been only recently assumed by the grand duke as an expression of the belief that Moscow was the historic successor to the empires of Rome and Byzantium.

Ivan grew up to become strongly aware of his semi-divine destiny, encouraged by the teaching of the church. With the connivance, and perhaps at the instigation of the Metropolitan Macarius, he rid himself of the nobles who had dominated him in his minority. Prince Andrew Shuisky was put to death. But the young man showed also a determination not simply to abase the boyars but in a more general sense to win the goodwill of his subjects. He initiated much needed reforms, made contacts with the west, encouraging contacts with England where the Russia Company had been founded for trade in 1555, and by making territorial gains, more particularly by the annexation of Kazan and Astrakhan, he pushed the borders of the grand duchy south and east, towards the Caspian Sea and the Ural Mountains.

By nature sexually promiscuous – and Ivan Timofeev stated that he had a homosexual affair with Bogdan Bel'skii – Ivan seems nonetheless to have had a strong affection for his first wife, Anastasia Romanovna Zakharyn, a daughter of an old boyar family. 'This emperor', an English visitor commented,

> doth exceed his [predecessors] in stoutness of courage and valiantness, and a great deal more. . . . [He] useth great familiarity, as well unto all his nobles and subjects, as also unto strangers. . . . And by this means he is not only beloved of his nobles and commons, but also held in great dread and fear throughout all his dominions. He delighteth not greatly in hawking, hunting or any other pastime, nor in hearing instruments or music, but setteth his whole delight upon two things: first to serve God, as undoubtedly he is very devout in his religion, and the second, how to subdue and conquer his enemies.

Ivan showed then every prospect of becoming not merely an able but a good ruler, careful for the interests of his people.

Then in 1553 he fell very seriously ill, so that for a time his life was despaired of. We do not know the exact nature of his illness but it may have been an attack of encephalitis, or even of a syphilitic nature. Whatever it was, it was evidently crucial for his future. During his illness he was much concerned to secure the succession for his infant son should he die but his plans were opposed by his cousin, Prince Vladimir of Staritza, who managed to win over, if temporarily, Ivan's own trusted advisers, the chamberlain Alexei Adashev and the court chaplain Sylvester. The episode strengthened the tsar's determination to crush any opposition to his will, and aroused his suspicion even of those hitherto in his confidence. On his recovery Ivan determined not merely to eliminate his critics but to break for ever the power of the boyars whom he regarded as enemies both of the tsar and the Russian people. Both Sylvester and Adashev were disgraced. The policy which he was henceforth to follow may appear rational and far-sighted, and so it has been interpreted: to set up a strong centralized state and to oppress and destroy his enemies within it.

After his illness in 1553 the tsar's character seems, however, to have undergone a steady deterioration which from time to time bordered on madness, more especially after the death of his first wife in 1560. Prince Semen Shakhovskoi praised the first part of his reign but in the second part he followed an evil path: 'Thus for sins he shewed himself to be the opposite [of the good ruler he had been]; he was filled with anger and fierceness, and began to persecute his servants evilly and mercilessly.' The *Khronograf* specifically links the change in Ivan's character with the death of his first wife Anastasia. He became increasingly obsessed with the semi-divine character of his power. 'The monarch', as he was to remind his enemy, prince Kurbsky, 'can exercise his will over the slaves whom God has given him. . . . If you do not obey the sovereign when he commits an injustice, not only do you become guilty of felony but you damn your soul, for God himself orders you to obey your prince blindly.' Such views were held by many contemporary rulers and do not by themselves constitute any indication of mental imbalance.

Simultaneously Ivan seems to have been beset by a deep feeling of insecurity which was perhaps rooted in his experience of childhood, enhanced by the attempts to frustrate his will when he was sick in 1553. Some facets of his personality, more especially the streak of sadistic cruelty, became more manifest, finding expression in fits of terrifying rage. 'Then did sweep upon the Tsar', as a contemporary described one such outbreak, 'as it were a terrible tempest, which set him beside himself and disturbed the peace of his godly heart. In some manner which I wot not it turned the mind, with all its plenitude of wisdom into the nature of a wild beast.' Daniel Printz von Bruchau said that in his rages Ivan 'foamed at the mouth like a horse', though when he calmed down he felt a sense of guilt for what he had done. Ivan Timofeev stated that Ivan 'was moved to evil as much by his nature as by anger'.

A further shift along the downward road of seeming mental imbalance occurred in 1564–5 when, because of the growing mistrust of his own courtiers, he left Moscow and retreated to the monastery of Alexandrovskya Sloboda, deep in a dark forest, 70 miles to the northeast. From there he wrote to the Metropolitan, denouncing the governing classes, both lay and clerical, and appealing for the support of the people whose champion he now claimed to be. He was entreated to return and by February 1565 was back in Moscow. Though he was only thirty-five years old he looked like an ageing man, his face wrinkled, nearly bald, with a straggling thin beard; in his rages he was prone to tear out his own hair.

He now inaugurated what was virtually a reign of terror, even if terror had a political purpose. He told Prince Kurbsky:

What you say about my alleged cruelties is an impudent lie. I do not put to death the strong men of Israel; I do not shed their blood upon the peoples of the Lord. I deal severely only with traitors. Until now the sovereigns of Russia have been free and independent. They have rewarded or punished their subjects as they have seen fit, without being answerable to any one. Never will this change. I am no longer a child. I need the grace of God, the protection of the Virgin Mary and of all the saints, but I ask no instruction from men.

To promote his policy he established a private army or bodyguard, the Oprichnina, which was to be absolutely obedient to himself. The Oprichniki were an early version of the secret police, ministers of terror who had the right to rob and torture with impunity, constituting a state within a state. 'He divided his dominions', so Shakhovskoi commented, 'given to him by God, into two pieces . . . and he ordered [those in] the other part to rape and murder [those in] that part.'

Once more the tsar left Moscow and returned to the Alexandrovskya Monastery which had been turned into a fortress. Here his life seemed to alternate between orgies of drunken licentiousness and seeming acts of contrition. For after listening to the prisoners being tortured, he would beat his head in penitence, praying for those whom he had had mutilated and killed. In a semi-blasphemous parody of religion, in some ways resembling the future antics of Peter the Great, he and his associates, he acting as abbot, Prince Viazansky as treasurer and the venomous Malyuta 'Baby' Shuratove, dressed in black cassocks worn under gold-embroidered tunics trimmed with marten fur, went from the torture chamber to the chapel, the tsar 'beaming with contentment'.

His married life had become unstable and tempestuous, underlining his egocentricity, insecurity and manic temperament. After his first wife's death he married a Circassian beauty, Maria, the daughter of Prince Temrink, but he soon tired of her illiteracy and uncouthness. After she died on 1 September 1569 he married on 28 October 1571 Martha Sobakin, the daughter of a Novgorod merchant, but she died two weeks later, 13 November, before the marriage had even been consummated. According to one account her death had been brought about by an excess of unbridled sexual passion on the tsar's part, but it seems more likely that she may have been seriously ill even at the time of the marriage. In this incident, as in many others, it is almost impossible to sort out what in Ivan's life history was hostile rumour and what may have been historical fact. The tsar's fourth wife was Anna Alexeevna Koltovskaya, but, wearying of her, he packed her off to the Tikhvinsky monastery where as Sister Daria she was to live safely for another fifty-one years. Perhaps she was the most fortunate of Ivan's wives.

Then, in defiance of canon law, he married without the benefit of the church Anna Vassilchikura but she soon disappeared and was replaced by Vasilissa Melentievna. Vasilissa, less sensible than the Tsarina Anna, took a lover, Prince Ivan Devtelev, who was subsequently impaled by the tsar's orders under his wife's window before she was despatched willy-nilly to a convent. When the tsar discovered that his seventh wife, Maria Dolgurukaya, was not a virgin when he married her, in his horror and anger he had her drowned the next day. His eighth and last wife was Maria Feodrovna Nagaya. More unfortunate and priapic than Henry VIII of England and even less happy in the children who survived his marriages, matrimonial bliss eluded him after the death of his first wife.

Ivan the Terrible, Tsar of Russia, in crown and robes (photograph: © The Hulton-Deutsch Picture Collection Limited, London)

Meanwhile the Oprichniki ensured obedience to the tsar's will. A personal or service nobility, drawn from all classes, they were placed above the law with a licence to fulfil the tsar's orders. 'The more the people detested them, the more confidence the sovereign shewed in them.' Indeed he took a personal delight in watching and even assisting at the execution of his enemies. Prince Michael Vorotyasky, who had fought successfully against the Tatars, was found guilty of witchcraft and was lashed to a stake between two fires which, according to the hostile and not entirely reliable account of Prince Kurbsky, Ivan himself helped to stoke.

Whole cities suffered the same fate as individuals. Suspecting that the people of the important commercial metropolis of Novgorod, some 3,000 miles north-west of Moscow, were aiming for autonomy, the tsar looted the city and massacred the inhabitants, many of whom were simply tossed into the near-freezing river. No one could defy his will with impunity. The city's archbishop, Leonid, was first sewn up in a bear skin and then hunted to death by a pack of hounds. When the Metropolitan Philip protested courageously against Ivan's tyrannical policy, in an outspoken sermon in the Dormition Cathedral in the Kremlin on 22 March 1568, the Oprichniki revenged their master seizing him as the Metropolitan was conducting a service in the Uspensky Cathedral; he was banished to the Otroch monastery where he was strangled in his cell by Malyuta Shuratove. From this time onwards Ivan followed a policy of brutal intimidation.

The people of Pskov suffered a fate similar to those of Novgorod. Even those in the tsar's own councils, whom he began to suspect of intriguing with his enemies in Poland, Turkey and the khanate of the Crimea, did not escape his wrath. The imperial chancellor, Ivan Viskovaty, was strung up on the gallows while members of the tsar's entourage took turns to hack off pieces of his body, Malyuta Shuratove starting with the chancellor's ear. The treasurer, Nikita Funikov, was scalded to death in a cauldron of boiling water.

It can hardly be denied that the policy of terror worked, nor did it cease when the tsar decided to disband the Oprichniki in the early 1570s. Was terror simply a means to a fulfilment of policy, to promote an efficient and centralized system of government, as could be argued in the case not merely of Ivan but of Peter and Stalin? Or was there an additional ingredient? Was it also an individual reflection of a personality that was fundamentally deeply disturbed, who in modern terms could be described as psychopathic?

After his illness in 1553, Ivan appeared a deeply disturbed man, disturbed at times to the brink of madness. His sense of personal insecurity, his basic mistrust, even of those who were his confidantes, his sadism, his uncontrolled rages suggested a highly abnormal personality. Henceforth, the tsar became addicted to the ingestion of mercury, which was kept bubbling in a cauldron in his room for his consumption.

There can be no doubt, as the exhumation of his body showed later, that he suffered from mercury poisoning and this, together with his ill-health and temperamental disposition, made him increasingly ill-balanced. It has been alleged that he was afflicted with diffused cerebral syphilis or syphilis of the aortic valve, and there were features of his personality which might well seem to fit such a diagnosis; nor, in view of his sexual promiscuity, would it be surprising that this was the illness which marred his personality and eventually destroyed him. Whether Ivan's problems were basically organic or psychological in origin, the events of his life served to deepen a personality disorder which may be traced back to childhood and was accentuated by illness in 1553 which ultimately transformed an able, intelligent statesman into a suspicious and cruel tyrant.

He had long looked older than his years, becoming shrunken and stooped with long white hair straggling from a bald pate onto his shoulders. He had been particularly shattered by the death of his son and heir for which he was himself responsible. In 1581 he had struck out with his cane at his son's third wife, Elena Sheremeteva when she was pregnant because, in Ivan's view, she wore clothing which he thought indecorous. She fell and later miscarried. When her husband protested at the way his father had treated his wife Ivan turned on him, inflicting a fatal wound. When his son died, the tsar suffered agonizing feelings of guilt, striking his head in grief against his son's coffin, and then roaming vacantly through the corridors of the palace searching vainly for his son.

By 1584 Ivan's health was collapsing. He suffered what was described as a 'decomposition of the blood' and 'corruption of the bowels'. His body swelled, the skin peeled off and gave a terrible odour. He found some relief in hot baths and did not easily give up his interest in life. Four days before he died he showed an English visitor, Jerome Horsey, his collection of precious stones. On 19 March 1584 he had his will read, and then ordered a chessboard to be brought to his bedside; as he was setting up the chessmen the tsar collapsed and died. The son who succeeded him, Tsar Feodor I, was a pious prince, nicknamed 'the Bellringer' because of his love of church services, but he seems to have been of feeble intellect and mentally retarded.

There is a striking resemblance between Ivan and his successor as tsar a century later, Peter the Great. Both were rulers of enormous energy and authority, who by their reforms wrought great changes in traditional Russia. They strengthened Russia's influence outside its borders, undertaking campaigns against the Turks and looking for outlets to the Baltic. Their personalities were almost equally bizarre. They were strangely or at least superstitiously devout but simultaneously found a curious pleasure in blasphemy. They liked drunken frolics and revelled in violence. Each killed his eldest son and heir, Ivan by mishap, Peter by deliberation. It seems very likely that in part their destinies were shaped by the difficulties they experienced in childhood when they were terrorized by their own violent mighty subjects, and both may have had their mental capacities distorted by serious illness. Their creativity was streaked by a lack of mental balance which could conceivably have been organic in its origin.

For Russian historians, whether tsarist or Marxist, Peter was inevitably a heroic figure. He was the man who cast off the shackles of the past; 'in his hand', as the Russian writer Chaadaev phrased it, 'Peter the Great found only a blank sheet of paper and he wrote on it Europe and the West, since then we have belonged to Europe and to the West.' He defied the still feudal boyars and introduced modern western ideas and customs into still traditional Muscovy. Though fundamentally a superstitious man, he proved a mortal foe to ecclesiastical conservatism. The more traditional Russian Christians, particularly the sect known as the Old Believers, readily identified their tsar with anti-Christ himself, condemning Peter for his western-style dress and dissolute style of life, for his new uniforms, and for his compulsory shaving of beards, which they criticized as a violation of the very image of God in man.

Peter was the most indomitable of men. If in some ways he appeared a carbon copy of Ivan the Terrible, he had greater self-confidence and an even stronger belief in his destiny. He did not merely restructure the state but as a great warrior redeemed the defeat which his army had endured at the hands of the Swedes at Narva by a glorious victory over the Swedish king Charles XII at Poltava in 1709. Against the Turks, like Ivan, he was somewhat less successful; but the territorial expansion of Russia became under his lead as much a factor in the making of world history as the country's seeming emergence from its medieval cocoon.

Even if it can be properly argued that Peter the Great's impact on Russia was less than has sometimes been thought, there can be little doubt that he was huge in every way. Nearly seven feet tall, he was astonishingly strong. He could twist silver coins with his fingers, and, though doubtless an agonizing experience for the victims, liked as an amateur dentist to extract his courtiers' teeth. He revelled in manual labour, was a skilled craftsman and cobbler. He walked so fast that his companions found it difficult to keep pace with him. He travelled far more widely than any previous Russian ruler, visiting England, Holland, Germany, absorbing lessons all the time, teaching himself German and Dutch, and wherever he went he displayed an endless curiosity.

Yet despite great physical stamina and a catena of achievements there was in Peter a dark side which seemed to falter on the fringe of madness. It displayed itself in his maniacal rages, in his acts of outrageous cruelty and in the boorish activities of his dissolute and drunken court. As with Tsar Ivan, some at least of the facets of Peter's character became more comprehensible in terms of his childhood and upbringing. The fourteenth child of Tsar Alexis, though the only son of his father's second wife, the youthful Natalia Narishkina, Peter was born in the Kremlin on 30 May 1672. He was four years old when his father died. Immediately Russia was plunged into twelve years of misgovernment and a power struggle between the boyars who supported one or other of the late tsar's wives. Alexis's immediate successor, Tsar Feodor III, was a feeble youth who died in 1682 six years after his accession. During his reign Peter's mother, Natalia, had been forced to go into virtual exile with her infant son at Pusluzersk; but her principal adviser, Sergeyvitch Matveyof (who was married to a Scotswoman, Mary Hamilton) won the favour of the tsar who wed his godchild. When, shortly afterwards, Tsar Feodor died, the notables demanded that the youthful Peter, now ten years old, should be proclaimed joint tsar with Feodor's brother and heir, the feeble-minded Ivan V.

Although this was what happened the position of Peter and his mother became precarious, for Ivan V's sister, the redoubtable Sophia Alexeevna was determined to oust Peter and his mother. She managed to win over the Muscovite garrison, the Streltsy and rid herself of Natalia's favourite Matveyof who was thrown from the palace balcony onto the spears of the soldiers waiting below. Sophia and her lover Prince Basil Golitsyn exercised power while Peter and his mother went again into hiding. Peter's life seemed to be in such danger that he fled precipitately by night from Preobrazhenskoe to the sanctuary of the Troitsa monastery where he collapsed in a state of terror and exhaustion. The humiliations which he experienced in his boyhood were always to be at the back of his mind.

In other respects there was perhaps nothing very remarkable about his childhood. He played with dwarfs, freaks from the Samoyed and Kalmuk plains who, garbed in raspberry coloured coats adorned with gold buttons and trimmed with white fur, drew the tsar in a miniature cart, barking, neighing, braying, cackling and farting as they did so. As he grew older, he became more keenly interested in military games, arranging mock battles between the stable boys, and experimenting with fireworks and other explosive devices, as a result of which the son-in-law of his Scottish favourite, Gordon, was burned to death.

At length there was a palace revolution which enabled him to relegate his half-sister to the dubious comforts of a nunnery while his half-brother, Ivan V, never more than a cipher, died in 1696. Peter now had the opportunity to initiate the plans which in the course of the next twenty years were to transform Russia into a great power, to wage successful war against the Swedes in the north and the Turks and Tatars in the south. In the process he reconditioned a nation, creating a new capital at St Petersburg, built a fleet, trained an army, remodelled the bureaucracy and made the church subservient to his will.

Yet in this man of creative genius there were bizarre streaks which seemed symptomatic if not of madness at least of deep psychological disorder. He was conventionally religious, for he attributed his success in war to God's favour. Yet the pursuit of the blasphemous and obscene became a favourite recreation. While this may have been no more than an attack on the conservatism of a church which as the upholder of traditional customs could be seen as a hostile critic of his reforming policies, in the clowning and frivolities in which Peter and his courtiers engaged there seemed a darker side.

Peter delighted to parody the ceremonial of the orthodox church. He formed the synod of the 'Most Drunken Fools and Jesters', the rules of which Peter, as a deacon of the order, helped to draw up; the first commandment characteristically read 'to get drunk every day and never go to bed sober'. The synod had a mock patriarch, Peter's old tutor, Nikita Zotov, described as the 'Most Clownish Father Josafat, Patriarch of Pressburg and the river Yamsa'. Members of the order were given obscene nicknames. The tin mitre which the so-called patriarch wore portrayed a naked Bacchus on a barrel. Vodka took the place of holy water. At Christmastide the mock-patriarch and his companions made an uproarious and drunken drive through the city on sleighs. During the season of Lent the members wore their coats back to front, rode on asses and bullocks or, if there was still snow, on sleighs drawn by pigs, goats or even by bears. On Shrove Tuesday 1699 there was a feast in honour of Bacchus at which the patriarch made the sign of the cross to bless the guests with two long tobacco pipes, an insulting gesture as the orthodox church had condemned the use of tobacco.

The 'drunken synod' became a permanent feature of the tsar's court. Peter was present in 1715 when the mock patriarch, now a senile octogenarian, was married to a young widow by a blind and deaf centenarian. When six years later, in 1721, Zotov died, a special ceremony was invented to mark both the election of his successor, Buturlin, and marriage to Zotov's widow. The tsar, who had heard of the legend of the so-called female pope Joan, devised what he thought would be an amusing prank to ascertain the sex of the two principals. Seats were made in which special holes were inserted which would enable Peter and the other participants to examine the private parts of the mock-patriarch and his wife. The tsar gripped Buturlin's genitals, shouting *'Habet foramen! Habet!'* ('He has an opening!') In the course of the orgy which followed the so-called cardinals sat in specially constructed boxes where they were obliged to drink a spoonful of vodka every quarter of an hour for the remainder of the night. When the dawn broke the tsar escorted a semi-nude girl, the 'princess-abbess' who carried a basket of eggs. Each of the drunken cardinals kissed the abbess's breasts before taking an egg which he cast as his vote for the patriarch. In reward for his office Buturlin was given the freedom of the tsar's cellars as well as lodgings in Moscow and St Petersburg.

Peter the Great as a young man, from a painting by Sir Geoffrey Kneller during his visit to England in 1697
(Royal Collection Enterprises, © Her Majesty Queen Elizabeth II)

How far this throws any meaningful light on Peter's psychology it is difficult to say. It could be that these goings on were little more then Peter's way of opposing what he held to be the hypocrisy of the Russian church or, even, according to contemporary Russian standards, of having good clean fun. It is significant of the extent to which such 'fun' involved taunting the old, the innocent, the harmless. It may have reflected an ever more deep-seated neurosis.

The dark shades of Peter's mind were perhaps better reflected in the violence and cruelty with which he treated his opponents. When, in 1687, he suspected that there was a plot against his power, involving his half-sister Sophia, he had the arms and legs of the plotters hacked off before they were raised to the scaffold and beheaded, their blood dripping on the corpse of the principal conspirator Ivan Miloslavsky. Three years later, after the rising of the Streltsy, Peter personally acted as one of the executioners, wielding an axe to strike off their heads. . . . He enjoyed watching the torturer at work and the whipping of women.

His treatment of his son and heir Alexis, in some respects comprehensible, underlined his psychopathic character. Alexis was the son of Peter's marriage to Eudoxia, a lady of whom Peter swiftly tired and had relegated to a nunnery. It has been suggested that Peter had homosexual inclinations, for the tsar apparently had such a dread of sleeping alone that if he did not have a woman he would press an orderly to his side. Such incidents point less to homosexual traits than to Peter's underlying neurosis. He was eventually to take as his permanent companion a German servant girl, Catherine, herself the cast-off mistress of the tsar's favourite, Alexander Menshikov, who was to be crowned as the tsarina.

His son Alexis proved an acute disappointment to his father, for in so many ways he was the opposite of all the things for which Peter stood. He compared his son to the servant in the Gospel who buried all his talents. Alexis was traditionally religious and made friends among the monks and other critics of his father's policies. Alexis had neither talent nor liking for military pursuits. His father arranged for Alexis to marry a plump German princess, Charlotte of Brunswick, but the tsarevitch neglected her for a mistress. When his wife died, he developed a passionate attachment to a Finnish servant girl Afrosinia.

Peter threatened Alexis that he must either mend his ways or be cut off like a gangrenous limb. Alexis, frightened by his father, promised that he would surrender his inheritance if he was allowed to become a monk. At last, in August 1716, the tsar, who was visiting Copenhagen, lost his patience and issued an ultimatum to Alexis, either to join him or straightaway go into a monastery. In desperation Alexis, accompanied by his mistress Afrosinia dressed in male clothes, fled to Vienna where he sought asylum from the emperor, and eventually made his way to St Elmo near Naples where he was squirrelled out by his father's envoy Peter Tolstoy who persuaded him to return to Russia. Alexis believed somewhat naively that he would be allowed to marry his mistress and give up his rights. He was arrested and brought to trial, in which he implicated, among others, his mother who was sent off to a harsher convent; the tsar ordered that her lover Glebov be impaled, wearing a fur skin to prolong his agony in the freezing cold of the Russian winter. Alexis received 40 strokes from the knout and died as a result.

How do we explain Peter's behaviour? Perhaps we do not need to do so, for his ability was unquestioned and the cruelties attributed to him were by no means unusual in the age or country in which he lived. Yet it is difficult to deny the existence in Peter's character of dark, elemental nervous spasms.

The Marxist historian Pokrovski attributed Peter's mental imbalance to the progressive inroads of syphilis. In 1706, according to a French source, he experienced what was euphemistically described as a 'disgrace in the courts of love', and he was apparently prescribed mercury. Yet, as with Henry VIII of England, there was really insufficient evidence of mental impairment to suggest that he was in the tertiary stage of syphilis in the closing years of his life.

There can be no doubt that when Peter was under stress, he developed a nervous twitch, varying in intensity, which affected the left side of his face. This could have been simply a hemi-facial spasm, paroxysmal and involuntary, affecting the left rather than the right side of the face. Normally brought on by emotional stress and fatigue, in general it appears to be unrelated to neurological illness. It seems, however, that there were occasions when in Peter's case this nervous twitch culminated in a convulsive fit and a loss of consciousness. Indeed, one of the things which he cherished in his future wife Catherine was her ability to soothe him when he felt the onset of such an attack. She laid his head in her lap until he fell asleep. When he woke refreshed, he did not remember what had happened earlier, a characteristic feature of epilepsy. 'His left eye, his left arm and left leg', Cardinal Kollonitz, the primate of Hungary, wrote portentously, 'were injured by the poison given him during the life of his brother, but there remains of this now only a fixed look in his eye and a constant movement of his arm and leg.'

This may well suggest that Peter was the victim of epileptic seizures, and even that the personality disorder from which he suffered was temporal lobe epilepsy. Although he was physically strong, he had constant bouts of ill-health. He was dangerously ill between November 1693 and January 1694 and suffered from a recurrence of fevers throughout his life. If the illness which put his life at risk was encephalitis this might also explain his predisposition to convulsive fits and the dysfunction of his brain and the violence to which it gave rise. In Peter's case as in Ivan's, in default of more definite evidence, such suggestions must be at best speculative. No doubt the long term effect of his traumatic experience as a boy and prolonged over-indulgence in alcohol also affected his health and outlook.

There were some signs at the close of his life that the tsar was losing his grip as a result of some deterioration in his mental faculties. 'No expressions', the Prussian minister told his king, 'are strong enough to give Your Majesty a just idea of the unendurable negligence and confusion with which the most important affairs are treated here.' The tsarina had herself become the victim of her husband's suspicious rage, for indiscreetly she had taken a lover, William Mons, the brother of one of Peter's discarded mistresses. Mons was executed on 14 November 1724 and his head was placed in spirits in Catherine's bedchamber as a memento of marital infidelity.

Peter's general health was failing, even though even in his last year he had enough zest to preside over the election of the new mock patriarch at the Drunken Synod, and to plunge into the cold, rough sea to help rescue a boat in difficulty. But in 1722 his physicians had diagnosed a stranguary and a stone; there was a blockage in the urethra and the bladder caused by muscle spasms which caused him severe pain. In the summer of 1724 an English surgeon Dr Horn, inserted a catheter and eventually a stone was passed. But, by mid-January 1725 as the shadows descended the dying tsar sought pardon for the ills he had perpetrated. On the early morning of 28 January 1725 he died of a painful bladder complaint and cirrhosis of the liver, a natural sequel to his over-indulgence in heavy liquor. His eyes were closed by his wife Catherine who was to succeed him as the tsarina of all the Russians.

The majority of Russian rulers after Peter the Great were to be men and women of character and even, as in the case of Catherine the Great, of some ability. Catherine herself was not a Russian but a German princess married to a youthful and imbecilic prince, Tsar Peter III, to whose violent death in 1762 she may well have been privy. Their son, Paul, who resented that he had been kept from the throne for three decades by his mother, was a psychotic who after five years' deranged rule was strangled with a scarf by one of the officers of his own bodyguard. Yet the true successor to Ivan the Terrible and Peter the Great was not really one of the Romanov tsars, the last of whom, Nicholas II, was murdered by the Bolsheviks in 1918, but the dictator Joseph Stalin in whom many of the features of Ivan and Peter, both men whom he greatly admired, reappeared with a vengeance.

X

The Bewitched King and His Legacy

Although it is normally easy for the skilled practitioner to diagnose physical disease, even the specialist may find it difficult to pinpoint the cause and character of mental illness. Yet the ills of body and mind are so subtly intertwined as to be apparently inseparable, and constantly react on each other. As in the case of the Russian tsars, physical illness may be a precipitating agent in upsetting the balance of the mind. While, in other cases, physical illness may not give rise to any severe mental impairment, yet it may, if no more than peripherally, affect the judgement of the mind.

The interrelationship of physical weakness and mental debility was exemplified particularly well in the seventeenth-century Spanish king, Charles or Carlos II, whose life was conditioned from birth by chronic ill-health. He was not in a conventional sense insane, but his physical decrepitude had its complement in mental weakness, even, if very intermittently, he showed sparks of political understanding, and even wisdom. The twin ills of Charles's body and mind, made his governance, in so far as it was governance at all, a disaster for his people.

Charles's personality, shaped so powerfully by genetic factors, was a testament to the importance of heredity in European politics. Inbreeding in royal families played a significant part in shaping the destiny of Europe. Plainly, certain physical illnesses can be passed from one generation to another. If, as Macalpine and Hunter insisted, George III was a victim of the metabolic disorder, porphyria, then, as they state, the disease may be traced back to Mary, Queen of Scots, circulated through the Stuart, Prussian and Hanoverian royal families and, from George III himself, descended to princes and princesses in the twentieth century. The congenital blood disease, haemophilia, which is passed on by females who do not themselves suffer from it to their male children, provides another instance of an inherited disease which has in recent history disastrously affected the royal families of Europe. Queen Victoria was herself a carrier, for one of her sons, Leopold, duke of Albany, three grandsons and six great-grandsons were all haemophiliacs. Through intermarriage haemophilia spread to the royal families of Spain and Russia. The tsarevitch, Alexis, heir to the last Russian tsar, Nicholas II, was a victim and it was his mother's search for a cure that led to her falling under the evil influence of Rasputin with such sinister consequences for Russia and the world.

153

In the sixteenth and seventeenth centuries royal inbreeding became pre-eminently a characteristic of the Austrian and Spanish Habsburgs. *'Tu, felix Austria nube; alii gerant bella'* ('You, happy Austria, marry; others wage wars') reads the sixteenth-century tag. The Habsburgs hardly ceased to wage wars, but they intermarried with enthusiasm to the ultimate detriment of their heritage. First cousins married first cousins; uncles married nieces. Philip II's fourth and last marriage, the union which eventually produced an heir to his Spanish throne, was to Anne, the daughter of the emperor Maximilian II, his cousin. His son, Philip III, married Margaret, the sister of the Habsburg emperor Ferdinand II. Their son, Philip IV, married first a French princess and then later in his life another Habsburg, his niece Mariana. The eventual fruit of all these marital endeavours was the last Habsburg king of Spain, Charles (Carlos) II, in whose personality the congenital deficiencies of inbreeding, physical and mental, were to be powerfully and disastrously concentrated. Although to some he appeared an idiot, he was not insane, and yet he was the victim of an inheritance which was in some sense warped physically and mentally.

Charles II's father, Philip IV, had fathered no fewer than fifteen children by his two wives; but of these children two miscarried, three lived only long enough to be baptized and six lived between two weeks and four years. The king who was not unjustifiably nicknamed *'El Rey Donjuanesco'*, fathered many bastards who, unlike his legitimate children, seemed to be relatively healthy. Of these the best known was the gallant and able Don Juan, even though it has recently been argued that he was actually not the king's child by the actress Ines de Calderon but the fruit of her affair with her current lover Medina de las Torres.

But while the bastard children of Philip IV flourished, the legitimate line was feeble to the point of extinction. The Spanish medical historian Gregorio Marañón held that Philip suffered from syphilis, sustaining a serious attack in 1627, and that syphilitic symptoms were present in his final illness. Whether Philip's 'sexual adventurism' undermined his capacity as king seems doubtful since for most of his reign he was an energetic ruler trying to cope with overwhelming problems, but his health could conceivably have had serious consequences for his offspring.[1]

The personal problem which Philip IV found it difficult to resolve satisfactorily was that of succession to his throne. His first wife, the French princess Isabella, suffered miscarriages. She left two children, a boy, Baltazar Carlos, immortalized in Velasquez's glowing portrait, and a girl, Maria Teresa who was eventually to marry her first cousin, the French king, Louis XIV. Baltazar Carlos was betrothed as a child to a cousin, Mariana, the daughter of the emperor as well as his father's niece, but in 1646 the prince died of smallpox shortly before his seventeenth birthday. His mother, the queen, had died three years earlier.

Bereft of a legitimate male heir, the widowed Spanish king, in some respects prematurely aged, felt it his duty to cast round for a new wife in the hope of siring a future king. His choice fell on his niece, the princess Mariana, who had been intended originally as a bride for his own son. When he married her in 1649, she was fifteen years old, thirty years younger than her husband, but she proved fertile. In 1649 she gave birth to Margarita Maria, who was later to be an empress of Austria, but what Philip wanted was not a daughter but a son. So news of the birth of a prince, Felipe Prospero, in 1656 was an occasion for great rejoicing throughout Spain. Unfortunately the sparkle of the fireworks soon faded, for Felipe Prospero was a sickly epileptic who died in November 1661. There was to be one last chance. To Philip's immense relief, depressed as he so often was in his closing years at the thought of his crumbling empire, its disasters as it seemed to him in some ways the sequel to his own misspent life, another son was born on 6 November 1661, the future Charles II.

So when four years later, in 1665, Charles became king, the omens for the future of his country were neither politically nor personally good. Philip IV had died on 17 September 1665, taking leave of his wife, Mariana, two days earlier and commanding the order of the Golden Fleece to be conferred on his four-year-old heir. 'May God,' he said feelingly, 'in his mercy make you happier than I have been.' When, however, his illegitimate son, Don Juan, asked to see the king who had earlier publicly recognized him as his son, he was rebuffed. 'Who asked him to come,' Philip had murmured. 'This is a time only for dying.'

To some it seemed as if it was not only the king who was dying but that the Spanish Empire was itself bleeding to death. Although there were to be some superficial signs of economic recovery in Charles II's reign in the shape of a rise in agrarian production and commercial expansion along the Cantabrian and Mediterranean coasts, the Spanish economy, more especially that of Castile, had been exhausted by continuous warfare; the currency was in chaos; industrial development was negligible; much overseas trade was under the control of foreign merchants. Spain's international prestige had waned for it had been forced to recognize the independence of the Low Countries, had lost Portugal and was overshadowed by the powerful France of Louis XIV. All foreign commentators agreed gloomily on Spain's impoverished state. 'If', the French envoy commented in 1689, 'one examines the government of this monarch . . . one will find an excessive state of disorder.'[2] What it needed was a skillful helmsman who could save the creaky ship from sinking. Although the significance of the Spanish king's personal influence over government must not be overstressed, the long reign of a physically sick and mentally retarded monarch can only be regarded as a major contribution to Spain's decline.[3]

Since Charles was still only a young boy of four, by his will Philip IV had sought to provide for the future government of his country by setting up a committee or junta to advise the queen mother, Mariana, who was to be regent and chief executive. A pious, narrow woman who was customarily dressed in the sombre garb of a widow or even of a nun, Mariana lacked the experience and the capacity to govern effectively, nor, devoted as she was to her son, had she any real understanding of the deep and difficult problems by which her adopted country was afflicted. She placed her trust in her confessor, a scheming Austrian Jesuit, Father Everardo Nithard. As Philip's will forbade foreigners from serving on the council of state, she managed to get Nithard naturalized and appointed Inquisitor-General.

But from the start of the regency Mariana's path was far from smooth, for she had to cope with the king's half-brother, Philip's bastard son, the ambitious, able and attractive Don Juan. Don Juan ousted the queen-mother's principal minister, the Jesuit Father Nithard but, not assiduous enough, he allowed the queen to confer power on yet another one of her minions, Fernando Valenzuela. It was in this hot-house atmosphere, in a bigoted court, governed by rigid etiquette, but riven by intrigue, distrust and political skullduggery, that the young king was brought up.

From the start Charles was a sickly, retarded child. His upbringing did nothing to help resolve the temperamental and physical problems which he had inherited, perhaps in view of their serious nature it could hardly have been expected to do so. For nearly four years he had to be breast-fed by a bevy of fourteen wet nurses. He was rachitic and unable to walk properly because his legs would not support him.[4] At the age of nine he still could not read or write, and his general knowledge throughout his life was to remain feeble. He was eight and a half before he went to his first hunt on foot and he did not ride a horse until 1671, though later in life hunting was to be one of his principal recreations; the carefully regulated battue affording him some pleasure as did the gentler art of music, which momentarily stilled the traumas by which his life was already engulfed. When he was ill with gastric fever in May 1671, his death was daily expected. He had persistent bouts of ill-health. His Habsburg jaw was so elongated that he found difficulty in masticating his food.

Some years later, in 1686, the papal nuncio wrote of Charles II that

he is short rather than tall; frail, not badly formed; his face on the whole is ugly; he has a long neck, a broad face and chin, with the typical Habsburg lower lip, not very large eyes of turquoise blue and a fine delicate complexion. He has a melancholic and faintly surprised look. His hair is long and fair and combed back so as to bare the ears. He cannot stand upright when walking, unless he leans against a wall, a table or somebody else. He is as weak in body as in mind. Now and then he gives signs of intelligence, memory and a certain liveliness, but not at present; usually he shews himself slow and indifferent, torpid and indolent, and seems to be stupified. One can do with him what one wishes because he lacks his own will.[5]

'Of the five Habsburg kings', Marañon later wrote incisively, 'Charles V inspires enthusiasm, Philip II respect, Philip III indifference, Philip IV sympathy and Carlos II pity.'

Yet when on 6 November 1675 Charles came of age, momentarily and rather surprisingly he showed a flash of energy, even a will of his own, which may indicate that with better training he might have showed gumption. Obviously resentful of his mother's dominating will, secretly he penned a letter to his half-brother, Don Juan (whom his mother and the council had now decided to send as viceroy to Sicily) requesting him to come to Madrid to help in the government. 'On the sixth (November)', the king wrote, 'I enter into the government of my kingdoms. I need your person at my side to help me, and rid me of the Queen my mother. On Wednesday the 6th at 10.45 you will be in my antechamber.' When, two days before, on 4 November, the king was presented with a decree which would have prolonged the powers of the queen mother and the governing junta, on the grounds of his own incapacity, the king actually refused to sign the document. On Don Juan's arrival at the palace, he was cheered by the mob and accompanied the king to the Mass and Te Deum. Did the palace revolution signify that the youthful monarch would become king indeed?

Far from it; it was to be the shortest day of dupes in history. After the religious service Charles paid a visit to his mother with whom he stayed for two hours. Emerging in great distress, tears welling down his cheeks, once and for all Charles's act of rebellion was at an end. 'Don Fernando Valenzuela', Sir William Godolphin reported, 'whispered me in the Ear and said all this Stir will come to nothing.[6]

The king's efforts to untie the apron strings which bound him to his mother had failed and he once more became thoroughly dependent upon her. He could not resist the pressures which she brought to bear upon him. Henceforth the king was to be a negative factor in his own government, rarely attending council meetings or giving orders on his own initiative. In fact the foundations of the queen mother's government were less than rock-solid, even though Don Valenzuela was in the saddle again, appointed captain-general of Granada and the obvious 'prime minister'. If the king himself acquiesced, many of the grandees denounced the favours Valenzuela enjoyed, and complained of the incompetence of his government. While Valenzuela might appear to hold all the cards, it was the king's half-brother, Don Juan, who remained the joker in the pack. A group of grandees demanded Don Juan's return (his own signature was actually the eleventh on the petition) and the dismissal of Valenzuela. On Christmas Day 1676 the unpopular minister fled to the royal apartments in the Escorial, but was later arrested and banished.

Don Juan's return to power was greeted warmly by his half-brother the king as well as by most of the grandees. It seemed possible that Don Juan might initiate reform in the government, and even train his young half-brother, the king, in his duties. The queen mother was ordered to leave Madrid and to reside in the Alcazar at Toledo while Don Juan set about the difficult, if not impossible, task of getting his half-brother to undertake the business of a king more seriously. He tried to teach him to write in a more literate fashion, and he was determined that the king should be seen by his people and attend the meeting of the Cortes. The king had rarely left the neighbourhood of Madrid, his furthest journey so far had been from Madrid to Aranjuez, but Don Juan arranged for him to go to Saragossa, the longest of the three journeys from his capital that he was ever to take.

Don Juan was well intentioned, conscientious and not without ability. It was within his powers to galvanize the Spanish government but the stars in their courses seemed to fight against him. Popular rumour, through the medium of satire, complained that he was tardy in initiating much-needed reform. The harvest failed with consequential famine in 1677; and the high price of bread made him unpopular. Plague struck many parts of Spain. Inflation was at its highest ever. The war with the French was ended but only at the cost of a humiliating treaty, signed at Nymwegen in 1678.

Don Juan strove for reform but time was not on his side. Above all he had to be eternally vigilant in the king's company lest Charles should return to his mother. He wanted Charles to attend the Cortes in the various parts of his dominions, in Aragon, Catalonia, Valencia and Navarre, but, apart from the journey to Saragossa, the king remained immobile. His mother's residence at Toledo, from which she bombarded her impressionable son with bitter missives of complaint at the treatment to which she had been subjected, became the focal-point for gatherings of the increasing number of disaffected grandees. Then Don Juan fell ill, probably with acute cholecystitis, for the autopsy after his death recorded that two stones had been found in his gall bladder, one the size of a walnut, the other of a hazel-nut. After battling with his illness for two months Don Juan died aged fifty on 17 September 1679.

Don Juan's death put paid to any hope of effective reform, and indeed to any possibility, remote as this doubtless was, of Charles himself taking up the reins of government. It was hardly surprising that four days after Don Juan's death the king was re-united with his mother at Toledo, and government relapsed into the usual uninformed incompetence. The spiral of mismanagement continued. Once more the financial situation plunged towards bankruptcy, and without the bankers' manipulation of the money supply the crown's credit would have collapsed totally. There was, however, nothing that anyone could do to overcome the financial shortfall. Between 1693 and 1699 the government was to suspend the repayment of state debts. 'The present exigencies of this monarchy,' Stanhope reported, 'are inconceivable. Most of the bills they have sent for Flanders have been lately sent back . . . I am assured . . . that upon no branch can be found a credit for 100,000 ducats, be the occasion ever so urgent.'[7] Nothing could be expected from the frail and feeble-minded monarch who was little more than a cipher in his kingdom.

Yet there was one aspect of the situation which directly involved the king and the future of the state: his own marriage. His doctors had already strongly recommended that in view of certain physical manifestations on the king's part, the time had come for Charles to marry. But who was to be the bride who would suffer his dubious embraces? Was it to be an Austrian princess, another Habsburg, as his mother wanted, or a French princess as Don Juan had originally favoured? Since the queen mother's candidate was as yet only five years old, the French princess, Marie Louise, a daughter of the duke of Orléans and a niece of Louis XIV, eventually proved to be the more acceptable candidate. Louis himself, in spite of being told by cipher that Charles was physically repulsive, approved an alliance which he thought would be profitable for France.

So the frail Spanish king made the second longest journey of his life, to meet his future bride at Burgos. His queen, Marie Louise, was a lively seventeen-year-old girl, ill at ease in a land whose language she did not speak and whose customs she found too rigid; as a symbol of French influence she was always to be unpopular with the Spaniards. She eventually did what she could to fulfil her duty as the king's wife, but without avail. For it seems that although the king attempted intercourse, he suffered from premature ejaculation, so that he was unable to achieve penetration. The French king, anxious about the future, asked to be kept closely informed about the most intimate details of the king's private life. 'Finally, sire', the French ambassador Rébenec told his royal master on 23 December 1688, 'she [the queen] once told me that she was anxious to confide in me . . . that she was really not a virgin any longer, but that as far as she could figure things, she believed she would never have children.' By stealth Rébenec managed to procure a pair of the king's drawers – 'he does not wear his shirts longer than the waist' – and had them examined by surgeons for traces of sperm; but the doctors could not agree about their findings.

The queen's own position was an unenviable one, for except when there were unconfirmed reports of her pregnancy, she remained deeply unpopular. Probably in part as a result of an excessive consumption of sweetmeats, which may have been a form of compensation for her failure to produce an heir, she became increasingly corpulent and so less attractive to her feeble husband. To her uncle the French king she wrote of her fear of being poisoned. She suffered illness, apparently of a gastric nature, in August 1687 and again in November 1688. On 8 February 1689 she had an accident while out riding and though apparently not seriously injured took to her bed, complained that she had been poisoned and a few days later, 12 February, she died.

Since there was no heir, the question of the king's re-marriage became a matter of urgency, both from the point of view of Spain and the great powers. Charles's mother once again looked longingly towards a possible Austrian connection. Mariana's brother, the emperor Leopold I, had a daughter but she was inconveniently too young, being only nine years of age, but Leopold's wife, the empress, had a sister, indeed three, and it was for one of these, Maria Ana of Neuburg, that the king, doubtless influenced by his mother, expressed a positive choice. Maria Ana's father, the Elector Palatine, Philip William, was a far from wealthy prince but to have one daughter the empress and another the queen of Spain was no negligible achievement, more especially as Maria Ana was soon to show herself ready to pillage her new country of everything she could lay her hands on, including works of art, to enrich her German family. So it was that Charles II made the third longest journey of his life, to Valladolid to greet his bride whom he married on 4 May.

What Maria Ana no more than Marie Louise could give her husband was a child. There were constant rumours of a pregnancy, perhaps circulated deliberately by members of her household, but fruit there was none. Although Maria Ana failed to give the country what it wanted, she was a woman with a strong will, determined to influence her country's government and sustain the Austrian Habsburg interest. She did not see eye to eye with her fellow countrywoman, the queen mother Mariana, but Mariana died of breast cancer on 16 May 1696 in the 'odour of misplaced sanctity'. The removal of the principal influence in Charles's short life meant that he became more and more the prey of the competing interests at his court.

From time to time Charles had periods of improved health and mental lucidity, but the general picture, as the poor man himself sensed, was one of slow but steady decay. The letters which foreign envoys sent home to their governments read like an oscillating temperature chart. 'His Catholic Majesty', Stanhope told Lord Nottingham in May 1693, 'is now well, and abroad again, for joy of whose recovery the 18th instant [there] was a masquerade on horseback by night with flambeaux, performed before the palace.' 'His Catholic Majesty', he wrote three years later, 16 September 1696, 'has been extreme ill these seven days; but, thanks to God, is now much better by taking the quinine, yet not so safe as his good subjects wish him.' Three days later he told the duke of Shrewsbury that the king was out of danger but

his constitution is so very weak, and broken much beyond his age, that it is generally feared what will be the success of another attack. They cut his hair off in this sickness, which the decay of nature had almost done before, all his crown being bald. He has a ravenous stomach, and swallows all he eats whole, for his nether jaw stands so much out, that his two rows of teeth cannot meet; to compensate which, he has a prodigious wide throat, so that a gizzard or liver of a hen passes down whole, and his weak stomach not being able to digest it, he voids in the same manner.[8]

Yet a fortnight later the English envoy was to report that the king's health had much improved. The improvement was not to last, for within a month he was again taken ill, and 'has had his fit every day since' – Stanhope was writing on 14 November 1696 – 'nor is he wholly clear in the intermediate space'. The festivities which had been arranged to celebrate his recovery were held in suspense.

The Grandees and Foreign Ministers were admitted into the King's bedchamber on his birthday, His Majesty being in bed. The ceremony passed in a low bow, without a word on our side . . . they sometimes make him rise out of his bed, much against his will, and beyond his strength, the better to conceal his illness abroad. He is not only extreme weak in body, but has a great weight of melancholy and discontent upon his spirits, attributed in a great measure to the Queen's continued importunities to make him alter his will.[9]

Yet, by next April, it was reported that he had killed seven wolves while out hunting. In October 1697 he and the queen were at the shrine of San Diego at Alcala (whose body had been employed, as it had been earlier in the case of Don Carlos, to bring about a recovery of the king's health) to offer thanks giving for a further escape from death.

The fluctuations in the king's health were inevitably matters of the greatest interest to the courts of Europe, more especially to those who had a personal stake in the succession to the Spanish throne. While the king literally tottered from one ceremonial function to another, rumour began to circulate that the king's health, more especially his impotence, may have been induced by supernatural agencies, in other words that he was diabolically 'possessed'.

As early as December 1688 the French ambassador Rébenec had reported to Louis XIV that 'a Dominican monk, friend of the King's confessor, received a revelation that the King and Queen were bewitched. I remark in passing, Sire, that the king of Spain has long since got into his head that he is bewitched.' Theologians had in fact long recognized that impotence could itself be a symptom of demonic possession.[10] Charles raised the question himself in an interview with Inquisitor-General Valladares in 1696; but the Council of the Inquisition had then decided not to investigate the matter further. In January 1698 the matter was, however, raised again, with a new Inquisitor-General, the austere ascetic Juan Tomas de Rocaberti.

High politics now began to have some bearing on the question. There were many who resented the powerful influence of the queen and her pro-Austrian policy, and those who looked towards France rather than Austria had an able spokesman in Cardinal Portocarrero, an energetic and ambitious priest of rectitude if of little scholarship; his library was described as 'one of the three virgins of Madrid', the other two being the queen and the sword of the duke of Medina Sidonia, reputedly a coward. Potocarrero was strongly critical of the queen and eager to undermine her influence. It was thought that one of the ways in which this could be done would be to change the king's confessor, Father Pedro Matilla, a man in whom the king had great confidence but regarded commonly as a creature of the queen, 'this army of vermin, or better swarm of devils' as Don Sebastian de Cores impolitely described the queen's following.

So Father Matilla retired to the seclusion of his monastery where he died within a month, and was replaced as royal confessor by Froilan Diaz, a respectable scholar who had been a professor at Alcala University. His appointment was to have profound consequences both for the king and his country. Diaz, who was much intrigued by the notion that the king had been bewitched, and that this explained his impotence, made contact with his friend Antonio de Arguelles who had apparently had some success in exorcizing a group of nuns disturbed by demonic possession at the convent at Cangas de Tineo in Asturias where he was chaplain. With the support of the Inquisitor-General, Tomas de Rocaberti, but without the approval of the local bishop. Tomas Reluz of Oviedo, Diaz sought Arguelles' help to try to discover what demonic agencies had caused the king's rumoured bewitchment. Arguelles agreed to Diaz's request. His instructions were contained in a coded letter in which the inquisitor was described as the *amo* and Diaz as the *amigo*. On 14 March 1698 Stanhope had written to the earl of Portland at Paris, hinting at the rumour that Charles was bewitched:

> The King is so very weak, he can scarcely lift his head to feed himself; and so extremely melancholy that neither his buffoons, dwarfs, nor puppet-shows . . . can in the least divert him from fancying everything that is said or done to be a temptation of the devil, and never thinking himself safe but with his Confessor, and two friars by his side, whom he makes lie in his chamber every night.

On 11 June he wrote again that the 'King will not bear to talk of business of any kind', and said that his relations with his wife were so strained that he believed that she actually designed to kill him.[11]

It was a week later, 18 June 1698, that Father Arguelles was told that he must write the names of the king and queen on a piece of paper which he was to keep sealed or concealed in his breast while he was exorcising the afflicted nuns. If an opportunity presented itself he was to ask Satan outright whether either of the two named on the paper in his breast was bewitched. The devil proved accommodating. The king was indeed bewitched 'and this was due to destroy his generative organs, and to render him incapable of administering the kingdom'.

The spell, made at moonlight and especially potent when there was a new moon, had been given to the king when he was fourteen years old in a drink. Father Arguelles reported his findings to his superior, recommending that the king should eat his food and digest it more slowly, that all his food and drink should be blessed before consumption, and that he should be sure to drink half a pint of olive oil a day, which was certainly sound and realistic advice. The confessor and the Inquisitor-General persisted in pursuing the matter further, endeavouring in vain to trace the witch. Casilda by name, who had prepared the charm. Arguelles found that he was getting drawn deeper and deeper into problems which he could no longer resolve. He told his correspondents that the nuns were proving difficult and that the devil, not called Beelzebub for nothing, had himself confessed that much of what he had said was a tissue of lies. All that the good father could advise was a close attention to the remedies already recommended, such as a change of all the king's bedding, furniture and clothing, and the dismissal of his physicians, all advice that could probably do no harm. It might be a good thing if the king changed his place of residence, he added. New physicians were appointed and the king went on a visit to the shrine of San Diego at Alcala.

Throughout the summer of 1698 the English envoy, Stanhope, who had kept up a running commentary on the king's health, confirmed the rumour that it was thought that he was likely to die in the very near future. The gazettes, he told his son, James, on 25 June, tried to give the impression that the king was in perfect health, but this was designed simply to gull the public.

> 'Tis true that he is every day abroad, but *haeret lateri lethalis arundo*; his ankles and knees well again, his eyes big, the lids are as red as scarlet, and the rest of his face a greenish yellow. His tongue is *travada* . . . that is, he has such a fumbling in his speech, those near him hardly understand him, at which he sometimes grows angry and asks if they all be deaf.[12]

Eighteen days later, on 29 June Stanhope reported that the doctors had diagnosed his illness 'as "*alfereza insensata*", which sounds in English, a stupid epilepsy'. On the evening of that day as the king walked with the queen in the garden he felt a swimming sensation in his head. When he retired to make his devotions he cried out to his gentleman-in-waiting, the duke of Uceda, that he was falling, and collapsed unconscious into the duke's arms, 'deprived of all sense'. Two other fits followed. 'There is', Stanhope told Chancellor Methuen of Ireland on 9 July, 'not the least hope of this King's recovery, and we are every night in apprehensions of hearing he is dead in the morning, though the Queen lugs him out abroad every day, to make people believe he is well till her designs are ripe.'[13]

These bizarre happenings have to be placed within the framework of the international scene, for it was in 1698 that the great powers tried to come to an agreed decision – without recourse to the devil – about the future of the Spanish Empire should Charles II die. By the first of such treaties to which the great powers were a party which had been negotiated at Vienna in 1668, it had been decided that in the event of Charles's death the emperor would get Spain, the Indies and Spanish territory in northern Italy, and the French would receive the Netherlands, the Franche-Comté, the Philippines, Navarre and Naples. As the balance of power in Europe shifted, especially after the accession of Louis XIV's enemy, William, the Dutch Stadtholder, to the English throne, so this solution became less acceptable, more especially to the French.

As the king's health declined, yet another treaty of partition was negotiated, though without the participation of the Spanish king. By this agreement the electoral prince of Bavaria, Joseph Ferdinand, who was the grandson of the Spanish king's sister, Margarita, would inherit the Spanish dominions outside Europe, the archduke Charles, the emperor's second son, would get Milan, and the dauphin, Louis XIV's heir, the Sicilies, some Italian territory and Guipuzcoa. If Joseph Ferdinand became the Spanish king, this would seemingly avert the danger of the Spanish empire being incorporated into either the domains of the French king or the Austrian emperor. What it failed to do was to take any account of the personal wishes of Charles himself. Meanwhile the Spanish court was itself the scene of a struggle between the embattled interests of the pro-Austrians, led by their ambassador Count Harrach, and aided and abetted by the queen, and of the pro-French led by Cardinal Portocarrero, both of whom tried to get the ear of the debilitated monarch.

While the great powers wrangled the king's confessors were still concerned to liberate the king from his diabolic possession. The queen, who had herself been exorcized in December 1698 to promote her fertility, was angered by the rumour which asserted that she had been responsible for bewitching the king. The death of the Inquisitor-General in June 1699 gave her the chance to rid herself of her enemies at court. She managed to get a tame cleric, Baltazar de Mendoza, the bishop of Segovia, appointed Inquisitor-General, and eventually Father Diaz was dismissed from his post as royal confessor. An interminable investigation into his conduct followed which was at last brought to an end by Father Diaz's acquittal four years after Charles's own death. To complicate the situation further the duke of Savoy despatched a Capuchin friar, Father Mauro Tenda, with some reputation as an exorcist to investigate further the supposed bewitchment of the king. He set off for Madrid where he soon became involved in a series of curious incidents which underlined the superstitious beliefs of the king and his wife, for he discovered that they had both secreted small bags of charms, hair, nail parings and the like, which they kept under their pillows. Father Tenda, who was evidently a self-assured priest, managed to win Charles's confidence and temporarily his health seemed also to improve. Stanhope, reporting in 1699 declared that the king seemed fit and vigorous. When he and the queen visited the sepulchres at the Escorial, the queen showed a surprising devotion to the body of the king's mother. 'They talk', he added, 'of a famous exorcist come from Germany who has dissolved several charms by which the king has been bound ever since a child; yet not all of them, but that there is great hope of the rest, and then he will not only have perfect health, but succession.'[14] 'Many people tell me', the king himself confided to Cardinal de Cordoba, 'I am bewitched and I well believe it; such are the things I experience and suffer.'

But the exorcists' confidence was soon to be sapped, in part as sequel to an odd incident which occurred when a crazy woman made an unauthorized entry into the palace and approached the king. Charles, alarmed by the unusual apparition, pulled out a piece of the true cross which he carried with him to ward off the powers of evil. A royal clerk, Don Jose de Olmo, was instructed to find out where the woman lived. He discovered that she lodged with two other women as crazy as herself, for they whispered that they kept the king locked up in a little box in their room. Father Tenda's help was invoked and together with Father Diaz the two priests were despatched to interrogate and, if necessary, to exorcise the women.

Long before these events had occurred, the king's health was failing fast. Shortly after his birth he had been described as having 'the most beautiful features, a large head, dark skin and somewhat plump' but on the verge of his thirty-ninth year he had become an emaciated figure suffering from a terminal illness. He had been a virtual invalid since birth, probably afflicted by a bone disease, acromegaly, the result of an inherited endocrine dysfunction, and occasioned by a tumour of the pituitary gland. This illness would explain his strange physical appearance, his over-large head, his exaggerated Habsburg chin, the nature of his extremities as well as his impotence. The illness gave rise to fits of dizziness and what seem to have been epileptic convulsions.

Although there were periods of remission in his degenerative malady, he had neither the intelligence nor the will to govern his empire about even the geography of which he was strangely ill informed. The nature of his upbringing, the inadequacy of his education, the stiff etiquette of his court, his dependence upon his mother, the psychology of his religious beliefs, helped to create a mentally retarded and hypersensitive monarch who was little more than a figurehead in the vast empire of which he was nominally the head; the only issue about which he felt strongly was the integrity of his dominions after his death. Describing the impression which the king made as he walked in the Corpus Christi procession, Stanhope wrote:

All who saw him said he could not make one straight step, but staggered all the way; nor could it be otherwise expected, after he had had two falls a day or two before, walking in his own lodgings, when his legs doubled under him by mere weakness. In one of them he hurt one eye, which appeared to bu much swelled, and black and blue in the procession; the other being quite sunk into his head; the nerves, they say, being contracted by his paralytic distemper.

The Spanish government was in a more chaotic state than ever, weakened by the process of decentralization which the king had assisted by creating a vast number of new nobles, and by bureaucratic incompetence. Trade, a foreign diplomat reported, 'is dead. There are 40,000 artisans out of work, beggars are dying of hunger and crimes are committed daily in the street for want of bread.'

Behind this crumbling façade the court was the scene of a power struggle between the queen and her Austrian supporters and the pro-French party headed by Cardinal Portocarrero. The precarious balance of power had been upset by the death in February 1699 of the seven-year-old electoral prince of smallpox. After his death Louis XIV and the English king William III negotiated on 11 June 1699 yet another treaty of partition. The Holy Roman Emperor Leopold's second son, Charles, would receive the major part of the Spanish Empire while Louis's son, the dauphin, would get what had been granted to him under the first treaty together with the duchy of Lorraine. The settlement was flimsy and unsatisfactory, for both the main parties distrusted each other, the emperor who was not a signatory called it unjust nor had the Spanish king been consulted.

The pitiful king was in the last stages of his illness. He was given extreme unction on 28 September 1700 and five days later, with Cardinal Portocarrero there to guide him, he dictated his last will and testament, bequeathing his empire in its entirety 'without allowing the least dismemberment of the Monarchy founded with such glory by my ancestors' to the grandson of Louis XIV, Philip, duke of Anjou. It was perhaps the most decisive, certainly the most important, act in his whole life. Just before 3.00 p.m. on All Saints' Day 1700 Charles II died. Within weeks Philip of Anjou was proclaimed king as Philip V, the partition treaty was torn up and Europe was plunged into thirteen years of bloody and costly conflict before his title was fully authenticated.

It is arguable that Charles II had only a peripheral and superficial impact on the history of Spain. For the first fourteen years of his reign he had been a minor and during the last two decades of his life he was little more than a cipher. Even if he had been in better health, he would still have been unable to resolve the economic and political problems which were a part of the legacy which he had inherited. Yet if he had been physically and mentally more vigorous, less under the thumb of his mother, he might have been better equipped to break the rule of the noble oligarchy and even to initiate needed reforms in his country's administration. His half-brother, Don Juan,

Charles II of Spain as a young boy, from an engraving by Larmessin, (photograph: Witt Library, The Courtauld Institute of Art, London)

Philip V, King of Spain, from an engraving by Pierre Drevet after Hyacinthe Rigaud (photograph: The Courtauld Institute of Art, London)

had shown some perspicacity during his brief period of government. Yet the task was a Herculean one which might well have daunted a prince of much greater capacity than Charles II. As it was his physical ill-health and mental frailty had proved to be a disaster for his empire, and in some sense for Europe as a whole.

The future history of the Spanish royal house was to show that, in terms of melancholy, retarded mentality and ill-health, the legacy of Charles II was as much pathological and psychological as territorial. For it was surely ironical that after thirty-five years of the decrepit Charles II Spain should have had as king for forty-six years Philip V, the grandson of Charles II's sister, Maria Teresa, who had married the French king, Louis XIV, and so was a great-grandson of Philip IV of Spain. In his veins there flowed metaphorically the accumulated 'toxic' genes and chromosomes of the houses of Habsburg and Bourbon. Understandably Philip V experienced intermittent attacks of manic depression which made it impossible for him to govern effectively or even, on occasions, at all.[15] Had he not had an extremely capable wife in Elizabeth Farnese and been served by a series of competent ministers, Philip might well have been a disastrous ruler of his great empire. Nor was his death in 1746 the end of the matter, for his son and successor, Ferdinand VI, suffered from a similarly debilitating mental illness. So for a century Spain lacked a monarch whose physical and mental health was equal to the responsibilities of government.

It had taken thirteen years of bloody war before the last will and testament of Charles II had been vindicated; thousands were to die and be maimed on the great battlefields of Europe – at Blenheim, Ramillies, Oudenarde, Malplaquet; Gibraltar was seized by the British; treasuries were exhausted and national debts piled high before the great powers, by the treaty of Utrecht in 1713, eventually accepted Louis XIV's grandson as king of Spain.

Philip V was a sombre, serious-minded and devout man. He was not, as Saint-Simon put it, 'born with any superiority of intellect nor did he possess the least trace of what is called imagination. He was cold, silent, sad and sober, knowing no pleasure except hunting, fearing society, fearing even himself, seldom coming forward, seldom attracted to others, solitary and retiring by preference and habit. He was inordinately vain, and could bear no opposition.'[16] But he was also very highly sexed, so that he flitted inappropriately and continuously from his confessor's closet to his wife's bed. His first wife, the lively, youthful Marie Louise of Savoy, momentarily diverted him from his serious and stuffy routine, inducing him to playing games like 'hide and seek' and the 'cuckoo game', but she died at the early age of twenty-six in February 1714. 'The king of Spain', Saint-Simon wrote, 'was much moved, but somewhat in the royal manner. They persuaded him to go out hunting and shooting, so as to breathe the fresh air. On one of these excursions, he found himself within sight of the procession that bore the queen's body to the Escorial. He gazed after it; followed it with his eyes, and went back to his hunting. Princes, are they human?'[17]

His widowhood was short, for in 1715 he married Elizabeth Farnese, the daughter of the duke of Parma, a redoubtable and highly intelligent woman who virtually replaced her comatose husband as the real ruler of Spain. She was never popular with her new subjects, for she distorted her adopted country's foreign policy to push forward the interests of her own Farnese family, and more especially of the children that she had by Philip. But she was utterly indispensable to her husband, and they were rarely parted from each other, sharing a 'small bed' together. She seems to have established her ascendancy over her husband by a form of sexual blackmail. 'The king's own nature', Saint-Simon commented, 'was her strongest weapon, and one which she sometimes used against him. There were nocturnal refusals, arousing tempests; the king shrieked and threatened, sometimes did worse. She held firm, wept, and on occasion defended herself.[18]

The king's ancestry was psychologically disturbing. His grandfather Louis XIV told him:

No other person will tell you what I can say to you. You yourself are witness of the nervous disorders originating in the indolence of the Kings, your predecessors: take warning by their example, and remedy, by an opposite conduct, the ruinous effects which they have entailed in the Spanish monarchy. But I confess to you with concern, that while you freely expose yourself to the perils of war, you want courage to combat this odious vice, which overpowers and prevents you from applying [yourself] to business.

The future was to show that Louis's fears were well grounded.

Philip became the victim of a deep melancholy from which it was difficult to rouse him. The first really serious attack apparently occurred in autumn of 1717 when he complained that he felt as if he was being consumed by a fierce internal fire, as if the sun was striking his shoulder and sending a piercing ray to the very centre of his body. When his physicians examined him they could find nothing wrong and assumed that he was suffering from delusions. The king became even more frenetic, declaring that death alone would prove whether he or his doctors were right. He was convinced that he was dying in mortal sin. The French ambassador somewhat more realistically attributed his troubles to the demands which he was making on his wife. 'The king', he reported, 'is visibly wasting away through excessive use he makes of the queen. He is utterly worn out.' The hypochondriacal delusions from which he suffered as well as the belief that current disasters were a divine punishment for his personal inadequacies were symptomatic of his manic depression. 'For the last eight months', his chief minister, Alberoni, commented, 'he has been showing symptoms of insanity, his imagination inducing him to believe that he is destined to die immediately, fancying himself attacked by all sorts of disease in him.'

Philip was so convinced that he was about to die that he would summon his confessor to his bedside at any time of the night or day. His ministers suggested that he should draw up a will making his wife, Elizabeth Farnese, the regent. The rumour of his illness percolated to foreign courts, stimulating the great powers to take steps to protect their own interests should his wife become regent or the king die. 'Three sly and artful French men' were intruded as his medical attendants while the queen, wishing to counter French influence, persuaded her father, the duke of Parma, to despatch his own physician, Dr Cervi, to attend her husband. It was only the outbreak of war with France and England, the two countries acting in unusual concert together against Spain, that at last roused the king from his lethargy.

But Philip's introspective melancholy was to recur, causing an internal political crisis which greatly taxed the queen's own resources. His religious scrupulosity once more reinforced his belief that the disasters befalling Spain were a divine retribution for his own failings. In the dim recesses of his mind, he came to the conclusion that he was in bounden duty obliged to resign his throne. He was not fit to govern the country, a conclusion which it hardly needed divine guidance to suggest was undoubtedly true.

Even before the end of 1723 rumour was sweeping through Paris that Philip was suffering from religious mania and was thinking of giving up the throne. The more sceptical wondered whether there might be other reasons for such a decision. Philip in his heart of hearts hankered after a return to his native France, and the delicate health of the young French king, Louis XV, continued to rouse in him hopes of succession to the French throne. But he could not be both king of France and Spain. If he was no longer king of Spain, then his chances of succeeding Louis would be the greater.

On 10 January 1724 Philip announced his decision to abdicate in favour of his son, Luis.[19] 'I have resolved', he declared, 'to retire from the heavy burden of governing this monarchy, in order to concentrate my mind on death during the time that remains to me and to pray for my salvation in that other and more permanent kingdom.' 'Thank God', he said, 'I am no longer a king, and that the remainder of my days I shall apply myself to the service of God and to solitude.'

Philip's retirement was something of a charade. Although he liked to don the habit of a Franciscan friar and announced modest cut-backs in his household, he chose as his retirement home the magnificent new palace of La Granja at San Ildefonso, the building of which had been a heavy drain on the Spanish treasury, having already cost some 24 million pesos. It was San Ildefonso which in practice continued to be the seat of government, for neither Philip nor his ambitious wife ceased to interest themselves in affairs of state.

In any case the new king and queen were hopelessly inexperienced. Luis was undoubtedly popular with the Spanish people '*el bien amado*', reputed for his qualities as an athlete and a dancer, but in other respects he was a young thug, poorly educated, brusque to women, given to strolling the streets at night and even finding fun in robbing his own gardens. He would burst unannounced into the private apartments of his wife's ladies-in-waiting. Sport rather than the art of government was his metier; his wife was equally frivolous in taste and so vulgar in manner[20] that Luis actually had her temporarily confined.

The dismay at San Ildefonso at the behaviour of the new king and queen can be imagined, so that Philip, ever scrupulous, now began to wonder whether in resigning the crown to an unsuitable successor he may in some way have been guilty of an offence against God. He deplored the infantile behaviour of his son, and even more so that of his daughter-in-law, and enquired as to whether if the marriage had not been consummated it might yet be annulled. He was fortunately rescued from this dilemma by the sudden death of his son from smallpox at the end of August 1724.

But Philip was now confronted by another dilemma. According to his act of renunciation, the throne should now pass to Luis's younger brother, Ferdinand, an opinion which even Philip's own confessor appeared to share. But this was an unwelcome outcome, not least to Elizabeth Farnese who had never been agreeable to the surrender of power which her husband's abdication had entailed. With her strong support, and prompted by the papal nuncio, Aldobrandini, Philip announced that he would resume the crown.

Philip had more than twenty years of rule in front of him, but it was Elizabeth Farnese who articulated her country's foreign policy, strongly biased in favour of her Italian interests, more especially those of her son, the future Charles III of Spain. The country's domestic economy remained largely stagnant. Meanwhile her husband continued periodically to be afflicted by fits of manic depression which in their own severe stages could easily slide into madness. He was seriously ill again in the spring of 1727, at times lethargic, at others passionate and excitable, acting violently towards his doctors and his confessor. When the queen tried to curb his religious devotions, which she thought excessive, he responded by trying to beat her. He screamed and sang and even bit himself. He suffered too from acute insomnia and loss of appetite, sustaining his vitality by consuming sweetmeats. Formerly obese, he became thin. He began to suffer delusions, believing that he could not walk because his feet were of different size, nor would he have his hair cut, which made the wearing of a wig difficult, or his beard shaved. The queen persuaded the court to move from Madrid to Andalucia where for five years from 1728 to 1733 it remained at the Alcazar of Seville.

Philip was still obsessively aware of his inability to fulfil his responsibilities, and continued to contemplate the possibility of a further abdication, a prospect which greatly alarmed the queen. He sent a letter to the president of the Council of Castile without consulting his wife, declaring that he wished to renounce the throne in favour of his son Ferdinand. The council hedged. The king, believing that the council had accepted his decision, told Elizabeth what he had done while they were out hunting. Elizabeth Farnese, much concerned, pressed him to recall the note, explaining that she thought that the clauses relating to herself and her children needed to be amended. Once the note of abdication was safely in her hands, she tore it into shreds and told her husband that she disapproved absolutely of his abdication which without her consent lacked legality.

The danger of his making an impulsive decision remained, so that pen and paper were kept as far as possible out of his reach. For a time he reverted to a semi-normal life, allowing himself to be shaved for the first time for eight months, and even concerned himself with the functions of government. Whether this was to the interests of his country may be doubted. It was certainly much to the inconvenience of his ministers as well as of his courtiers, for 'His Catholic Majesty', as the English envoy Sir Benjamin Keene told Waldegrave on 6 April 1731, 'seems to be trying experiments to live without sleep.' He supped at 3.00 a.m., retiring to bed at 5.00 a.m. He rose to hear Mass at 3.00 p.m. But then he changed the pattern of his day, going to bed at 10.00 a.m. and rising at 5.00 p.m.

In 1730 news reached the Spanish court that the king of Sardinia had decided to abdicate. The queen and her advisers were greatly worried lest Philip might try to follow his example (though the Sardinian monarch had resigned his throne to marry his mistress). They tried to represent to Philip that the Sardinian king's abdication showed that he was really insane. But, by August 1732, Philip once more retired to bed, would not even rise to have his meals, would speak only to his immediate servants and would not have his hair cut or his nails pared. Keene told the duke of Newcastle on 17 October 1732 that 'we are now properly without any government, or even the form of it, for he has not seen either of his ministers or his confessor near twenty days past, and consequently there has been no Dispatch.'

By Easter 1733 there were some signs of returning normality. His son, Ferdinand, managed to persuade his father to be shaved, to have his linen changed and to take an emetic. By the summer the English envoy could report that the king 'has continued to apply himself to business, so that the government is now again on a regular footing, and as to his health, I never saw him look more cheerful and more of speech'. It was, however, only an intermission. The court was itself split by intrigue, for the queen resented the influence which her step-son, Ferdinand, seemed to be gaining over the king. 'I believe indeed', the indefatigable English envoy commented,

> she would willingly have avoided this recourse to the prince, but the king may be too long accustomed to the queen's tears to be moved by them, and as those of the prince were new they could not well fail to make an impression. Besides by the

precautions she had taken to keep anyone from approaching the apartment there is no doubt that she had a design to do by force what the king at last consented to; and to authorize her to proceed to such means, it was prudent to try all other ones, and convince the prince himself of the necessity of obliging the king to take care of his health.[21]

His return to normality was short-lived. Early in 1738 he was described as 'disordered in his head'. He remained morosely taciturn, though there were occasions when shrieks from his room betokened delirium. 'It must end in an abdication', Keene had earlier told the chief English minister, the duke of Newcastle, but Philip remained resolutely king, strongly dependent upon his wife. 'When he retires to dinner', Keene again recounted to the duke of Newcastle on 2 August 1738,

> he sets up such frightful howlings as astonished everyone at the beginning, and have obliged the *confidants* to clear all the apartments as soon as he sat down to table; and as the queen cannot be sure of his behaviour, she does not fail to keep him within doors, insomuch that they do not take the air in their favourite garden of S. Ildefonso as they used to do heretofore. His diversion at night is to hear Farinelli [the Italian singer Carlo Broschi] sing the same five Italian airs that he sang the first time that he performed before him, and [he] has continued to sing every night for near twelve months together. But your Grace will smile when I inform you that the king himself imitates Farinelli, sometimes air after air, and sometimes after the music is over, and throws himself into such freaks and howlings that all possible means are taken to prevent people from being witness to his follies. He had one of these fits this week, which lasted from twelve till past two in the morning. They have talked of bathing him, but fear they shall not persuade him to try that remedy.[22]

Farinelli later told Dr Burney that he had sung the same four songs, two of which were '*Pallido il sole*' and '*Per questo dolce amplesso*' by Hasse, until the king's death. It has been reckoned that he must therefore have sung these songs some 3,600 nights in succession.

And so the years passed, the king slothful, devout and dull, still devoted to the wife who determined the policy of his empire. It was a tragi-comedy, underlined by the king's repeated bouts of manic depression, brought to an end only by a massive stroke which he suffered on 9 July 1746. The marquis d'Argenson commented:

> Philip died of chagrin and corpulence, which he had contracted by excessive indulgence to his appetite, which was more regular than moderate. He was laborious without doing anything useful. No man has ever given such an example

of the misuse of marriage, allowing himself to be ruled by his wife, who ruled him badly. His queen had compelled him to sacrifice the honour and wealth of Spain to conquer domains in Italy, and God has decreed that she should never enjoy them.[23]

With her husband's death and the accession of her step-son Ferdinand Elizabeth Farnese's power was brought to an end.

But Ferdinand's accession hardly changed the character of the monarchy. The new king, fourth but only surviving son of Philip's first marriage, was a pasty-faced man, vacant in expression, short and stocky in appearance, 'as stout and robust' so Keene said, 'as those that love him can wish him'. He showed a measure of wise statesmanship in concurring with his ministers that Spain required a period of peace and reconciliation. But he had inherited his father's temperament.[24] He was lazy by nature, finding respite from depression in plays, opera – he and his wife were patrons of Scarlatti and Farinelli – and other amusements. In other respects he was moody, suspicious and irresolute, and like his father in depression he went daily in apprehension of violent sudden death.

He was as uxorious as his father, depending completely upon his wife, Barbara, the daughter of King John V of Portugal. 'She was', Archdeacon Coxe commented, 'homely in her features and the original elegance of her shape was lost in corpulence.'[25] This was something of an understatement, for her skin was pockmarked, her lips were thick and she was a sufferer from chronic asthma. Her temperament seems to have been as neurotic as that of her husband, for her own royal house of Braganza was not free of mental disturbance. Like her husband she went daily in fear of sudden death which her asthmatic tendency may have encouraged. She was also fearful that if her husband died before her she would be plunged into poverty, and to avert this catastrophe became excessively avaricious, leaving a considerable fortune to her brother, Pedro of Portugal, when she died on 27 August 1758.

Her death seems to have hastened her husband's relapse into manic depression. He remained in seclusion at his palace of Villaviciosa de Odón, withdrew from company and would not eat, taking only soup for nourishment, nor sleep. He took to beating his unfortunate servants. 'There is', the English ambassador Lord Bristol commented,

a melancholy in the king which nothing can divert, and such a settled taciturnity prevails that no directions can be given, nor any order issued. . . . He will not be shaved, walks about without any covering but his shirt, which has not been changed for a surprising time, and a night gown. He has not been in bed for ten nights, nor is he thought to have slept five hours since the second of this month and that only in intervals of half-an-hour. He declines lying down, because he imagines he shall die when he does so.

Ferdinand did not long survive his wife. He tried to commit suicide with a pair of scissors, begged for poison, but eventually died a natural death in his forty-seventh year on 10 August 1759.

No Spanish monarch was in the future to be as physically decrepit as Charles II or as much the victim of depressive insanity as Philip V and Ferdinand VI. Indeed Ferdinand's successor, his half-brother Charles III, Philip's son by Elizabeth Farnese, once an heir to the grand duchy of Tuscany and later king of the Two Sicilies, was to prove an able and enlightened prince. Yet metaphorically, it would appear, the genes conspired to deprive the Spanish Bourbon house of the capacity for good government. Of later kings Charles IV was a well-intentioned but feeble monarch, brow-beaten by his wife, Maria Luisa, the lover of the chief minister Godoy. 'What', the king asked Godoy, 'have my subjects been doing today?' 'He never grew to maturity', writes the most recent historian of his reign, 'remaining infantile in knowledge and judgement, unable to distinguish between supporters and scoundrels'.[26] Goya's splendid portrait of this royal family points unerringly to the fundamental disability and simplistic futility of the Bourbon line. Charles's son, Ferdinand VII, was a died-in-the-wool reactionary, while Ferdinand's daughter, Queen Isabella II who came to the throne at the age of three became a politically conservative and sentimentally pious woman with a 'rough and somewhat mealy look'. As a result of diplomatic manipulation she was unhappily married at sixteen to her cousin, an effeminate Bourbon prince, Francisco de Asis, an immature young man who liked to play with his dolls even in adult life, and who was so much a hypochondriac that he refused to see anyone whom he suspected of having a cold. Attached as Isabella was, perhaps obsessively, to a nun, Sor Patrocinio, who had supposedly experienced the stigmata, the queen looked for compensation for her unhappy marriage elsewhere. 'The Queen', the Prince Consort wrote, 'has her lovers. Her mother, Christina, wanted to press a lover on her, one according to her wish.' There can be little doubt that for many centuries, apart from the dubious effects of inbreeding, there was a long-persisting neurasthenic streak in the Spanish royal family which had repeated political repercussions for the country over which it ruled.

XI

Florentine Frolics

The Medici, unlike the Habsburgs and the Bourbons, were not a royal family, but as Italian princes, politically sagacious and culturally minded, they ruled Florence, apart from a brief period in the early sixteenth century, from the 1430s until the death of the last grand duke, Gian Gastone, in 1737. Florence probably reached its apogee under the skilful guidance of the real founder of the family's fortunes, the great merchant prince, Cosimo dei Medici, and his grandson, Lorenzo the Magnificent. Their wide banking network made the Medici a force in the economy and politics of western Europe, and even after their interests had diminished the Medici long remained a dominant power in Italy. The family supplied two popes, Clement VII and Leo X, as well as a constant bevy of cardinals, and two of the most influential of the queens of France, Catherine dei Medici and Marie dei Medici. Florence was itself superbly enriched by fine buildings, paintings and sculptures which the patronage of the Medici and their supporters provided. As grand dukes of Tuscany the Medici wielded a despotic authority and presided over a luxurious court.

By the late seventeenth century the Florentines, like the Medici family itself, were suffering from a hardening of the arteries, for they were living on the reputation and resources of a glittering past. The Medici court was still opulent and extravagant in its expenditure, and its princes were the patrons of art and culture. Yet this was in some sense a façade which failed to screen Tuscany's failing economy and political impotence. The country had long ceased to be a focal point for a flourishing industry, and its agriculture was in a bad way. Its citizens were heavily taxed to finance the costly court and to provide the subsidies which the grand duke had to pay to foreign powers. The burden fell heaviest on the middle men, the farmers and merchants who always had been the mainstay of the Tuscan economy. As a consequence there was growing poverty and unemployment. The great religious festivals and secular pageants which diverted the Florentines could not conceal effectively the city's festering economic blight.[1]

In effect Florence had become politically impotent. On his tours abroad Grand Duke Cosimo III who ruled from 1670 to 1723 had been greeted with ceremonial solemnity befitting a noble prince; and to his delight he won from the emperor the right to be entitled Royal Highness instead of Highness (a title which, to his vexation, the emperor had already bestowed on the duke of Savoy), and to be called *Serenissimo* 'the Most Serene', but such honours were merely nominal. Florence had become a third-rate power and its army was small and its navy, once substantial, was practically non-existent. That Florence remained at peace and comparatively free from foreign interference was because it was not to the interest of the great powers to intervene. But they were poised like vultures around the fading Medici line, and Florence was a stool pigeon quite incapable of effectively defending itself.

Grand Duke Cosimo III ruled Tuscany for fifty-three years. While his governance was neither particularly good nor bad, it was affected by certain facets of his own character which are in some sense vital to understanding the nature of his son and successor, the last grand duke, Gian Gastone. Brought up by a pietistic mother, unhappily married to his father Grand Duke Ferdinand, who ruled Florence from 1621 to 1670 and much preferred the embraces of his handsome young page Count Bruto della Molara, Cosimo became a narrow, serious-minded and zealous *dévot*, better suited to an ecclesiastical than to a secular career. Even as early as 1659 he was said to have exhibited 'the symptoms of a singular piety . . . he is dominated by melancholy beyond all that is usual. . . . the Prince is never seen to smile.' His life was a perpetual church-crawl, for he would visit five or six churches a day, and his greatest delight was to take part in religious processions. Edward Wright wrote that in his latter years the grand duke had 'a machine in his own Apartment, whereon were fix'd little Images in Silver, of every saint in the Kalendar. The Machine was made to turn so as still to present in front the Saint of the Day, before which he continuously perform'd his offices.' 'His zeal', he added, 'was great for gaining Proselytes to the Romish Church'.[2] Probably the event in his life which afforded him the greatest satisfaction was his appointment by the pope as a canon of St John Lateran, a privilege which enabled him to touch the holy relic of St Veronica's handkerchief, which Christ had supposedly used on his way to the cross, and which bore dimly his mystical features. Cosimo was proud to have his portrait painted dressed in his canon's robes. In 1719 he was to dedicate his country as a result of divine guidance to the 'governance and absolute dominion of the most glorious Saint Joseph'.

Such religiosity, a not wholly unfamiliar aspect of Florentine society, might have been innocuous if it had not found expression in legislation. The grand duke was intolerant in his attitude to unorthodoxy in both morals and belief. He tried to ban female actresses, prohibited men from entering houses where there were unmarried girls and imposed a formidable and intolerant series of anti-Semitic decrees. Intermarriage between Christians and Jews was forbidden; Christians were not even to occupy the same house. A Jew who went with a non-Jewish prostitute was fined 300 crowns, while the prostitute was liable to be flogged in public, naked to the waist. In November 1683 Christian nurses were forbidden to suckle Jewish babies. The grand duke sought so to control schools and the university that anything capable of being interpreted as a challenge to orthodoxy was outlawed. He ordered Bandinelli's statue of Adam and Eve to be removed from the cathedral because it was indecorous.

Cosimo had married Marguerite Louise d'Orléans, a niece of Louis XIII of France and so a cousin to Louis XIV, in what must have seemed diplomatically an excellent choice which *prima facie* offered every opportunity of prolonging the Medici line, an objective which long dominated Cosimo's thoughts. 'She will yield such fruits', Cosimo was told, 'as will console your old age and perpetuate your Highness's pedigree.'

In fact few better examples of marital incompatibility could be found than Cosimo's marriage to Marguerite Louise. The bridegroom was an austere and gloomy man, so averse to physical contact that some suspected that he might be a homosexual. 'He sleeps', Princess Sophia of Hanover reported, 'with his wife but once a week, and then under supervision of a doctor who has him taken out of bed lest he should impair his health by staying there over long.' Contrariwise his wife was beautiful, extremely lively, physically energetic and, as became the daughter of Gaston d'Orléans, proud, stubborn and selfish.

Married by proxy at the Louvre in Paris, she journeyed to Italy by sea and was greeted by her new subjects in a ceremonial as costly as it was gorgeous. But Marguerite Louise had few illusions. She had been obliged to leave a lover, Prince Charles of Lorraine, in Paris and she had wanted to be a queen, not a grand duchess, and she had no liking for her new country. She found the Florentines constrained and uninteresting, and her husband unbearable. Cosimo's father packed off her French attendants and brought to bear every pressure he could to make her do her duty; eventually an heir, Ferdinando, was born in 1663.

But the future grand duchess still resented her fate. She was sent to cool off at Poggio a Caiano where she told the French queen that she was 'deprived of every convenience, buried alive in appalling solitude', though in fact she was surrounded by a numerous court. A visit from her former beau, Prince Charles, did not reconcile her to married life, though his own marriage brought their relationship to an end. When she discovered she was pregnant, she tried to induce a miscarriage, but eventually a daughter, Anna Maria, was born in August 1667. Marguerite Louise demanded passionately that she should be allowed to return to France. When she refused to share her husband's bed, her cousin, Louis XIV, told her to behave herself. Cosimo was despatched on a series of expensive foreign tours, presumably in the mistaken belief that absence makes the heart grow fonder, but at least he and his wife resumed marital relations in a manner of speaking and their third child, Gian Gastone, was born on 24 May 1671. Eventually the grand duchess got her way and on 12 June 1675 she left Tuscany for France, never to return.

The tumultuous nature of their relationship must have been the more irritating to the grand duke since the interest of his life was to assure the future of the dynasty. Although Cosimo was to live to a very ripe old age, he was hypochondriacal and so apprehensive that he might die that he was much concerned with securing the succession to the Medici line. Fate, however, showed that he was to be no more successful in arranging the marriages of his children than his father had been in marrying him to the redoubtable Marguerite Louise, indeed less so since none of them was to have offspring. Cosimo's heir, Grand Prince Ferdinando, was married to a Bavarian princess, Violante, a union for which her husband lacked enthusiasm. No sooner was the marriage arranged than Ferdinando set off for Venice in search of more satisfactory pickings, whether male or female. Aware of his son's weakness, Cosimo sent him a warning letter:

> I wish you to promise to abstain from diversions that are damnable to the soul . . . likewise that you will avoid becoming indecently familiar with musicians, comedians (reputed as infamous people), and take no part in the conversations, and still less in the entertainments of courtesans.[3]

But what Ferdinando, a talented aesthete, enjoyed was precisely 'becoming indecently familiar with musicians'. His tutor had already banished from his household a singer, Petrillo, who had taken his fancy; but in Venice he found a substitute in a *castrato*, Cecchino de Castris who acquired great influence over him. If Ferdinando had been content with *castrati* it would have been better for his health, for on another visit to Venice he caught a syphilitic infection and came back in the company of a female singer the Cotton Girl 'La Bambagia'. Long before he died, for he predeceased his father by ten years, his memory gone, his faculties disordered, he had become a victim to general paralysis of the insane induced by syphilis. He had become, someone said, a 'martyr to Venus'.

Since it was soon apparent that Ferdinando would not be blessed with offspring, the grand duke turned his attention to the marriage of his daughter, Anna Maria. Her father's attempts to get her a husband had failed with Spain, Portugal, Savoy and the dauphin, in the latter case partly as a result of the machinations of her mother, the grand duchess; but at last at the emperor's suggestion she found in some sense a suitable husband in the Elector Palatine, Johann William, a widower, three of whose sisters were the empress, and the queens of Portugal and Spain, and three of whose brothers were bishops. But the elector's life had not been free from stain. His wife had a miscarriage which was put down to the 'disorders contracted from her husband, for although he esteemed and loved her well, he was frequently, through the generous warmth of his heart, diverted by extraneous amours'.[4] The electress went to Aix-la-Chapelle to take the baths 'to promote fecundity', but in vain.

So the grand duke's younger son, Gian Gastone, remained the hope of the family. As a child he had suffered neglect, for his mother, who had no time for him, had left the country when he was four. He was in some respects a studious and solitary youth, whom Lami had described as a 'most learned prince . . . a follower of Leibnitz in philosophy and not one to let priests and monks lead him around by the nose'. But he suffered evidently from some form of deep depression. Contemporaries noted that he often seemed so taciturn and sad, weeping alone in his chamber, that they wondered whether he was wholly sane. 'I am very surprised', the Jesuit Father Segnieri commented, 'to hear that Prince Gian Gastone has now lost faith in everyone.'

When Gian Gastone was twenty-three, his father decided that it was time for him to marry. His choice fell on a wealthy widow, Anna Maria, daughter of the duke of Saxe-Lauenburg and widow of the Count Palatine. She was a boorish, disagreeable woman, sluttish in taste, fearsome and formidable in form with a 'coarse ill-favoured aspect and ungainly massive limbs'. Her only apparent interests were in hunting and horses and her Bohemian estates. She had no particular wish to remarry and had no intention of living in Florence. It was indeed a condition of the marriage that she, and presumably her husband, would continue to live in Bohemia.

Gian Gastone's reaction to married life was one of horror. He took an immediate dislike to the Bohemian countryside, to the smell of horses and to possible intercourse with his coarse wife. For comfort he turned to his intimate friend, his lackey Guiliano Dami, a man of humble birth who became his lover and later his procurer and who was to exert great influence over him for the remainder of his life. By 1698 he could bear his wife's household no longer and travelled to Paris, ostensibly to see his mother who received him coldly.

He returned to his wife's castle at Reichstadt and tried to persuade her to winter in Prague. When she refused he went without her, accompanied by Dami. Here at least for a time he could cast into oblivion the grim household at Reichstadt and the austerities of the grand ducal court in a round of sensual pleasures. According to a contemporary:

There were scores of fresh young students in Prague, smooth-chinned Bohemians and Germans, who were so impecunious they wandered begging from door to door. In this wide preserve Guiliano [Dami] could always hunt for amorous game and introduced some new and comely morsel to the Prince. There was also no small number of palaces at Prague belonging to great and opulent nobles. These had regiments of retainers about them in their households, footmen and lackeys of low birth and humble station. Guiliano induced His Highness to seek his diversions with these . . . so as to choose any specimen that appealed to his singular sense.[5]

So Gian Gastone acquired a taste for 'rough trade' which he was never to lose.

News of these pursuits, together with heavy gambling losses which landed him in debts he could ill afford, for his father kept him on short commons, filtered through to his wife who in turn reported them to his sister the Electress Palatine. She informed the grand duke but Gian Gastone still persisted in his manner of life, wandering the streets at night and drinking in low taverns. Through such frivolities he could temporarily put out of his mind his repellent wife and his sanctimonious father, but alcoholism and sexuality were a sinister cure for acute depression.

From time to time Gian Gastone returned to Reichstadt with the best of intentions. He wrote to Cosimo on 18 April 1699:

Your highness must learn that nineteen days after the marriage ring was given, if not earlier, my Princess began to give me samples of her capriciousness, peevish faces and sharp words, because I would not leave Dusseldorf, now and then saying a number of impertinent things about me and my people. . . . She is haughty and vain enough to trample on everybody and govern everybody, believing that she is the greatest lady in the world, because she owns these clods in Bohemia . . . it would certainly be impossible for me to stay with her in the most delicious spot in the world. . . . According to her servants she has always been the same, in widowhood as in wedlock with my predecessor [the Count Palatine], who was despatched into the other world by excessive drinking to dissipate the rage and disgust he suffered on her account.[6]

Gian Gastone was acutely aware of the irony of his position. His mother had left his father because she found him unbearable. Her son had left his wife because he found her unbearable.

When the emperor urged Gian Gastone 'to try and overcome his great aversion to living with his wife in that horrid solitude', Gian Gastone declared that he had tried to live amicably with his wife but without success. Reichstadt in summer was bad enough; in winter it was unendurable.

In October 1703 he moved to Hamburg where he stayed until the following February finding there fleshly diversions unavailable at Reichstadt. But when he moved on to Prague he seemed utterly depressed, inert and withdrawn, spending most of his time simply gazing out of the window. He would not even sign letters because he had taken an acute dislike to his writing table. Pretty young faces and 'rough trade' seemed alone capable of diverting him from his melancholy. By 1705 he was back in Florence permanently. There no longer seemed any possibility of his wife joining him there nor indeed of any children being born to him or to his brother or to his sister.

In an attempt to provide for the succession the Grand Duke Cosimo, like a drowning man then grasped at a straw, if so inappropriate a word can be used to describe his obese brother, Cardinal Francesco Maria. The cardinal was everything that his brother was not: hedonistic, generous to a fault, gluttonous and worldly. There had indeed been a curious reversal of roles; the bigoted grand duke was more suited to an ecclesiastical, the cardinal to a secular career. He had accumulated great wealth from his many benefices but his ecclesiastical duties sat lightly. So far he had shown little taste for female company, indeed rather the reverse; but his brother persuaded him to seek a dispensation from holy orders that he might marry and hopefully sire an heir to the grand duchy. He was permitted to retain his many sources of income. In any case marriage was one of the few pleasures that he had not experienced.

The proposed bride was Eleonora, the daughter of Vincenzo Gonzaga, duke of Guastella. 'Look to your health', the electress wrote to him, 'that you may give us the consolation of a little prince.' It was good advice for though the cardinal was only forty-eight years old he was a mountain of flesh, paunchy and pock-marked, suffering from gout and catarrh. Eleonora found him so repulsive that at first she would not even submit to his embraces. She did all she could to get away from him; but fortunately an overtaxed constitution had done its job and the cardinal died on 3 February 1711, and with his death Cosimo's last hope of a direct male heir perished. All he could do was to take vengeance on his brother's 'lackeys, pages and grooms, most of whom had been cherished in their youth by the said Prince for their comeliness; and after they had grown to man's estate . . . serving him as pimps and procuring him other handsome lads and companions. . . . He vastly enjoyed watching others perform. . . . Some were expelled from the state, others went to the galleys.[7] As for his widow, Eleonora, she found the embraces of her French footmen more seductive than those of her elderly husband and had two illegitimate sons, Mignon and Francesco. Horace Mann wrote to his friend Horace Walpole:

> Can you forgive her that all the entreaties, all the handsome young fellows put in her way during the Cardinal's lifetime should not prevail upon her to procure such an advantage to Tuscany [through the birth of an heir], and that after his death she should fuck with her footmen to increase the number of the *innocenti* [the children who were sent to the hospital for orphans].[8]

Gian Gastone alone was left, for Ferdinando died two years later. In a desperate effort Cosimo tried to ensure that should Gian Gastone predecease him his sister the Electress Anna Maria should succeed to the grand duchy, but the emperor interposed to say that as Cosimo's states were imperial fiefs the grand duke could not provide for the succession in this way. It was worrying that Gian Gastone's own health was giving some cause for concern. 'He does not appear capable of any great application', a

A bust of Gian Gastone, Grand Duke of Tuscany (Uffizi Gallery; photograph: Fratelli Alinari)

French visitor, Guyet de Merville, wrote in 1719. 'He never opens a letter, to avoid having to reply to it. This kind of life might bring him to a very advanced age, did he not suffer from asthma and aggravate his infirmity by the quantity of potent cordials he consumes. There are even people who believe that he will die before his father.'[9]

Gian Gastone's life-style had now taken on its curious and unusual shape. 'He is a good prince', Montesquieu who visited Florence in December 1728, commented, 'endowed with brains, but very lazy, rather addicted to the bottle'. ('*Il aime un peu à boire, même des liqueurs*'). But Montesquieu praised his kindly and compassionate nature, even if, as he thought, his indolence and perverted tastes made him easily the prey of unscrupulous adventurers. '*Du reste, le meilleur homme du monde*' was his conclusion.[10] '*Il mondo va da se*' seemed to epitomize his outlook on life.

At last on the Vigil of All Saints 1723 the aged grand duke died and Gian Gastone, now fifty-two and in many respects prematurely aged, succeeded him. The once slender, attractive young man had become stout and heavily jowled. He had little interest in governmental matters but he chose his ministers well, so that Florentine government was in some respects better and certainly more liberal than it had been in his father's time. The heavy hand the church played in protecting orthodoxy and morality became more relaxed. Where Cosimo had been prodigal in his expenditure on ecclesiastical objectives, Gian Gastone was sparing. The Council of Four was abolished and the old secretariat re-established. His father's draconian legislation was reversed, so much so that the Jesuits were now to criticize the university of Pisa as a centre of heretical teaching. Galileo was restored to a place of honour, and the works of Gassendi were allowed to be published. There was some lightening of the heavy load of taxation. The accession of Gian Gastone marked a more enlightened and liberal system of government, though the infirmities from which Florence suffered could not be cured by a stroke of the pen. In practice the grand duke appeared to be an absentee landlord. The state, as Montesquieu noted in 1728, had '*une domination assez douce. Personne ne connoît et ne sent guère le Prince et la Cour. Ce petit pays a, en cela, l'air d'un grand pays.*'

The grand duke was incapable of changing his topsy-turvy manner of life. In summer he lived on the ground floor of the Pitti Palace; the donkey which brought him peaches was ushered into his bedroom. In the winter he was carried to an upper room. The Baron de Pollnitz, who visited Florence in 1731, paid his respects to his sister, the electress, 'very retir'd . . . continually at her Devotions', and was surprised to learn that the grand duke wished to see him, for he had been told that 'it was very difficult to get an audience'.

'I found', he wrote in November 1731, 'the Great Duke sitting upright in bed, accompany'd by several lap-dogs, with nothing on but a Shirt without Ruffles, and a long Cravat about his Neck of coarse Muslin; His Cap was very much besmear'd with

Snuff; and truly there was nothing neat nor grand about him. By his Bed-side there stood a Table in form of a Beaufet, upon which there were Silver Buckets that contain'd Bottles of Liquors and Glasses.'[11]

'The Grand Duke', he wrote, 'lay snug in his Bed, not that he was sick, but out of pure Indulgence. 'Tis now twenty-two months since he went out of his Palace and above seven since he put on his Cloaths . . . he dines at five o'clock in the Evening, and sups at Two in the Morning. He always eats alone, commonly in his Bed and spends two or three Hours in Table Talk with Joannino and some young fellows called *Ruspanti*.'

In practice the grand duke looked at the world through a more or less permanent haze of intoxication. 'By now he was accustomed to drink exceeding deep: not only of heady wine and fiery liquor, but also of *rossolis* which is a mulled and syrupy cordial confected of raisins and other ingredients of most potent quality, mixed up with sugar and spice. He protracted his cups till late and after dinner was always brutified.'[12] He had been known to tumble from his horse when he was drunk. When he went to a reception given by his sister-in-law Princess Violante, he was so drunk that he talked obscenities and was eventually pushed vomiting into his coach.

His bedchamber became the centre of his existence. Guiliano Dami, who had become royal chamberlain, assisted by two footmen, Gaetano and Francesco Nardini, acted as pimps and panders for the grand duke's pleasures, taking a good rake-off for their services. They sought out young men and boys 'unruly and unclean' but 'graced with an alluring eye and the countenance of an Adonis'.[13] These were the *ruspanti*, so called because they were paid a fee, from one to five ruspi, which they collected on Tuesdays and Saturdays, for their services. They were, de Pollnitz said, 'pensioners to the Grand Duke . . . all their business is to attend the Grand Duke whenever he sends for them at Dinner or Supper. . . . They wore no livery . . . and they are only known by their Locks, which are always very much curl'd and powder'd', presenting a strange contrast to the grand duke himself.[14]

The cosmopolitan *ruspanti* of whom there were some 370, some even well born, some women, took part in indecent entertainment at the prince's whim. They had to be pretty, young, strongly sexed, and sufficiently immune to good taste and a sense of smell to endure the dubious embraces of their master. It was Gian Gastone's habit to invite the chosen lad to his bed-chamber, examine his teeth to see if they were white and regular, then ply him with drink, *rossolis* in particular, then grope and feel his private parts to see if they were well shaped and likely to blossom rapidly. 'If they did not seem to penetrate sufficiently, he would shout: "Press in, boy, press in."' Thereafter he would call him 'you', and finally descend to the familiarity of 'thou', hugging dandling, kissing, and being kissed in return, mixing together mouthfuls of wine and tobacco smoke.[15] He bestowed on his 'rough trade' noble titles for the nonce and called them his ministers of state while they were invited, indeed expected, to call him by every opprobrious name of which they could think, and even pummel him if they so wished.

While it was the task of Dami and his companions to scour the poorer parts of the city for suitable candidates, the grand duke's passion was sometimes aroused simply by seeing an attractive youth, either in the palace or on his rare trips into the city. Learning, for instance, that a young barber had a fiancée, he invited him to bring her to the palace, dallied with each of them and had them consummate their relationship while he watched. There were evidently some occasions when he got more than he bargained for. He had been so attracted by the muscular prowess of a Bohemian bear-leader, Michael Henzchemic and the youthful charms of his two assistants that they were enrolled among the *ruspanti*. On one occasion at midnight the grand duke was seized with a sudden desire to have the bear-leader. When Henzchemic was tracked down he was already very drunk. He was brought back to the palace and with the grand duke consumed more wine until Gian Gastone vomited on Henzchemic's face and chest. The bear-leader was so enraged that he pummelled Gian Gastone with his fists until the grand duke's cries brought help. But Gian Gastone rarely bore any grudge against his assailants. He seemed actually to relish the vomit as well as the bawdy stories with which he was regaled. At times there were a dozen or more *ruspanti* in his bedchamber, engaged in an orgy of sex.

In 1730 the grand duke sprained his ankle and took to his bed, from which except on very rare occasions, he was not to move for the next seven years. Once he ventured out at two in the morning to the public baths of St Sperandino and stayed there for five hours.

The Revd Mark Noble, a late eighteenth-century historian of Florence, wrote:

It is impossible to give much of the personal history of the Prince who, from mere indolence and sloth, was never dressed for the last thirteen years of his life, and who never left his bed for the last eight. His appearance was singularly whimsical; he received those whom he suffered to approach him, in his shirt, without ruffles, a cravat of considerable length, made of muslin, none of the finest, and a night-cap, all of which were besmeared with snuff.

The late Earl of Sandwich acquainted this writer that this 'filthy' habit so far grew upon Gian Gastone towards the latter part of his life, that to stifle the disagreeable smells of his bed, the room was covered entirely, when his lordship was introduced to His Royal Highness, with new-gathered roses.[16] But the perfume of roses, new or otherwise, can hardly have overcome the stench of the grand duke's bedchamber for the bed was often verminous, the sheets were soiled and the room stank of tobacco, drink and excrement. The grand duke was wholly oblivious of his appearance; his finger and toenails were unpared. Double-chinned and paunchy, he still wore a large and dirty periwig with which on one occasion he was seen to wipe the vomit from his face.

What confidence can be placed in these tales which come from the pen of a hostile critic who plainly had the Roman historian Suetonius' account of Tiberius in mind when he was writing, is not entirely clear. If in some respects they may seem too reminiscent of the modern tabloid press, the general picture has the hallmark of accuracy. When the prince de Craon, whose son incidentally was said to be guilty of 'ruspantism', as representative of the grand duke's eventual heir Francis of Lorraine called on him in January 1737, he found Gian Gastone in a 'condition worthy of pity; he could not leave his bed, his beard was long, his sheets and linen very dirty, without ruffles; his eyesight dim and enfeebled, his voice low and obstructed, and altogether the air of a man who had not a month to live'.

Gian Gastone had become a negligent ruler, an alcoholic with seemingly perverted tastes. Yet he had been a promising youth and by disposition was humane and kindly. He must surely have been the victim of a personality disorder which circumstances, an upbringing without affection, a distant and austere father, and an unhappy marriage, had all conspired to turn into the wreck of a man. His father was melancholic. It seems highly probable that Gian Gastone may himself have suffered from a depressive illness. When he returned to Florence in 1705 he had lived in semi-seclusion, sometimes spending the night simply gazing at the moon. The strange distractions in which he indulged were the answer to a depression which annulled his interests in the affairs of state, self-indulgence which alleviated the prodigal boredom and sadness of existence.

But what of the future of Florence? Lacking direct heirs, Gian Gastone seemed as concerned as his father had been to provide for the future succession to the grand duchy. Ten years before he had become grand duke the ending of the War of Spanish Succession had destabilized Italy and made it again the prey of the great powers. Like his father, Gian Gastone sought to maintain Florence's neutrality, much to the indignation of the interested parties, more especially Spain and Austria. 'To the Grand Duke's physical stupidity', the Spanish ambassador, Father Ascanio, wrote in exasperation to the duke of Parma on 2 January 1725, 'which has been seen on divers occasions over a long period, lying motionless as a lunatic, is added his political stupidity, in which H[is] H[ighness] perseveres no less than his government, ignoring all that happens in the world relating to this Court, believing this to be the best policy to avoid any entanglement and enjoy the benefit of time'.[17]

In 1731 the great powers came together at Vienna and agreed that in the event of Gian Gastone's death the duchy should pass to Don Carlos, duke of Parma, son of Philip V of Spain and Elizabeth Farnese. As Don Carlos was at least half-Italian as well as young and fair in appearance he made a favourable impression on Gian Gastone. 'He said some days ago', de Pollnitz wrote, 'after he had signed his last will and testament, declaring Don Carlos of Spain his successor, that he had just got a son and heir by a dash of his pen, which he had not been able to get in thirty-four years of marriage.'[18] But he took less kindly to Don Carlos's habit of shooting with bows and arrows at the birds depicted in the fine Gobelins tapestry hangings of his room in the Pitti Palace, seldom missing the target. Gian Gastone gave orders for the tapestry to be removed and replaced by a damask hanging with a gold fringe explaining that 'as the weather was growing warmer, he was fearful that the Prince's health might have suffered by the heat of the winter furniture'.[19]

Don Carlos's plans did not in fact materialize for as a result of the War of the Polish Succession, in the subsequent game of princely musical chairs, Don Carlos became king of the Two Sicilies and was replaced as heir to the grand duchy by Francis Stephen, then duke of Lorraine, the husband of Maria Teresa, the heiress of the Habsburg Empire, and himself the future emperor Francis I. In the face of the pressure exerted by the great powers Gian Gastone was impotent. The Florentines were even prevented from celebrating the major feast days commemorating the great days of Medici rule. His city was occupied by foreign troops. But he did manage to get Francis Stephen to promise that Florence would never be incorporated into the Austrian empire. It was perhaps the most important act of his life, for it guaranteed Florence's future independence. It was also one of his last acts. By June 1737 he was seriously ill, suffering from a large stone in the bladder, and on 14 July his funeral took place with sumptuous pomp in the duomo. If the duke had been an ineffective ruler death had redeemed his reputation with the Florentines, he was carried to his tomb with all the ceremonial of which the city of pageantry was capable:

> Ah yes, 'tis true I've heard the sad lament:
> Great Cosmo's seed this day at last is spent;
> Your end, Oh Florence, I know is now decreed.

His sister, the Electress Anna Maria, lived on in the Pitti Palace for six more years, dying on 18 February 1743. 'All our jollity is at an end, our Carnival overset', Horace Mann told his friend Horace Walpole, 'the Electress died about an hour ago . . . The common people are convinced that she went off in a hurricane of wind; a most violent one began this morning and lasted for about two hours, and now the sun shines as bright as ever. This is proof; Besides for a stronger, just the same thing happened when John Gaston went off.'[20] By her will she bequeathed all the personal possessions and property of the Medici to the city of Florence 'for all eternity'. In so doing the electress had made amends for her brother's frolics and the Medici could be said to have repaid the Florentines for the loyalty they had given the family over three hundred years.

XII

Mad George

There were periods in George III's long reign of sixty years, periods which were comparatively short in duration, when the balance of his mind was evidently disturbed, between mid-October 1788 and March 1789, in February–May 1801, in February–June 1804 and in October 1810; thereafter he lapsed into a state of seeming senile dementia to the onset of which it is possible that his earlier mental trouble may have predisposed him. The exact nature of his illness, its cause and character, baffled contemporary observers: it was, said one, a consequence of 'some prevailing irritating acrimony'; another, that it was a form of delirium or the result of a simple 'peculiarity of constitution'. Some of his actions might even suggest that George III was a victim of schizophrenia or, like Henry VI of England and Philip V of Spain, of a manic-depressive illness, but the symptoms of his malady did not seem to fit particularly well with either diagnosis. Whatever the nature of his complaint, there could be no doubt that in his illnesses he behaved like a lunatic. During his major attack in 1788 his doctors agreed that he suffered from some form of temporary insanity and some feared that he would never recover. *'Rex noster insanit*, Our king is mad', was the crisp verdict of one of his own physicians, Richard Warren.

Earlier instances of royal madness have shown that mental illness can be an aftermath to an organic illness. Some twenty years ago two distinguished medical historians Ida Macalpine and Richard Hunter reached the conclusion that George III was never in a clinical sense mad but was the victim of a hereditary metabolic disorder, variegate porphyria, which had many outward symptoms characteristic of schizophrenia or manic-depressive illness. It was, they argued, a disease which had affected to a greater or lesser degree his ancestors, and which was to afflict some of his close relatives and later descendants. In his case the king's mental trouble was a consequence of a bodily illness, not the effect of plain insanity. Their learned and brilliant exposition cannot be lightly discarded, even though the evidence may still be insufficiently conclusive to make their diagnosis final.

There were few signs even if George III was fundamentally of a nervous disposition that he was the victim of mental debility during the first twenty-eight years of his reign. His early life had not revealed any fundamental physical or mental weakness, though as early as 1758 two years before he became king Lord Waldegrave commented on his neurotic temperament: he had, he said, 'a kind of unhappiness in his temper. . . . Whenever he is displeased . . . he becomes sullen and silent, and retires to his closet not to compose his mind by study or contemplation, but mainly to indulge the melancholy enjoyment of his ill humour. Even when the fit is ended, unfavourable symptoms may frequently return.[1]

After he became king he had some short periods of ill-health which some later historians believed unjustifiably to be precursors to his later neurosis. In 1762 Horace Walpole told his friend Horace Mann that the 'king had one of the last of these strange and universally epidemic colds, which however have seldom been fatal; he had a violent cough and oppression in his breast, which he concealed, just as I had. . . . Thank God he is safe, and we have escaped a confusion beyond what was ever known. . . . We have not even any standby law for the regency.'[2]

Three years later, in 1765, he had a similar complaint, the chief symptoms of which were a violent cough, fever, a fast pulse, hoarseness, tiredness, insomnia and painful stitches in the chest. Horace Walpole wondered whether he might not be suffering from consumption and hazarded to Lord Holland that he 'wasn't likely to live a year'. 'The king', Walpole wrote to Horace Mann on 26 March 1765, 'has been extremely ill, with a fever, violent cough, and a humor fallen on his breast. He was blooded four times; recovered enough to take the air, but caught new cold and was cupped last Friday.'[3]

Twenty-three years elapsed before he was struck down again by a serious illness, the onset of which was, however, not dissimilar to the sickness that he had experienced in 1762 and 1765: a bad cold, fever and hoarseness of voice. Between times he had proved to be one of the most conscientious of British monarchs. He had had to deal with a series of crises, political and personal, which could well have weakened a stronger constitution than his own. There had been two major wars: the Seven Years War with France and the War of American Independence, the first triumphant, the second disastrous. Relations with parliament had been often difficult, and the problem of trying to find a reliable and competent first minister was only to be resolved by the appointment as prime minister of the young William Pitt in 1784. In Queen Charlotte he had an affectionate and caring wife, but his sons, more especially 'Prinny', George, prince of Wales, were to give him cause for anxiety by reason of their extravagance and dissipation. Although there was nothing, political or personal, to cause him undue stress in 1788, cumulatively in the past he had experienced numerous problems which might be expected in time to take their toll.

He became ill in early June 1788 with a 'bilious fever, attended with violent spasms in his stomach and bowels', but he appeared to recover and went to Cheltenham, highly reputed as a spa, to recuperate and to drink the mineral waters. The king seemed in good spirits. He enjoyed watching Mrs Jordan play the part of Roxelana in *The Sultan* at the local theatre and attending the Three Choirs Festival at Worcester.

'Never did schoolboys enjoy their holidays equal to what we have done on our little excursion', the queen told Prince Augustus. But a month after the king's return to Windsor in August, there were ominous signs of a major breakdown in his health. He complained to his doctor, Sir George Baker, 'of a very acute pain in the pit of the stomach shooting to the back and sides, and making respiration difficult and uneasy', and of cramps in the muscles of his legs as well as a slight rash on his arms. These symptoms seemed to disappear before Dr Baker gave him a thorough examination, and he attributed his trouble to a chill brought on by his keeping on wet stockings.

But the remission was only temporary and was a precursor to a serious and baffling illness, mental and physical in its manifestations. The king, Baker noted, has 'some yellowness in the eyes and urine bilious' (that is, unduly dark in colour) and a pain in his stomach. More alarming still were hints of a coming nervous breakdown. The king felt it increasingly difficult to concentrate and gave vent to sudden paroxysms of passion. He was quite unlike his normal self. 'In the afternoon of 22 October 1788', Baker reported, 'I was received by His Majesty in a very unusual manner, of which I had not the least expectation. The look of his eyes, the tone of his voice, every gesture and his whole deportment represented a person in the most furious passion of anger.'[4]

When Fanny Burney, who was acting as one of the queen's ladies-in-waiting, met him the following Saturday morning (25 October) she commented that 'He spoke, with a manner so uncommon, that a high fever alone could account for it, a rapidity, a hoarseness of voice, a volubility, an earnestness – a vehemence – it startled me inexpressibly.'[5] 'He is all agitation, all emotion, yet all benevolence and goodness.' Always a talkative man, he now suffered from 'incessant loquaciousness', so that he would chatter on, speaking rapidly, for hours at a time; 'yesterday se'night', Lord Sheffield wrote, 'he talked incessantly for sixteen hours, to divert him from which they endeavoured to turn to writing, at length he began to compose notes on Don Quixote.' Not surprisingly his voice became very hoarse. He slept very badly, sometimes not at all, once being wakeful for as much as seventy-two hours.

The onset of what was then termed delirium became inexorable. While the king had his occasional good day in the course of which he managed to fulfil some of his duties, the deterioration in his health alarmed his family as well as the ministry. He was experiencing, as Sir George Baker put it, 'an intire alienation of mind' which made it increasingly impossible for him to exercise his responsibilities. 'His pulse is weaker and weaker', the Prince of Wales's comptroller, Captain Payne, reported, 'and the doctors say it is impossible to survive it long.' At the end of November the doctors thought that it was advisable that he should be moved from Windsor, where he loved to be, to Kew which he disliked, for Kew had the advantage of being more secluded than Windsor and closer to Westminster, the seat of government. The king went reluctantly, moving to what seemed to him virtual imprisonment in an uncomfortable and freezingly cold house.

He was, however, entering a fantasy world, the prey of hallucination, though often acutely aware of the agonizing position in which he was placed. 'He fancies London is drowned and orders his yacht to go there', Lord Sheffield told Mr Eden.[6] He bestowed high honours on pages and menials, and composed fanciful letters to foreign powers on imaginary causes. His equerry, Greville, noted that once the king 'got a pillow case round his head, and pillow in bed with him which he called Prince Octavius, who he said was to be born this day'.[7] His language was sometimes uncharacteristically obscene. He became so excitable that he sometimes struck out violently at those around him.

In particular he developed a curious fixation on the countess of Pembroke, formerly Lady Elizabeth Spencer, a staid lady-in-waiting to the queen, whose husband in 1762 after six years of married life, disguised as a sailor, had eloped on a packet boat with a Miss Kitty Hunter, a daughter of a lord of the Admiralty, 'and since that date [he] has had amorous connections with several ladies of less note.' The king fantasized that he was married to Lady Pembroke. He even told his wife, speaking in German (which was another aberration characteristic of his condition), that he did not really like her, that he preferred another, that she was mad and had been so for thirty years. He was determined 'for reasons he then improperly explained' that he would not admit her to his bed until the year 1793. When the queen sent him a present of a bunch of hot-house grapes on 11 January 1789, George asked what queen it was who had sent them. 'Was it queen Esther?' 'No,' they replied, 'it was your wife.'[8] When, two days later he was playing picquet with one of his doctors he scribbled across the card:

> O dear Eliza [Lady Pembroke] ever love thy Prince
> Who had rather suffer death than leave thee.

He said she was his Queen of Hearts, and when the card came his way he kissed it. He told Dr Willis that he had devised a new doctrine of the Trinity, the persons of which were God, Dr Willis and Eliza. He asked Greville to get Paley's *Philosophy* from the royal library which he thought would tell him that though 'Man might have one wife, yet that Nature allowed more'.[9] When he was feeding the queen's dog, Badine, he said that he liked her because she was fonder of him than of the queen whom he had never really loved. 'Whatever fever his Majesty has had', Windham wrote on 26 November 1788, 'has been only symptomatic, and not at all the cause of his disorder which is pure and original insanity. The symptoms of this have been increasing by slow degrees, and for a considerable period.'[10]

His doctors were at a loss as to how best to cope with the king's illness. Contemporaries were aware that mental ill-health could be either organic in origin, the result of brain disease, or psychological, the effect of temperament, strain or physical factors, or might indeed be a combination of both. 'Madness with respect to its cause is distinguishable into two species,' William Battie wrote in his *Treatise on Medicine*, 'viz. Original and Consequential. . . . The first is solely owing to an internal disorder of the nervous substance: the second . . . owing to the same . . . being disordered *ab extra*.'[11] The first was thought by its nature to be incurable lunacy; the second, though characterized by mental derangement and delirium, might be cured.

George's doctors were self-evidently at a grave disadvantage. They had no adequate clinical instruments, and etiquette prevented them from making a systematic and close personal examination of their patient. Their conclusions were along traditional lines as Lord Grenville's account of their diagnosis on 20 November 1788 demonstrated:

> The cause to which they all agree to ascribe it, is the force of a humor which was beginning to show itself in the legs, when the king's imprudence drove it from thence into the bowels; and the medicines which they were then obliged to use for the preservation of his life have repelled it upon the brain. . . . The physicians are now endeavouring . . . to bring it down again into the legs, which nature had originally pointed out as the best mode of discharge.[12]

Since they seemed unware of the best way to treat their royal patient, given that his illness appeared to have settled in his mind, with some reluctance his doctors agreed to call in a contemporary expert on the treatment of the insane, Dr Francis Willis, who was to be assisted by his sons. Willis had studied at Oxford, first at Lincoln and then at Brasenose College, and had taken his MD at Oxford, but this did not in itself constitute a licence to practise or even to be a guarantee of good medical knowledge. Willis who was ordained had, however, a genuine interest in medicine, acting as a general practitioner and physician to the General Hospital at Lincoln before he opened his asylum at Greatford near Stamford in 1776. Here he acquired a considerable reputation. 'Almost all the surrounding ploughmen, gardeners, threshers, thatchers and other labourers were attired in black silk breeches and stockings', so a visitor described the asylum and its inhabitants, 'and the head of each was bien poudrée, frisée et arrangée. These were the doctor's patients and dress, neatness of person and exercise being the principal features of his admirable system, health and cheerfulness conjoined towards the recovery of every person attached to this most valuable asylum.'[13] On the recommendation of Lady Harcourt, whose mother he had treated successfully, Dr Willis was brought to the notice of the royal family.

Dr Willis and his sons have had a bad press. When the king first met him, on Friday 5 December 1788, he took an instant dislike to him. 'Sir, your dress and appearance bespeaks you of the Church,' the king said, 'do you belong to it?' 'I did formerly,' Willis replied, 'but latterly I have attended chiefly to Physick.' 'I am sorry for it,' the

Interior view of a lunatic asylum in the eighteenth century (photograph: The Wellcome Institute Library, London, © The Trustee of the Wellcome Trust, 1993)

king commented, showing some agitation, 'you have quitted a profession I have always loved, and you have embraced one I most heartily detest.' Willis replied, 'Sir, our Saviour himself went about healing the sick.' 'Yes, yes,' the king responded testily, 'but had not £700 a year for it.'[14] The Willises were certainly to do well financially out of the king's illness. Later, in 1792, Dr Willis was to be given the high fee of £10,000 to treat the mad Queen Maria I of Portugal, but without success.

Yet George III may have owed his recovery in health, if he owed it to anyone, more to the Willises than to his personal physicians. Francis Willis was undoubtedly a formidable man with a withering stare with which he reputedly managed to keep his patients under control. He was as firm in his treatment of the royal household as he was of the patients in his own asylum, even censoring letters to the king and taking government documents to George personally.

There is no doubt that he submitted the king to a harsh regime, involving the use of a strait jacket and a special restraining chair which the king called pathetically his 'coronation chair'. On occasions Willis had his patient tied to his bed. Yet in a number of ways Willis showed greater understanding of how to treat the mentally ill than some of his contemporaries. He believed indeed in discipline but it was discipline allied to sympathy. 'When I was first summoned to attend George III', he admitted later, 'I gave great offence to the Queen by my method of treating his malady. As death makes no distinction in his visit between the poor man's hut and the prince's palace, so insanity is equally impartial with her subjects. For that reason, I made no distinction in my treatment of persons submitted to my charge. When, therefore, my gracious sovereign became violent, I felt it my duty to subject him to the same system of restraint as I shoud have adopted with one of his own gardeners at Kew; in plain words I put a straitcoat on him.' Hostile as he was to Willis, George seemed to respond to his treatment. 'Dr Willis', Greville remarked, 'remained firm, and reproved him in nervous and determined language, telling him he must control himself or otherwise he would put him in a strait waistcoat. On this hint Dr Willis went out of the room and returned with one in his hand . . . the king eyed it attentively and alarmed at the doctor's firmness began to submit. I was much struck with the proper manner and the imposing style of the authoritative language which Dr Willis held on this occasion.'[15]

Although Willis was never to win the king's confidence, fundamentally he was a humane man who realized that insanity as he understood it could not be cured simply by the application of purgatives and the use of force. As soon as the king showed signs of improving health, he gave him more latitude, allowing him, for instance, to pare his nails with his own penknife and to handle his own razor while Mr Papendick shaved him, a degree of freedom which the royal physicians deplored. They, more especially Richard Warren, were pessimistic about the king's possible recovery, whereas the Willises were hopeful that he might regain his health. When the king was again ill in December 1810 Robert Willis told a parliamentary committee that the nature of the king's illness made recovery possible:

> I consider the king's derangement more nearly allied to delirium. . . . In delirium, the mind is actively employed upon past impressions. . . . There is also a considerable disturbance in the general constitution: great restlessness, want of sleep, and total unconsciousness of surrounding objects. In insanity, there may be little or no disturbance, apparently, in the general constitution; the mind is occupied upon some fixed assumed idea. . . . Taking the king's insanity, therefore, and delirium, as two points, I would place derangement of mind somewhere between them. His Majesty's illness, uniformally, partakes more of the delirium than of the insanity.[16]

The doctors in 1788 needed every ounce of optimism which they could muster. George's illness had precipitated a political crisis of some magnitude. Since he was unable to take responsibility for government, his son, the prince of Wales, had to step in. 'As the poor king grew worse', Fanny Burney observed, 'general hope seemed universally to abate; and the Prince of Wales took the government of the house into his own hands.'[17] Nor were the prince and his brother, the duke of York, aided and abetted by the king's doctor, Richard Warren, who was a supporter of the Whigs, averse to exploiting the situation to further their own interests. The Whig Party saw in the king's illness an unforeseen opportunity for getting rid of William Pitt and his Tory supporters and gaining control over the government.

The prince of Wales whose profligacy and extravagance had led to strained relations with his father gave his support to the Whigs and their leader, Charles James Fox. If the king was likely to be incapacitated for some time, conceivably for the remainder of his life, a regent would have to be appointed to rule in his stead.[18] It was obvious to the Whigs that George, prince of Wales, was the man to hold the office.

All that William Pitt and the Tories could do, apart from praying for the king's recovery, was to employ delaying tactics and seek to limit the powers of the regent should the bill come before the House of Commons. The Tories were in practice helped by the comparative lack of solidity in the Whig ranks. The prince of Wales was himself a capricious and doubtful ally, though an indispensable one since if he became regent he would become the giver of preferment and patronage. The Whigs were themselves split by factions and Charles James Fox was an unreliable leader.

For the moment everything seemed, however, to be going their way. They were convinced that the king would not recover. 'An entire and speedy recovery', Lord Loughborough reassured the Whig leader, 'seems to me beyond the reach of any reasonable hopes.' Loughborough himself put forward the proposal which Fox was to adopt that the prince of Wales had an undoubted and legal right to be the regent. But even the Whigs were not quite sure about the powers which the regent should have, while the Tories sought to make sure that any regency would be of limited duration. The death of the Speaker of the House of Commons, Cornwall, on 2 January 1789 made the issue an even more pressing one since the appointment of a new Speaker had to be confirmed by the king or his representative. On 12 February a Regency Bill drawn up by Pitt passed the House of Commons; but by that time there were signs that the political crisis was in its final stages as the king's health began slowly to mend.

The flickers of light were becoming more pronounced. On 2 February 1789 Fanny Burney had been walking in the gardens at Kew when to her alarm she saw the king coming towards her, attended by two of his doctors. 'What was my terror', she confided to her diary, 'to hear the voice of the king himself loudly and hoarsely calling after me, "Miss Burney! Miss Burney!" Heavens how I ran! My feet was not sensible that they touched the ground.' At last, begged to stop by Dr Willis, Fanny desisted. When the king came up to her he greeted her very cordially and spoke rationally. 'Why did you go away?' he asked. Then he told her that he intended to make some new ministerial appointments.[19]

The king's restoration to health was a matter for great celebration throughout the nation. Although he was still very easily tired, he stood up well to the three hours' ordeal of a thanksgiving service in St Paul's Cathedral on St George's Day 1789, observing feelingly to the archbishop of Canterbury, 'My Lord, I have twice read over the evidence of the physicians on my case, and if I can stand that, I can stand anything.'

The service at St Paul's took place only a few months before the storming of the Bastille in Paris, an event which symbolically released an era of revolution and international war which was to affect the domestic and foreign politics of every nation. The king's health seemed to stand up well to the strains created by these stirring events, and it was twelve years before he had a renewal of his trouble, which could have been conceivably brought on by an unexpected change of ministry in 1801 and a proposal to introduce a bill to free the Roman Catholics from the penal legislation imposed on them, a law which the king saw as a breach of his coronation oath.

The old symptoms reappeared in February 1801 – stomach pains, muscular weakness, hoarseness, a fast pulse, sweating, insomnia and delirium; once again his urine was unusually dark in colour. 'I have', the king commented to General Garth when they were riding together, 'not had any sleep this night, and am very bilious and unwell.' Once again the royal physicians believed that he might have caught a chill by sitting over long in a very cold church, but there were soon indications that the events of 1788 were to repeat themselves. He was emotionally labile, sometimes bursting into tears, showing anger and constantly fidgeting. 'If he attempted to play the game of drafts he unconsciously turned the board about incessantly; if a table cloth was laid, he also turned it round and round unable to keep his hands still. . . . In the same manner his state of nerves seemed to compel him to roll up his handkerchiefs . . . on which in some days he had not less than 40 or 50.'[20]

To the king's horror the Willises were recalled. George III, Thomas Willis complained naively, had 'imbibed a prejudice against us'. As in 1788 they were optimistic about his chances of recovery, and in a comparatively short time he did become quieter, slept better and talked more rationally. 'He was afraid,' the king said, 'he had been ill for a long time,' but he did not know how long. On 14 March 1801 he was well enough to receive Pitt and three days later to preside over a meeting of the Privy Council.

Although his health improved slowly, he was still much depressed and when the prince of Wales saw his father for the first time in four weeks on Sunday 19 April, the king 'continually and repeatedly talked of himself as a dying man, determined to go abroad. . . . to make over the Government to the Prince. . . . He took the Prince to the room, the scene of the late confinement, and complained of the treatment he had experienced in terms the most moving.'[21]

The Willises had been supposed to leave at the end of March but partly at the request of the king's daughter, the Princess Elizabeth who was still worried by her father's state of health, to the king's fury they stayed on. Almost literally they 'kidnapped' their royal patient and kept him in virtual confinement until mid-May. 'I spoke to him', Thomas Willis wrote, 'at once of his situation and the necessity there was that he should be immediately under control again. His Majesty sat down, turning very pale . . . and looking very sternly at me exclaimed, "Sir, I will never forgive you whilst you live." '[22]

By early June he was, however, sufficiently recovered to go to Weymouth to recuperate. 'Sea-bathing', as he told his friend, Bishop Hurd of Worcester on 20 October 1801, 'has had its usual success with me, and in truth it was never more necessary, for the severe fever I had the last winter left many unpleasant sensations. . . . These are nearly removed. I am forced to be very careful and to avoid anything of fatigue. . . .'[23]

Three years later, in February 1804, he had another short attack, again allegedly brought on by a chill caused by wearing wet clothes. When the prime minister, Henry Addington, wanted to send for the Willises the dukes of Kent and Cumberland, the king's sons, refused to allow them access on the grounds that if the king saw them this would produce in the king 'an irritation of mind for which the worse consequences might be apprehended'. In their stead another 'mad-doctor', Samuel Simmons, physician to St Luke's Hospital for lunatics, was summoned to supervise the treatment of the king; but his methods were similar to those employed by the Willises, and he was to be no more popular with the king than his predecessors had been. This attack was, however, relatively short in duration and by the end of March a bulletin announced, somewhat prematurely, that 'His Majesty is much better and in our opinion a short time will perfect his recovery.'

The king continued in fact to be in an extremely irritable state of mind, being particularly vexed by that 'horrible doctor' Simmons. Once more the Whigs, accusing William Pitt and the ministry of concealing the true state of the king's health, began to talk of a regency. But by the end of July 1804 George was well enough to prorogue parliament and he went again to recuperate at Weymouth. His physician, Sir Francis Milman, thought it better that he should not bathe in the open sea. Once again the strain on his wife and family had been considerable, resulting in a virtual separation between the king and his wife, for Queen Charlotte took an aversion to the renewal of marital relations, causing the king, perhaps the most chaste of the Hanoverian monarchs, to say jokingly that he might have to take a mistress.

Such attacks were inevitably taking their toll on the king's health, mentally as well as physically, more especially as he was by now not very far short of his seventieth birthday. Whatever the nature of the king's illness, it had made irremediable ravages on his constitution, even after his apparent recovery. The burden of his royal responsibilities as the long and bloody war with France continued, with significant contingent political and economic effects for his own people, weighed heavily on him. His sight was beginning to fail, and his ability to concentrate diminished. In 1810 his favourite daughter Amelia became seriously ill and eventually died.

Shortly after the subdued celebrations on 25 October 1810 which marked the fiftieth anniversary of the king's accession to the throne, his malady returned. So critical was the political situation and so uncertain the chances of his recovery that the events of 1788–9 seemed about to repeat themselves as Lord Grenville commented in a letter to Lord Grey:

> That attack began about 22 October, this about 25th. Parliament was then prorogued to the 20 November, now 23rd. . . . In the two attacks in 1801 and 1804, a Parliament was actually sitting, the thing was in some degree kept from public observation, but in this instance, as in 1788, it must . . . be brought forward.[24]

Given the king's age, seventy-two, his failing eyesight and his deteriorating health, the chances for a full recovery seemed slim. Reluctantly the king's physician, Sir Henry Halford, decided that recourse would have to be made to Simmons, who arrived at Windsor with four assistants and demanded 'the sole management of the king', a request which was at first refused. But the king acted so violently that he had again to be put in a strait-waistcoat. He had quiet periods when he played airs upon a harpsichord which had belonged originally to Handel, but he rambled incoherently and once again became obsessed by his infatuation for Lady Pembroke, now herself an old lady of seventy-five; she was to live to be ninety-three 'They refuse', he complained, 'to let me go to Lady Pembroke although everyone knows that I am married to her; but what is worst of all, is that that infamous scoundrel Halford [his physician] was at the marriage, and now has the effrontery to deny it to my face.' He swore five times on the Bible that 'he would be faithful to his dear Eliza who had been faithful to him for fifty-five years'. 'Lady Pembroke', Henrietta, Lady Bessborough had written in September 1804, 'says the king persecutes her with love letters, and that she has been obliged to write very seriously to him to desist – elle l'a furieusement attendu – but certainly in favour of his taste, she is the handsomest woman of 70 I ever saw.' He talked of founding a 'female order', possibly along the lines of the Order of the Garter, a notion which his contemporaries thought singularly distasteful.

It had become plain that a regency was now a political necessity. The prime minister Spencer Perceval tried to reassure the king 'that the same course nearly had been pursued as that which had been approved by His Majesty after his illness in 1789, so as to provide his finding everything as nearly as possible upon recovery in the same state as before.' Although the king found it difficult to concentrate he commented on the proposal sensibly. The prince of Wales, on the advice of Sir Henry Halford who warned him that a change of government might have adverse effects on his father's health, left the ministry unaltered. Almost imperceptibly George III had ceased for all practical purposes to be king.

It might well have been kinder to the old man to have tried to indulge his whims and to have kept him within the context of family life, but as his mental disorder apparently deteriorated into senile dementia he was kept under restraint and separated from his family, living in a world of his own deranged imagination, losing, as Lord Auckland put it:

all the vestiges of partial reasoning and recollections which had hitherto been preserved through the whole of his illness, engrossed by the wildest and most extravagant fancies. He imagines that he has not only acquired the power of living forever, but that he can call from the dead whomsoever he pleases, and makes them of any age. . . . In short he appears to be living . . . in another world, and has lost almost all interest in the concerns of this.[25]

For the remainder of his like he existed in this solitary other world. The regency had become permanent. His wife, Queen Charlotte died in November 1818 but her death passed him by. He was now blind as well as deaf. He had occasional paroxysms when he talked endlessly, once for some sixty hours, but for the most part his life was calm, his only amusement 'the inexhaustible resources of his distempered imagination'. When his son, the duke of York, came to visit him at the end of November 1819, he found that his father was 'amusing himself with playing upon the harpsichord and singing with as strong and firm a voice as ever I heard . . . but we must not conceal from ourselves that His Majesty is greatly emaciated within the last twelve months . . . the frame is so much weaker that we can no longer look forward to his being preserved to us for any length of time.'[26] At Christmas 1819 the paroxysms returned and at 8.32 p.m. on the evening of 29 January 1820 George III died.

Is it possible at this distance of time to reach any conclusion as to the nature of the illness by which King George III was afflicted before he was caught up in the cobweb of senile dementia? Contemporaries were plainly very perplexed. Some even blamed the mineral waters of Cheltenham Spa which he had been drinking shortly before he fell seriously ill in 1788. 'The king's late disorder', the *London Chronicle* reported 'was owing solely to his drinking the waters of Cheltenham' which, Horace Walpole observed, were 'the most violent of all lotions and stronger than Madeira and Champagne', capable of 'deranging' the intellect for months.[27]

The evidence is plainly insufficient in its detail to make any exact diagnosis of the

George III in old age as he was in his final illness, from an engraving by Charles Turner (photograph: The Wellcome Institute Library, London, © The Trustee of the Wellcome Trust, 1993)

king's illness possible. We are left seeking a balance between possibilities and probabilities. Even if the cause of George III's mental trouble was organic, psychological ingredients must surely have had a part to play. Beneath his stolid exterior George had always been a nervous, highly strung man. The impression created by the cartoonists of 'Farmer George' is belied by his interest in and patronage of the arts. He was a very sensitive man who could be easily upset, though he might not show it. There may well have been no immediate occasion for his breakdown, except possibly in 1801 when the issue of Roman Catholic Emancipation was a cause of anxiety, but stress accumulates through the years, and may seek an outlet when least expected. If there was no single event in 1788 to explain the serious illness of that year, the past two decades of his reign had been in many respects politically fraught, not least by the War of American Independence. There is, as we have seen earlier, an intangible and inextricable relationship between bodily and mental ill-health so that it would still not be historically improper to find in George's illness deep psychological fissures.

In more recent times it has been asserted that George III's illness was manic-depressive in its character; and some at least of his actions and attitudes appear equally to have been of a schizophrenic nature. In 1967 the current interpretations of George III's illness were challenged by the exhaustive research of two medical historians, Ida Macalpine and her son Richard Hunter. In an article printed originally in the *British Medical Journal*[28] they suggested that the king suffered from a rare metabolic disorder, acute intermittent porphyria, a diagnosis which they amended in their subsequent book *George III and the Mad Business* to an attack of an alternative and even more severe form of the same illness, variegate porphyria.

Porphyria is a little known disease, rampant within a community in South Africa where it appears to have been introduced by a Dutch burgher in 1688 and which was subsequently disseminated among some eight thousand of his descendants, and found also in Sweden.[29] It seems possible that its characteristic symptoms which included fever, hoarseness of voice, abdominal pain, rapid pulse, loss of appetite, wasting of the muscles, insomnia and more especially a discoloration of the urine (which appeared after it had been left standing as red or reddish-brown or even purplish in colour), may have, as in other diseases, changed over the generations. In the debate which followed the publication of Macalpine and Hunter's book, some experts on porphyria declared that it had been originally a comparatively innocuous disease, causing most noticeably a sensitivity of the skin, which did not greatly affect the vigour or judgement of those afflicted by it. Its growing severity was in part attributed to the treatment of patients by modern drugs, notably the sulphanomides, which apparently led to more pronounced and dangerous symptoms, among them stupor, hallucinations, manic outbreaks and paralysis of the limbs. While one contemporary expert on porphyria accepted the conclusion that mental disturbances, such as George III experienced, could be a symptom of a sufferer from variegate porphyria, there were those who were sceptical of the supposition that insanity had been a characteristic feature of the disease in past ages.

To support their conclusions Macalpine and Hunter rallied a remarkable catena of historical evidence, tracing the earliest onset of porphyria to Mary, Queen of Scots, and finding its dissemination among her descendants. On the substantial and detailed evidence of James I's physician Sir Theodore de Mayerne they concluded that, like his mother, James too was a victim of porphyria. Subsequently they traced its course through the illnesses and deaths of a number of James I's descendants, his son and heir, Henry, prince of Wales, in 1612, of Charles II's sister, Henrietta, duchess of Orléans, at the age of twenty-six in 1670 and possibly of her daughter, Marie Louise, the first wife of Charles II of Spain. The last Stuart monarch, Queen Anne, was another sufferer; though her only surviving son, William, duke of Gloucester, succumbed to smallpox. Through James I's daughter, Elizabeth, the 'Winter Queen' of Bohemia and her daughter, the Electress Sophia of Hanover, skipping the first two Hanoverian kings, it passed to her great-grandson, George III and his sister, Caroline Matilda, queen of Denmark. Through either Sophia's daughter, Sophia Charlotte, queen of Prussia, or George I's daughter, Sophia Dorothea, the wife of Frederick William I of Prussia, porphyria was transmitted to Frederick William's son, Frederick the Great of Prussia.

The hereditary taint was passed on by George III to at least four of his sons, George IV (and possibly to his daughter the princess Charlotte who died at the early age of twenty-one in childbirth in 1817), Frederick, duke of York, Augustus, duke of Sussex and Edward, duke of Kent, the father of Queen Victoria. Although Victoria may have acted as a carrier of haemophilia, she does not appear to have transmitted porphyria to her many descendants, or at least only conceivably to one of them, for Macalpine and Hunter claimed that two members of the Hanoverian royal family, then living, were sufferers from porphyria.[30] They did not provide detailed evidence or names; but they were clearly referring to German princesses and it seems highly likely that they had also in mind an uncle of queen Elizabeth II, all of whom have since died.

It is *prima facie* difficult to refute findings based on such an imposing array of evidence, but certain doubts, expressed by some critics at the time, remain. Experts on porphyria have, for instance, disagreed as to whether in the past insanity was a likely manifestation of the disease and, for instance, whether diarrhoea or constipation was a feature of the illness. That George III suffered from a looseness of the bowels as a result of the over-use of purgatives, then thought to be a necessary part of the treatment, might even account for the discoloration of the urine. The discoloration of the urine was perhaps the most vital part of the evidence put forward by Macalpine and Hunter who also drew attention to the description of James I's urine as being of the colour of Alicante or port wine, but this may not be in itself sufficient to prove that George III was a sufferer from variegate porphyria since such discoloration can occur as a sequel to other medical conditions such as kidney disease or renal calculi from which the king suffered. Nor is it known whether the urine sample was discoloured as the king passed it or whether it changed colour, as is apparently the case with porphyriacs, after it had been left standing for some hours. All this does not specifically confute the conclusion that George III was a victim of variegate porphyria, but it suggests that it would be arbitrary to accept this as an ascertained fact.

The hefty evidence which traces the dissemination of porphyria among the descendants of Mary, Queen of Scots is perhaps more open to criticism because it is not beyond question that Mary, Queen of Scots and her son, James VI and I, were victims of the disease.[31] While it is true that many of the symptoms of the illness from which James I suffered might well suggest that he was the victim of a metabolic disorder, there are equally good reasons for supposing that he was afflicted by disease of the kidneys, which would account for the reddish coloration of his urine, and haematuria, aggravated by crippling arthritis, as his doctor Mayerne suggested. There is a substantial amount of doubt in attributing the death of George III's sister, Caroline Matilda of Denmark to porphyria and indeed of the deaths of some of the others in the royal gallery.

Moreover, if porphyria was the hereditary disease which afflicted George III it still seems surprising that it went through thirteen generations without giving rise to more than a few scattered incidents spread over centuries. It should, given the example of the porphyriac group in South Africa, have been much more widely distributed among the royal families concerned. Even the chance of a dominant gene surviving for so many centuries without mutation appears arithmetically slim. Furthermore if George III was the victim of acute variegate porphyria, his must surely have been an atypical and very severe case, for some of the other members of the royal families discussed by Macalpine and Hunter never suffered even remotely the mental agonies which he experienced.

It is doubtful whether the argument can be taken further. It is plain that in its symptoms porphyria can mimic other diseases, but Macalpine and Hunter's thesis, if in some respects flimsy, cannot be wholly refuted. Yet there is still surely room to wonder whether his illness may not at least have been in part psychological in its origin, and even to hold that he may still conceivably have been the victim of schizophrenia or a manic-depressive illness.

Except for the historians of medicine, the precise nature of George III's illness may be of no great importance, for its practical effects were the same whether the king suffered from variegate porphyria or from manic-depressive insanity. The king's behaviour, his logorrhea, his hallucinations, his violence, demonstrated that by normal criteria he was insane, and as a result during his illness he was so incapacitated that he could not govern and even had to be placed under restraint.

In one respect, however, the nature of his illness influenced the way in which historians have sought to interpret the reign of George III. If he was the victim of a life-long nervous and mental ailment which from time to time erupted into madness, then such disorder could well have impaired his political judgement throughout his life. If, on the other hand, he suffered from only occasional attacks of porphyria, then it was more likely that except during the attacks themselves his judgement would have been normal. Some earlier historians found in the king's nervous disorder an explanation for what they believed to be his attempts to recover the lost powers of the crown, for his treatment of ministers whom he did not like, such as Grenville and Chatham; and even attributed to it in part his responsibility for the outbreak of the War of American Independence, its prolongation and its disastrous conclusion. Such views, however, no longer hold water, not because George III did not have in his mind the seeds of madness but because historians were themselves mistaken in their interpretation of the policies he followed.

Certainly it is right, as his biographer, John Brooke, has strongly argued, that George III should be liberated from the image of the mad king which for so long held sway.[32] For the greater part of his reign he was a responsible and conscientious monarch. Yet it cannot be denied, whether the reasons for the onset of madness were organic or psychological, that for a few brief periods of his reign George III was mad, so mad that he could not govern his country. Had he not recovered from the most serious of these attacks in 1789, the prince of Wales would have become regent, probably replacing the Tory government of William Pitt by a Whig administration, possibly under Charles James Fox. What effect this would have had on the fast developing situation in a Europe let loose by revolution and war it is of course impossible to say, but it could have had serious effects for England. It did not happen and even though the later attacks provided the king's ministers with some anxious moments they were not for the country of critical importance. Ultimately George III's madness was a personal rather than a public tragedy.

XIII

Danish Charade

It seems historically ironical that George III's exact contemporary Christian VII of Denmark, who was married to his sister, Caroline Matilda, should have been a victim of madness. Until the close of his long life George III's mental illness, severe as it was in its manifestation, was sporadic in its impact, but for the greater part of his reign Christian VII was undoubtedly mad, even if he had his lucid periods. The irony may not end there, for if Macalpine and Hunter's verdicts were to be accepted, Christian's wife, Queen Caroline Matilda, like her brother, George III, suffered from porphyria and was to die from it an an early age.[1]

The Danish and the Hanoverian royal houses were closely related, for Christian's mother, Louisa, was a daughter of George II. When Christian visited England in 1768, people commented on his close resemblance to the British royal family. 'He is . . . extremely like the Royal family,' Lady Mary Coke wrote, 'but the one he resembles most is Prince Frederick' (the youngest brother of George III who died at the age of fifteen in 1765).[2] Horace Walpole said that the Danish king strutted exactly like his grandfather, George II, or a cock-sparrow.[3] The princess of Hesse averred that he reminded her more than anybody of the king's father, Frederick, prince of Wales, 'but that he curls his hair so high'. There in a sense the likeness ended, unless there were genetic factors at work, except in political terms. For if George III's madness caused a political crisis, the lunacy of his brother-in-law created not merely a political emergency but harbingered a moving personal tragedy.

The Danish monarchy, unlike that of Great Britain, was not a constitutional government, but, by the *lex regia* of 1665, an autocracy. The government of this small country could be affected decisively by the personality of its king as was demonstrated by the rule of Christian VII's grandfather, Christian VI, a well-intentioned man of very moderate ability, much influenced by his strong-minded, pietistic wife, Sophia Magdalena; he sought to impose a heavy-handed puritanical orthodoxy on his people, closing the theatres, banishing actors and upholding a strict Sabbatarian regime. Christian's son Frederick V, a big, burly man with a red face and a blueish pimpled nose, who became king in 1746, reacted against the inflexible rule of his father, and under his lead and that of his charming and popular English wife, Louisa, the court became a centre of gaiety rather than of gloom. Their second heir, Christian, was born on 29 January 1749. Two years later, to her husband's great grief, Louisa herself died.

Although six months later Frederick found a second wife in Juliana Maria of Brunswick, the king became a dipsomaniac, neglected affairs of state and his life-style became increasingly debauched. Affectionate by nature, so much so that he never lost the regard of his people, he became physically ill and even mentally disturbed before he died.

It is against this sombre background that Christian's upbringing has to be placed, and it goes some way to explain the schizoid features of his personality. His mother had died when he was two and his relations with his step-mother were never close. Verdicts seem to differ as to whether his step-mother, Queen Juliana Maria, was scheming and cold-hearted, or retiring and devout; but her affections were focused predominantly on her son, Frederick, Christian's half-brother, a weak and deformed prince for whose future his mother was certainly ambitious. That Christian had a damaged childhood seems plain enough. Void of affection, he was left to the mercy of his preceptors, the chief of whom, Ditlev Reventlow, was a brutal bully who did not hesitate to terrorize his young charge. He sometimes beat the young boy until he was found on the floor foaming at the mouth. Reventlow called him his 'doll': 'Let's go to show my doll,' the tutor said grimly as he gripped him by the hand to show him to the court.[4] In his task Reventlow was assisted by a dour Lutheran pastor, Georg Nielsen. Subjected to ignominy and physical abuse, the prince came to believe that he was an inmate of a prison rather than a resident in a royal palace.

This situation was to change for the better with the arrival in 1760 of another tutor, the twenty-eight-year-old Vaudois Swiss, Elie-Salomon François Reverdil, who had come to Copenhagen as a professor of mathematics two years previously. He was a sensible, compassionate man who tried to instruct his pupil in philosophy and the principles of benevolence, but he recognized that though Christian was a good linguist who spoke Danish, French and German and seemed to possess a lively intelligence, he was temperamentally a difficult and retarded student whose education had been singularly narrow, so that he was very inadequately prepared for the work of government. Much later in his life Reverdil, who died at Geneva in 1808, the same year as his former pupil, wrote his memoirs which form one of the principal sources for our knowledge of the young Danish prince.

It is fair to say that Reverdil's judgements may have been over-coloured by his experience of Christian in later life, but even if this bias is taken into account what he has to say suggests that as a young boy Christian displayed some signs of incipient insanity. Reverdil became, in his own words, 'the saddest of employees, a madman's keeper'. The boy was seemingly haunted by a deep feeling of insecurity and inadequacy. Fear always remained a characteristic feature of his personality, so that even as an adult he gave way to pressure from others stronger than himself. Simultaneously he developed early an abnormal concern with physical toughness.

Physically rather a weakling, short and slender in build, he tried to compensate for his deficiencies by creating a macho image of himself. The king's diminutive physique may well have been a significant ingredient in the development of his disturbed personality. He had to try to live up to his own idealistic image of himself. He wanted, he said, 'a perfectly tough body' and frequently examined his limbs and chest to see whether he was achieving this objective.[5] 'Men', so the psychologist W.H. Sheldon observed, 'whose temperament differs widely from that which accords with their physique are particularly subject to psychological conflict, since they are at odds with their own emotional constitution.'[6]

To call attention to himself he indulged in schoolboy pranks. He blackened his face and hid under the table at which his aunt, Princess Charlotte Amalie, was dining and terrified her by emerging shrieking. He threw powdered sugar over the head of his staid grandmother, Queen Sophia Magdalena, and a departing Lutheran pastor found that he had been struck on the head by a bun thrown by the crown prince.

As he grew older he replaced his tutors with the more indulgent company of his equerry, originally his page, Sperling, and his valet Kirchoff who introduced him to the more sensual pleasures of adolescence. Reverdil commented primly, 'We will throw a veil over the disorders in which Sperling would encourage him', but he added that they undoubtedly contributed to the onset of his madness. The Danish psychiatrist V. Christiansen who published his classic study of Christian's madness in 1906, attributed its onset, humorous as this now seems, in part to over-indulgence in masturbation.[7] He found an outlet for his aggressive instincts by stalking the streets of Copenhagen by night, showing off with pride a watchman's 'morning star', a club with iron spikes, which he had snatched as a trophy in a brawl in the dark streets of his capital.

When he was sixteen negotiations were opened for his marriage to his thirteen-year-old cousin, George III's sister, Caroline Matilda. In the disturbed diplomatic climate of a Europe still overshadowed by the bitter rivalries engendered by the Seven Years' War, the British saw the marriage with the future king of Denmark as a useful bastion against French influence and a reassurance of British power in northern Germany and the Baltic. The English envoy to Denmark, Titley, reported enthusiastically that Christian was 'very amiable, genteel . . . well grounded in the study of the law of nature and in general theology . . . [possessing] a manly countenance, a graceful and distinguishing figure'. What struck him most forcibly, as it did others, was his close resemblance to the English king as a young man. Although the engagement was announced to the British parliament on 10 January 1765, the marriage was not expected to take place for two years, a plan which had to be changed by the sudden death of Frederick V in 1766 and Christian's accession to the throne.

Christian's bride, Caroline Matilda, was a posthumous child, born four months after the death of her father, Frederick, prince of Wales, and brought up by his widow, the princess Augusta. She was ingenuous but attractive, with a porcelain sort of prettiness.[8] Her husband who shared her fair hair and light blue eyes, was not unprepossessing in appearance. They were perhaps *prima facie* not all that ill-matched.

The young princess was greatly depressed when she learned that her marriage was to take place sooner than she had expected, for since by Danish custom she could take no English ladies-in-waiting with her, for her it meant going into virtual exile. The ceremony was timed to take place at 7.00 p.m. in the drawing room at St James's Palace, the duke of York acting as proxy for the bridegroom, on Wednesday 2 October 1766. Nothing happened before 8.00 p.m., the 'poor little Queen', as Lady Mary Coke explained, 'being so overcome that she was obliged to remain in the state bed-chamber till she cou'd recover herself'.[9] The queen wept bitterly at her departure for her new country.[10]

When she arrived she was received with 'universal applause and affection', and the English envoys at Copenhagen wrote glowingly of her and her husband. Mr Titley said that Christian showed 'a most lively understanding' and Mr Cosby praised 'the masterly ease and dignity with which he expressed his sentiments'. In fact Christian had already tired of his wife with surprising swiftness. 'He said', Prince Charles of Hesse reported, 'she was excessively pretty, but as his Majesty is not always of the same mind, and the day of his marriage, which was five days after her arrival, he was a good deal out of humour.' 'The princess', the French ambassador, Ogier, told his government, 'has produced hardly any impression on the king's heart; and had she been even more amiable, she would have experienced the same fate. For how could she please a man, who most seriously believes that it is not fashionable (*'n'est pas du bon air'*) for a husband to love his wife.'[11] Yet, whatever he felt, Christian did his duty and in August 1767 Lady Mary Coke could report that she was glad that Caroline Matilda was not only 'very much liked' but was 'breeding, to the great joy of that nation'. The future Frederick VI was born on 28 January 1768. In practice Christian was already in the early stage of incipient schizophrenia.

Thrust by his father's death into a position of absolute power, remembering the humiliations to which he had been subject as a child, Christian determined to be, as the English envoy put it, 'thoroughly Master of his Affairs'. His father's ministers, though for the moment he retained the services of the able Count Bernstorff, were relegated to the shelf, Count Moltke being replaced by Count Danneskjold. Whether he was up to his royal responsibilities was, however, soon to be a matter of some doubt.

In fact the king's interest in government was slight. Freed from tutelage, he wanted most of all to indulge himself in those things which gave him the most satisfaction,

Christian VII during his visit to England in 1768, from a painting by Nathaniel Dance (Royal Collection Enterprises, © Her Majesty Queen Elizabeth II)

sexual and sensual. He found an apt preceptor and companion in the youthful Count Conrad Holcke, a young 'jackanapes' as Walpole called him, who readily pandered to his needs and who proved to be the evil genius of his early years as king. It was Holcke who provided him with a mistress Anna Catherine Benthagen, or Sløvet Katrine, more titillating than his demure English wife.[12]

Sløvet Katrine became the king's mistress, attended the theatre with him and sat in the royal box; when Reverdil remonstrated with the king over this he was told to return to Switzerland. She accompanied the king on his roistering expeditions disguised as a naval officer. In November 1767 at a masked ball at the Christianborg Palace it was commented that 'The king danced with no one else the whole evening.' The king showered gifts upon her and made her a baroness.

Holcke aided and abetted him in less savoury practices. Christian had elements of sado-masochism in his character which were probably expressions of his progressive mental illness. He was fascinated by public executions, and went incognito in Sperling's company to watch the execution of a Saxon, Moerl, for theft. There were times when Christian believed that he might himself be an incarnation of Moerl. At other times he played at mock executions and had a rack devised on which Holcke was ordered to beat him until he bled.[13]

The king's strange behaviour as well as his seeming infatuation with Katrine led to a growing coolness with his wife who found a strong champion in her doughty lady-in-waiting, Madame von Plessen. She had a caustic tongue, spoke of Christian as the 'Sultan' and was courageous enough to tell his secretary that she thought 'his conduct towards the Queen was of a nature that could only be tolerated by low women and in houses of ill fame'. Christian believing that Madame von Plessen was creating a barrier between his wife and himself, banished her, so greatly saddening the queen who found herself deprived of one of the very few friends at court she could really trust.

Within two years the king had done much to destroy the popular goodwill which had greeted his succession. There was public anger at the outcome of some of the king's nightly forays in the course of which, accompanied by Catherine, he had destroyed a brothel. His advisers told him forthwith that if he did not dismiss Catherine there would be a revolution. Christian, at heart a coward who was always ready to divest himself of a friend if there was a threat against himself, banished Catherine to Hamburg where she was later sent to prison.

Alienated from his wife and unpopular with his subjects Christian decided on a European tour, which included England, though he had no intention of taking his wife with him. His brother-in-law, George III, who had heard rumours of his misconduct, viewed the trip with less than enthusiasm. 'He [King Christian] is now opposite', the English envoy Gunning reported, 'in all respects from what he promised at his first setting out as is possible. Parts, however, are not wanting. I dread the consequences of the present project, though contrary perhaps to our expectation some good may result from it.'

So the young Danish king, accompanied by a suite of fifty-four persons, including Count Holcke and his chief minister Bernstorff, set out for England in May 1768, the king supposedly travelling incognito as the count of Travendal. At Hamburg the company was joined on 6 June 1768 by Johann Friedrich Struensee as travelling physician. Tall, broad-shouldered and highly intelligent, Struensee was in many respects unconventional, sceptical, liberal but egocentric. He was accustomed to read in bed by the light of two candles resting in the hands of a skeleton. His meeting with King Christian was as ominous for his future as for that of Denmark.

The royal party reached Calais and boarded the English yacht *Mary* which George III had provided for the crossing; but on their arrival at Dover on 9 August 1768 they found that no coaches had been arranged for their journey, so they had to avail themselves of hired carriages.[14] Christian was certainly not in the best of humour when the municipal and cathedral authorities greeted him at Canterbury, for he disliked formal ceremonies of this kind, and he remarked to Bernstorff that 'the last king of Denmark who entered Canterbury laid that city in ashes and massacred its inhabitants'.

Nor was his English brother-in-law in London when he arrived at the lodgings in the Stable Yard at St James's Palace placed at his disposal, accommodation of which the Danish courtiers were strongly critical – 'By Heaven!' Count Holcke was heard to exclaim, 'this will never do; it is not fit to lodge a *Christian*!' George III who had gone to Richmond appeared on the scene some time after his brother-in-law's arrival.[15] But their interview did not last much more than twenty minutes and though the English king gave an allowance of £84 a day to pay for his brother-in-law's board and had ordered the gold plate to be brought from the Tower for his use, his own entertainment was of a formal and limited nature, a family dinner party, a ball at the Queen's House and a 'farewell entertainment' at Richmond Lodge on 26 September.

But what George III lacked in enthusiasm was made up by the welcome given to Christian by the aristocracy and the admiring shouts of the populace. The princess Amelia gave a great evening party at Gunnersbury House with over a hundred guests, who in the pleasant warmth of an August evening, walked on the terrace, watching a magnificent display of fireworks, which was followed by a supper and a ball, led by the king dancing with the duchess of Manchester. He was wearing a splendid suit of silver silk embroidered with silver thread and his politeness, even though he did not shine at country dancing, was such that, wrote Lady Mary Coke, 'it convinces me he has sense, and can act properly when he pleases'.[16] There was, however, already an undercurrent of criticism and Lady Talbot judiciously if affectionately nicknamed him 'the Northern Scamp'.

This particular festivity actually proved too much for the king, who for the next day or so was indisposed, as a result, so Lady Mary Coke surmised, of eating too much fruit, causing him to refuse an invitation to dine with the imperial ambassador, even though the king called at his residence, pale of face, dressed exquisitely in blue and white silk, to chat with the ladies. But the round of festivities, of parties and masked balls went on.

What seemed astonishing was the enthusiasm of the populace, perhaps, however, understandable in view of the gratuities which the king flung profusely at the cost of the Danish treasury. Christian undoubtedly wallowed in his popularity; 'I suppose he does not dislike the pleasure the people have in looking at him.' He arranged to dine in public in the banqueting-hall at St James's; he dressed in the morning with the window sashes down, so that he might be seen by the passers-by.[17]

The king's visit was supposedly educational. In pursuit of enlightenment arrangements were made for him to travel outside London.[18] He proved popular the length and breadth of England, even the illustrious universities of Oxford and Cambridge presenting him with honorary doctorates.

In general, given his youth, it was thought that he had conducted himself well, though he left a distinctly mixed impression behind him. When he went to see the opera, the *Buona Figliola*, Lady Mary Coke commented disapprovingly that he not only stood for the first act but 'lean'd over the Box with his elbows and head. . . . He picked his Nose which you know is neither graceful nor royal. Towards the latter end he seem'd excessively tired and gaped very much.'[19] Walpole commented caustically to Sir Horace Mann that at the play *The Provoked Wife*, 'he clapped whenever there was a sentence against matrimony, a very civil proceeding when his wife is an English princess'.[20]

There was certainly a seamier side to his visit. After dark the king and his boon companions crept out from St James's Palace disguised as sailors to explore the lower haunts of the city. 'He is certainly amorous', Walpole told Strafford, reporting gossip as he loved to do, 'but stays so short a time, that the ladies who intend to be undone must not haggle. They must do their business in the twinkling of an *allemande*, or he will be flown.'[21] For a time he installed an actress, a 'stripper' would be a more appropriate term, at St James's, 'that Strange Girl', Lady Mary Coke wrote, 'that you remember was used to put herself out upon the Stage, almost all her clothes off'.[22] The king and his companions vandalized the lodgings at St James's, smashing the furniture and causing much damage.

Yet, all told the visit from the king's point of view was a success. He was given a great send-off. Escorted by the city officials he sailed down the Thames from Westminster to the Temple in the state barge. Generous in his gifts to high and low, he left London on 12 October 'followed by the sincerest blessings of enormous crowds who ran after his carriage for miles out of the city'. These were shouts which were to re-echo in the king's mind in the empty years which were to follow.

His travels were not quite over, for from England he crossed to France where he received almost as ecstatic a welcome. 'We are taking the life out of this poor little Dane', Madame du Deffand told Walpole. He was bombarded with parties and entertainments, and fêted by both the Académie des Sciences and the Académie Française where the Abbé Voisenon recited a poem in his praise. Yet his trip revealed some disconcerting if fleeting glimpses into the king's aberrant personality. Although Louis XV, a connoisseur in such matters, had provided a bevy of actresses for his pleasure, the king seemed curiously indifferent, even hostile, to such company; possibly because he had been affected by some venereal complaint. Perhaps more sinister was the report that the king's speech was often rambling and sometimes incoherent. Behind the facile façade there were at least some hints of a lack of mental balance.

When he returned to Denmark in January 1769 he was greeted by his wife at Roskilde, and for a time their relationship seemed to be on a better footing. Caroline Matilda liked to dress in male riding costume, wearing a scarlet coat and buckskin breeches. Although the more strait-laced were highly critical, the queen's attire appealed to the king's macho tastes. 'The king', Reverdil said, 'was a great friend of everything militating against Court etiquette and was exceedingly pleased with the Queen's new dress', but, he added, 'dressed as a man she appeared far too small.'[23]

Then, in October, she fell ill. A dropsical condition, said some; a venereal complaint caught from her husband, said the uncharitable. Very conceivably it may have been a minor nervous breakdown, to which her husband's bizarre behaviour may well have contributed. The queen, the English envoy Gunning reported obscurely on 4 November 1769, showed

> some unfavourable symptoms . . . though there appears no immediate danger, yet the situation the queen of Denmark is at present in, is too critical not to make it highly necessary to obviate the worse symptoms, and as this happy effect depends very much upon His Majesty's own care, I believe she would be wrought upon by nothing more successfully than by some affectionate expostulation from the King, upon the very great importance of her life.

With some difficulty she was prevailed upon to consult Struensee, now the king's physician in ordinary, reluctantly because she suspected that it was he who had been instrumental in introducing her husband to a new mistress, Madame Birsette von Gabel, an unfortunate young woman who was shortly to die, in August 1769, giving birth to a stillborn child. But Struensee not only restored the queen's health but

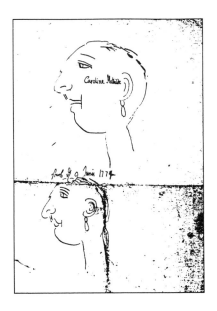

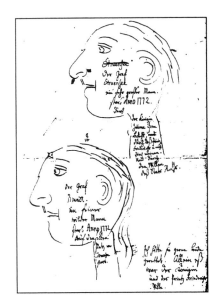

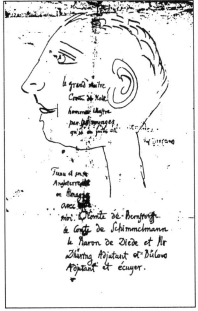

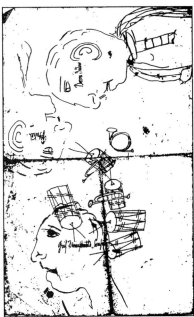

Sketches by King Christian VII: *top left* Queen Caroline Matilda. The date given for her death of 9 June 1774 is wrong: she died on 10 May 1775; *top right* his ministers, Struensee and Brandt. The second half of the inscriptions read: 'died at the behest of Queen Juliane and Prince Frederick and not through my will or the will of the council of the State'; and, 'I would have saved them if I could. It was all done at the will of the Queen and Prince Frederick.'; *bottom left* his chamberlain, Count Holcke. Part of the inscription reads: 'a man made illustrious by the voyages which he made with me to France, England and Germany'; *bottom right* his courtiers, Count Danneskjold and Baron Bülow (Royal Danish Archives)

injected her with a new found confidence and interest in life. He also successfully inoculated her son, the crown prince Frederick, against smallpox, a procedure which was criticized by more conservative churchmen and doctors. Some ten years older than the queen, Struensee exerted a powerful fascination over her, so that they became ever more intimate.

Struensee was himself a man of contradictions. He was politically ambitious and yet full of enlightened rationalism. He had come to dominate the impressionable king, whose schizophrenic propensities were becoming daily more evident. 'The king', Struensee told Caroline Matilda, 'will have to be ruled by someone. And it would be more to my interest that he should be ruled by Your Majesty than by another.' At first Christian seemed to fall completely under Struensee's domination. At his insistence the king dismissed his former advisers and installed Struensee as head of a secret cabinet, assisted by Enevold Brandt. Struensee introduced an amazing mass of reforming legislation which transformed every aspect of the national life, abolishing the censorship of the press and striking out at the vested interest of the civil service, the treasury and the church. He entered on a policy of retrenchmant reducing expenditure on the court and abolished nearly fifty religious holidays. It was inevitable that there should be a hostile reaction to a minister who himself flaunted his newly won authority, living in some state and attended by footmen dressed in white and scarlet livery.

The validity of what Struensee was trying to do, his indubitably far-sighted if unpopular reforming forays into the social, economic and religious infrastructure of Danish life, lay ultimately in the unrestricted monarchical authority of the Danish crown. If Christian supported Struensee, he could be, and he thought that he was, unassailable. He was installed in a ground-floor apartment at the Christianborg Palace, and appointed to the office of 'Director of Requests', a post which gave him supreme authority over all departments of state, the heads of which had to communicate with the king only by writing. On 15 July 1771 Christian signed a decree appointing Struensee 'Privy Cabinet Minister' and giving the minister's orders the 'same validity as those drawn by our own hand. They shall be immediately obeyed'. Christian's dependence upon Struensee was itself a sign of his own mental weakness.

For the fundamental snag in this situation was the deteriorating mental health of the king himself. He was prey to hallucinations. At times he questioned his own birth, suggesting that he was really the offspring of his mother's love affair with Lord Stanhope. At other times he claimed to be a son of the king of Sardinia or of a counsellor of the French parlement whom he had met in Paris; more ludicrously that the empress of Russia was his mother and even that his own wife was really his mother. At other times he held that he was a changeling who had been substituted at birth for the true prince. Frederick V was not his real father and though Struensee tried to reassure him by pointing out his resemblance to his grandfather Christian VI he still insisted that he was not the rightful king, and imagined on one occasion that the royal council was to proclaim his illegitimacy, an announcement which would be preceded by a thunderclap or even by an earth tremor. Although he was passionately concerned to preserve and protect the royal dignity, he declared that he had no wish to be king, that he found the royal duties onerous, and on his tour of Europe he suggested to Struensee when they were at Antwerp that they might run away together.

He was still obsessed with his physique, using every method he could think of to toughen his body, pinching the skin, pummelling it and in other ways seeking to make it impermeable as marble, immune to blows from the sword or gunshot. A real man, he held, would readily submit his body to physical torment, even to martyrdom. He jumped high in the air, and ran round the palace gardens at all times of the day and night, banged his hands and even his head against the wall until the blood ran. Sometimes he rubbed snow or ice and even gunpowder on his stomach and on another occasion applied burning pieces of firewood to his skin.

His vivid imagination ran riot, and he indulged in an ever-changing kaleidoscope of fantasy, punctuating it with acts of real or imagined violence. He found an outlet for his aggressive desires by smashing the windows of his own palace and breaking up the furniture of the state rooms. 'This morning the king', Count Rantzau wrote to Gahler on 20 June 1771, 'has been walking alone with his young friends. As there is no longer any furniture in his own apartment, he made sorties on next door's furniture. This morning he made a tour of all the rooms of us others, opening them up and looking inside. They finished by taking two windows off their hinges and throwing them below. One had either to laugh or cry but it made the atmosphere at dinner dreadful.' This cannot itself have been much helped by the king's habit of keeping dinner waiting for some hours and often rising abruptly before the dinner had ended; the servants were instructed to try to hold down the king's chair. In his vandalistic rampages Christian was helped by a black page, Moranti, a native from the Danish colony on the Gold Coast, and by his female companion, who one Sunday flung the contents of one of the rooms of the Hirscholm Palace from the balcony to the courtyard below. The king was apparently only just prevented from hurling Moranti and his dog Gourmand, to whom Christian was actually devoted, down as well. The young monarch liked nothing better than to fight with Moranti, rolling with him on the floor biting and scratching, though Christian was rarely beaten except by his own wish.

This masochistic element in his personality explains a strange encounter involving Struensee's colleague, Brandt, who always did what he could to humour the king. When Brandt was sitting at dinner at the royal table, the king suddenly shouted threateningly, 'I am going to thrash you, Count, do you hear me?' Brandt made no reply but when dinner had ended Struensee and the queen both remonstrated with the king for insulting Brandt without provocation. 'He is a poltroon', Christian shouted, 'and I will make him submit to my will.'

Later that evening Brandt went himself to the royal apartment and challenged the king to a duel. Christian accepted the challenge, rejected swords or pistols but agreed to a fist fight. In spite of the king's liking for punishment, he had this time taken on more than he had bargained for. He was so badly beaten that he was left writhing on the floor, begging for mercy. Brandt 'battered him without pity, insulted him with words and threatened him in the rudest way; he cursed him, wrestled with him and reduced him to asking for quarter. At last he left him much bruised and even more terrified.'[24]

More often the violent imagery was an output of his imagination. He spoke of running amok in the palace, intending to kill the first person he met, insulting people by spitting at them, slapping them on the face or even throwing plates and knives at them. He imagined himself running down the streets breaking windows, killing the passers-by, frequenting brothels, fighting with watchmen and associating with wicked persons in the most perverted of activities. Waking in the morning he would declare that he had killed six or seven people in the night. Mindful perhaps of his affair with 'Gaiters Catherine', he conjured up another mistress whom he called De la Roquer. According to Christian she was tall, robust and strong, resembling a man more than a woman, with large hands, a debauched and drunken creature with whom the king imagined that he roamed the streets, beating up people and in his turn being beaten up and getting drunk. His nights were often wakeful and he would chatter for hours on end about his fantasies to those who would listen. He tried to search out men of like mind to himself, those whom he dubbed '*Comme-ça*', actors, soldiers, sailors and drop-outs.

His Swiss tutor, Reverdil, who had returned to court found him at first lucid and sensible but closer acquaintance revealed that his mind was very confused. ' "You are Brandt", he said to me; then, giving over to a rapid and incoherent prattle, he repeated several verses of *Zaire*, which we had read together four years previously. Then he said "You are Denize; you are Latour", French actors who had been in his service; at last he realised that it was myself.'

Reverdil commented that the king's moods fluctuated wildly, passing quickly from a state of wild excitement to one of deep depression. The English, Christian said in an elated moment, had regarded him as a god; and as a king he thought he really eclipsed all other monarchs. Then his mood changed, and he spoke of himself as '*der kleine Mann*', and even contemplated doing away with himself. As they walked beside the palace lake the king exclaimed, 'But how can I do it, without making a scandal? And if I do, shall I not be even more unhappy? Shall I drown myself? Or knock my head against the wall?' Reverdil thought it best to try to humour him. 'Do', he told the king, 'as you think best.' The next day the king suggested that they might go for a row on the lake. 'I should like to jump in', he said sadly, 'and then be pulled out very quickly', adding in German (for normally they conversed in French), '*Ich bin confus*' ('I am confused'); '*Es rappelt bei mir*' ('There is a noise in my head'); '*Er ist ganz übergeschnappt*' ('I am not quite myself'). When at his request Reverdil tried to read to him, he was unable to concentrate. As he sat staring in front of him, he murmured, 'Struensee, is he the Queen's *cicisbeo*? Does the king of Prussia sleep with Matilda? Or is it Struensee?'[25]

Such vivid fantasies appeared to be part of the problem of identity which haunted him. If he was not his father's son, was he not one of six special beings born morally blind whose objectives could only be achieved through self-indulgence in debauchery and self-torment, not because such activities gave pleasure but because they were an aspect of his true objective in life? The ordinary things of life, like the people around him, were an illusion. Was there not, he asked of Struensee, a beyond after death different from that which the teachers of religion and philosophy provided?

Although fundamentally his disposition was cowardly, in compensation he sought to present a macho image to the world, believing that the truly courageous man would stick at nothing. He had indeed moments when he seemed normal, but he was subject to sudden changes of mood when he vented his anger against those nearest to him. He was so mistrustful and suspicious and so easily took offence that even his closest servants were liable to instant dismissal. He would not stand any contradiction and grew angry if those around him tried to persuade him that his fantasies were imaginary. Their advice might momentarily reduce him to melancholy and even to tears but it was of no lasting effect. He listened neither to his wife nor to Struensee nor to Brandt nor to his chamberlain, Warenstalt; indeed he even obliged Warenstalt to accompany him on an expedition to the town, roaming the streets and breaking windows, among them those of his former tutor, Count Reventlow.

Bernstorff suggested to Struensee that the king's excesses were the product of adolescence which he would outgrow, but Struensee knew better. He advised the king to take cold baths, but without avail; it seems likely that opium may have been administered as a sedative from time to time. Struensee had acquired such an ascendancy over the mind of his royal master that it was he whom the king requested to search his bedchamber to ensure that no assassin was hiding in the room. But Struensee had a growing band of enemies, not merely among the courtiers but more especially among those who were jealous of the authority he wielded and who resented the reforms which he had made in the government of Denmark.

Struensee's power thus depended ultimately on the goodwill of an increasingly deranged prince whose indiscretions and dissoluteness for obvious reasons the queen and the ministers sought to conceal. Because of the king's extravagant behaviour they tried, naturally enough, to limit access to his presence to those who would understand the state of his mind. By so doing they gave ammunition to their critics who believed they were enslaving and making a tool of the king. It was rumoured that Christian was being drugged. But if Struensee was able to keep the true state of affairs at court screened from the public, he could not conceal his own misdemeanours, the news of which soon reverberated through the courts of Europe. Although Struensee had had another mistress in Madam von Gahler, the wife of General Peter von Gahler, twenty-seven years younger than her husband, the queen was absolutely infatuated with her lover and, presumably aware of the king's confused state of mind, threw caution to the wind:

> The queen hardly ever took her eyes off him, insisted on his presence at all gatherings and allowed him, publicly, to take liberties which would have ruined the reputation of an ordinary woman, such as riding in her coach and walking alone with her in the garden and woods.[26]

Struensee showered her with gifts, a pair of scented garters and his miniature, which she wore around her neck in daytime and at night placed in a book which she put under her pillow. He had the king institute a special order of chivalry which bore her name.

Yet there were spies everywhere, hostile both to the queen and the minister. When a daughter, the princess Louise, was born to Caroline on 7 July 1771, the lampoonists and satirists of Copenhagen questioned its paternity. Writing from Vienna, Lady Mary Coke observed that their queen's scandalous behaviour was bringing her Danish subjects to the point of revolt, in favour of the Hereditary Prince Frederick.[27]

'There was no Dane', Reverdil observed, 'who did not regard it as a personal insult to be subjected to a power whose sole foundation was scandal in the royal family.' The press, freed from censorship, indulged in satirical condemnation of the minister who had given it its freedom. Struensee had made enemies at every level of society, and his own arrogance lost him supporters, even from among his own friends. Sir Robert Murray Keith wrote on 6 October 1771, 'The populace love the king, and are extremely averse to the delegation of his power to a man whose rise is so unbecoming. . . . He has now become vulnerable from every quarter, and some who did not dare to look at him, now shake off their deep submission, together with that awe which was so necessary for the support of his unbounded authority.'[28]

Few revolutions have been so well heralded, so that even its leading victims discussed beforehand what they might do if they fell from power. Caroline Matilda wondered whether she might have a future as a singer. But when the revolution

Princess Louise and her sister, Caroline Matilda (right), the Queen of Denmark, painted in 1767 by Francis Cotes (Royal Collection Enterprises, © Her Majesty Queen Elizabeth II)

actually came, it was engineered by a small, amateurish band of conspirators. The rumour that Struensee designed to procure the abdication and even death of the king, in order to marry the queen and take over supreme power, percolated to the Frederiksborg Palace where the dowager queen, Juliana Maria, and her own decrepit son, the Hereditary Prince Frederick lived. Frederick's tutor, Ove Guldberg helped hatch a conspiracy to get rid of the hated minister.

The occasion was to be a masked ball at the palace on the evening of 17 January 1772. At four the next morning the principal conspirators all gathered in the queen dowager's apartment. Unarmed they were led by one Jensen to the king's bedchamber where they woke up the king's valet Brieghel. As the king's door was locked, he took them to a secret entrance which at first, to their trepidation, he refused to open. In their consternation the plotters showed signs of panic: Guldberg dropped one of the candles; the queen mother nearly fainted and her son flopped into a nearby chair. Rantzau who had kept his nerve explained to the valet that their object was to save the king from his enemies and on guaranteeing the king's safety they were allowed to enter his room.

When Christian saw them, he burst into sobbing and shrieked with terror 'For God's sake, gentlemen, what have I done; what do you want of me?' His step-mother reassured him, saying that no harm would come to him providing he signed the papers which they had prepared. They went upstairs to the Hereditary Prince's room where without more ado and hardly understanding what he was doing the king signed the requisite orders for the arrest and imprisonment of Struensee, Brandt and his own wife.

There was no doubt that what was taking place was popular with the people. 'Glorious, eventful night', Suhm wrote in an open letter to the king, 'future Homers and Virgils shall sing thy praise, so long shall the fame of Juliana and Frederick endure, but not increase, for that is impossible.' While the king had not been unaware of his wife's infidelity, his total loss of perspective on reality seems to have led him to acquiesce in it. To reassure the public Christian, looking sullen and vacant, was driven the next day in his gilded coach through the streets of Copenhagen. On his twenty-third birthday, 29 January, he went to the theatre to two French plays, *L'Ambitieux* and *L'Indiscret* which, by innuendo, reflected on his wife's relationship with the minister, but there was such a crush at the theatre that the king rushed away and the queen dowager fainted.

The unfortunate victims of the *coup d'état* were treated harshly. The queen and her daughter were imprisoned in considerable discomfort at Kronborg. Struensee and Brandt were confined in harsh conditions, the fallen minister fettered to the wall in such a way that at night he could not even rise from his bed. An investigative commission which the new government set up to review the evidence found that, among other charges, Struensee's 'unlawful intimacy with the Queen had gone so far as is possible between two persons of different sex'. By challenging the king's powers and issuing edicts which lacked the royal signature Struensee had broken the *kongelov*, the fundamental law of the land. In prison Struensee's mood fluctuated, but he was apparently comforted by a new-found faith transmitted to him by a Lutheran pastor, Dr Munter.[29] Christian had no qualms about signing the death warrant of his chief minister and wife's lover, and the night before the execution of Struensee and Brandt was entertained by the Italian opera.

The queen, who was declared to be divorced from the king, was sentenced to life imprisonment in the castle of Aalborg. While many English people like Lady Mary Coke condemned Caroline Matilda for her 'infamous' conduct, her brother, George III, could hardly ignore the harsh treatment to which the Danes had subjected his sister. Under threat of force, the queen was released and allowed to take refuge at Celle in Hanover, for George III was unwilling to allow her to return to England. Although she was granted £5,000 a year by the British government, she found her exile tedious and depressing. But she did not altogether lack champions, foremost among them a twenty-three-year-old Englishman, Nathaniel Wraxall, 'the purest orang-outang in England' as a contemporary described him, who plotted to overthrow the government of the queen dowager and restore Caroline Matilda. It was a vain if gallant gesture for which George III lacked enthusiasm, and was brought to a close by Caroline Matilda's own death on 11 May 1775, shortly before her twenty-fourth birthday, probably from typhus or scarlet fever. Macalpine and Hunter found in her illness symptoms of porphyria and believed that this was the sickness from which she had suffered periodically before and from which she now died; but the evidence is inconclusive.[30]

Caroline Matilda's death had at least diminished the possibility of an embarrassing political situation for both Denmark and England. Once the revolution had taken place Danish politics reverted to their former sluggish state. Walpole was more or less correct in suggesting that both Queen Juliana Maria and her son did not 'excel the king in capacity'.[31] They plundered the treasury to reward their supporters and brought Struensee's reforming policy to an end; there was a return to the old ways as the censorship of the press was restored and other restrictive and oppressive practices were revived, among them a return to labour services for the peasants and the use of torture in judicial procedure.

After the revolution Christian exercised only a nominal authority. He lived more or less in complete seclusion, making only token appearances. He had given way to the pressures exerted by the queen dowager and her son, but resented what they had done. Shortly afterwards he made some crude, childlike portraits, among others, of Struensee and Brandt, whom he somewhat curiously described as '*eine feiner wilder*

Mann', asserting that their deaths were the responsibility of Queen Juliana and Prince Frederick and not the result of his will or the will of the council of state. He would have saved them if he could (*'Ich hatte sie gerne beide gerettet'*). He also drew two somewhat ambiguous and unflattering portraits of his wife, her gender revealed only by her earrings, the date of her death wrongly inscribed.[32] Christian seems not to have comprehended fully either the captivity or death of his wife; on one occasion he ordered the horses to be made ready so that he could go to meet her. He was dragged out only in periods of semi-lucidity when affairs of state seemed to demand that he put in an appearance as the titular head of state or when his signature was required to legitimize government decrees.

One such occasion occurred in 1784 when his son the Crown Prince Frederick resentful of the reactionary and unpopular government of his step-grandmother and her repulsive son, prevailed upon his father to attend the council of state in order that he might append his signature to a document dismissing the ministry. Once he had done this Christian rushed from the room, followed in almost equally precipitate haste by his half-brother, Prince Frederick, who was obliged to surrender the authority which he had wielded.

Christian still had more than twenty years of life in front of him, but he lived in seclusion and his public appearances were rare. 'I was much struck', commented one who had attended a royal levée, 'by the venerable appearance of the monarch as well as by the marked homage and respect with which he was treated. . . . The return of his malady evinced itself in a singular manner. While in the midst of the most cheerful conversation and when, apparently quite collected, he suddenly ran across the apartment and saluted the first person he met with a violent slap in the face.'[33]

The English philosopher and economist, the Revd T.R. Malthus watched him reviewing his troops in June 1799:

Towards the end of the review I got near the king's tent and saw him quite close. . . . He is treated quite as an idiot. The officers about the court have all orders not to give him any answer. Some of the party observed him talking very fast and making faces at an officer who was one of the sentinels at the tent, who preserved the utmost gravity of countenance and did not answer him in a single word. Just before the royal party left the tent the Prince rode up at full speed, and his father made him a very low bow.

'The king', he commented later, 'is very fond of the parade of royalty, and appears extremely displeased when any thing like a want of proper respect is shewn to him. He is to be answered only by a bow, and this rule is kept with great strictness.'[34]

Despite the king's madness Denmark, with Andreas Bernstorff as its chief minister enjoyed a long period of liberal government, a measure of increased prosperity and a period of peace until the outbreak of the Napoleonic Wars threatened the League of Armed Neutrality which the Danes together with other Baltic powers had espoused. As a consequence of the Danes' attempt to preserve their neutral stance and fearful of the pressure that Napoleon was bringing to bear upon the Danes, the British fleet twice bombarded Copenhagen, causing heavy casualties, the last occasion in September 1808.

Ironically Christian ended his shadowy existence some months before the British bombardment of his capital, on 15 March 1808.[35] In a curious and elaborate charade, which had lasted forty years, he remained the head of the government, his royal powers laid down by the Danish *lex regia*. Although the crown prince, the future Frederick VI, wielded the real power and had done so for a quarter of a century, he had never been offically the regent. It was ironical, given Christian's past history, that he should have died the very year that Denmark declared war against Great Britain, the country which had given him a wife and where four decades earlier, before his mind became deranged by chronic schizophrenia, he had, at least in his own opinion, enjoyed a great triumph, and at the hands of which shortly after his death his country experienced a major humiliation.

XIV

The Swan King

Ludwig II, king of Bavaria from 1864 to 1886, was the last European monarch whose madness was to make a significant impact on the cultural and political heritage of the modern world. A cross standing starkly in the shallow waters of Lake Starnberg where, certified as mad, he drowned himself or was drowned in June 1886, commemorates this most bizarre of monarchs. Ludwig's eccentric behaviour became a legend in his own lifetime. The Wittelsbach family to which he belonged was one of the oldest ruling families in Europe, rulers since the Middle Ages of the large south German kingdom of Bavaria, for their princes, long entitled electors, had become kings in 1806. Bavaria was to become reluctantly a part of the German empire in 1871 but its rulers retained the title of king until the ending of the First World War swept all Germany's princes from their thrones, not entirely into oblivion, for there were, and are still, many Bavarians who cherish the memory of the past.

Ludwig's father Maximilian had become king of Bavaria in 1848 following the abdication of Ludwig I, whose personal and political indiscretions had aroused such opposition that he had been obliged to give up the throne. There was nothing in Ludwig's parentage or immediate ancestry to suggest what the future had in store for him, but even as a boy he was very sensitive.

He was rarely seen by his parents and was brought up by nursery maids and governesses, of one of whom, Fraulein Meilhaus, he became very fond. He seems, by and large, to have been a lonely child who was largely left to his own devices and imagination, something which in Ludwig proved to be intensely vivid.

His imagination was more especially gripped by the image of the swan, an emblem which was to haunt him throughout his life. The royal castle at Hohenschwangau, the high house of the swan, situated in the Bavarian Alps, high above the glittering mountain lakes, the Schwansee and Alpsee, had been rebuilt by Ludwig's father Maximilian, and was dedicated to the legend of Lohengrin. Lavish frescoes that adorned its walls depicted a swan drawing the boat in which sat Lohengrin, the knight of the Holy Grail whom Ludwig was to identify with himself.

Even as a teenager, he had developed an intense admiration for the composer, Richard Wagner, a passion which was to dominate his life. He first saw *Lohengrin* performed on 2 June 1861, then *Tannhäuser* and in 1863 the *Ring*. It was said, even by Wagner himself, that Ludwig had no real ear for music, but the young prince was spellbound by the themes which dominated Wagner's operas, more especially the search for the Holy Grail. Wagner's music was to generate a series of fantasies which Ludwig sought to convert into reality, eventually with tragic results. 'The simplest reading of the situation', the leading British authority on Wagner commented, 'would seem to be this – that even as a boy Ludwig had a romantic vision of himself, as king, leading the German people along ideal paths, and that the Wagner writings simply happened to strike into that vision at the critical time and with tremendous impact.'[1] Wagner himself nicknamed the king Parzival, 'my son in the Holy Spirit', simple and wise, called by destiny to succeed to the Grail kingship.

After his father's sudden death in 1864, the immature young prince was given the opportunity to convert his vision into reality. Ludwig was very tall and radiated immense charm. He had rich curling hair, regularly waved, which he wore long, perhaps to cover his over-large ears, traces of a moustache on his upper lip and extraordinarily expressive eyes. 'He was', his minister of justice, Eduard von Bomhard commented shortly after his accession, 'mentally gifted in the highest degree, but the contents of his mind were stored in a totally disordered fashion.' 'I was struck', Bomhard recalled, 'by the way in which every now and then, just when his expression and whole demeanour seemed to show contentment he would suddenly straighten up and – looking around him with a serious, even stern, expression – would reveal something dark in himself that was in complete contrast to the youthful charm of a moment ago. I thought to myself "if two different natures are germinating in this young man," as it seemed to me from the very first conversation with him, "may God grant that the good one may be victorious."'[2] The minister had unconsciously glimpsed Ludwig's schizophrenic nature.

For the future of the Bavarian state and the Wittelsbach royal line Ludwig's marriage soon became a matter of urgency. The king liked female company and treated his women friends as his confidantes, more especially the beautiful Austrian empress, Elizabeth, whom he was prone to regard as the incarnation of his heroine Marie Antoinette. For six years he had an intimate friendship with the actress Lilla von Bulyowsky. But in the nineteenth-century world a king must marry a royal princess. Ludwig announced his engagement to Sophie, the sister of the Empress Elizabeth. 'Oh, how wonderful it will be', 'the eagle', as Ludwig called himself, wrote to his 'dove' Sophie from his eyrie of Hohenschwangau on 25 August 1867, his twenty-second birthday, 'when We Two shall be here alone in the rapturous Hohenschwangau.'

Then only a few days later he confided to his former governess, now the Baroness Leonrod, that he could not proceed with the marriage. He had, he told her, 'tossed off the burdensome bonds' and was breathing again 'fresh air after a dangerous illness'. 'She would not have done for my wife: the nearer the date of the wedding came the more I dreaded my intended step.' 'I see', he wrote to Sophie, 'that my true and faithful brotherly love is now, and always will be, deeply rooted in my soul, but I also see that it is not the love which is necessary for a matrimonial union.' Her parents were naturally scandalized by Ludwig's action; the unhappy Sophie was to marry the French duc d'Alençon and meet a violent death. But Ludwig simply wrote in his diary: 'Sophie got rid of. The gloomy picture fades. I longed for, am athirst for, freedom. Now I live again after this torturing nightmare.'[3] The collapse of Ludwig's matrimonial plans was an ill omen for the future.

Ludwig's real nature was homosexual. His intimates were young men of whom the chief was for many years Prince Paul von Thurn und Taxis. Passionately devoted to each other, they exchanged gushing, romantic letters. 'May sweet dreams be with you and may everything that is dear to you on this earth be present', Paul wrote to the king on 13 July 1866. 'Sleep well, angel of my heart, and give one more thought to your most faithful Friedrich', the nickname which Ludwig had conferred on his lover.[4] Yet Ludwig was temperamental, demanding and ultimately inconstant. The romance faded as Paul made a morganatic marriage and was disowned by his family.

Long before that, at the time that Ludwig had broken off his engagement to Sophie, he had discovered a new lover, Richard Hornig, who in the summer of 1867 accompanied him to Paris. Hornig was a twenty-six-year-old equerry, blue-eyed, with blond wavy hair, an excellent horseman 'with a leg for a boot'. 'It is a pity', Prince Hohenlohe wrote on 8 July 1869, 'that the king's talents are lying fallow, and that he confines himself more and more to the bad company of the horse-breaker, Hornig.' '*Vivat Rex et Ricardus in aeternam*', the king wrote in his secret diary in 1872,[5] but Hornig's marriage brought the affair to an end.

There followed a succession of others, the cavalry officer, the Baron von Varicourt, the actor Josef Kainz and men of lower social status like the royal lackey Alfonso Welcker. It is impossible to say when romantic friendship elided into physical intimacy but rumour was rife and excerpts from the secret diary suggest that Ludwig was self-indulgent, only to suffer subsequent feelings of guilt and remorse.*

In spite of the dramatic events that were at this time shaping the future of Germany, Ludwig was largely indifferent to politics, though there were circumstances which required his active participation. In the Seven Weeks War between Prussia and Austria the Bavarians had sided with the Austrians and had suffered a major setback at the

---

*The 'secret diary' which Ludwig kept between December 1869 and June 1886 was lost in the destruction of the Residenz by British bombing in 1944. Some extracts, probably taken down by the Bavarian prime minister, Johann von Lutz, were published in 1925 and were used by Chapman-Huston in his biography *A Bavarian Fantasy* (1955). Some of the surviving entries, cryptic and hieroglyphic, speak of Ludwig's having 'fallen', and then having resolved to live a 'purer' life.

hands of the Prussians at Kissingen where the Bavarian commander in chief was killed. Ludwig, obsessed by notions of medieval chivalry rather than modern warfare, had so little enthusiasm for the war that he wondered whether he should abdicate in favour of his brother, Otto. His wish was in part stimulated by his desire to be with Wagner in Switzerland. Wagner himself, more patriotic and nationalistic than the king, advised Ludwig to 'heed his warriors'. So the king made some visits to the front line before he retreated with Prince Paul to the pleasures and parlour games of Roseninsel. On the day that war had been declared Prince Hohenlohe wrote in his diary:

[The king] sees no one now. He is staying with Taxis and the groom Völk on the Roseninsel and lets off fireworks. Even the members of the Upper House, who were to deliver an address, were not received. . . . Other people do not trouble their heads about the king's childish tricks, since he lets the Ministers and the Chambers govern without interfering. His behaviour is, however, imprudent, since it tends to make him unpopular.[6]

A few months later, on 18 August 1866, Hohenlohe commented that

the King is busy devising scenery for the opera, William Tell, and is having costumes made for himself, dressed in which he parades his room. Meanwhile it is a question whether his kingdom is to lose [as a result of its defeat by the Prussians in the Seven Weeks War] the thirty thousand inhabitants of Franconia and the seven hundred thousand of the Palatinate.[7]

Within four years Bavaria was at war again but on this occasion helping the Prussians against the French. Neither Ludwig nor his ministers were a match for Bismarck's manipulative policy. Reluctantly, if at the price of a subsidy, the king accepted the German imperium resulting in the proclamation of the Prussian king William I as German emperor at Versailles. Ludwig's interests in the normal functions of government remained still at a superficial level. He delighted in ceremonial. He loved military uniforms, though, as an English visitor commented, he wore his hair too long to be really 'militaristic'; but kingship had become increasingly a pageant restricted to the court and the king himself.

So he lived to an ever-increasing extent in a world of his own making, engaged in patronizing Wagner and the theatre, and in building decorative palaces which, though not all were finished, remained his most substantial heritage to posterity. And at the root of his fantasy life were the medieval legends embodied in Wagner's operas.

Ludwig may have been unmusical but the composer's combination of drama, folk history and the setting in which his operas took place had seized the king's heart and mind. Here was to be found, as Ludwig saw it, the true genius of the German nation which it was his duty, privilege and pleasure to patronize. 'In Germany', the king assured Wagner, 'we must raise the banner of pure and holy art so that it flies from the battlements, summoning German youth to rally around it.'[8]

Intent on putting his patronage into practice he sent his secretary Pfistermeister to track Wagner down. When at last Pfistermeister found him in Stuttgart, he assured him of Ludwig's unlimited support if he would only come promptly to Munich. 'Dear, gracious king', the composer responded on 3 May 1864, 'These tears of heavenly emotion I send to you to tell you that now the marvel of poetry has come as a divine reality into my poor, love-thirsty life! And that life, in its last poetry and tones, belongs now to you, my gracious young king, dispose of it as you would your own property!'[9] This was the first letter of a long correspondence which passed between the two men, over-effusive and emotionally highly charged. While the phraseology might even suggest a homosexual relationship, this seems unlikely. While Wagner was highly sexed, his many affairs were heterosexual as his relations, for instance, with Cosima von Bulow, an illegitimate daughter of Franz Liszt, twenty-four years younger than himself, show. Besides, Wagner was thirty years older than his patron and far from good-looking. Ludwig was cruelly intolerant of anyone whom he considered ugly and only had eyes for pretty young men and women.

Nonetheless their close and even passionate relationship meant much to both men, for it enabled Wagner to live and compose in comfort, and Ludwig to find his destiny in the myths which Wagner was setting to music. Wagner wrote of the king after he had been presented to him: 'He is also so beautiful, spiritual, soulful and splendid that I fear his life must run away like a fleeting, heavenly dream in this common world.' The dream was to turn ultimately into a nightmare.

The Bavarians might appreciate Wagner's music but they criticized the extravagant favours which their king showered upon him. Wagner lived in opulence as the arbiter of the arts for the future of which he had radical and expensive plans, including the creation of a new music school and the building of a new theatre, for which the king's purse and patronage were essential. The chief minister, Baron von der Pfordten, a university professor and a conservative lawyer, neither appreciated Wagner's music nor the radical political views he had once espoused, and was deeply suspicious of the king's extravagant expenditure and its effect on the Bavarian treasury.

Even Wagner's relations with the king were not free from friction, strong as was the bond between them, for Wagner could be devious and dishonest while Ludwig was demanding and temperamental. They continued, however, to write to each other in ecstatic terms. 'My Unique One! My Holy One!', the king commented after seeing the first performance of *Tristan* on 10 June 1865, 'How blissful! – Perfect. So overcome

Ludwig II of Bavaria as a young man (The Mansell Collection)

with delight! – To drown . . . to sink-unconscious-highest pleasure-Divine work! – Eternally true-to beyond the grave.'[10] On 21 June Ludwig wrote from his Alpine retreat:

Long since the daylight has sunk down and disappeared behind the high chain of mountains; peace reigns in the deep valleys, the ringing of the cow-bells, the song of the cowherd rises upward to my joyous solitude. The evening star sends its gentle light from afar, showing the wanderer his way out of the valley and once again reminding me of my Dear One and his divine works. In the distance, at the end of the valley, rises the church of Ettal out of the dark green of the pine woods. The Emperor Ludwig the Bavarian [Holy Roman Emperor in the early fourteenth century] is said to have built this church after the plan of the Grail Temple at Montsalvat. There the figure of Lohengrin revives anew in my vision; and there I see in my mind Parzival, the hero of the future, searching for salvation, for the single truth. How my soul longs and thirsts for such works as can re-create those spirits for us.[11]

'I long for you', he wrote on 21 August,

only when I think of my dear one and his work am I truly happy. . . . How are things with you just now, up there in the joyful wooded heights? Dear One, please grant me a request! I beg of you. Tell me something of your plans for 'Die Sieger' and 'Parzival'! I am yearning to hear. Please quench this burning thirst! Oh how null is the world! How wretched and vulgar so many men! Their lives revolve in the narrow circle of everyday banality. Oh, if only I had the world behind me![12]

The king seemed totally absorbed in his protégé. While Wagner inspired by Ludwig's request, began to write the libretto for *Parzival*, the king withdrew from public gaze, refusing, for instance, to attend official gatherings on the plea of being unwell but continuing to go to the theatre. After a performance of Schiller's *William Tell* he made a special visit to the lake of Lucerne, travelling incognito (though he was soon recognized) to the scene of the play's events, evidently identifying himself with the hero.

Wagner stayed with Ludwig at Hohenschwangau which he called the 'Grail castle', 'protected by Parzival's sublime love'. 'He', Wagner wrote, 'is I, in a newer, younger, lovelier, re-birth: wholly I, and himself only to be beautiful and powerful.' They made a trip together into the Tyrol and on 14 August the king wrote to Cosima, still naively unaware that she was Wagner's lover (though the second name of his illegitimate daughter Isolde was Ludowika named after the king):

Let us take a solemn vow now to do all it is in human power to do to preserve for Wagner the peace he has won, to banish care from him, to take upon ourselves, whenever possible, every grief of his, to love him, love him with all the strength that God has put into the human soul! O, he is godlike, godlike! My mission is to live for him, to suffer for him, if that be necessary for his full salvation.[13]

These grandiose sentiments were all very well but they served mainly to express how far the king was already advancing into a dream world of his own creation. There was a riding tide of criticism in Bavaria at Wagner's extavagance, anger worsened by Wagner's own unsubtle intervention into Bavarian politics. Even the besotted king could not withstand the hurricane. 'Your Majesty', Pfordten wrote on 1 December 1865, 'now stands at a fateful parting of the ways: you have to choose between the love and respect of your faithful people and the "friendship" of Richard Wagner.'[14] With sadness in his heart the king ordered Wagner to leave Munich for Switzerland. If Ludwig had been obliged to abdicate the throne, he would have been in a far weaker position to patronize and subsidize his friend; with Wagner in Switzerland he could, and did, provide for him. Just before he left, Ludwig wrote, 'My love for you will never die, and I beg you to retain for ever your friendship for me.'[15]

Their relationship, though never entirely devoid of friction, continued to sustain the king. Wagner, with Cosima who had deserted her husband, lived in comfort in a delightful villa at Triebschen near Lucerne where Ludwig was to visit him. His creative powers remained as vibrant as ever. The king attended the rehearsal and the first performance at Munich of *Die Meistersinger*; and it was the composer himself, seated by his side, who rose and bowed to the rapturous applause, an action construed by conservative opinion to be a breach of court etiquette. 'I was', the king wrote, signing his letter with his hero's name, 'Walther', 'so moved and carried away that it was impossible for me to join in with the profane expression of praise through hand-clapping.'[16] On the 23 September Wagner sent a finely bound score of *Die Meistersinger*, with a dedicatory poem reflecting their close relationship, to mark Ludwig's twenty-third birthday.

There was then some gap in the correspondence, and even some measure of disagreement, and they were not to meet for eight years. But on the outbreak of the Franco-Prussian War Wagner, much more patriotic than his patron, sent Ludwig a poem of homage, praising Bavaria's support for Germany. The two men met again at Bayreuth, where the completion of the theatre had been made possible by a generous loan from the king, in August 1876 for the premiere of the *Ring*. After the performance Ludwig wrote:

I came with great expectations; and, high though these were, they were far, far exceeded. . . . Ah, now I recognize again the beautiful world from which I have held aloof; the sky looks down on me again, the meadows are resplendent with colour, the spring enters my soul with a thousand sweet sounds. . . . You are a god-man, the true artist by God's grace who brought the sacred fire down from heaven to earth, to pacify and sanctify, and to redeem![17]

When, at the close of *Götterdammerung*, Wagner stepped on to the stage to greet the audience he said that the Bayreuth festival had been 'embarked again in trust in the German spirit and completed for the glory of the king of Bavaria, who had been not only a benefactor and protector to him but a co-creator of his work'.[18]

When, in November 1880, the Bavarians celebrated the 700th anniversary of Wittelsbach rule, Wagner came to Munich to attend a private performance of *Lohengrin*. It was the last occasion on which the king and the composer saw each other, for Ludwig did not go to the first performance of *Parzival* in 1882 because of ill-health, nor did he actually see it until 1884, by which time Wagner was himself dead. Ludwig was greatly shaken when he heard of Wagner's death and though he did not go to his funeral, he ordered all the pianos in his castles to be wreathed in black crepe. With Wagner's death a living thread in Ludwig's own life snapped, even if the themes of his operas continued to be uppermost in the king's mind.

Ludwig's fantasies found concrete expression in the fairy-tale castles which he was building at great cost to the Bavarian treasury. In 1868, with *Lohengrin* and *Tannhäuser* still fresh in his mind, the king conceived the notion of building a castle which would enable him to express the themes voiced in these operas in stone. They were to be stage sets immortalized. The first site was dramatically located on a hilltop only half an hour away from Hohenschwangau and named after Ludwig's death Neuschwanstein. 'The spot', he had told Wagner, 'is one of the most beautiful that one could ever find, sacred and out of reach, a worthy temple for the divine friend. There will also be reminders of *Tannhäuser*.'[19]

With its battlements and turrets, its dramatic situation, Neuschwanstein is a piece of giant stage scenery. Ludwig took an intense personal interest in its erection, often irritating the architects with sudden changes of mind, more emotionally than rationally motivated. The Singers' Hall was decorated with murals from the story of the Grail, taken from Wolfram von Eschenbach's medieval romance, *Parzival*; the throne room paid pictorial homage to sacred kingship. It was a shrine which Wagner was never to see and in which the king himself was never to stay until he was on the brink of madness.

Shortly after Neuschwanstein had been commissioned, Ludwig planned to build another royal palace, different in its function and appearance, Linderhof. This was to

Neuschwanstein Castle, upper Bavaria, one of Ludwig II's castles (German National Tourist Office, London)

be an act of homage to his great hero, Louis XIV of France, whom he sought to emulate as a patron of the arts, sometimes imitating his dress and manner of walk and talking to imaginary guests in French. On 7 January 1869 the king wrote to his former governess, Baroness Leonrod:

> Near the Linderhof, not far from Ettal, I am going to build a little palace with a formal garden in the Renaissance style, the whole will breathe the magnificence and imposing grandeur of the Royal Palace of Versailles. Oh, how necessary it is to create for oneself such poetic places of refuge where one can forget for a little while the dreadful times in which we live.[20]

Linderhof was a small palace faced with white ashlar, baroque in style and full of decorative fancies, lavish, colourful and charming, a wedding-cake extravaganza; over the fireplace there was a marble group entitled 'The Apotheosis of King Louis XIV of France'. In the gardens there were some fanciful follies: a hunting lodge where Ludwig and his companions dressed in bear skins and drank mead; a Moorish kiosk, Turkish in design; an artificial grotto in which a kaleidoscope of colours, as in some early disco, wrought an ever-changing spectrum upon an artificial waterfall and a lake with waves artificially created by machinery.

Most sumptuous of all was Herrenchiemsee, situated on the Herren island in Bavaria's largest lake, the Chiemsee. Like Linderhof it was inspired by Louis XIV's palaces rather than by the *Niebelungenlied* and was a horizontal building of great beauty modelled deliberately on Versailles. Its gallery of mirrors even outstripped its counterpart, being some ninety feet longer. Herrenchiemsee was, however, left unfinished, partly because it was actually designed as a skeletal structure and partly because the money ran out. The foundation stone was laid on 21 May 1878 but the king was only to spend some nine days there, between 7 and 16 September 1885.

There were other buildings which Ludwig built or restructured, all of them exotic and symbolic, many of which never got beyond the drawing-board and the king's fertile imagination. Of these Falkenstein would have been the most dramatic; it was designed as a Gothic fable like Neuschwanstein, a majestic Disneyland structure of pinnacles and towers located on a mountain top overlooking the world, a tribute to the cloud-cuckoo land in which the king came more and more to live.

In all these ventures Ludwig may seem to be no more than one of the world's major eccentrics, a romantic who tried to give concrete expression to the products of his imagination, which by virtue of his position and fortune he was able to do. But behind the mask there were more dangerous forces at work which displayed the steady disintegration of his personality.

As his mental capacities deteriorated he became increasingly capricious. He paid lip

The gallery of mirrors at the Palace of Herrenchiemsee (German National Tourist Office, London)

service to the ideals of democratic monarchy but sometimes he behaved like a despot. He gave ludicrous orders to punish his servants for minor misdemeanours which were usually not implemented. They were told that they must not look him full in the face and when his valet Mayr disobeyed he was ordered to wear a black mask.

It has been suggested that Ludwig may have suffered from an organic brain disease originating with a syphilitic infection. His father, who died of typhoid, was said to have contracted syphilis in Hungary as a young man, but the evidence for such a supposition is tenuous. How promiscuous Ludwig's own life had been is unclear, but while a syphilitic complaint is possible, it seems improbable.

There may conceivably have been genetic features in his ancestry which suggested that if conditions were favourable his mind might lose its balance. Among his mother's ancestors were the mad prince Ludwig IX of Hesse-Darmstadt who died in 1790, and his daughter Karoline who experienced hallucinations. His aunt on his father's side, Princess Alexandra, had to be confined to a mental home, believing that she had swallowed a glass piano. More pertinently his younger brother Otto became completely insane. Ludwig wrote to the Baroness Leonrod on 6 January 1871:

> It is really painful to see Otto in such a suffering state which seems to become worse and worse daily. In some respects he is more excitable and nervous than Aunt Alexandra, and that is saying a great deal. He often does not go to bed for forty-eight hours. He did not take off his boots for eight weeks, behaves like a madman, makes terrible faces, barks like a dog, and at times says the most indecorous things and then again he is quite normal for a while.[21]

His condition gradually worsened. 'He suffers', the king wrote on 20 October 1871, 'from a morbid over-excitement of the whole nervous system which is quite terrible.' The British chargé d'affaires at Munich, Sir Robert Morier, reported on 30 May 1875 that Otto was plainly the victim of religious hallucinations and that at the recent festival of Corpus Christi, dressed in a shooting jacket and a wide-awake hat, he had broken through a cordon of soldiers and thrown himself on the steps of the high altar, confessing his sins in a loud voice until with some difficulty he was persuaded to retire to the vestry. 'From all I hear', Sir Robert commented, 'there is no doubt that he will have to be treated as seriously out of his mind. On the whole it is certainly as well that this scene did not occur in St George's Chapel [Windsor].'[22] Although Otto protested vigorously to his brother against the restraints placed upon him, by 1878 he was incurably insane and had to be confined to the royal castle of Fürstenried where he was to reside until his death thirty-eight years later.

A striking change was taking place in Ludwig's own physical appearance. The slim youth who, though not strictly speaking handsome, had so impressed people by charm had by his thirties become an obese and unattractive man, who looked older than his years, with thinning hair and a straggling moustache. For one who had sought to banish ugliness from his existence, a glance at his own reflection must have been itself traumatic.

Ludwig's personality may have been temperamentally disposed to the onset of schizophrenia. Even from an early age the dividing line between fantasy and reality had been very blurred. His doctor reported that as a boy he had imagined that he heard voices as he was playing a game of billiards. The overpowering influence of the legend of the Grail on his mind pushed him further and further over the brink of sanity. He imagined himself to be Lohengrin, and wore the costume of the swan knight. On the Alpsee the king arranged a flood-lit tableau in which his close friend Prince Paul was ferried across the lake as Lohengrin in a boat drawn by an artificial swan to the sound of music from the opera while the king looked on.

He withdrew more and more from the public gaze into a private world. Instead of attending the public performances at the theatre in Munich, the theatre had to come to him in the form of theatricals in his own castles. Increasingly he became a nocturnal animal. In February 1868 it was reported that he had spent an entire night riding round and round the Court Riding School. Like Philip V of Spain, he turned night into day, waking at 7.00 p.m. in the evening and supping in the early hours of the morning to the discomfort of his courtiers and the ministers who came to consult him. He liked to travel at night and was sometimes glimpsed in the deep winter snow moving at high speed in a decorated sleigh, a lantern at the prow and two footmen perched perilously behind, the king himself an incongruous figure in a bowler hat.

His behaviour was becoming eccentric to the verge of insanity. He had his grey mare to dinner and allowed her to smash the dinner plates. He ordered his stable quartermaster, Hesselschwerdt, to recruit Italian bandits who were then to kidnap the crown prince of Prussia while he was on holiday at Menton. They were to keep him chained and feed him on bread and water. Equally fantastic were the journeys which he ordered his henchmen to make to find some enchanted land or island, a Shangri-la where Ludwig could live a life of contemplation in undisturbed seclusion, 'completely independent of seasons, men and needs of all kinds'. At his orders royal officials scoured the globe – Tenerife, Samothrace, Egypt, even Afghanistan (which one of them, Leher, reported to Ludwig had a 'certain similarity to our beloved Alpine landscape'), Brazil, the Pacific islands, Norway; but what Ludwig wanted was not simply an estate which belonged to someone else but an independent land which he could call his own, a land of Prester John. His servants indulged his whims but they did not take them seriously, and sometimes simply disregarded his more capricious commands.

There seemed to be two Ludwigs: one was charming and sociable, could be active and even politically sensitive, careful of the welfare of his people; but the other was dreamy, moody, inconsiderate and withdrawn, increasingly immersed in a world of fantasy. And the second Ludwig was steadily taking over. 'So long', Prince Hohenlohe commented, 'as the King is encouraged by the sycophancy of the Court and the Government officials, so long will he continue to regard himself as a demi-god who can do what he pleases and for whose pleasure the rest of the world – at any rate Bavaria – was created.'[23]

The public became increasingly critical of a king they so rarely saw, of his extravagant building operations, of his rumoured affairs with cavalrymen, of his strange manner of life, while his ministers were alarmed by his mounting expenditure. Although the king was in receipt of a subsidy from Prussia, his building operations had landed him in a desperate financial situation. By early 1884 he owed 7½ million marks. For the moment a loan was arranged through the good offices of the finance minister Emil von Riedel from a consortium of south German banks. But the king showed no signs of slowing down his building plans and by early 1885 he was nearly twice as much in debt. Von Riedel remonstrated strongly with him when he asked for a further loan, telling him that the state could afford no more and that he really must practise economy. Ludwig was as recalcitrant as ever. 'If a certain sum is not obtained (in about four weeks) Linderhof and Herrenchiemsee, my property will be legally confiscated! If this is not forestalled in good time I shall either kill myself promptly or else leave immediately and for ever the accursed land where such an abominable thin4 could happen.'[24] He even urged Count Durckheim – this on 28 January 1886 – to get together an armed force to defend him. Ludwig's agents made desperate approaches to secure further loans – to a mysterious rich Persian, to the duke of Westminster, to the king of Sweden, the sultan of Turkey. He even contemplated a plan which would involve robbing the Rothschild bank in Frankfurt. In April 1886 the gas and water company took a claim for non-payment of their bills to court.

As a final move he consulted Bismarck who advised him to place his problems before the Bavarian parliament which would surely do something to assist the king in his critical needs. The king's ministers, themselves aware that parliament might not respond, advised Ludwig to come to his capital to strengthen his chances. But instead of returning to Munich the king planned to dismiss the ministry, using his servants, among them his barber Hoppe now influential in court circles, to find new ministers, naturally without avail.

Matters had now reached crisis point. Ludwig had proved himself to be more than an extravagant luxury. He had become a potential political menace. He must go. Since his heir, his brother Prince Otto, had been mad for many years, a regency was necessary; and with some reluctance the king's sixty-five-year-old uncle Prince Luitpold was persuaded to take on this role. The Bavarian minister in Berlin, Count Lerchenfeld, explained the situation to Bismarck. 'If', Bismarck agreed, 'the king was unfit to rule because of mental illness, then, in all conscience, I could see no reason to keep him on the throne.'

What followed had all the ingredients of a tragi-comedy, if increasingly the greater emphasis was on the tragic elements. The chief minister, von Lutz, bewildered as to how best to deal with so unusual and so awkward a situation, consulted a leading Bavarian alienist, Dr Bernard von Gudden, professor of psychiatry at the university of Munich and director of the District Mental Hospital for Upper Bavaria. Von Gudden, who was a humane man as well as a highly experienced doctor, diagnosed the king's case, even though he had not seen the patient personally, as one of advanced paranoia.

The medical report which von Gudden submitted was used as evidence to support the king's deposition. Von Gudden's appraisal, dated 8 June 1886, pronounced the king to be 'in a very advanced state of insanity' which was incurable in its character, which made him 'incapable of exercising government . . . for the entire remainder of his life'. It was extraordinary in the circumstances that such a final judgement should have been passed without any recourse to a personal confrontation with the patient. 'The mental powers of His Majesty', the medical committee of three doctors reported, 'are disrupted to such an extent that all judgement is lacking, and his thinking is in total contradiction to reality. . . . Gripped by the illusion that he holds absolute power in abundance and made lonely by self-isolation, he stands like a blind man without a guide at the edge of an abyss.'[25]

But how to inform the 'blind man' of this verdict? On 9 June 1886 the specially constituted commission, headed by Baron von Creilsheim, with four other dignitaries, Dr von Gudden and his assistant, accompanied by medical orderlies, set out for Neuschwanstein. At one o'clock in the morning Count Holnstein, who had been named as one of the king's two legal guardians, discovered that the king's coachman, Fritz Osterholzer, was attaching horses to the royal carriage; fearful that the king might be attempting a getaway, Holnstein ordered the coachman to stop what he was doing, informing him that Prince Luitpold was now the country's ruler. As a loyal servant of the king Osterholzer immediately hurried to the castle to tell his master, whom he found pacing up and down the Singers' Hall reciting verses from Schiller. As soon as Ludwig heard what was happening, he ordered the gates to be barred and the royal guard to be reinforced by police from nearby Fussen.

Ludwig II of Bavaria in middle age (The Mansell Collection)

So when on a wet and chilly summer afternoon the commissioners eventually arrived at the castle they found the gates closed and were refused admission. While they sat disconsolately in their carriages, one of the king's admirers, herself an occasional inmate of a mental home, the colourful Baroness Spera von Truchess, arrived at the castle and gained entry. She advised the king to leave for Munich, but he refused. She was in the castle (it was seven hours before she could be persuaded to leave) while the commissioners drove back to Hohenschwangau where on the king's orders they were then arrested by the local police. They were detained in the gate lodge where they were not best pleased to learn that the king had ordered them to be blinded, flogged and starved, but the secretary to the commission managed to make his way back to Munich where he alerted the government as to the course of events. The ministers at once ordered the release of the commissioners, and issued a proclamation confirming Prince Luitpold's appointment as regent.

Had Ludwig been more fully aware of his predicament he might yet have saved himself, but he was indecisive and inert. He would not return to Munich where he still had a loyal following. He thought of taking his life, but his aide-de-camp refused to go to a chemist's shop to purchase the requisite poison.

At midnight on 11 June Dr von Gudden reappeared followed by his assistant and five medical orderlies, and a posse of police. Fearful of an attempt at suicide, for it was rumoured that the king had talked of throwing himself off the castle tower, they ambushed Ludwig as he came out of his room to mount the staircase to the tower. He was escorted back into his bedroom. 'How can you declare me insane when you have not examined me?' was his pertinent question to von Gudden. But the doctor escorted the king, as he had been told to do, to his other residence at Berg where he arrived at midday on Saturday 12 June.

It was at Berg, situated by the waters of Lake Starnberg, that Ludwig was to be interned. The place had been so prepared that there was no avenue for him to escape. Outwardly he appeared calm. Von Gudden who believed that his patients should be treated sympathetically allowed the king as much liberty as he thought feasible, permitting him to take a walk in the morning so long as he was followed by his orderlies at a discreet distance. If he wanted to take an evening stroll, von Gudden said that he might do so as long as he went with him. When his fellow doctors expressed their doubts as to the wisdom of such a decision, von Gudden dismissed their remonstrances with a laugh.

At 6.45 p.m. on 12 June 1886 the king and the doctor set off together to walk beside the lake. They must have looked an odd pair, the towering king and the diminutive doctor. When by eight o'clock they had not returned a search party was formed. Darkness fell. It began to rain. Then, about ten, in the shallow water by the lakeside the king's jacket and overcoat were discovered, his umbrella nearby. The king's body was found in the water face down. His watch had stopped at 6.45 p.m. Von Gudden was a few paces away, floating in the muddy shallows of the lake.

What had happened precisely remains mysterious. The story, which has been discussed endlessly, has all the makings of a detective mystery. Why were the king's jacket, coat and umbrella thrown aside? Ludwig's followers, unready to accept a verdict of suicide, believed that the king might have been killed accidentally or even deliberately. Some said that Ludwig had not been drowned but had been chloroformed by the doctor, who had used the bottle of chloroform he carried with him on the king to still his agitation. In the ensuing struggle the king had died and the doctor had collapsed from a heart attack. But as the king was the stronger and younger man, the story seems very improbable.

It is just possible that when the king set out on his walk with von Gudden there was, as has been suggested, a plan of escape. But the only evidence to support this story rests on the report that a boat had been seen moving up and down the lake in the rain without apparent purpose, and that there were marks of carriage wheels outside the castle gate. It seems much more probable that with his mind in a state of turmoil the king on the spur of the moment cast away his umbrella, threw off his coat and jacket and jumped in the lake in a suicidal gesture. Von Gudden tried to save him, but in the ensuing struggle the king prevailed and both drowned. The bodies drifted slowly towards the shallow waters where they were found. Suicide had been in Ludwig's mind for some time, and though the possibility of a cure had been discussed, knowing the fate of his brother Otto, the future must have seemed to the king impossibly bleak.

And so the body of King Ludwig II was laid to rest on 19 June 1886 after a solemn requiem in the crypt of St Michael's church; later a vase containing his heart was placed with the other relics of his ancient family in the Votive Chapel of Alt-Otting.

Did Ludwig's unconventional life-style and disturbed mind make an impact upon German history? Had he been more politically interested, had he been a sounder statesman, it is just possible that Bavarian history might have taken a different course, even conceivably that Bismarck's plans for the unification of Germany would have gone less smoothly. Yet even if he had been a more normal monarch, it seems historically doubtful whether he would have been a match for Bismarck. What Austria had failed to do, Bavaria with stronger leadership could hardly have done. Ludwig, sane or insane, was politically little more than a figurehead. As mental troubles more and more overwhelmed him he came to inhabit a never-never land increasingly remote from his own kingdom, but because he was a king endowed with regal powers he was able to people his court with sycophantic minions, to build his dream castles at the expense of his country's treasury and push back the harsh political realities of his time to the side lines. In his search for the Holy Grail of his imagination he had become ultimately a sacrifice to the illusions which had come more and more to occupy his deranged mind.

He was not to be the last king of the long Wittelsbach line, for ironically he was succeeded by his long-mad brother, Otto, who remained sovereign at least in name until he was dethroned in 1913 by his cousin, Ludwig III, the last Bavarian monarch; but in many respects, mad as he became, Ludwig II was surely the most tragic and possibly the most creative member of his ancient family.

XV
'An Infirmity' of Politicians

In an age of monarchy the personality and health of the ruler could be a matter of supreme importance to his people, for the sort of man he was and the extent to which his decision making affected his policies and his judgement helped to shape his peoples' lives for good or ill. In a democratic or semi-republican age where autocratic monarchy has ceased to exist and constitutional monarchs exercise a very limited authority the problem may well be of only nominal significance. Although monarchy still survives in Great Britain, Holland, Belgium, Spain, the Scandinavian countries and Japan, royal power has in practice been so reduced that monarchy has everywhere become a mere shadow of its former self. The genetic factor, salient when European families were linked by close ties of intermarriage, is no longer a matter of import.

Real power has passed into the hands of presidents and dictators, of prime ministers and politicians, subject as they too may well be to pressure from business and other interests. In countries where democracy exists, there is normally some form of constitutional procedure, a limitation on the term of office, or a regular electoral process, which can act as a safeguard against major abuse of power and position resulting from the failing health, mental and physical, of a formerly responsible politician. By and large, politicians who experience nervous breakdowns or who display signs of incipient madness are a rare phenomenon, and in fact they are usually induced to resign their office before they can do damage.

Historically speaking, then, the phenomenon of a powerful or responsible politician the balance of whose mind is in doubt is comparatively rare. But it is not wholly unknown. Its potential dangers may, for instance, be demonstrated by the case of the earl of Chatham, William Pitt the elder, whose health was never good and whose last ministry was terminated by a severe nervous breakdown which made him temporarily the victim of manic-depressive insanity. In the suicide of the British foreign secretary, Lord Castlereagh, in 1822 there was another instance of a severe mental breakdown which led to hallucinations and eventual insanity.

Pitt's medical history had never been good, for he was the victim of gout, probably a legacy from his father and grandfather, and was subject to attacks of severe depression and acute insomnia, even in his finest days as Britain's leader against France in the Seven Years' War when his ill-health had occasionally damaging effects on his conduct of cabinet government. 'I am indeed much out of order', he wrote in

1754, 'and worn down with pain and confinement: this gout which I trusted to relieve me has almost subdued me.'[1] His not infrequent absence from cabinet meetings gave scope for intrigue among his cabinet colleagues; but his great reputation and his political skills were such that much as the young king, George III, disliked him, he offered him the prime ministership in 1766.

His acceptance was disastrous, for though, as ever, Pitt made a gallant attempt to dissemble, his rare appearances in the British House of Commons, his legs swathed in red flannel, leaning on a stick, were a theatrical reminder of the forces of decay which were impinging on his mind. There were complications, possibly Bright's disease, which spelt not merely inactivity but real mental derangement in the form of manic-depressive insanity. His love of display became so extravagant as to bring him to the brink of bankruptcy: in April 1767 he ordered his architect, Dingley, to add thirty-four bedrooms to his residence, North End House, and to acquire any property which was likely to interfere with his view from it. Yet he himself had become a virtual recluse, sitting day after day in a little room at the top of the house, unwilling to communicate, even with his wife. He had his food left in a hatch outside his room so that he should not glimpse the servants who brought it. 'His nerves and spirits', so wrote his colleague the duke of Grafton, 'were affected to a dreadful degree, and the sight of his great mind bowed down and weakened by disorder . . . [made] the interview truly painful.'[2] Chatham recovered, as a result of his wife's care rather than his doctor's advice, but the disorder was the culmination of a long history of ill-health which had dogged him from early days.

Chatham was not the only notable English minister to suffer an acute breakdown in health while in office. The brilliant foreign minister, Lord Castlereagh, who had played a very prominent part in negotiating the peace settlement at the end of the Napoleonic Wars, suffered a mental breakdown in 1822. The crisis seems to have been precipitated partly by stress, brought on by his own public unpopularity, but he had also been greatly affected by, indeed had become obsessed with, a recent scandal. This resulted from the arrest of the bishop of Clogher who had been apprehended in a London tavern, the White Hart in St Alban's Place, Westminster, with his purple episcopal breeches down in flagrant intimacy with one John Moverley, a private soldier of the first regiment of guards. Without the least justification, Castlereagh suspected that he too was in danger of being charged with homosexual offences. He told the king, George IV, who sensibly refused to take his remark seriously, that he might as a result become a 'fugitive from justice' and have to flee to the 'ends of the earth'. Castlereagh's mind had been overwrought for weeks, leading to bouts of amnesia, while his handwriting had become indecipherable. His doctors, worried by the outcome of the insidious approach of madness, ordered his razors to be removed from his room, but on 12 August 1822 he cut his throat with a pen-knife.[3]

The problems facing twentieth-century politicians and their constituents are somewhat different from those which faced Chatham and Castlereagh. Most politicians holding responsible office are not schizophrenic or mad, though as we shall see later an exception may have to be made in the case of those who exercise dictatorial power. Yet, even so, the balance of their minds may still be decisively and sometimes disastrously affected by the ill-health of which they are the victims.

It has been an underlying thesis of this book that there is often an inextricable relationship between physical and mental ill-health, and that to try to separate one from the other is artificial. Yet it is important to recognize that ill-health, whether physical or mental, does not naturally inhibit creativity or political or academic achievement. Both Franklin Roosevelt and John F. Kennedy were American presidents of exceptional capacity; the mathematician Stephen Hawking of Cambridge University shows how physical disability does not necessarily inhibit superb intellectual creativity. Nor is madness itself of necessity sterile, especially in the realms of art and literature. From the cases which we have been reviewing it may well have appeared that mental imbalance reacts in a negative and disastrous way on the personalities of the rulers and the process of government. Yet there are circumstances in which it may promote creative projects. The Roman emperor Nero had a positive and creative side to his personality. The Russian tsars, Ivan and Peter, were in some respects as statesmen brilliantly creative. Ludwig of Bavaria's fertile imagination harbingered an artistic output.

Yet if we admit that neither physical nor, up to a point, mental illhealth precludes the possibility of positive achievement, broadly speaking where physical ill-health is allied to a personality disorder public policy and governmental responsibility may well be adversely affected.

'Since 1908', Hugh L'Etang wrote in 1969, 'eleven out of thirteen British premiers and six out of eleven American presidents have had illnesses when in office which have incapacitated them to some degree.'[4] Sir Henry Campbell-Bannerman who resigned the British premiership in April 1908 was already suffering from cerebro-vascular disease when he took office, collapsed in November 1907 and from the end of January 1908 was confined to his bed, unable even to consult his colleagues. Bonar Law, appointed prime minister on 24 October 1922, was in the first stages of cancer of the larynx, but resigned when he realized the nature of his illness. Ramsay Macdonald, the first Labour prime minister, exemplifies the case of a politician whose slow but steady physical deterioration affected his mental processes.[5] Soon after the national government which he headed had been formed in 1931 he had a slight collapse and an even more decisive breakdown in health occurred after England abandoned the gold standard. After two successful operations for glaucoma in 1932 he made a slow recovery but complained of suffering from 'brain-fag'. 'My trouble', he wrote on 26

December, 'is not a cold or anything like that, but just a complete breakdown from top to toe, inside and out, like the wonderful one horse choice.' 'The depression', he wrote the next day, 'has been one of the blackest and has affected everything. . . . The strain is at last telling on me . . . I have crossed the frontiers of age. . . . I walk as an old man, and my head works like an old man's. . . . How long can I go on?'[6]

Out of loyalty to his followers, a sense of duty and of misguided indispensability, Macdonald injudiciously stayed on. He suffered from insomnia and acute depression. 'At night my mind (is) like a pool which seeks to be quiet but which is stirred by springs at the bottom.'[7] Once early in 1933 he was observed to look nervously over his shoulder in the House of Commons, later explaining that in his perturbation he feared that a man in the public gallery was going to shoot him. At a disarmament conference in Geneva he lost the thread of his speech and told his audience 'Be men, not mannequins.' His speeches, always prolix, evaporated in a cloud of waffle and confusion. 'He has lost all grip', Lloyd George's secretary, Tom Jones, commented in February 1934, 'and moves from one vagueness to another.' 'Only a melancholy passenger in the Conservative ship' was Attlee's comment; 'inane and gaga' was Harold Nicolson's crisp judgement.

By the middle of March 1934 the prime minister confessed that he was 'a machine run down; stupid in mind and can do no work and sick in body'.[8] In the hope of recuperation he indulged in foreign travel but he remained 'very tired and stupid, head a mere log, no memory, yawning all day'. His writing deteriorated and he forgot names, made awkward slips of the tongue and his diary was marred by spelling mistakes. He was only sixty-nine when he retired in 1935 but he seems to have been a victim of Alzheimer's disease, the onset of which was very slow but sure.

Winston Churchill who led Great Britain to victory through the dark and dangerous days of the Second World War was a very different sort of personality from Macdonald. He was an enigmatic character, better attuned to leadership in war than in peace, whose judgement was occasionally affected prejudicially by his mental and emotional make-up.[9] The child of a fashionable beauty and a politically preoccupied father, he had been largely disregarded by his parents, and such neglect helped in some ways to condition his future career. His characteristic arrogance and egocentricity took shape in early youth, instilling in him the will and obsessive desire to succeed. His political career, fluctuating in character, was in part an answer to the traumas of his childhood. Like some other members of his family, including the first duke of Marlborough, he was a cyclothymic, swinging easily from one mood to another, passing from elation to a despair which was capable of holding him in thrall for long periods of time. His career was to reach its apogee in his flamboyant leadership of the Second World War. With its ending, he seemed like a stranded whale, and an ageing whale at that.

Even in the war years there were slight signs of a steady slowing up of his mental processes, hardly surprising in view of the immense stress under which he laboured as well as several bouts of ill-health. Between November 1943 and August 1944 he had three attacks of pneumonia with consequential exhaustion. 'God knows', Lord Alanbrooke wrote in his diary on 4 December 1941, 'where we should be without him, but God knows where we shall go with him.'[10] On 28 March 1944 Churchill seemed 'quite incapable of concentrating for more than a few minutes and keeps wandering continuously'. By December 1947 his personal physician, Lord Moran, felt that Churchill was 'living in the past and impatient of change . . . he was sliding almost imperceptibly into old age'. Even as early as April 1941 he had looked 'very depressed and desperately tired – in a sort of coma almost. His speech was rather slobbery and very slow. . . . It was a terribly depressing interview. The general atmosphere of sycophancy and the old man's lack of grasp and understanding apparently, made me leave to walk home convinced for the first time that we could not win the war.' But Churchill possessed the ability to bounce back triumphantly. 'He is either on the crest of the wave or in the trough,' General Ismay wrote in 1942, 'either highly laudatory or in the hell of a rage.' His native tenacity, the charisma of his leadership, something not far short of genius in his make up, enabled him to keep the 'black dog' of depression sufficiently at bay to carry the nation to victory.

It was to be a different story after the war ended. In July 1945 the Labour Party took office, but Churchill was returned to office in October 1951. His health was already deteriorating and affecting his mental processes as his physician Lord Moran made plain in his much criticized reminiscences.[11] He had suffered a series of small strokes, in August 1949, in February 1952 and in June 1953, leaving him with some facial weakness and slurred speech, 'scarcely comprehending what he was called upon to do, finding it difficult to concentrate or to compose his speeches'. The last stroke had occurred at a dinner for the prime minister of Italy on 23 June 1953 but though it was plain that he had experienced a further, in some sense incapacitating, attack his doctors and politicians combined to keep its seriousness from the public, even though the *Daily Mirror* asked in mid-August 1953 'whether Sir Winston Churchill is fit enough to lead us'.

Behind the façade he was a shadow of his former self. His speech was slurred and he walked with difficulty. He read little but novels, spent much of his time playing bezique, found it difficult to concentrate and was increasingly forgetful of names and occasions. Although he recognized his declining powers, he was unready to resign, in part because he had little confidence in his probable successor, Anthony Eden, himself an ill man, nor had he any wish to go to the House of Lords. Although his active political life was at an end, no one felt able to tell him that he must resign. 'Thus, for three months, Britain had neither an effective Prime Minister nor a Foreign

Secretary.'[12] But his performance at the Conservative Party conference at Blackpool was such that those closest to him realized that his resignation was required in the interests of the nation. On 6 April 1955 he resigned. Although he had another decade of existence before him, his real life had come virtually to a close.

Churchill was surely justified in having doubts about his successor, Anthony Eden, for although he was a man of great gifts there seems to have been a basic instability in his disposition to which a bout of severe ill-health shortly before and during his prime ministership contributed. 'Anthony's father', as R.A. Butler put it, 'was a mad baronet and his mother, a very beautiful woman. That is Anthony – half mad baronet, half beautiful woman.' His mother had wished originally to marry Francis Knollys but had been dissuaded from doing so by the future Edward VII. An unconventional woman – there were those who rumoured that Anthony's real father was George Wyndham – she was thoughtless and extravagant. 'By her profligacy and imprudence, she was not only to destroy Windleston [the family home] but totally to alienate her children.'[13]

Anthony's father, Sir William Eden, known with some justification as the 'bloody baronet', was a man of excessive ill-temper and so intolerant and passionate that to some he seemed to be on the brink of madness. 'Not bloody lamb again', he shouted as a loin of lamb was served for lunch before throwing it out of the window. He had many talents, was the best horseman in the county, one of the best shots and an amateur boxer of repute and withal a civilized and cultivated man. 'Nature', his son Timothy wrote, 'had showered upon him with an uncontrolled hand her gifts and her curses alike and without control he received them all, and without control he expended them.'[14]

In spite of his talents, intelligence, ability and charm, Anthony Eden never properly threw off the legacy of his inheritance and the traumas of his upbringing which stress and physical ill-health made horrific in their effects. As Foreign Secretary in Churchill's government in 1952 he required a gall bladder operation, but unfortunately the 'knife slipped', accidentally cutting the biliary duct with the result that Eden experienced a high fever. A second operation was judged necessary from which he nearly died. On the advice of an American specialist, Dr Richard Cattell, he underwent a third operation, lasting eight hours, at Boston in the USA to unblock the bile duct.[15] He recovered but had suffered irreparable damage, for while the operation restored Eden's circulation, he was henceforth liable to a flare-up of acute obstructive cholangitis or Charcot's intermittent fever. When Eden became prime minister he was technically not a sick man but his health was precarious, so that at moments of stress he became unduly irritable and suspicious, and his judgement showed some signs of impairment.

These physical and neurotic tendencies may help to explain what many believe to be his disastrous handling of the Suez crisis in 1956. He appeared, so some of his colleagues asserted, 'intoxicated with drugs',[16] not surprisingly since his doctors dosed him alternately with amphetamines and tranquillizers which may well have promoted his striking changes of mood. The neurophysical effects of the bile duct obstruction were even more significant, and the combination of physical ill-health and political stress had the worst possible personal and political effects.

The crisis came at the end of August 1956 when Anthony Eden suffered a high fever followed by periods of lassitude and agitation. 'The Suez Canal', as his wife, Clarissa, put it, 'was flowing through the drawing room.' Although Eden's own doctors were unsure as to whether their distinguished patient was very ill or simply suffering from acute exhaustion, at the invitation of Ian and Ann Fleming, the Edens went to recuperate at their house, Goldeneye, in Jamaica. Their stay led the rebarbative Randolph Churchill to comment that the only parallel to the position of the British troops then in Egypt was Hitler's refusal to withdraw his army from Stalingrad, but 'that Hitler did not winter in Jamaica'. When the prime minister returned it was evident that he lacked the capacity to carry out his duties effectively. 'For a moment he was looking directly at me,' a government official phrased it, ' . . . I saw in his eyes a man pursued by every demon.'[17] On 8 January he resigned and was succeeded by Harold Macmillan whose own resignation was later to be brought about by ill-health caused by bladder trouble, a decision which in later life he regretted.[18]

This brief survey of British prime ministers hints at some disturbing features. It appears that in the approach to power and in the conduct of policy temperamental considerations may be as important, perhaps more so, than the avowed principles to which politicians claim to adhere and which in some cases may be a reflection of their own inner traumas. It is less a question of 'naked ambition', though this on occasions may play a part, than the extent to which policy may itself be moulded by inner and personal problems. It may be difficult, even impossible, to illustrate such a thesis by references to special occasions or particular decisions, but there are depths concealed from public view which at times give rise to some degree of mental incompetence or at least inept judgement.

The supposition that a politician can be judged without reference to his mental and physical health or to the aberrant features of his private life seems historically fallacious. Even Lloyd George's competence as a prime minister and leader of the Liberal Party cannot be wholly divorced from his sexual indiscretions; Asquith's tenure of office was affected by the nature of his private personality. Churchill's cyclothymic disposition made him a fitting leader in war, though even in this respect he made some disastrous judgements influenced less by rational considerations than by emotional impulses, but he was an unfortunate politician in time of peace. Anthony Eden's personality, shaped by heredity as well as by physical illness, meant that the Suez crisis was as much a personal as a public predicament.

The survey suggests that elevation to high office, and a lengthy tenure of it, may make a psychological impact on the office-holder, tending to distance the politician from his or her constituents, and leading to an increasingly insecure grasp of political reality. The lengthy tenure of office which Margaret Thatcher enjoyed as Conservative prime minister helped to bring about some diminution in her political insight as well as apparently producing an obsessive concern to retain her authority over cabinet, party and country.[19]

In Britain prime ministers, affected by incapacitating ill-health or diminishing mental grip, have normally been persuaded sooner or later to resign, and in any case possess far less power than their American counterparts. The American experience has by and large been less happy, the power which an American president wields providing even greater potential for adverse effects on government, more especially when the president is himself the victim of physical illness with prejudicial effects on his mental powers. It is a phenomenon which the latter years of the presidency of Woodrow Wilson demonstrate particularly well.

A successful if temperamental president of Princeton University, his upbringing affected by a difficult home background, Wilson was unquestionably a man of high ideals and marked intellectual power. His health, however, had been long in doubt, for between 1874 and 1910 he had had already some twelve serious illnesses, among them three nervous breakdowns and he early showed clear signs of arterial degeneration.[20] When, in 1913, Wilson succeeded Theodore Roosevelt as president, his then doctor, Weir Mitchell, aware of Wilson's state of health, expressed doubts as to whether he would be able to complete his term of office.

Although in the early years of his presidency Woodrow Wilson seemed in good fettle, pushing through important domestic legislation, there were some warning signs in the shape of blinding headaches, kidney trouble and haemorrhage of the retina which suggested that he was suffering from hypersensitive vascular disease. His failing health seems to have accentuated some of the characteristic features of his personality. His inflexibility and unreadiness to compromise, which had already led to bitter disputes when he was president of Princeton University, became more pronounced. Wilson had brought America in 1917 into the First World War, and the part which he was to play at the subsequent Peace Conference at Paris in 1919 was to be affected vitally by the president's deteriorating health and impaired judgement.

It was plain that by 1919 Wilson was 'experiencing rapid cognitive and emotional changes on the basis of hypertension and cerebro-vascular disease' as the blood flow in the brain diminished.[21] 'I never', one of his close associates, Gilbert Close, commented, 'knew the President to be in such a difficult frame of mind as he is now. Even while lying in bed he manifests peculiarities.'[22] Irritability, some failure of memory, tunnel vision, increasing petulance and secretiveness led to difficulties with

President Woodrow Wilson (© The Hulton-Deutsch Picture Collection Limited, London)

his colleagues Clemenceau and Lloyd George at the Peace Conference, to a break with his trusted adviser, Colonel House, and a seeming inability to keep the American people properly informed about what he was trying to do. 'His lack of contact with the people and their leaders', Herbert Hoover said, 'separated him from the reality of which sound compromises are made.'[23]

In particular Wilson showed a lack of preparedness and a failure to comprehend matters of detail, fastening his whole attention almost obsessively on the proposal for forming the League of Nations and its covenant, committed to the somewhat unrealistic notion that this would resolve the world's outstanding political and economic problems. Idealism had run riot to the loss of reality. Already a tired man, his health worsened after he became seriously ill either with the severe influenzal virus or encephalitis which was sweeping Europe and America between 1917 and 1919.

After he had played his part in signing the peace treaty he sailed home a shattered man. When in late September he spoke at Pueblo he shambled on to the platform and much of his speech was 'mumbled; he mouthed certain words as if he had never spoken them before. There were long pauses. He had difficulty following the trend of his thought. It was a travesty of his usual brilliant delivery and fine logic.'[24]

Shortly afterwards Wilson had a severe stroke, compromising his vision and paralysing his left side. Common sense and political wisdom should have dictated that he resign but his doctor, Cary Grayson, abetted by his second wife, Edith Galt Wilson, kept the consequences of the president's seizure from the people, putting mistaken personal loyalties in front of the national interest. The public was kept deliberately in the dark. The president himself may have been unaware of the serious character of his illness, for he may well have been suffering from anosognosia, unawareness of illness, which is symptomatic of certain brain disorders, such as a thrombosis or blood clot in the right cerebral hemisphere.

The decision to continue was both tragic and disastrous personally and politically, for it meant that for two years, from October 1919 to March 1921, the American government was in practice rudderless. The helmsman, over-protected by his wife and physician, lived in comparative isolation, shielded from any real contact with the outside world. For seven months he did not meet the cabinet; for a month he was unable to read a newspaper. His thinking was confused and for hours at a time he would simply stare into space. When eventually Wilson met his cabinet, on 13 April 1920, he had not, in Herbert Hoover's opinion, 'recovered his full mental and physical vigour'.[25] As a result of his deteriorating health he had been overtaken by an organic loss of intellectual power; he was suffering from dementia. The brain damage affected his personality, for he became obstinate, querulous, lacking in grasp and emotionally labile. When Stockton Aston was reading to him in the autumn of 1920, the president 'would begin sobbing, when there didn't seem to be anything . . . to call for it'. The Senate had already refused to ratify the main plank in his political programme, the establishment of the League of Nations.

Yet against all common sense he sought the democratic nomination for the third time in the summer of 1920. Not surprisingly Warren G. Harding won an overwhelming victory. Harding's presidency was to be marked by corruption and scandal, which he tried to screen or at least cast into oblivion by playing cards and drinking. Whether the stress contributed to his premature death is not plain but it could have promoted the coronary disease which culminated in an apoplectic stroke from which he died on 2 August 1923. Wilson outlived him, dying on 3 February 1924. In Wilson's case the onset of ill-health had been politically disastrous, both for himself and his country, though as a personality and as a president he stood head and shoulders above Harding.

Wilson's ill-health, if ominous in the long run, did not appear to have sapped his political judgement in his earlier years, nor did this happen in the case of Franklin D. Roosevelt, whose achievement was to prove a spectacular triumph of mind over body. Born of an aristocratic and wealthy family, for his uncle Theodore had been president in the earlier years of the century, he had married his fifth cousin, Eleanor, an attractive and intelligent woman, in 1905 when he was twenty-three. He became a lawyer, entering political life as a Democratic senator for the New York State Senate in 1910. Vigorous and forceful, fair and handsome, he was a strong supporter of Wilson and stood as an unsuccessful candidate for the vice-presidency in 1920.

In August 1921 he and his family went on vacation to their summer home on the island of Campobello in New Brunswick, Canada. After an afternoon's sail, he helped to fight a forest fire on a neighbouring island, and, overheated by his exertions, cooled off by swimming in a nearby lake. Later he swam again in the cold waters of the Bay of Fundy and sat for some time in his damp bathing suit. As a result he went down with a severe chill, with a high temperature and pain in his back and legs. Vacationing in the neighbourhood was a distinguished octogenarian surgeon, W.W. Keen, who had twenty-eight years earlier played a vital part in salvaging President Grover Cleveland's life and political reputation.[26]

Keen, who was unacquainted with poliomylitis or infantile paralysis, diagnosed Roosevelt's illness as 'lesion of the spinal cord' and recommended vigorous massage, which was in fact the worst kind of treatment for such an illness. Two weeks later, Roosevelt, still in great pain with the paralysis spreading rather than abating, was treated by a doctor from Boston, Robert W. Lovett, who made a correct diagnosis and halted the massage.

Roosevelt's recovery was only partial. He tried every conceivable exercise that might help to strengthen the muscles, spending much time at Warm Springs in

Georgia, a warm pool with a constant temperature of 88°F which gave him some relief. But he was never to recover the use of his legs, could not walk without heavy metal braces or stand without assistance. Psychologically his illness presented him with a challenge which he met with vigour and determination. 'Franklin's illness', Eleanor Roosevelt commented, 'proved a blessing in disguise; for it gave him strength and courage he had not before. He had to think out the fundamental of living and learning the greatest of all lessons – infinite patience and never-ending persistence.'

In June 1924 he went to nominate A.L. Smith as the Democratic candidate for the presidency, unsuccessfully as it happened, and his courage in attending the convention in a wheel-chair attracted high praise and was a long-term preliminary to his own nomination for the presidency in 1932.

Of Franklin D. Roosevelt's achievements it is needless to speak of the New Deal, of the recovery of the American economy, of his sympathy for the underdog and the disabled which his own condition may well have helped him to understand the better, of the part he played in world politics, culminating in 1941 in America's entry into the Second World War. Yet it was perhaps inevitable that sooner or later his infirmity should take its toll. Even before he was struck down, his good health had been somewhat sporadic: he had had typhoid in 1912, appendicitis in 1914, tonsillitis in 1916, quinsy in 1918, pneumonia in 1918 and a tonsillectomy in 1919, which was thought by some to have reduced his immunity to polio.

As president he had a punishing work load and by 1943, if not before, his stamina was beginning to be sapped and his judgements became less sure.[27] How far deteriorating health affected his decision making just prior to and immediately after America's entry into the Second World War it is difficult to establish, but there were hints that his powers of leadership were in fact beginning to wane and the decisiveness of his judgement was less sure, as was shown by the inconsistency of his policy towards Japan before the attack on Pearl Harbour on 7 December 1941, which gave him the justification he sought for entry into the Second World War.

The signs were more visible after the Teheran Conference in 1943 where he established a cordial relationship with Stalin which may in part account for the policy he was to follow at Yalta two years later. On his return he seemed 'bone-tired' and 'gave the impression of being exhausted'. A young cardiologist Dr Howard Bruenn carried out an examination at the Bethesda National Hospital at the end of March 1944 which showed that the president was suffering from metabolic hypersensitive encephalopathy, manifested by momentary episodes of impaired consciousness and confusional states. His face appeared grey, his finger tips and his lips looked blue and he had difficulties with his upper respiratory tract, suggesting that he was suffering from chronic pulmonary disease and congestive heart failure as well as from hypertension. His physician, Dr Ross McIntire, incidentally recommended to him by

Woodrow Wilson's doctor, Cary Grayson, more or less suppressed the report, so that as a result of McIntire's misleading announcements about his health the public was kept deliberately misinformed, as earlier had been the case with Woodrow Wilson.[28]

But encephalopathy and attendant ills were steadily to vitiate Roosevelt's powers of leadership and to affect his political and military judgement. There were already, if intermittently, signs of this in his growing fatigue, clouded consciousness, a degree of intellectual impairment and some behavioural aberrations, 'the mouth' as Jim Bishop put it, 'being left open unconsciously, and thought processes were sometimes left unfinished, with sentences dangling'.[29] It is not easy to give specific examples of how this affected public affairs, but his endorsement of the Morgenthau plan for the future of Germany at the Quebec Conference at the end of August 1944 could conceivably have been a case in point. Roosevelt was beyond question a very ill man when he accepted nomination for an unprecedented fourth term of office and was elected.

So that when he went to the Yalta Conference with Stalin and Churchill in March the omens were poor. 'He was', Dr Roger Lee of Boston said, 'irascible and became very irritable if he had to concentrate his mind for long. If anything was brought up that wanted thinking out he would change the subject. He was, too, sleeping badly.' Lord Moran, who had accompanied Churchill, described Roosevelt as a 'very sick man. He has all the symptoms of hardening of the arteries of the brain in an advanced stage, so that I give him only a few months to live.'[30] 'Cordell (Hull) and I', Jim Farley wrote, 'agreed that he was a sick man . . . and should not be called upon to

Churchill, Roosevelt and Stalin at the Yalta Conference of 1945 (© The Hulton-Deutsch Picture Collection Limited, London)

make decisions affecting his country and the world.' But 'he looked dead after his return from Yalta' and lapsed into seeming lassitude; his speech to Congress was a dismal affair, halting, ineffective and confused.

Whether Roosevelt's performance and policy were the manifestations of his ill-health is more a matter of controversy. While with hindsight his seeming readiness to appease Stalin and to give a virtual green light to Russian control over eastern Europe may appear ill-judged, he may well have been in better command of his material than some later commentators have supposed.[31] In his treatment of Stalin he seemed to show an understandable naiveté but momentarily at least, in spite of his appearance, he may have continued to serve his country well. On 1 April he died of a massive stroke, to which his ill-health had long predisposed him, at Warm Springs in Georgia. While Roosevelt's pre-eminence as a political leader is not in dispute, it is certain failing health eroded his judgement.

Some of his first lieutenants were in even less good fettle mentally and physically than the president. By a curious psychological quirk Roosevelt appointed to government office men who, though able and intelligent politicians, were in some respects in a worse state of health than himself. Take, for instance, the men who served Roosevelt and his successor Truman as Secretaries of the Navy. Claude A. Swanson, appointed secretary in 1933, was so frail that he could hardly stand without support, had to be assisted in and out of the cabinet office, was unable to hold a cigarette and spoke so indistinctly that he could hardly be heard or understood. 'In his physical condition', Harold Ickes wrote of a function at the White House in January 1937, 'he cannot stand for long. Finally he began to weaken in his legs and his cane slipped on the smooth floor. He fell in a dead faint.' 'Swanson's continued membership in the Cabinet', he commented later, 'when everyone knows he is neither physically nor mentally qualified to serve, must create a bad impression.' 'For two or three years', Ickes wrote at the time of his death in July 1939:

> Swanson has been more dead than alive. For months on end he has not been able to attend Cabinet meetings or go to the office. He has spent many weeks in the Hospital completely incapacitated. He cannot walk into the Cabinet room alone and he has to sit there until his aide comes and lifts him out the chair and helps him to totter out to his car.[32]

But, in spite of his feeble physique – perhaps because of it – Swanson was an exceptionally aggressive and influential politician who urged Roosevelt to make war on Japan after the bombing of the gunboat *Panay* in 1937.

Swanson's immediate successors were not in all that better shape. Frank Knox died of a heart attack in April 1944. In 1947 Truman appointed James Forrestal who had earlier attracted Roosevelt's favourable notice. Militantly anti-communist and anti-Semite, he eventually broke down under stress. Sleeplessness, digestive problems and anxiety so dogged him that he became increasingly paranoic, so distrustful that he would not admit visitors without powerful scrutiny. He came to believe that even the beach umbrellas were bugged. Hesitant, indecisive and depressed, he flung himself to his death from the sixteenth floor of the US Naval Hospital at Bethesda on 22 May 1949.[33]

Roosevelt's Secretary of War in 1940 was described as a 'very tired decayed old man' of seventy-three, rigid and inflexible, a sufferer from insomnia who, in spite of waning powers, remained in office until September 1945. His colleague as Secretary of State, Cordell Hull who retired at the age of seventy-three after twelve years of office, was afflicted by fatigue, arteriosclerosis and diabetes; he was so sensitive to cold that he kept his office like a greenhouse. His judgements were not always reliable, but he was commonly regarded as the president's mouthpiece.

Even more influential in world affairs was Roosevelt's intimate adviser, Harry Hopkins. Harold Ickes commented on 20 September 1941:

Bill Bullitt ruefully remarked to me that the President had to have someone near him who was dependent upon him and who was pale and sick and gaunt. He had had such a person in Louis Howe and now another in Harry Hopkins. Bill insisted that the two resembled each other physically, being cadaverous and bent and thin.[34]

Hopkins was very closely associated with Roosevelt from the time of the New Deal to the very end of the president's life when Hopkins's advice may have been crucial in the decision making at Yalta. When Moran met him in Washington in December 1941 he was horrified by his appearance. 'His lips are so blanched', he wrote, 'as if he had been bleeding internally, his skin yellow like stretched parchment and his eyelids contracted to a slit, so that you can just see his eyes moving about restlessly, as if he was in pain.'[35] Hopkins had had a very long history of ill-health: a peptic ulcer in 1936, cancer in 1939, fatty diarrhoea and protein deficiency; and he was eventually to die of haemochromatosis, a disease of the digestive tract. Illness left Hopkins prostrate and made him both irritable and impulsive in judgement.

In the person of President John F. Kennedy America's destiny seemed to many to experience a revival. Young, vigorous, handsome and well born, he possessed a charisma that was not easily shattered. Some of the glitter has worn off with the passing of the years. He was a habitual womanizer: 'I wonder', he once observed to an astonished, not to say embarrassed Harold Macmillan, 'how it is with you, Harold? If I don't have a woman for three days, I get a terrible headache.'[36] His assassination was to serve his political and personal reputation well, perhaps unduly so. For his attractive, even seemingly macho exterior screened continuing physical weakness and acute pain which may well have had consequences for his political judgements which were sometimes less than well balanced. In the Bay of Pigs affair Kennedy had become convinced that Cuba, as a political satellite of Soviet Russia, constituted a danger to the security of the United States. He knew that Cuban exiles were being trained by the CIA in Guatemala, and approved a decision, against expert advice, to launch an invasion of the island; but the landing on the Bay of Pigs proved to be a fatal error; the Cubans shattered the would-be invading army. Kennedy had been warned against going ahead with such a 'wild idea', as Dean Acheson called it; and he had badly miscalculated. His decision to go to Dallas in 1963 was ill conceived and even foolhardy, for he knew well that it was a centre of strong anti-administration feeling and that the visits of Adlai Stevenson and Senator Fulbright had caused near-riots. His only comment to his brother had been that this would make his trip more exciting.

Kennedy suffered constantly from pain which required the administration of steroids, local anaesthetics and stimulants.[37] He had left Princeton University without finishing his course because of infectious hepatitis. He was at first declared unfit for military service but he was allowed eventually to join the navy where the injury which he had originally received playing football at Harvard was made worse when a Japanese destroyer rammed his ship. Subsequently his left heel was built up and he had to wear a comb-type brace.

Even more importantly he was affected by a renal malfunction of the adrenal glands, Addison's disease, which caused weakness and inability to fight infection and conceivably had repercussions on his mental judgement. He was always much concerned to screen his physical infirmity. To disguise the onset of Addison's disease he sun-bathed and used sun tan lotion to conceal its symptomatic brown pigmentation. The disease made surgery for his back problem difficult, and even after he underwent spinal surgery he was to experience agonizing pain. At the time of the presidential election in 1960 President Lyndon Johnson, to whose recent heart attack Kennedy had alluded in a speech which he made at the Democratic convention held at Los Angeles, countered by asserting that Kennedy was a victim of Addison's disease. It was a charge which at the time his supporters vehemently denied, but the fatigue, emotional instability, depression and irritability from which he suffered were among its characteristic symptoms. He was able in part to control his illness by taking steroids but these in themselves may have promoted psychiatric complications. He was treated with stimulants such as procaine and with amphetamines, without realizing the potentially dangerous side-effects of the pain-killing drugs with which he had to live for the remainder of his life.

His leading medical adviser became a then fashionable New York practitioner, Dr

Max Jacobson, who treated many celebrities, among them Truman Capote and Tennessee Williams. Jacobson, whom Kennedy nicknamed 'Dr Feel Good', was to accompany Kennedy to Vienna where he was to meet the Soviet leader, Khrushchev. There is some reason to suppose that the drugs which Jacobson administered were prejudicial in their effects, and in April 1975 his licence was taken away by the New York State Board of Regents on some forty-eight charges of unprofessional conduct.[38]

It would be possible to speculate on the psychological and health problems which have confronted America's more recent presidents. There seems, for instance, to have been something of a megalomaniacal streak in Richard Nixon: 'Look,' he said to a fellow traveller in the presidential aircraft as it circled over Washington and the White House, 'look at all this! And it's all mine!' Mrs Reagan's recourse to astrology seems to epitomize the office of a highly popular but elderly president whose grip on affairs of state had long seemed minimal. Enough, however, has surely been said to show that even in the Land of the Free the holders of the highest office were not free from blemish.

Health problems did not affect Mackenzie King, the prime minister of America's neighbour, Canada, but King was to be, as his diary shows, the victim of psychological aberration in the shape of strange beliefs – recourse to spiritualism, table-turning, necromancy – which dominated his private life.[39] While it has been asserted strongly that such beliefs did not significantly affect his political judgements, it seems more than probable that there were times when they filtered through his intensely private existence into the public domain.

William Lyon Mackenzie King was probably the most successful Canadian politician of the twentieth century, enjoying a term of prime ministerial office longer than that of any other Commonwealth prime minister, including Sir Robert Walpole. In spite of crises and divisions within his party, without being an outstanding speaker and lacking all personal charisma, he had welded the Canadian Liberal Party into a formidable political phalanx. Outwardly his career appeared to be one of almost unparalleled success.

Yet personally King was an enigmatic and complex character. During his early life, and indeed long after her death in 1917, he was dominated by the figure of his mother, Isabel Grace, a daughter of William Lyon Mackenzie, a leader in the rebellion of 1837, from whom Mackenzie King may have inherited his deep interest in liberal and social reform. He appears even as a young man to have been a lonely figure. He was not uninterested in women and like W.E. Gladstone took some interest in the rehabilitation of prostitutes to whose wiles he may occasionally have succumbed. He had a passionate but apparently not a homosexual friendship with a fellow student, Bert Harper, whose early death by drowning as a result of his trying to rescue a skater was an unalloyed grief to him. Thereafter Mackenzie King was very much a loner with few

Mackenzie King, Prime Minister of Canada (© The Hulton-Deutsch Picture Collection Limited, London)

close friends, living an inner life within the portals of Laurier House or his country estate at Kingsmere where he acted as a country squire.

Realistic and even ruthless as a politician, his real world became in middle age extra-terrestrial, a world of the spirits whom he was to evoke through the agency of mediums, table-tapping, dreams and numerology. On earth he fastened all his affection on his Irish terrier Pat. 'Little Pat', he wrote in 1931, 'came from the bedroom and licked my feet – dear little soul, he is almost human. I sometimes think he is a comforter my dear mother has sent me.'[40] 'Little Pat', he wrote in 1939 on the day Britain declared war against Germany ' . . . is "the little angel dog" who will one day be a "little dog angel".' Pat was to live for another two years, dying at the ripe age of seventeen, before he achieved this distinction. As he was dying King sang aloud to him 'Safe in the arms of Jesus', 'looking at dear mother's picture as I sang'. He was succeeded by another Pat who filled a similar role. 'Before going to bed', he wrote on Christmas Eve 1944, 'I had a little talk with Pat, in his basket. We spoke together of the Christ-child and the arrival in the crib.' When, in 1947, King George VI gave King the high honour of the Order of Merit, King confessed to his diary that his dogs were more deserving of the honour than himself.

His obsessive interest in spiritualism developed comparatively late in his political life, for it was during the election campaign of 1925 when King was already fifty-one years old that he met a medium, Mrs L. Bleaney of Kingston, who was to have a great effect on his philosophy of existence. 'The influence of the talk with that woman', he wrote, 'is strange, it has brought me very near to the dear ones in the Great Beyond, what seems now more like the Great Omnipresent, Here and Now.' 'You will', Mrs Bleaney told him, referring indirectly to the election, 'pass safely through into a perfect clear atmosphere where you will once again breathe the pure sweet air of freedom and justice after a hard fight', words which King thought a 'truly wonderful vision of a situation which could have been foreseen only through spiritual vision'.[41]

Seven years later at a seance arranged by a widow of a Canadian senator, a Mrs Fulford, at Brockville, he met another medium, a Mrs Etta Wright, who put him into touch with the departed, his mother, Sir Wilfrid Laurier and other politicians. 'There can be no *doubt* whatever', he wrote, 'that the persons I have been talking with were the loved ones and others I have known and who have passed away. *It was the spirits of the departed.*'[42]

From this time forward such communications played a dominant part in his life. On his trips to Europe and England in particular he consulted other mediums who greatly widened his acquaintance with the departed, leading to conversations with, among others, Leonardo da Vinci, Lorenzo dei Medici, Pasteur who prescribed for his dog Pat's heart condition, Lord Grey of Falloden, Gladstone and Rosebery. In January 1935 he was in touch with the spirit of his grandfather who assured him that 'You will be Prime Minister this year in June. . . . Get ready for the long struggle. . . . Go to bed early whenever you can, eat lightly, drink no spirits or wine, try to pray all you can.' His grandfather's prediction was confirmed by the spirit of Sir Wilfrid Laurier though perhaps understandably he got the figures of King's actual majority wrong.

On a trip to Europe King met Hitler and had the foresight to warn him that if there was war the British Empire would stand together, but in other ways he warmed to the Führer. 'I am', he wrote on 27 March 1938, 'convinced he is a spiritualist – that he has a vision to which he is being true – his devotion to his mother – that Mother's spirit is I am certain his guide.'[43]

After the outbreak of the Second World War there seemed to be fewer allusions to spiritualistic matters in his diary, possibly because the spirits were apparently less well informed about the future course of events. His father had told him that Hitler had been shot by a Pole: and his mother had predicted that there would be no war. But he continued to have psychic experiences, and at one seance his parents told him of Pat's safe arrival in the beyond and his meeting with his friends the Pattesons' dog Derry.

With the ending of the war he continued to be active in spiritualistic matters, recording on a visit to England that 'President Roosevelt [who had died recently] took up most of the morning' and was very complimentary to him. 'You have', he told King, 'that slow Scotch way with you. You are *not* clever. You are wise!'[44] Sir Wilfrid Laurier commented that he knew that Churchill liked him 'very much'. King George V confirmed that the visit which his son George VI and Queen Elizabeth were to make to Canada was 'due to their affection for you'.

It has been reiterated that King did not allow these extra-terrestrial interests to intrude into his political life or affect his political judgement. 'Never', his friend Joan Patteson said, 'did he allow his belief to enter into his public life.'[45] Yet his beliefs played so prominent a part in his private life that they could not help but shape his public career. When in 1944 there was an acute cabinet crisis over the issue of conscription, King commented that it was 'wholly the power from beyond' that had saved the day.

What is even more disturbing is the extent to which this powerful political leader allowed his life and judgement to be so strongly influenced by what was plainly the intellectually banal and the spiritually trite and silly. It underlined too King's boundless egocentricity. His spirit guides told him in general what he wanted to hear. The messages he sought were projections of his own wishes. 'The combination of simple-mindedness and egoism', C.P. Stacey wrote, 'leaves one slightly breathless . . . [leaving] the ineradicable impression of a limited intelligence.'[46] The guidance from the unseen world seeped into his unconscious and helped to mould his ideas. Mackenzie King may have been a political giant but his extremities were feeble; fortunately for Canada he did not heel over.

This survey has surely shown that there may be a significant correlation between physical ill-health and mental incapacity which in politicians holding positions of great authority can have deleterious consequences for those whom they govern. For the twentieth-century world the problem of political incapacity has perhaps been made the more difficult by man's increased longevity, which has resulted in a decided increase in gerontic leadership. Although Gladstone was still prime minister in 1894 in his eighty-fifth year and Pope Leo XIII was pope until his death at the age of ninety-three in 1903, the influence exerted by old men in politics has been relatively greater in the twentieth century than in the past. Both Pilsudski in Poland and Hindenburg in Germany were affected by advancing senility.[47] Konrad Adenauer was chancellor of Germany in 1963 at eighty-seven. General Franco, dictator of Spain, died in office in 1975 in his eighty-third year. The Ayatollah Khomeini, virtual ruler of Iran and in some sense its evil genius, was still dominant until his death in 1989 in his eighty-seventh year. Hirohito was emperor of Japan from 1926 until his death at eighty-seven in 1989. At the age of eighty-nine in 1993 Deng Xiaoping continued to preside over China with his elderly cronies. Ronald Reagan completed his third term of office at the age of seventy-five. President Mitterand of France was re-elected until the age of seventy-nine. Old age, it has been often said, brings wisdom and experience, but it also promotes an inflexibility of mind and an inability to absorb or construct new ideas which may well be of disservice to the governed; it can also bring a physical decline which, often illustrated above, triggers mental deterioration.

By and large the majority of the electorate in most countries seem normally to have a simple faith in the physical and mental capacity of the man or woman whom they have elected to high office, a faith which subsequent events may not justify. The more democratic the electoral process the greater the possibility of preventing abuse, but as Rousseau admitted reluctantly if realistically the general will is not infallible. The people's choice is not necessarily the right one, for they may be swayed by purely ephemeral emotions or by the superficialities of the media or by the tortured rhetoric of an injured mind. Awareness of such possible dangers may be the best possible safeguard against the damage that mental imbalance or physical ill-health may do, but there is no infallible nostrum for ensuring that the people will elect good governments or that those who govern will resign when their capacities fail. The only effective remedy is eternal vigilance, the only relevant advice summarized in the old Latin tag *cave emptor*.

XVI
Madmen in Jackboots

More than any other period the twentieth century has been an age of dictators who have let loose an explosion of human misery and destructive war unparalleled in the annals of the past, even by an Attila or a Genghis Khan. Such a phenomenon requires more than an historical explanation.

That is not to say that historical developments have not played an essential part in the rise of dictators and their continuance in power. It was historical circumstances that provided the dictators with the opportunity to win power: the turbulence of the Russian Revolution provided the opportunity for Lenin's ascendancy and the context for Stalin's brutal dictatorship; the feckless politics of 1920s Italy paved the way for the fascist hegemony of Mussolini; and the swingeing terms of defeat that occasioned the dreadful depression and hyperinflation of post-First World War Germany set the scene for Hitler's assumption of supreme power. Yet a purely historical explanation may be insufficient to illuminate how and why it was that they sought power, and why, when they acquired it, they so abused it.

Lord Acton's oft-quoted maxim that power always corrupts and absolute power corrupts absolutely may not be axiomatically true. There have been absolute sovereigns in the past, such as Louis XIV of France, or even dictators in the twentieth century such as Salazar of Portugal and Franco of Spain who may have ruled without great profit to their peoples but who did not seem abnormal personalities.

Yet the great dictators seem to fall into a category of their own, so obsessed with the possession of power that it supersedes all else. And in such cases a power psychosis seemed eventually to pervert and subvert the personality. 'The pathological mind', Harold Lasswell observed in his now classic book *Psychopathology and Politics*, 'is like an automobile with its control lever stuck in one gear; the normal mind can shift.'[1] The dictator is a politician with a one-track mind, intoxicated by power, seeking to impose his will and his values upon all his subjects and eliminating all those who will not accept them. The pursuit and retention of power becomes the sole object of his existence.

What may be the features of his personality which pave the way for this development? Freud explained mental disintegration in terms of childhood, tracing frustration back in some instances to pre-natal experience. The cases which we have examined already make it plain that a deprived or damaged childhood may be of critical significance in the evolution of future neuroses or psychoses. Childhood and adolescence are, then, a formative process in the development of the psychopath or sociopath, some of whose features most of the dictators display.

A distinguishing feature of the lives of the dictators has been the impoverishment of their childhood and adolescence, not merely in material but in familial terms. Hitler, Mussolini and Stalin all came from a wretched and unhappy home background, with a devoted mother and a father whom they hated. Youthful rebellion led them into trouble with the authorities, causing lasting resentment. Deprived of affection, insecure, humiliated in adolescence, unable to form a happy sexual relationship, they were to seek compensation for their damaged self-esteem in the pursuit and abuse of power.

It would, of course, be ludicrous to suppose that all children with such backgrounds are likely to become dictators, juvenile delinquents or psychopaths. Yet in the dictators' early environment the seeds of the future had been planted, awaiting the opportunity which their native intelligence and ability were able to exploit. The forest of tares was to come later.

Is it possible to explain their development in physical as well as psycho-analytical terms? Stalin was pock-marked and partly deformed. Mussolini was over-concerned to present a macho image of himself. Hitler had an almost feminine physique. Both Mussolini and Hitler were suspected of having a syphilitic infection, apparently without confirmatory evidence. Hitler's doctor said that he had caught encephalitis at Vinnitsa in 1942, and as a result of his doctor's ministrations he was certainly the victim of amphetamine abuse. The precarious nature of Mussolini's health in later years may have affected his mental balance. Physical health can be, as we have seen, a significant ingredient in mental impairment. The ruthless actions of the Turkish dictator, Kemal Atatürk, become more comprehensible in the light of the fact that he suffered from Korsakoff's psychosis, a form of organic brain disorder, a result of thiamine deficiency brought about by alcoholism, which tends to loss of memory and, as a compensatory factor, to the invention of imaginary activities.[2] From time to time health problems may have been an exacerbating factor in the dictators' minds but in themselves they are insufficient to explain their disordered personalities.

The clue, then, to their natures lay first in the development of the dictators' propensities, then in the way in which circumstances allowed them to abuse power to the extent of bringing them to the brink of madness itself. For the dictator power became an obsession, taking precedence over all else, giving them the opportunity to vent long-felt grievances, to fulfil personal ambitions and to give rein to their unconscious impulses, so that private concerns became rationalized into public issues. What may have been personal grievances were outwardly presented as an ideology designed for the public welfare which was propagated with great skill to win public enthusiasm for the dictators' policies. It is a fascinating aspect of mass psychology that millions of normal men and women were gulled and enchanted so that they too became seemingly committed to a personal, even maniacal cause. To buttress his image the dictator needs self-aggrandizement, whether it finds its outward expression in unlimited adulation, in flamboyant ceremonial or in grandiose architecture. He needs too to suppress all opposition, whether real or imaginery. But in the midst of a sycophantic court and unstinted adulation, the dictators mentioned remained, as they had done throughout their lives, figures isolated from reality, flawed personalities who in their self-deception could make decisions which might well be ultimately suicidal and self-destructive. Stalin died in his bed but there were rumours that like Tiberius his death may have been hastened.[3] Hitler committed suicide in the Berlin bunker. Mussolini was ignominiously hanged by the Italian partisans. Ceausescu and his wife were shot after a summary trial. These dictators may not have been clinically insane but as personalities they were dangerously abnormal.

If there is a prototype of twentieth-century dictatorship, then the Italian dictator, Benito Mussolini, must surely be a leading candidate.[4] Broad-shouldered, muscular, scowling, Napoleonic in stance, his very appearance expressed the role he had deliberately fashioned for himself, epitomizing the cult of 'ducismo'. He fostered a macho image of himself as a virile, tough, athletic figure, seen driving a fast car, riding a horse, flying an aeroplane. To Hitler's disgust, he even had himself photographed in the semi-nude. When he was inspecting a line of soldiers he would make rapid strides rather than walk. In similar fashion he ordered those who were to be interviewed to sprint to his desk and after dismissal to run out at the double, as they did so giving him the Roman salute with which he had replaced the handshake (for he had an almost morbid dislike of physical contact).

'If a man is told a hundred times a day that he is a genius, he will eventually believe in his own infallibility.' So it was with Mussolini and indeed with most of his fellow dictators. Women held up their babies to receive his blessing. It was rumoured that he had halted the flow of lava from Mount Etna by his will power alone. A new town was to be called Mussolinia. He saw himself at least as an equal of Napoleon and Jesus Christ. He was a superb illusionist who sought for many years successfully to conceal the physical and mental crevasses below the surface.

How significant were these 'crevasses'? Some believed, as with earlier tyrants, that he was the victim of syphilis which he had contracted when he was teaching at Tolmezzo on the Austro-Italian border in 1905–6, four years before Paul Erlich introduced treatment for syphilis with organic arsenic compounds. Much later Count Ciano and his chief of police wondered whether his central nervous system had not been affected by syphilis, explaining his unaccountable judgements; but the Wasserman test which he had taken showed a negative result. His physical health progressively deteriorated, doubtless making an eventual impact on his judgement. But the key to understanding Mussolini lies less in his physical than in his mental make-up.

Mussolini, his British biographer, Denis Mack Smith, has observed, 'was not mad but simply trying to impress people as a man of power'.[5] Yet in this power-complex there seemed to be ingredients that brought him within the no man's land of the mentally disturbed. Megalomaniac or paranoic, he was pathologically narcissistic and egocentric. 'His first consideration', the British ambassador commented, 'is Mussolini, his second is the fascist regime, his third Italy.' His lack of conscience, his dim view of human nature, his ruthlessness, his inner loneliness suggest at least that Mussolini had some of the characteristics of the typical psychopath.

His over-structured sense of his own importance was something which ballooned with success, and was evidently a compensation for a deep feeling of inferiority and insecurity which he experienced in childhood and adolescence. Born on 29 July 1883 at Predappio, a village in the Romagna, his father was the local blacksmith, an idle fellow who only worked when he felt like it, an early socialist, an anti-clerical, a womanizer and an alcoholic, very different from Mussolini's mother, a devout Catholic who became the bread-winner of the family, and who was later to assume the status of a cult figure in whose memory schoolchildren sang the *Felix Mater*. It was an unhappy background, even if Mussolini, like his fellow dictator Hitler, was tempted to exaggerate the deprivations from which he suffered in childhood, but plainly he had a bleak and insecure home. School life offered no recompense, for the regime of the school which he attended at Faenza, run by a religious order, was harsh and austere, while Benito himself was a violent and undisciplined pupil. He seemed to his contemporaries to be a bully. If he won a bet, one commented, he asked for more than his due, and if he lost he tried to avoid paying. In a fit of temper he stabbed a fellow student at supper and was expelled.

Manhood brought little brighter prospect. His upbringing made him a socialist and an anti-clerical. He had managed to secure an educational diploma and a job as a temporary teacher before he moved to Switzerland, probably to avoid the draft for military service. He was in Switzerland for two years, living penuriously and described in the Swiss police records because of his extreme socialist views as an 'impulsive and violent man'. Although, like his father, a womanizer, he had few intimate friends. To some at least he seemed not wholly sane.

The outbreak of the First World War was for him as for Hitler the pathway to salvation. Abandoning his Marxist politics he became overtly patriotic and, like Hitler, rose to the rank of corporal before he was invalided out in June 1917. The war had filled him with national fervour and bitter contempt for Italy's ruling politicians. Post-war discontent and malaise fostered both his political ambition and the burgeoning of his pyschopathic aggression.

By exploiting a situation in which the forces of liberal democracy appeared feeble and nerveless, Mussolini acquired power by intimidation and political gerrymandering. For twenty years he was to be '*il duce*'. His powers of leadership, intelligence and vitality and his massive achievements cannot be gainsaid, but the longer he remained as the unquestioned head of state, the greater the adulation he demanded and received, and the more remote became his grip on reality. The psychopathic features of his personality became the more pronounced, in the ruthless extermination of his critics, in his massive egocentricity, and in his readiness to use war as a weapon in his philosophy of politics and life. Given what was happening, the fascist rejuvenation of Italy, the fulfilment of what Mussolini thought to be its imperial destiny of which the Ethiopian war was an expression, and then the alliance with Hitler which preceded Italy's entry into the Second World War, it may not have been so very obvious that the cracks beneath the surface of his macho image were widening. Two features of his personality were, however, surely playing an ever greater part in his life: deteriorating physical health with adverse effects on his mental balance and political judgement, and a growing gap between the icon which he made for himself and the historical reality within which it had to operate.

He sought to keep the stigma of ill-health at a distance. While it seems unlikely that he was actually later the victim of syphilis of the central nervous system his health was worsening. As early as 1925 he had vomited blood and collapsed in his car, suffering from a severe gastro-duodenal ulcer. Four years later he was treated for an internal haemorrhage and was kept on a liquid diet, involving his drinking three litres of milk a day. His health was such that, like Hitler, he became a frugal eater, abstaining from alcohol and tobacco. When he visited North Africa in 1942 he was afflicted by serious internal pains which his doctors diagnosed as worms and amoebic dysentry but which was more likely to have been a peptic ulcer. In the most critical period of the war, in January 1943, he lived on sedatives and liquids.

His faltering grip on reality was more serious, suggesting the possible onset of a brain disorder. When the Second World War broke out, he appeared strangely indecisive and even incoherent while his country was fatally ill-prepared. He tried to brazen out his shortcomings, meeting with Hitler, who was critical of the Italian war effort at Feltre in July 1943; but his performance was pitiful, and as the two dictators met for the first time Allied bombs fell on Rome. When King Victor-Emmanuel, advised of his deteriorating powers, asked for his resignation, he did not resist.

After Marshal Badoglio succeeded him, Mussolini was incarcerated on the island of Ponza and later at La Maddelena where apparently he spent much of his time reading a life of Christ, and finding a curious analogue between Iscariot's betrayal and the treatment to which he had been subjected. From this situation he was rescued by a lightning raid by the Germans who made him the head of a puppet government under

German protection. But his capacity for leadership had evaporated in the collapse of his past hopes and his dwindling grip on reality. While his health had temporarily improved, he spent much of his time at the lakeside resort of Gargnano on the lake of Garda, improving his German, translating Wagner's *Ring* into Italian and making notes on Plato's *Republic*. He was infinitely depressed by the prospect of an Allied victory but could do nothing to avert it. 'I challenged the world but it proved too strong for me. I despised other men and they are taking their revenge.' In a last desperate bid he joined a group of Germans who were trying to make their way to Austria but he was apprehended by Italian partisans at Dongo at the head of the lake of Como and summarily executed together with his mistress, Clara Petacci. In a clinical sense he was not mad, but in his attitude to life, he appears psychopathic, affected to an ever-increasing degree by a syndrome which brought him more and more within the no man's land of the mentally disturbed.

There is a striking similarity between his career and that of the German dictator Hitler.[6] Both men had a deprived childhood and a humiliating adolescence. Both men found a purpose and philosophy in their experience of war, and on the seed-bed of economic disorder and political futility reared the tree of a new political order for their peoples. Both were the victims of deteriorating health,[7] and became steadily more bizarre in their behaviour.

The British historian, A.J.P. Taylor, observed of Hitler that 'all his activities were rational' while Neville Chamberlain exlaimed after meeting him on 7 September 1938 that Hitler showed 'no signs of insanity, but many of excitement'. This was not, however, the impression which Hitler made on others. As early as 1930 Sir Robert Vansittart described him as this 'half-mad and dangerous demagogue'. Eight years later the British ambassador, Sir Neville Henderson, called him a 'mystic, a psychopath or a lunatic; perhaps one, perhaps both, perhaps all three'. In the summer of 1942 Albert Speer confessed that Hitler 'often gave the impression of being mentally impaired'.

It is plain that as with Mussolini, indeed more obviously so than in Mussolini's case, his childhood environment and early life may help to explain the development of what we may describe as his personality disorder. His father, Alois, who was a senior collector in the customs, was a strict disciplinarian and an inveterate smoker, which may explain Hitler's life-long detestation of tobacco, who never had an intimate relationship with his son. Although a womanizer, Alois married Klara Polzl, a girl twenty-three years younger than himself, in 1885; Hitler was born four years later in April 1889. Denied affection by her husband, finding consolation in her Catholic faith, Klara's life was an unhappy one, redeemed only by the deep love which her son felt for her. Her death from breast cancer in 1907 four years after her husband's decease was a traumatic blow to young Adolf. Hitler remained a solitary

Hitler at Berchtesgaden, Germany, 1937 (courtesy James Kyle)

figure and, apart from a romantic affair with a niece who subsequently committed suicide, and his later relationship with Eva Braun, Hitler never had many intimate women friends.

In his childhood he was a 'loner' and as such he was in many ways to remain, without real intimates, finding compensation in the unconscious images of his mind. The services which he attended at his mother's church where he was a chorister were to make an indelible impact less by the content than by the magic and ceremonial of the Mass; 'I used', he said later, 'to intoxicate myself with the splendour of the service.' Here may have been the seeds of that love of panoply and ceremonial which gave to the Nuremberg rallies a religious albeit pagan symbolism. At school he was thought to be argumentative and self-opinionated. It is at least arguable that this desire to vindicate the shortcomings of his childhood led in part to his making a decisive impact on a world which in early life had treated him roughly.

In many respects he remained immature and even childlike throughout his life. He got on better with children (and animals) than with adults, with whom he was sometimes ill at ease. He had a liking for childish things, for sweets and chocolates – he used to put seven spoonfuls of sugar in his tea – for going to the circus and to the cinema, where his enduring favourites were *Snow White and the Seven Dwarfs* and *King Kong*. He liked reading stories about American cowboys and Indians, especially the adventure stories of Karl May, a German who wrote about the American frontiers which he had never visited. Other habits, ingrained in him in boyhood, remained with him throughout life. The fantasies of childhood were to persist into adult life.

In adolescence he found the world a sad and hostile place. After his mother's death he went to Vienna where he made a small fluctuating income from the sale of his paintings; but although they revealed a modest artistic talent, he was refused admission to the local school of art, constituting yet another humiliation. At one stage his life-style sank very low and he found himself living with down and outs in a hostel.

It was in reaction to his inability to create a satisfactory niche in society that negatively he began to develop his anti-Semitic views and positively to be deeply stirred by the music of Wagner and the ideas which it incorporated. He was swayed particularly by hearing at Linz a performance of Wagner's *Rienzi* in November 1906; 'there was' his friend, August Kubizek, commented, 'something strange about Hitler that night. It was as if another being spoke out of his body, and moved him as much as it did me . . . it was a state of complete ecstacy and rapture.' Of all the early emotional and intellectual influences which shaped Hitler's mind Wagner's music, with its romantic Germanic folk mythology and neopaganism, was probably the most powerful and enduring. In 1939 he was to tell Frau Wagner that his political career had been inaugurated the day that he listened to *Rienzi*, and it was the overture to *Rienzi* which he ordered to be played at all major Nazi rallies. It is not surprising that one of his most treasured possessions should have been a letter which Wagner's patron, Ludwig II of Bavaria, had written.

From a degrading life of failure Hitler, like Mussolini, was rescued by the outbreak of the First World War. He was at Munich and at once joined up. War seemed to offer him an opportunity for service, a function and purpose which peace failed to provide. 'To me those hours appeared', he wrote, 'like a *deliverance* from the vexatious moods of my youth.' If his comrades found him serious and humourless, he was courageous, capturing four Frenchmen singlehanded and though he was never commissioned, like Mussolini ending his war service as a mere corporal, he twice received the award of the Iron Cross. When the armistice occurred in November 1918, bringing this compensating life of purpose to an end, he was extremely upset. 'I had not cried since the day I had stood at the grave of my mother.'

The immediate post-war years, set against the background of defeat and the unduly harsh peace settlement of Versailles, with their sorry tale of depression, unemployment and galloping inflation, provided Hitler with his entry into politics. He attributed Germany's defeat, the 'stab in the back' less to the generals than to the politicians and selfish sectional interests, which he conceived to be predominantly Jewish in origin. The party which he had formed, the National Socialists, made a violent but unsuccessful attempt to seize power in November 1923. Although the Beer Hall putsch failed, it gave Hitler a halo of martyrdom, even though he was only to serve nine months of his prison sentence, and an opportunity to publicize his aims. Within ten years he was the undisputed leader of the National Socialist party, crushing all opposition by fair and foul means, and was accepted by the senile German president, von Hindenburg, as the chancellor and Führer of Germany.

His meteoric rise can be explained in terms of the political and economic crisis which had left Germany in so desperate a state. He gave the nation back its self-respect as well as a real measure of prosperity. The evils of anti-Semitism and the later horrors of the concentration camps were screened from a grateful public or at least cast into oblivion. Even the outbreak of the Second World War was represented by his more devoted followers as being forced on the nation. In his early years Hitler seemed to respond to the political and social needs of his people, but his hypnotic hold over them may seem at first sight puzzling, if not inexplicable. The answer to his success seems to lie in Hitler's basic psychology and the evangelical message associated with it. He was a superb performer who staged his theatrical rallies with a masterly hand, employing the glowing pomp of a semi-religious ceremonial, so mesmerizing his audience. His semi-messianic role was supported by the glitter and glamour, the flags, music and uniforms of charismatic pageantry. He was well able to judge the mood of his audience and to move it to a passionate response.

Like many a religious prophet, he had developed a message simplistic in nature, which he articulated in his book *Mein Kampf* which showed incidentally that he was more skilled in the spoken than the written word. 'I believe,' he said in 1938, 'that it was God's will that [from Austria] a boy was sent into the Reich and that he grew up to become the leader of the nation.' 'Just like Christ, I have a duty to my own people.'

The roots of his message were to be found in a medley of uncritical readings of philosophy and history and in his earlier experience of life and in a cast of mind that was fundamentally unstable. At its base was his profound belief in the historic destiny of the Aryan race, for, as he wrote, 'blood is the cement of civilization'. 'All life', he affirmed at Chemnitz on 2 April 1928, 'is bound up in three theses, struggle is the father of all things, virtue lies in blood, leadership is primary and defensive.'

The corollary to this doctrine which became Hitler's overmastering obsession was that the principal obstacle to the fulfilment of his grand design was the evil conspiracy of Judaism to the obliteration of which he devoted all his efforts. 'The Jew is the personification of the Devil and all evil.' 'The mixture of races is the original sin of the world.' He was even worried personally by the possibility of his having a Jewish ancestry, based on a rumour that his father might have been the illegitimate son of Maria Anna Schikelgruber, a servant girl who had been seduced by a member of the Jewish family, the Frankenbergers.

Is it possible to explain the psychology which led to such bizarre conclusions and ultimately to a cost higher in human misery than any history had previously known? Was there any possibility of an organic disease which might have affected the balance of his brain? As with Mussolini, there was a suggestion which had the support of his masseur Felix Kersten that Hitler was the victim of neurosyphilis, but the Wasserman test which he took on 15 June 1940 had proved to be negative. Although Hitler had a morbid interest in sex, he may have been impotent. His niece Geli, with whom he had hints of an affair, asserted that he was affected by a 'masochistic coprophilic perversion', which involved getting sexual gratification through the act of defecation or urination upon his exposed head; but this, like the talk of a syphilitic infection, cannot be corroborated. Similarly ill-founded seems the suggestion made by his own doctor, Theodore Morell, that as a result of encephalitis Hitler had become a victim of manic-depressive insanity.

But with Dr Morell we are on firmer ground for while his reminiscences are often unreliable his notebooks[8] show that Hitler suffered for many years from a gastro-intestinal complaint, evidently chronic cholecystitis or disease of the gall-bladder, which gave him intense pain in the right part of the upper abdomen. As a result he had adopted a near-vegetarian diet and became a compulsive taker of the tablets which Dr Morell prescribed. Morell, who had been appointed his personal physician in 1936 was a supposed specialist in dermatology and venereal diseases but has been more accurately described by Trevor-Roper as a 'quack' and a 'charlatan'. He prescribed drugs for Hitler's complaint which, as in the case of President Kennedy, had ultimately very adverse effects. On Morell's advice, Hitler took up to sixteen tablets a day of Dr Koestler's Anti-Gas pills which contained strychnine and atropine. Morell administered methamphetamine, orally and intravenously, affording Hitler some temporary relief and investing him with a sense of well being. He recommended two golden vitamin tablets, containing caffeine and pervitin, which he ordered in immense numbers for Hitler's consumption. While many of these tablets were harmless and their effects innocuous, the cumulative consequences of Hitler's physician's polypharmacy, promoting amphetamine toxicity, may well have seriously disordered his nervous system, causing excitability and irritability, restlessness, insomnia, tenseness, volubility, poor judgement and a state of paranoia, all of them characteristic features of Hitler's personality.

There is, moreover, ample evidence to suggest that in the closing years of the war in other more physical ways Hitler's health was going downhill steadily, for latterly he had some of the physical symptoms of Parkinson's disease which may have affected his judgements adversely. In the later stages of the war he made impulsive and sometimes inexplicable decisions which had disastrous consequences for the German war effort. Electrocardiagrams indicated that he may also have been suffering from a 'rapidly progressive coronary arteriosclerosis' which would again explain the at times seemingly confused state of his mind.

Such symptoms, which were in the main developments of his later years, cannot by themselves explain the excesses of Hitler's personality, his paranoia and megalomania, his distrust of others, his hardness and brutality outside his small domestic circle, his obsessive belief that he was privileged by destiny to fulfil his objectives. Rather we are left with the conclusion that Hitler's character and the policies to which it gave rise can be accounted for mainly in terms of a personality disorder. In a well-argued essay Dr Park suggested that he may have been the victim of a psychomotor epilepsy emanating from the temporal lobe. 'His personality profile', he writes, 'is consistent with that form of psychomotor seizure victims', giving rise to unexplained fears, dreamlike delusions, speech automatism, aggression and paranoia. But there was no EEG evidence for such a disorder, and many of the symptoms mentioned above are typical of other personality disorders.[9]

Doubtless the humiliations which he had experienced in boyhood and early manhood led him to seek compensation by creating a world of grandiose fantasy. He was and remained an essentially solitary man who did not find it easy to make close friends. The only friend of his youth, August Kubizek, he broke with; and another of his familiars, Ernst Rohm, he was to sentence to death. His subordinates were often men of inferior quality, either physically, intellectually or morally: Hermann Goering, responsible for the Luftwaffe, was a morphine addict; Himmler a hypochondriac; Streicher, the gauleiter and editor of *Der Sturmer*, a sexual pervert; and Goebbels had a club foot. Eva Braun, the companion whom he was to marry on the eve of his suicide, was, as it were, a sponge who could absorb and still his ill-humour (as did his listening to Wagner's music). She was largely indifferent to politics and her role seems to have been like that of an affectionate and faithful dog.

In his boundless eccentricity he would brook no opposition. His anger found expression in outbursts of seemingly manic rage. When a Swedish visitor, Birger Dahlems told him in 1939 that England was likely to go to the defence of Poland 'his speech became more and more garbled, his whole behaviour gave the impression of a person who was not at all himself'. General Guderian, who was German Chief of Staff, described how in February 1945 he found Hitler with his 'cheeks flushed with rage, his whole body trembling . . . beside himself with fury and having lost all self-control. After each outburst of rage, Hitler would stride up and down the carpet edge, then suddenly stop immediately before me and hurl his next accusation in my face. He was almost screaming, his eyes seemed to pop out of his head and the veins stood out on his temples.' Eugene Dollmann, a henchman of Himmler, recalled how at a mention of the Rohm plot of 1934, he 'leapt up in a fit of frenzy, with foam on his lips . . . he ranted wildly about terrible punishments. . . . [He] raged for a full half hour; the visitors thought he must be mad.'

In Hitler's case as in Mussolini's his mind's grip on reality became steadily looser. That he lived more and more in a dream world of his own illusion was an expression

Mussolini and Hitler, about to deposit a wreath at the Temple of Hermes (© The Hulton-Deutsch Picture Collection Limited, London)

of his unbalanced mentality. He, like the Roman emperors of old, had subsumed a semi-divine status, 'the ultimate sense of the dynamic and *volkreich* being', 'a mystical and magnetic force drawing together *Volk* and State', 'the incarnation of the Spirit of the People, and it is only through this interpretation that the people are led to a full realization of itself.' Such ideas were the children of a fevered imagination, the outcrop of a disordered mind, rather than the reflections of a process of ratiocination. His final days were spent in the isolation of the remote fortresslike Wolfsschanze or in the Berlin bunker where, with his whole world toppling about him, he concentrated his attention on a model for the rebuilding of his native town of Linz.

Although Hitler may not have been mad in the clinical sense, even more than Mussolini he seems to hover on the brink of sanity. It may be that his personality was moulded by a conjunction of different developments, his childhood and early life, the pharmacological toxicity, the onset of Parkinson's disease. Robert Waite has suggested that many of the symptoms which he displayed were those of what is now called a borderline personality disorder.[10] Ultimately the secret to understanding Adolf Hitler lies in the deep wells of his unconscious.

By the side of Hitler and Mussolini, the third great dictator of the twentieth century, Joseph Stalin appears an elusive, secretive, mysterious personality, only rarely given to popular demonstrations or displays of rhetoric.[11] Stalin produced, and 'not on me alone', Sukanhov, later one of his victims, wrote 'the impression of a grey blur, dimly looming up now and then, and leaving no trace behind him.' But, no less than Mussolini and Hitler, he became the centre of a cult which portrayed him as a kindly, fatherly figure, smoking his pipe, fond of children, simple in his tastes. 'I want to howl, roar, shriek, bawl with rapture at the thought that we are living in the days of the most glorious, one and only, incomparable Stalin! Our breath, our blood, our life – here, take it, O great Stalin,' wrote the writer Alexei Tolstoy.[12] Children at school were taught to chant:

> Within the walls of the Kremlin there's a fellow
> He knows and loves all the land;
> Happy and fortunate are you because of him:
> He is Stalin and great is his name![13]

His statue, 16.5 metres tall, mounted on a pedestal some 33 metres high, dominated the capital of Soviet Armenia.

Like Mussolini and Hitler he had the capacity to bewitch and deceive his people. As a tyrant his record was even worse in the terms of the terror he instigated, the wanton murders and savage imprisonments in gulags and labour camps with which he maintained his regime, the endless procession of people, at least five million of them, he had had liquidated. On a single day in December 1938 he was to sign 3,182 sentences of death. The image popularly disseminated was light years away from the reality. His claims to genius of a sort cannot be denied. He was certainly a masterly organizer and manipulator, if brutal and ruthless in his methods. If at some stage in his career he had become genuinely attracted to the more idealistic qualities of Marxist dialectic, such idealism had been quickly subordinated to the pursuit of power, the elimination of criticism and the imposition of policy.

Stalin was in a direct line from Ivan the Terrible and Peter the Great, both men whom he held in high esteem. Talking with the film director Sergei Eisenstein and the actor who played the part of Ivan in Eisenstein's film, Stalin praised the tsar as a 'great and wise ruler who protected the country from the infiltration of foreign influence and tried to bring about the unification of Russia'.[14] Like Peter he saw himself as the creator of a new social structure of which he was himself the personal embodiment. Even his banquets bore on occasions some resemblance to the meetings of Peter's 'drunken synod', marked by drunkenness and horseplay. Stalin liked childish practical jokes such as having rotten tomatoes placed on the chairs on which his guests sat. The Yugoslav Milovan Djilas remembered how on one such occasion the guests were ordered to guess what was the outdoors temperature under the threat of drinking a shot of vodka for every error out of line.[15]

There was, as we have seen, an element of psychotic neurosis, if not worse, in the characters of Ivan and Peter, supplemented by the effects of organic disease. What of Stalin? Superficially he gives the impression of a startling if unattractive normality, less openly histrionic than either Mussolini or Hitler, a cold, calculating politician in pursuit of power. It has been suggested that he suffered from some degree of ill-health, a thyroid gland deficiency, myxoedema, which may be accompanied by some degree of mental aberration.[16] He had a slight physical deformity, the second and third toes of his left foot were joined and as a result of blood poisoning his left elbow was permanently stiff (for which reason he was apparently passed unfit for military service in 1916), but until his closing years he showed no very obvious signs of mental or physical degeneration.

Contemporaries do not seem to have doubted that Stalin was sane. His daughter Svetlana declared firmly that 'under no circumstances could one call him neurotic'. It was only after Stalin's death that Khrushchev, who described Stalin's mind as 'morbid' and 'sickly' stated that in his latter years Stalin was mentally unbalanced. 'It was during the war that Stalin started to be not quite right in the head.'[17] Shostakovich commented that he was mentally unbalanced, adding 'there's nothing odd about that, there are lots of crazy rulers, we've had our share in Russia.' Some evidence of such mental derangement, one of his biographers commented, came from a report compiled by the British Embassy stating that when his doctor was ordered to conduct a medical examination a number of men similar in appearance to Stalin were ordered to present themselves, so that he would not know which one was actually Stalin.[18] It seems unlikely that Stalin was in the ordinary sense of the word 'mad', but the story of his life, his pursuit and abuse of power, leaves an impression of abnormality which verges on the psychotic. We are left with the inescapable conclusion that Joseph Stalin was very likely what we should call a psychopath or sociopath.

His childhood shows the psychopath in the making. Born Iosif Vissarionovich Djugashvili in 1879 in the small Georgian town of Gori in a wretched hovel, later transformed by his henchman, Beria, into a marble shrine, Stalin, like Hitler and Mussolini, had a damaged upbringing with a father whom he hated and a mother who loved him. His father, Vissarion, was a ne'er do well cobbler, his mother Ekaterina Geladze. There was a persistent legend that attributed Stalin's paternity to a well-known Russian explorer, Nikolai Prezhevalsky, who had a brief affair with his mother, but, apart from Stalin's physical resemblance to Prezhevalsky, there is no confirmatory evidence. Vissarion was a drunkard who beat his wife and son, lost his business and became a factory worker at the Adelkhanov leather factory in Tiflis before he was stabbed to death in a drunken scrimmage in 1890 when Stalin was eleven years old. Although his mother beat her son, she was ambitious for his future, saved and scraped, working as a seamstress and laundress, to send him to the church school at Gori, for she remained a devout Christian. Stalinist legend was later to stress the loving relationship between mother and son, but the evidence for this is tenuous. When his mother died he did not attend her funeral nor allow a cross to be placed on her grave. He was, however, plainly an intelligent boy who by his mother's efforts, for his father had wanted him to work in a factory, went first to the church school at Gori and then at fifteen became a seminarian at Tiflis with the objective of becoming a priest. 'What a pity', she told him shortly before her death in 1936, 'you never became a priest.'

Stalin hated his father. 'Undeserved dreadful beating', so a school contemporary of his, Josef Iremashvili wrote later, 'made the boy as hard and heartless as the father himself. Since all people in authority over others owing to power or seniority seemed to him to be like his father, there soon arose in him a vengeful feeling against all people standing above him. From childhood on the realization of his thoughts of revenge became the aim to which everything was subordinated.' 'The alien force', as Robert Tucker put it, 'that his father represented had somehow been internalized within him.'[19]

His attitude to his mother was ambivalent. 'He was devoted', Iremashvili commented 'to only one person – his mother', but the evidence for deep affection is limited. She certainly slaved for him and lavished affection, but how far he really loved her is more doubtful. It may well, however, have been his awareness of his mother's faith in him which helped to invest him with the self-confidence which led to his unquestioning belief in his own capacity.

The little we know of his schooldays suggests that he was both a loner and a bully; in the words of Iremashvili, he was 'an unbalanced unrestrained and passionate character when he decided to go for something or achieve something. He loved nature, but never loved a living being. He was incapable of feeling pity for man or beast. Even as a child he greeted the joys and tribulations of his fellow schoolboys with a grimace. I never knew him to smile.' 'As a child and youth', he added, 'he was a good friend so long as one submitted to his imperious will'; he early idealized himself and identified himself with heroic figures in the fictional stories which he enjoyed reading, such as the courageous outlaw Koba who avenged his wrongs upon his enemies in Alexander Kazbegi's romantic novel *The Patricide*; Stalin for a time took the nickname of Koba.[20]

Although the young seminarian was reputed for his singing voice and initially for his regularity in attending the services, the seminary had little lasting influence over him, save by the harshness of its routine to confirm his growing anti-clericalism. 'He', so an inspector's report noted, 'several times spoke up to the inspectors. In general pupil Djugashvili is rude and disrespectful towards persons in authority, and systematically fails to bow to one of the teachers.' He gradually lost interest in and neglected his work and was attracted increasingly to radical political propaganda. Later he said it had been for this that he had been expelled from the seminary in 1899, but more probably it was because of his failure to turn up for an examination. It is possible that the format of the seminary's theological teaching, its rigid indoctrination of belief by rote, may have been carried over by Stalin both in the way he accepted and later transmitted Marxist dialectic.

His childhood had left him with a deep resentment not merely of authority but at the environment in which he had been brought up. He was a Georgian who never lost entirely his Georgian accent, but, perhaps in unconscious revenge for the treatment which his native state failed to give him, he treated Georgia unsympathetically, suppressing a nationalist rising there with brutal force in 1921. His feeling of inferiority may have been buttressed by his own physical unattractiveness, for he was short, no more than 5 ft 4 in tall, and pock-marked. His later behaviour, a recent writer has declared:

reflected an unconscious and irrational desire to alleviate anxieties caused by an impaired narcissism, stemming from the 'extreme dissimilarity of his relationships with his physically abusive father and his fanatically devoted mother,' which made 'inner conflict' inevitable. . . . [He] worshipped himself and hated himself. The first he externalized by promoting a narcissistic cult of personality. The second he dealt with by instituting a reign of terror, by turning the hatred outwards, especially towards objects that reminded him of his own latent homosexuality.[21]

Such an explanation may well seem speculative and far-fetched but it remains very probable that his future attitude towards his fellow men lay less in his conversion to Marxism than in the experiences of childhood and adolescence.

His rise from being a radical agitator and political prisoner to secretary of the party and so in fact if not in name head of state in the wake of Lenin's death is a matter of history. Once he had acquired power, the power which might be seen as a compensation for the shortcomings of early years, he emerged as a cold, egocentric, ruthless, self-contained politician, riding roughshod over his opponents. Bukharin commented:

He is unhappy at not being able to convince everyone, himself included, that he is greater than everyone; and this unhappiness of his may be his most human trait in him. But what is not known, but rather something devilish, is that because of his unhappiness he cannot help taking revenge on all people but especially those who are in any way higher or better than he . . . he is a small-minded, malicious man – no, not a man, but a devil.[22]

Comparing him with Lenin Boris Bazhanov declared that while both 'had a maniacal thirst for power', Stalin 'may have aspired to power to exploit it like a Genghis Khan, without burdening himself with suppositions such as "And what might this power be for?"'[23]

From the start of the Russian Revolution the Bolshevik leaders, Lenin and Trotsky, had made terror an instrument of policy both in the attainment and maintenance of power, so that Stalin's governance might seem only to differ from theirs in matters of degree, in his remorseless liquidation of his supposed enemies, of the kulaks, of the Church, of his own colleagues. 'I was remembering my friends and all I saw was corpses,' Shostakovich said, 'mountains of corpses.' Such was his pathological elimination of all who stood or were thought to stand in his way, consigned to labour camps or gulags or simply tortured and shot, that even in the 1930s some doubts might be raised as to his sanity. 'It is difficult', Professor McNeal admits, 'to demonstrate his insanity in the late 1930s on the existing evidence, and yet difficult to believe that his psychological condition was normal around 1937.'[24]

In the process of returning Russia to its introverted insularity, Stalin was effectually to help ruin its economy, to promote a Bolshevik imperialism which saw the absorption of the Baltic states and to repress any genuine democratic feeling until the age of *perestroika* in the 1990s. It was ironical that through a fatal mistake on Hitler's part, the Russo-German pact collapsed, and Stalin became the ally of Roosevelt and Churchill whom he consistently deceived and outmanoeuvred. Even the war, which did demonstrate in some sense Stalin's powers of leadership, and the fantastic sacrifice which the Russian people had to endure in the face of the German onslaught could not obliterate the fatal malaise with which he had injected his country.

Single-minded and ruthless, Stalin was obsessively suspicious, fearful of conspiracy and assassination. The food which he ate had first to be tasted; the tea that he drank was taken from sealed packets opened only by a special servant. Even the air in his apartment at the Kremlin had to be tested for toxic particles.

Stalin appears as a man without any real friends, incapable of caring, unloved and without compassion. It was said that he had some affection for his first wife, Ekaterina Svanidze whom he had married in 1902, but she died giving birth to a son, and there were apparently occasions on which he treated her violently. 'This creature' he was reported to have said at her funeral, 'used to soften my strong heart. When she died all my warm feeling for people died with her.' He emerged, in the words of one of his English biographers, Alex de Jonge, as a 'psychological cripple, excluded by his handicap from the world of feeling, an exclusion that fired his capacity for envy and hatred'.[25]

He married again, his secretary, Nadezhda Allilueva, a devoted communist, who apparently shot herself in a fit of acute depression (her sister and her brother suffered from schizophrenia) at the age of thirty-one in 1932. Stalin did not remain celibate but he had no close companion. His relations with his children were distant and even hostile. His son Yakov, desperate at his father's treatment of him, made an unsuccessful attempt at suicide and angered his father by marrying a Jewess. Captured by the Germans, an event which his father esteemed a disgrace, he was apparently shot by the prison guards when he refused to re-enter his hut at curfew at the prison camp at Sachsenhausen which ironically later became a Russian death camp for the Germans. Vasily, a philanderer, an obvious disappointment to his father, died an alcoholic. His daughter Svetlana whom he treated with some affection so long as she obeyed him rebelled against his strict regime and married a Jew as her first husband. Stalin appears to have taken little or no interest in his eight grandchildren.

The principal elements of the psychopath seem to fit Stalin's character perfectly. He experienced paternal rejection and a humiliating childhood. He was an intelligent and able man who did not suffer from delusions or hallucinations and appeared to behave rationally, but he was wholly egocentric, never accepting blame or capable of guilt. He manipulated people to suit his own ends but seemed able to convince them through plausible explanations of his policy that he had their interests at heart. He was incapable of feeling for others and readily sacrificed all who opposed him. This lonely man had indeed the instincts of the psychopathic American mass murderer. He lacked all affectional ties. His sex life was impersonal and superficial. He seemed pathologically incapable of personal warmth and compassion, his life devoted to the pursuit of power until in late 1952 high blood pressure and attendant troubles brought on the stroke which killed him.

Nicolae Ceausescu, who with his wife Elena, was executed in the Roumanian revolution in December 1989, had a career which in some respects seemed in microcosm to resemble that of Stalin. A peasant upbringing had made him into a radical socialist. By trade originally a cobbler he attained supreme power, eliminating his opponents, and governed Roumania for twenty-four years as a tyrannical despot in the name of a Marxist creed which, whatever it had meant to him in his early years, became a screen for externalizing his personal ambitions. He evidently became more and more the victim of the legend that he had himself created. Surrounded by an army of sycophants who applauded their leader like so many robots, the *conducator* as he liked to be called became 'our lay god, the name for history and eternity'.

Oblivious of his people's impoverishment, he and his wife adopted a luxurious lifestyle and to commemorate their achievement readily destroyed some sixteen churches, three monasteries and hundreds of houses in Bucharest to create a boulevard of socialist victory and a palace which in its size and splendour was to surpass Versailles. For Ceausescu the Roumanians were the descendants of the ancient Dacians and he himself the successor to the emperor Trajan, an unworthy choice since in character

Nicolae Ceausescu, Romanian president (© The Hulton-Deutsch Picture Collection Limited, London)

and performance he seemed more closely to resemble Trajan's predecessor, Domitian. Megalomaniac as he was, like Stalin, he was always fearful of the possibility of conspiracy. He had his food tasted and changed his suits frequently lest they might be impregnated with poison. His critics were given short shrift. Evidently the more he enjoyed power, the more he entered a fantasy world of his own. Whether he did in fact suffer from a basic personality disorder we have as yet insufficient evidence. 'Like Faust', it has been said of the hypo-manic politician, 'the demon he has evoked seems to be his abject slave and gives him all the elation of omnipotence – but only so long as he desires what the demon wishes. If he once allows himself to grieve for the Gretchens of his career, his demon slave at once becomes his fearful master and brings about his own destruction.'[26] 'Ceausescu', the Roumanian dramatist Eugene Ionesco declared, 'is a madman. His wife, thirsty for power, is also mad, and their son is an idiot, and it is these three who are being allowed freely to torture 23 million people.'[27]

The genus dictator, of which Mussolini, Hitler and Stalin were prototypes, and Ceausescu the most recent European example, seems to be a political phenomenon peculiarly characteristic of the modern world. Nor has such tyranny been confined to Europe. The Ugandan leader, Idi Amin, by some suspected of suffering from syphilis, showed many signs of imbalance, even if basically tribal feeling may account for his cruel and violent rule. The Libyan leader, Colonel Muamaar Gaddafi, reportedly the victim of more than one nervous breakdown, appears to have shown a lack of mental balance both in his actions and public pronouncements which suggests an element of insanity. The Central African ruler, the Emperor Bokassa I, was without doubt on the brink of madness, seemingly visualizing himself as the incarnation of Napoleon.

The latest recruit to this bizarre gang might be the president of Iraq, Saddam Hussein, who in his ruthless pursuit of power and fanatical Arabism trampled on civilized values. He was born in 1937 of a relatively humble family, for his father died when he was young and his uncle, an army officer, treated him violently and showed him little affection. A failure at school, he soon became identified with the objectives of the Arab Baath Socialist Party, and was in the future to overcompensate for the trials and tribulations of his youth and adolescence. Like Stalin he became trained in the art of political assassination, seeking to win his spurs in the murder, bungled though it was to be, of the communist-backed military ruler, Abdel Karim Quassem. A professional political agitator, he pursued his single-minded aims with success, propagating an image which through the cultivation of anti-Zionism and anti-Americanism made an appeal to many Arabs. Never in fact a professional soldier, for he had initially failed to gain admission to the military academy, he nonetheless portrayed himself as a military man dedicated to creating a single Arab nation under his own leadership, though as a good propagandist he adapted his role to suit his audience. Although he was himself a Sunni, he apparently fabricated his descent from the martyred founder of the Shia sect, the Imam Ali, and seemed to see twentieth-century Iraq as the legitimate successor to the Assyrian and Babylonian empires the ruins of which still litter his desert. Like others of his ilk, he sought to make his mark in building for posterity, erecting the great Monument of Victory in Baghdad where his two bare hands grasp the scimitars of war in a portentous archway to commemorate eight years of bloody war with Iran.

All judgements on living dictators must, of course, be highly speculative. There is insufficient evidence on the state of their bodily and mental health to make any conclusions possible. It would in any case be facile to suppose that every so-called tyrant or dictator is mad or even unbalanced. It could be argued that such men are merely outsize, ambitious, self-seeking politicians, capable of convincing themselves as well as their peoples that they somehow incarnate the true interests of their nations. Yet their actions leave us uneasy, even if the evidence is less than adequate to describe them as mentally unbalanced, for the ways in which they act seem to point unerringly to the manifestation of distinctive psychopathic qualities.

The dictator has a simplistic but distorted view of the world with paranoid undertones. For him the world is inhabited by good men and good ideas of which he is himself the embodiment, and by bad men and bad ideas which threaten his integrity and which must be destroyed. Indeed, because of his obsessively suspicious nature, representing a fundamental sense of inferiority and insecurity, the 'good men' can easily become 'bad men' and consequently need to be eliminated. The dictator is above all concerned to repair a basic lack of self-esteem by grandiose achievement, his desire for self-aggrandizement promoted by flamboyant ceremonial and by buildings designed for posterity. So Hitler constantly utilized the offices of the architect Speer to redesign Berlin. The dictator rationalizes his private aspirations by stressing his public and patriotic objectives. Since he cannot endure humiliation, criticism or insubordination, friends as well as foes may fall victim to his whims. In fulfilling his inner needs, both in his march to power and after its attainment, he will use terror and intimidation to liquidate his rivals and to defeat his opponents. He imposes his will by force and propaganda as well as by argument. In so doing he creates a personal mythology, designed purposely to enhance his heroic qualities, which has little or no basis in reality. He becomes the victim of self-deception which may very likely lead to his own destruction as well as bringing about untold suffering to others. The dictator lives, in words which Money-Kyrle used to describe the politician, 'in a kind of private jungle, full of false friends and treacherous enemies always waiting to entrap him, and against whom he must constantly defend himself by means of his superior ability. The basis of his illness is the conceptual distortion of the truth about the world.'[28]

The lives of the twentieth-century dictators serve to underline what broadly speaking has been the theme of this book, the extent to which bruised personalities who are entrusted with positions of great authority may make decisions and initiate policies which affect, often detrimentally, the lives of millions of their fellow human beings. The impact of a Hitler or a Stalin, let alone other malignant figures of our own age whom we have not considered, a Mao-tse-tung or an Ayatollah Khomeini, may indeed be incalculable.

Although it has become fashionable to interpret history in terms of social movements and impersonal forces, the historian ignores the personal aspect of history at his peril. Even if a leader seems only to be apparently expressing the aspirations of a social movement, the power which he or she exercises at any given moment may be sufficiently decisive to influence, even conceivably to change, the course of history. We have shown that such decisions may sometimes be less the result of ratiocination or of political idealism than the externalization of private desires, on occasions shaped by physical illness or mental imbalance.

What may be even more disconcerting, as we have observed earlier, is the extent to which the normal man or woman in the street can be hoodwinked or conned into giving his or her enthusiastic support to the most dreadful causes, sheltering under some patriotic, religious or other idealogical umbrella. There is unfortunately no guarantee that the crowds will not at some time in future history cheer hysterically yet another deranged dictator or some other dim-witted politician as the saviour of their country's wrongs.

'Mad World! Mad Kings! Mad Composition!' as Shakespeare had the Bastard say in *King John*. Are there any lessons to be learned? Although the mad kings and queens have gone, now no more than faded spectres who have retreated into a long-forgotten past, the problems which haunted their aberrant personalities and which in part promoted their own instability have not entirely disappeared. There is still the smell of gunpowder, if not of even more obscene odours, on the blasted heath of world affairs, still an abundance of crazy politicans, parading their personal obsessions and ambitions under the screen of altruism and patriotism, still a pack of dictators wielding immense power and kept in office by the terror which they can let loose and by the favour of a populace whom they have bewitched. Naked terrorism, blind in its total irrationality, streaks through the countryside of Northern Ireland and the once thriving towns of the Lebanon, Bosnia and umpteen other places. If misplaced religious enthusiasm, though still malignantly active in some quarters in Islam, has become happily a dying cause, social and political issues are capable of evoking irrational responses. In an age of supposed toleration, the persecution of minorities, based almost always on premises that are irrational, whether of coloured peoples, of homosexuals, of Jews or of any who depart from a supposed norm of conduct, continues. Men and women still speak in terms of the ultimate insanity of war, oblivious of a past which has shown repeatedly the uselessness of the human sacrifice which war ingests.

When shall we ever learn? 'If men could learn from history, what lessons it might teach us!', Coleridge wrote in 1831, 'But passion and party blind our eyes, and the light which experience gives is a lantern on the stern which shines only on the waves behind us!' It is terrifying that no less in 1993 than in the early days of ancient Rome the populace seems ready to accept and applaud the facile promises which their leaders parade before them. It may be that men and women as individuals seem often incapable of knowing what is in their true interest, and possibly if they did, they would be impotent to implement it. There are signs that in some respects even *perestroika* may be a false dawn. ''Tis a mad world, my masters.'

Yet it would be wrong to end on too pessimistic a note. If it appears often as if men and women have been caught captive in a stream of history which they cannot control, the victims less of a divine providence than of secular predestination, this study has none the less shown that individuals do in practice play a pre-eminent part in moulding the historical process. There is at least some comfort that it lies within the capacity of a vigilant and educated electorate to question the illusory idealism of self-seeking politicians and to save the nations from being bamboozled by men and women who, whatever the power of their rhetoric, are unfit to be invested with political responsibility.

Notes

Introduction

1. e.g. H. Zinsser, *Rats, Lice and History*, London, 1945; L.F. Hirst, *The Conquest of Plague*, Oxford, 1953; W.H. McNeill, *Plagues and Peoples*, Oxford, 1977.

2. II Kings, 19: 35–6; Herodotus, *History*, ii, p. 141.

3. J.F.D. Shrewsbury, The Plague of Athens, *Bulletin of the History of Medicine* (1950), pp. 1–25; P. Salway and W. Dell, The Plague at Athens, *Greece and Rome*, XXIV (1955), pp. 62–70; D.L. Page, Thucydides' Description of the Great Plague at Athens, *Classical Quarterly*, III (1953), pp. 97–119; E.W. Williams, The Sickness at Athens, *Greece and Rome*, XXVI (1957), pp. 98–153; Sir William MacArthur, The Plague of Athens, *Bulletin of the History of Medicine*, XXXII (1958), pp. 242–6; R.J. Littman and J. Littman, The Athenian Plague: Smallpox, *Transactions of the American Philological Association* (1969), 261–75; J.F.C. Poole and A.J. Holladay, Thucydides and the Plague of Athens, *Classical Quarterly*, n.s. XXIX (1979), pp. 282–300; James Longrigg, The Great Plague of Athens, *History of Science*, XVIII (1980), pp. 209–25; J.F.C. Poole and A.J. Holladay, Thucydides and the Plague: A Footnote, *Classical Quarterly*, n.s. XXXII (1982), pp. 235–6; J.A.H. Wylie and H.W. Stubbs, The Plague at Athens 430–428 BC: Epidemic and Epizootic, *Classical Quarterly*, n.s. XXXIII (1983), pp. 6–11; J.F.C. Poole and A.J. Holladay, Thucydides and the Plague: A Further Footnote, *Classical Quarterly*, n.s. XXXIV (1984), pp. 483–5.

4. Thucydides, *History of the Peloponnesian War*, II, cc. xlviii–liv.

5. Procopius, *History*, II, c. xxii.

6. Bede, *Ecclesiastical History*, III, cc. 27, 30; J.F.D. Shrewsbury, The Yellow Plague, *Journal of the History of Medicine*, IV (1949), pp. 15–47; Wilfrid Bonser, Epidemics during the Anglo-Saxon Period, *Journal of the British Archaeological Association*, 3rd ser., IX (1944), pp. 55–70.

7. P. Ziegler, *The Black Death*, London, 1969; J.F.D. Shrewsbury, *A History of Bubonic Plague in the British Isles*, Cambridge, 1970; J. Hatcher, *Plague, Population and the English Economy 1348–1530*, Cambridge, 1977; for a survey of plague and its social effects in later periods, Paul Slack, *The Impact of Plague in Tudor and Stuart England*, London, 1985. For the responsibility of the black rat as one cause of the disease, see Graham Twigg, *The Black Death; A Biological Reappraisal*, New York, 1985; David E. Davis, The Scarcity of Rats and the Black Death, *Journal of InterDisciplinary History*, XVI (1986), 55–70.

8. Donald R. Hopkins, *Princes and Peasants: Smallpox in History*, Chicago, 1983; Ann G. Carmichael and A.M. Silverstein, Smallpox in Europe before the Seventeenth Century, *Journal of the History of Medicine*, XLII (1987), pp. 147–68.

9. Percy M. Ashburn, *The Ranks of Death: A Medical History of the Conquest of America*, New York, 1947; E.W. Stearn and A.E. Stearn, *The Effect of Smallpox on the Destiny of the American Indians*, Boston, 1947; Peter Gerhard, *A Guide to the Historical Geography of New Spain*, Cambridge, 1972; H.F. Dobyns, An Outline of Andean Epidemic History to 1720, *Bulletin of the History of Medicine*, XVIII (1963), 493–515; D. Alden and J.C. Miller, Out of Africa: The Slave Trade and the

Transmission of Smallpox to Brazil, 1560–1631, *Journal of InterDisciplinary History*, XVIII (1987), pp. 195–223.

10. A. Briggs, Cholera and Society in the Nineteenth Century, *Past and Present*, XIX (1961), 76–96; R.J. Morris, *Cholera, 1832, The Social Response to an Epidemic*, New York, 1976; Francois Delaporte, *Disease and Civilization: The Cholera in Paris, 1832*, trans. A. Goldhammer, Cambridge, 1986; Richard J. Evans, *Death in Hamburg: Society and Politics in the Cholera Years*, Oxford, 1989.

11. S.N. Brody, *The Disease of the Soul, Leprosy in Medieval Literature*, Ithaca, N.Y., 1974.

12. C. Quétel, *Le Mal de Naples: Histoire de la syphilis*, Paris, 1986 trans J. Brodrick and B. Pike, London, 1992; Alfred Crosby, *The Columban Exchange: Biological and Cultural Exchanges of 1492*, Westport, Conn., 1972; Francisco Guerra, 'The Problem of Syphilis' in *First Images of America*, ii, 845–51; Richard Davenport-Hines, *Sex, Death and Punishment*, London, 1990.

13. ibid., p. 6.

14. See Dennis Altman, *AIDS and the New Puritanism*, 1986; Randy Shilts, *And the Band Played On*, New York, 1987; E. Fee and D. Fox, Contemporary Historiography of AIDS, *Journal of Social History*, XXIII (1988), pp. 303–14.

15. Norman Cohn, *The Pursuit of the Milennium*, London, 1957, pp. 124–38.

16. J. Barger, *Ergot and Ergotism*, London, 1931.

17. J.G. Fuller, *The Day of St. Anthony's Fire*, London, 1969.

18. C. Turnbull, *The Mountain People*, New York, 1972.

19. e.g. W. Sargant, *The Battle for the Mind*, London, 1957.

Chapter 1 The Wilderness of the Mind

1. *King Lear*, III, vi; IV, vi.

2. Roy Porter, *A Social History of Madness*, London, 1987, 38–9.

3. Roy Porter, *Mind's Forg'd Manacles, A History of Madness in England from the Restoration to the Regency*, London, 1987, pp. 1, 20.

4. Basil Clarke, *Mental Disorder in Earlier Britain*, Cardiff, 1975, p. 226.

5. Isidore of Seville, *Differentiarum*, 2, 17, 48; ed. W.M. Lindsay, Oxford 1911; *Patrologia Latina*, XXXIII, cols 77–8; *Etymologiarum Sive Originum*, lib. iv 5; *Pat. Lat.* LXXXIII, cols 184–5.

6. Valentinus, *Epitome of the whole course of physicke*, London, 1612, p. 9.

7. Daniel 4: 28–37; Penelope E.R. Doob, *Nebuchadnezzar's Children: Conventions of Madness in Middle English Literature*, New Haven, Conn., 1974.

8. Cf. John Saward, *Perfect Fools*, Oxford, 1980; M.A. Screech, 'Good Madness in Christendom' in *The Anatomy of Madness*, ed. W.P. Bynum, Roy Porter and Michael Shepherd, London, 1985, pp. 25–39.

9. Chaucer, *Nun's Priest's Tale*, lines 123ff.

10. E.J. Arnould, *Le Livre de Seyntz Medicines*, London, 1940.

11. Bede, *Two Lives of St. Cuthbert*, ed. B. Colgrave, Cambridge, 1940, c. 16.

12. Felix's *Life of Guthlac*, ed. B. Colgrave, Cambridge, 1956, c. 42.

13. *The Book of the Foundation of St. Bartholomew's Church in London* ed. N. Moore, Oxford, 1923.

14. E.A. Abbott, *St. Thomas of Canterbury, His Death and Miracles*, London, 1898, Vol. I, pp. 263–4, 269, 314; Vol. II, pp. 46–7.

15. Clarke, *Mental Disorder*, pp. 164–5; P. Grosjean, *Henrici VI Angliae regis miracula postuma*, Brussels, 1935; R. Knox and S. Leslie (eds), *The Miracles of King Henry VI*, Cambridge, 1923; B. Woolf, *Henry VI*, London, 1981, pp. 351–8.

16. Leges Henrici 78, 7: *Insanas et ejusmodi maleficos debent parentes sui misericorditer custodire.*
17. E.G. O'Donoughue, *The Story of Bethlehem Hospital*, London, 1914. Patricia Alldridge, 'Bedlam. Fact or Fantasy', in *The Anatomy of Madness*, Bynum, Porter and Shepherd, pp. 17–33.
18. M. Foucault, *Madness and Civilization*, London, 1967.
19. Porter, *Mind's Forg'd Manacles.*
20. Thomas Willis, *The Soul of Brutes*, Works, XII London 1684 pp. 206; Clarke, *Mental Disorder*, p. 294.
21. Porter, *Mind's Forg'd Manacles*, p. 32.
22. G. Zilboorg, *A History of Medical Psychology*, New York, 1941; I. Macalpine and R. Hunter, *Three Hundred Years of Psychiatry*, London, 1963.
23. e.g. Frank R. Ervin and Vernon H. Mark, *Violence and the Brain*, London, 1970; B. Kaada, 'Brain mechanism related to aggressive behaviour' in *Aggression and Defence*, ed. C.D. Clements and D.B. Lindsley, Berkeley, 1967.
24. Constantin von Economo, *Encephalitis Lethargica: Its Sequelae and Treatment*, trans. K.O. Newman, Oxford, 1931.
25. Claude Quétel, *Le Mal de Naples. Histoire de la syphilis*, Paris, 1986.
26. M.T. Tsuang and Randall Vanderamy, *Genes and the Mind. Inheritance and Mental Illness*, Oxford, 1980.
27. Anne Harrington, *Medicine, Mind and the Double Brain, A Study in Nineteenth-Century Thought*, Princeton, N.J., 1987.
28. For an interesting medical interpretation see John Butterfield and Isobel Ann Butterfield, 'Joan of Arc: A Medical View', *History Today*, VIII (1958), p. 628. For a fuller treatment see Marina Warner, *Joan of Arc*, London, 1981.
29. Gordon Claridge, *Origins of Mental Illness*, Oxford, 1985.
30. Sir George Pickering, *Creative Malady*, London, 1974.
31. K. Salzinger, *Schizophrenia: Behavioral Aspects*, New York, 1973; S. Arieti, *Interpretations of Schizophrenia*, New York, 1974; W.M. Mendel, *Schizophrenia, The Experience and its Treatment*, London, 1976; Manfred Bleuler, *The Schizophrenic Disorders*, trans. S.M. Clemens, New Haven, Conn., 1978; K.F. Bernheim and R. Lewine, *Schizophrenia*, New York, 1979; S.A. Shapiro, *Contemporary Theories of Schizophrenia*, New York, 1981; Gottesman and Shields, *Schizophrenia*, Cambridge, 1982; Ming Tsuang, *Schizophrenia*, Oxford, 1982.
32. Claridge, *Origins of Mental Illness*, p. 113.
33. Stanley W. Jackson, *Melancholia and Depression*, New Haven, Conn., 1986.
34. M.H. Stone, *The Borderline Syndromes*, New York, 1980.
35. Hervey Checkley, *The Mask of Sanity*, New York, 1982; Checkley considers Alcibiades as an example of a historical psychopath (pp. 197–203); S.B. Gaze, *Criminality and Psychiatric Disorder*, 1976; Michael Craft, *Psychopathic Disorders and their Assessment*, Oxford, 1966.
36. K. Magid and C.A. McKelvey, *High Risk*, New York, 1987, p. 21.
37. C. Petit-Dutaillis, *The Feudal Monarchy in France and England*, London, 1936, p. 79.

Chapter 2 Roman Orgies

The reliability of many of the Roman historians has been questioned. Tacitus and Suetonius were writing long after the events which they described; they were anti-imperialist in attitude and republican in sympathy. Both Dio Cassius and Herodian have been described as gossipy and anecdotal. Yet the force of their writing, and the stories they tell, if they need to be questioned, must be admitted. Dio Cassius was a contemporary historian of the events of the late second and early third centuries. Herodian probably wrote in his old age, in the late 240s; but he may well have been an eye-witness of some of the events he records, for he was in Rome, for instance, between 188 and 193, and though his history is not free from error, in many respects he seems a reliable and conscientious writer.

See R. Syme, *Tacitus*, Oxford, 1958; F. Millar, *A Study of Cassius Dio*, Oxford, 1964.

1. Suetonius, *Lives of the Caesars*, I, xlix, liv.

2. G. Marañon, *Tiberius*, London, 1956; Robin Seager, *Tiberius*, London, 1972; B.M. Levick, *Tiberius*, London, 1976.

3. Marañon argues that Tiberius was sexually timid: *Tiberius*, 9–19, 198–203.

4. Seneca, 100, VI, 32.

5. Suetonius, II, lxv.

6. ibid., III, xxiii.

7. Tacitus, *Annals*, III, iv.

8. Tacitus, *Annals*, VI, i. The unreliability of the rhetorical and anecdotal histories of Suetonius, Tacitus and Dio Cassius is stressed by F.B. Marsh, *The Reign of Tiberius*, Oxford, 1931.

9. Suetonius, III, xliii, xliv, lxii.

10. Marañon, *Tiberius*, 212.

11. J.P.V.D. Balsdon, *The Emperor Gaius*, Oxford, 1934; the most recent study is Anthony Barrett, *Caligula: The Corruption of Rome*, London, 1990.

12. Seneca, *De Consolatione ad Polybium*, XVII, 3.

13. Suetonius, IV, xxii.

14. Philo, *Legatio*, 76ff.

15. Suetonius, IV, xxii.

16. ibid., xix.

17. ibid.

18. ibid., xlvi, xlvii.

19. ibid., IV, lv.

20. A.T. Sandison, The Madness of the Emperor Caligula, *Medical History*, II (1958), 202–9; C. von Economo, *Encephalitis Lethargica*, Oxford, 1931; Henry Brill, Postencephalitic States or Conditions, *American Handbook of Psychiatry*, 2nd edn., ed. Sylvano Arieti, Vol. IV, New York, 1975, pp. 152–65.

21. A. Momigliano, *Claudius: the Emperor and his Achievement*, Cambridge, 1961; Barbara Levick, *Claudius*, London, 1990.

22. M.T. Griffin, *Nero, the End of a Dynasty*, London, 1984.

23. ibid.

24. Dio Cassius, LXXIII, 15.

25. Herodian, *History*, I, xiv, 8.

26. Dio Cassius, LXXIII, 17ff; Herodian, *History*, I, xv, 5.

27. ibid., 8–9.

28. ibid., xvi, 4–12.

29. The cause is obscure but Herodian mentions stomach trouble which led him to halt his troops 'while he went off with a single attendant to relieve his trouble' (IV, xiii, 4).

30. A very readable novel about these events is Alfred Duggan, *Family Favourites*, London, 1930.

31. Herodian, *History*, V. iii.

32. Dio Cassius, LXXX, 14.

33. ibid., 13.

34. ibid., 16.

35. Herodian, *History* V, vii, 6.

36. *American Diagnostic and Statistical Manual*, 1980, pp. 315–17.

Chapter 3 Medieval Trilogy

1. C. Petit-Dutaillis, *The Feudal Monarchy in France and England*, London, 1936, pp. 215–16.

2. *American Journal of Insanity*, LXVI (1910), pp. 445–64.

3. A.B. Steel, *Richard II*, Cambridge, 1962.

4. S. Painter, *The Reign of King John*, Baltimore, Md., 1949; W.L. Warren, *King John*, London, 1961; J.C. Holt, *The Northerners*, Oxford, 1961; J.C. Holt, *Magna Carta*, Cambridge, 1965.

5. Gerald of Wales, *De Principis Instructione*, *Opera*, ed. G.F. Warner, viii, Rolls Series, London, 1891, p. 301.

6. ibid., p. 309.

7. Arnulf of Lisieux, *Letters*, ed. F. Barlow, Camden Society, 1939, No. 42, p. 73.

8. *Materials for the History of Becket*, ed. J.C. Robertson, Rolls Series, London, 1882, Vol. VI, p. 72.

9. Roger of Wendover, *Flores Historiarum*, ed. H.G. Hewlett, Rolls Series, London, 1886, Vol. I, pp. 316–17; Painter, *King John*, pp. 270–1.

10. Richard of Devizes, *Chronicles of the Reigns of Stephen, Henry II and Richard I*, ed. R. Howlett, Rolls Series, London, 1884–90, pp. 111, 408.

11. Ralph of Coggeshall, *Chronicon Anglicanum*, ed. J. Stevenson, Rolls Series, London 1875, p. 138.

12. Annals of Margam in *Annales Monastici*, ed. H.R. Luard, Rolls Series, London 1864, p. 27.

13. ibid., p. 27.

14. Roger of Wendover, *Flores Historiarum*, p. 482.

15. Chalfont Robinson, *American Journal of Insanity*, LXVI (1910), pp. 445–64.

16. Hilda Johnstone, *Edward of Carnarvon*, Manchester, 1946, p. 124.

17. ibid., p. 86.

18. R. Higden, *Polychronicon*, ed. J.R. Lumby, 1882, Vol. VIII, p. 298.

19. Hilda Johnstone, The eccentricities of Edward II, *English Historical Review*, XLVIII (1933), p. 265.

20. Sir Thomas Gray, *Scalacronica*, ed. J. Stevenson, Edinburgh, Maitland Club, Vol. XL 1836, p. 75.

21. G.L. Haskins, *Speculum*, XIX (1939), pp. 73–81.

22. *Amis and Amiloun*, ed. M. Leach, Early English Texts Society, 1937; G. Mathew, *The Court of Richard II*, London, 1968, pp. 138–9.

23. *Chronica Monasterii de Melsa*, ed. E.A. Bond, Rolls Series, London 1867, Vol. II, p. 355.

24. Higden, *Polychronicon* VIII, p. 29.

25. ibid., p. 296; for a recent assessment see J.S. Hamilton, *Piers Gaveston, Earl of Cornwall 1307–12; Politics and Patronage in the reign of Edward II*, Hemel Hempstead, 1989.

26. *Vita Edwardi Secundi*, ed. N. Denholm-Young, London, 1957, p. 15.

27. T.F. Tout, *The Place of Edward II in English History*, rev. edn, H. Johnstone, Manchester, 1936, pp. 12–13n; Hamilton, *Piers Gaveston*, p. 75.

28. Marc Bloch, *The Royal Touch*, trans. J.E. Anderson, London, 1973, pp. 56–7.

29. *Chron. de Melsa*, II, pp. 335–6.

30. A.W. Goodman, *Cartulary of Winchester Cathedral*, Winchester, 1927, No. 233, p. 105.

31. J.R. Maddicott, *Thomas of Lancaster*, Oxford, 1970, p. 259ff.

32. Natalie Fryde, *The Tyranny and Fall of Edward II*, 1321–26, Cambridge, 1979.

33. ibid., pp. 163–4; G.O. Sayles, *Select Cases*, Selden Society, London, 1957, IV, p. 155.

34. Fryde, *Tyranny and Fall*, p. 15.

35. The account occurs in John Trevisa's translation of Higden's Latin *Polychronicon* (VIII, pp. 324–5); Trevisa was vicar of Berkeley.

36. G.P. Cuttino and T.W. Lyman, Where is Edward II? *Speculum* LII (1978).

37. A.B. Steel, *Richard II*, Cambridge, 1941; R.H. Jones, *The Royal Policy of Richard II*, Oxford, 1968; Anthony Tuck, *Richard II and the English Nobility*, London, 1973.

38. Steel, *Richard II*, p. 279.

39. *King Richard II*, III, ii, 54.

40. *Eulogium Historiarum* ed. F.S. Heydon, Rolls Series, London, 1863, III p. 378.

41. V.H. Galbraith, A New Life of Richard II, *History*, XXVI (1942), pp. 223–39.

42. Steel, *Richard II*, pp. 174–5.

43. Adam of Usk, *Chronicon*, ed. E. Maunde Thompson, London, 1904, p. 30.

44. *Dieulacres Chronicle*, in *Fourteenth Century Studies* eds. M.V. Clarke and V.H. Galbraith, Oxford 1937, p. 173.

Chapter 4 The Royal Saint

R.L. Storey, *The End of the House of Lancaster*, London, 1966; B. Wolffe, *Henry VI*, London, 1981; R.A. Griffiths, *The Reign of Henry VI*, London, 1981.

1. P. McNiven, The Problem of Henry IV's Health, *English Historical Review*, C (1985), pp. 761–72.

2. E.M.W. Tillyard, *Shakespeare's History Plays*, London, 1944.

3. S.B. Chrimes, The Pretensions of the Duke of Gloucester in 1422, *English Historical Review*, XLV (1930), pp. 101–3.

4. G.L. Harriss, *Cardinal Beaufort*, Oxford, 1988.

5. *A Chronicle of London*, ed. N.H. Nicholas, London, 1827, pp. 111–12.

6. *Chronicles of London*, ed. C.L. Kingsford, Oxford 1905, p. 285.

7. Wolffe, *Henry VI*, p. 41.

8. John Blacman, *Henry the Sixth,* ed. and trans. M.R. James, Cambridge, 1919.

9. Storey, *The End of the House of Lancaster*, p. 34; *The Brut*, ed. F.W.D. Brie, EETS, 1905/8, Vol. II, p. 485; *Excerpta Historica*, ed. S. Bentley, London, 1833, p. 390; C.A.F. Meekings, Thomas Kerver's Case, *English Historical Review*, XC (1975), pp. 331–45.

10. Storey, *House of Lancaster*, pp. 34–5.

11. John Whetehamstede's view of the king: *Registra Abbatum Monasteri Sancti Albani*, ed. H.T. Riley, Vol. I, pp. xvii, 248–61; Vol. II, pp. xvi–xvii.

12. R.F. Hunnisett, Treason by Words, *Sussex Notes and Queries*, XIV (1954), pp. 117–19.

13. Bale's Chronicle, *Six Town Chronicles*, ed. Ralph Flenley, Oxford, 1911, p. 140.

14. Whetehamstede, *Registrum*, I, p. 163.

15. Storey, *House of Lancaster*, p. 136.

16. *Paston Letters*, I, ed. J. Gairdner, Edinburgh 1910, pp. 263–4.

17. J.R. Lander, Henry VI and the Duke of York's Second Protectorate, *Bulletin of the John Rylands Library*, XLIII (1960), pp. 46–69.

18. *Rotuli Parliamentorum* V, pp. 241–2.

19. Basil Clarke, *Mental Disorder in Earlier Britain*, Cardiff, 1975, pp. 180–3.
20. *Paston Letters*, I, pp. 315–16.
21. *Foedera*, ed. J. Rymer, V, pp. 366.
22. Clarke, *Mental Disorder*, p. 184; Lander, *Henry VI and the Duke of York*, p. 51.
23. *Paston Letters,* I, p. 352.
24. *Rotuli Parliamentorum,* V, p. 453.
25. R.L. Storey thought this a possible diagnosis *(House of Lancaster,* pp. 136n, 252n.); Basil Clarke held that it was the most likely diagnosis *(Mental Disorder,* p. 186*),* but it was questioned by John Cole in *Welsh Historical Review* (1977), pp. 356–7. John Saltmarsh called Henry's illness depressive stupor *(King Henry VI and the Royal Foundations of Cambridge,* Cambridge, 1972, p. 11); Wolffe concluded that 'there is insufficient information' *(Henry VI,* pp. 270–1n.*).*
26. *Henrici VI Angliae Regis Miracula Postuma,* ed. Paul Grosjean, Brussels, 1935; *The Miracles of King Henry VI,* ed. and trans. Ronald Knox and Shane Leslie, Cambridge, 1923; Clarke, *Mental Disorder,* pp. 151–75; Wolffe, *Henry VI,* pp. 354–5.
27. ibid., p. 352.

Chapter 5 Happy Families

A. Brachet, *Pathologie mentale des rois de France*, Paris, 1903. Two recent studies: F. Autrand, *Charles VI*, Paris, 1986; R.C. Famiglietti, *Royal Intrigue: Crisis at the Court of Charles VI 1392–1420*, New York, 1986. Famiglietti has an excellent first chapter on Charles's psychosis, and lists the articles that have been written on his madness (p. 205 n. 2).

1. Brachet, *Pathologie mentale des rois de France*, p. 601.
2. *Chronique de Froissart*, ed. G. Reynaud, Paris, 1849, XII, p. 236.
3. H. Kimm, *Isabeau de Bavière, reine de France*, Munich, 1969; J. Verdon *Isabeau de Bavière*, Paris, 1981; C. Bozzolo and H. Loyau, *La Cour amoreuse, dite de Charles VI*, Paris, 1982, Vol. 1.
4. E. Jarry, *La Vie politique de Louis de France, Duc d'Orléans*, Paris, 1889; F.D.S. Darwin, *Louis d'Orléans*, London, 1936.
5. Brachet, *Pathologie mentale des rois de France*, pp. 621–4; *Chronique du religieux de St. Denis (R.S.D.)* ed. L. Bellaguet, Paris, 1839, Vol. II, p. 18. On Clisson, A. Lefranc, *Olivier de Clisson*, Paris, 1898.
6. *Oeuvres de Froissart*, ed. Kervyn de Lettenhove, Brussels, 1871, Vol. XV, p. 27.
7. *R.S.D.*, II, p. 18.
8. ibid., p. 20.
9. *Oeuvres de Froissart*, XV, p. 37.
10. For accounts see *R.S.D.* II, pp. 18–24; *Oeuvres de Froissart*, XV, pp. 26–48.
11. ibid., p. 42.
12. *R.S.D.*, II, p. 20.
13. *Oeuvres de Froissart*, XV, pp. 48–9.
14. ibid., pp. 77–8.
15. ibid., pp. 84–92.
16. *R.S.D.*, II, pp. 86–8.
17. ibid., p. 404.
18. Famiglietti, *Royal Intrigue, pp. 12–13.*

19. *Commentaries of Pius II*, ed. Adrian van Heck, Vatican City, 1984.

20. Juvenal des Ursins, *Histoire de Charles VI*, ed. Theodore Godelay, Paris, 1614, p. 220.

21. *R.S.D.*, III, p. 348.

22. Heidran Kimm, *Isabeau de Bavière*, Munich, 1969, p. 143.

23. Des Ursins, *Histoire de Charles VI*, p. 237.

24. Famiglietti dismisses the charge of adultery against the queen *(Royal Intrigue,* pp. 42–5) stating that the rumours, more specially of her supposed affair with Louis d'Orléans, appeared only later in the fifteenth century in a remark in a chronicle by Jean Chartier *(Chronique de Charles VII,* ed. Vallet de Viriville, Paris, 1858, Vol. I, pp. 209–10), composed before Chartier's death in 1464, and in a pastoral poem, 'Le Pastoralet', a fictional account designed to glorify Duke John the Fearless of Burgundy, possibly written between 1422 and 1425. The affair is alluded to by Jacques Dex in his *Chronicle of Metz* (c. 1438) and by the Flemish monk Adrien de But, writing between 1478 and 1488.

25. *R.S.D.*, VI, p. 72: Le Fèvre de Saint-Rémy, *Chronique*, ed. Morad, Paris, 1876–8, Vol. I, p. 292.

26. There is no reliable evidence but the marquis de Sade in his *Histoire d'Isabelle de Bavière, reine de France,* written in 1813 but only published in 1953 (ed. Gilbert Lely, Paris, 1953), claimed to have seen at Dijon a transcript of the trial in the course of which de Bosredon revealed under torture the queen's misdemeanours; the transcript was apparently destroyed in the French Revolution. De Sade's book is highly coloured and inaccurate.

27. *R.S.D.*, II, pp. 88–90.

28. ibid., pp. 542–6, 662–8.

29. ibid., III, pp. 114–16.

30. *Les Demandes faites par le roi Charles VI avec les responses de Pierre Salmon,* ed. G.A. Crapelet, Paris 1833, pp. 97–100; quoted in P.S. Lewis, *Later Medieval France*, London, 1968, p. 113.

31. *Choix de pièces ined.*, 1153; quoted in Lewis, *Later Medieval France*, pp. 113–4.

32. A. Coville, Jean Petit, *La Question du tyrannicide au commencement du XVe siècle*, Paris, 1932.

33. Richard Vaughan, *John the Fearless*, London, 1966, pp. 263–86.

34. Vale, *Charles VII*, pp. 8, 10–11, 27, 93–4, 135–6; Chastellain, *Oeuvres*, ed. Kervyn de Lettenhove, Brussels, 1863, vol. 11, pp. 181, 185–6; Brachet, *Pathologie mentale des rois de France*, pp. 64–6.

35. L. Ipcar, *Louis XI et ses médecins*, Paris 1936; on Louis's character, Lewis, *Later Medieval France*, pp. 116–19.

36. C. Petit-Dutaillis in *The Cambridge Medieval History*, Vol. VIII, pp. 274–5.

Chapter 6 Spanish Madness

Lives of Queen Juana include: M. Prawdin, *The Mad Queen of Spain*, London, 1938, which has an over-optimistic view of Juana's sanity: G. Imann, *Jeanne la Folle*, 1947; A. Rodríguez Villa, *La reina Doña Juana la Loca*, Madrid, 1944; Amarie W. Dennis, *Seek the Darkness*, 1953; M. d'Hulst, *Le Mariage de Philippe le Beau avec Jeanne de Castile*, 1958; Isabel's will is printed in *Testamento y codifico de la reina Isabel la Catolica*, ed. L. Vázquez de Parga, Madrid, 1969; for her husband Philip the Handsome's journeys to Spain: M. Gachard, *Collection des voyages des souverains des Pays Bas*, Vol. I, Brussels, 1876; Voyage de Philippe le Beau en Espagne en 1501, par Antoine de Lalaing, pp. 121–340; Deuxième voyage de Philippe . . . en 1506, pp. 389–430.

Fundamental is M. Gachard, *Don Carlos et Philippe II*, 2 vols. Brussels 1863. See also L. de Cabrera de Cordova, *Relatio vitae mortisque Caroli Infantis Philippi II*, Madrid 1715; M. Fernández de Navarrete, *Colección de documentos*, Vols XXVI, XXVII, Documentos relativos al Principe D. Carlos, 1842. There are modern biographies by Ghislaine de Boom, *Don Carlos*, Brussels, 1955, and C. Giardini, *Don Carlos*, 1956. Opposite, controversial views appear in Viktor Bibl, *Der Tod des Don Carlos*, Vienna/Leipzig, 1918, and Felix Rachfahl, *Don Carlos: Kritische Untersuchungen*, Freiburg-im-Breisgau, 1921. Manuel Fernandez Alvarez, *Don Carlos: Un Conflicta generacional del siglo XVI*.

1. Gachard, *Don Carlos et Philippe II*, I, p. 5.
2. ibid., p. 23.
3. ibid., p. 25.
4. *Calendar of State papers, Elizabeth, 1563* (Foreign), ed. J. Stevenson, London, 1869, p. 85.
5. Gachard, *Don Carlos et Philippe II*, I, p. 152.
6. *C.S.P. Elizabeth, 1562* (Foreign), ed. J. Stevenson, 1867, p. 483; Gachard, *Don Carlos et Philippe II*, I, p. 145.
7. ibid., p. 34.
8. ibid., p. 153.
9. ibid., II, pp. 395–6.
10. Brantôme, *Oeuvres Complétes*, ed. L. Lalanni, Paris, 1866, Vol. II, pp. 105–6.
11. Gachard, *Don Carlos et Philippe II*, pp. 72–92; *C.S.P. Elizabeth, 1562* (Foreign), p. 10.
12. Dionysius Daza Chacón (*c.* 1510–96), military surgeon to the Emperor Charles V, wrote *Pratica y teorica de cirugio en romance y en latin*. Valladolid, 1595. A translation of his account of Don Carlos's illness is in C.D. O'Malley, *Andreas Vesalius of Brussels 1514–64*, Berkeley, 1964, pp. 407–19.
13. ibid., pp. 296–302. Shortly before his death O'Malley gave the annual faculty research lecture at the University of California at Los Angeles in April 1969 on Don Carlos of Spain: A Medical Portrait.
14. *C.S.P. Elizabeth 1562*, p. 28.
15. ibid., pp. 29–30.
16. ibid., p. 32.
17. ibid., p. 29.
18. Gachard, *Don Carlos et Philippe II*, I, pp. 126–41; *Collecion de Documentos Inéditos*, Vol. XXIV, Madrid, 1834, pp. 515–53.
19. Lucio Ma Núñez, *Documentos sobre la curación del principe D. Carlos y la canonisación de San Diego de Alcala*, Arch. Ibero-Amer. 1914, pp. 424–6.
20. Gachard, *Don Carlos et Philippe II*, I, p. 89n.
21. ibid., p. 155n.
22. ibid., pp. 228–9.
23. ibid., p. 151.
24. ibid., II, pp. 418–20.
25. Brantome, *Oeuvres Complètes*, ed. L. Lalanni, Paris, 1848, pp. 125–7.
26. Gachard, *Don Carlos et Philippe II*, II, p. 390.
27. L.P. Gachard, *Lettres de Philippe II à ses filles les infantes Isabelle et Catherine*, 1884.
28. Gachard, *Don Carlos et Philippe II*, II, p. 403.
29. ibid., p. 450n.
30. ibid., p. 554.
31. ibid., p. 596.
32. *C.S.P. Elizabeth, 1556–8* (foreign), ed. A.J. Crosby, London, 1871, p. 513. On 28 August Cecil was informed that 'The Cause of his sickness was that for certain days he had eaten nothing, and had drunk

much cold water, and gone bare-legged by reason of the heads, whereby his stomach grew to such weakness that it was not able to keep any sustenance it received' (ibid., p. 534).

33. *The Apologye or Defiance of the Most Noble Prince William*, Delft, 1581.

34. De Boom, *Don Carlos*, pp. 118–19.

Chapter 7 Great Harry

F. Chamberlain, *The Private Life of Henry VIII*, London, 1930; J.J. Scarisbrick, *Henry VIII*, London, 1968; L. Baldwin Smith, *The Mask of Royalty, Henry VIII*, London, 1971; G.R. Elton, *Henry VIII*, Historical Association pamphlet, 1962; Carolly Erickson, *Great Harry*, London, 1979; Jasper Ridley, *Henry VIII*, London, 1984; Sir A.S. MacNalty, *Henry VIII, A Difficult Patient*, London, 1952; J.F.D. Shrewsbury, Henry VIII: A Medical Study, *Journal of the History of Medicine* (1952), 141–85; J. Dewhirst, The Alleged Miscarriages of Catherine of Aragon and Anne Boleyn, *Medical History*, 28 (1984), 45–56.

1. J.C. Flugel, 'On the Character and Married Life of Henry VIII' in *Psychoanalysis and History*, ed. Bruce Mazlish, Englewood Cliffs, N.J., 1963, pp. 124–49.

2. For a recent interpretation see Peter Gwyn, *The King's Cardinal*, London, 1990.

3. Peter Martyr, *Opus Epistolarum Petris Martyris*, Epist. DXLV; *Letters and Papers*, I, pt ii (1920) no. 3581, p. 1486.

4. Eric Ives, *Anne Boleyn*, Oxford, 1988, p. 56.

5. *Letters and Papers*, VIII (1885), no. 263, p. 104.

6. ibid., X (1887), no. 200, pp. 70–1.

7. ibid., no, 427, p. 172.

8. Edward Hall, *Chronicle*, ed. H. Ellis, London, 1809, Vol. I, p. 319.

9. *Letters and Papers* IV, pt ii (1872), no. 4358, 4546, pp. 1981, 1985.

10. ibid., no. 4597, p. 2003; *Love Letters*, ed. H. Savage, 1949, XVI.

11. *Letters and Papers*, IV, pt ii (1872), no. 4428, p. 1938.

12. MacNalty, *Henry VIII. A Difficult Patient*, p. 67.

13. See the interesting but unconvincing arguments of Ruth M. Warnicke, *The Rise and Fall of Anne Boleyn*, Cambridge, 1989, pp. 191–233. G.W. Bernard has argued that Anne was guilty of adultery and that this explains Henry's violent reaction (The Fall of Anne Boleyn) *English Historical Review*, CVI (1991), pp. 584–610, but has been refuted by E.W. Ives, ibid., CVII, pp. 651–74.

14. *Calendar of State Papers, Spanish* V, pt ii (1888), no. 17 p. 29.

15. *Letters and Papers*, X (1887), no. 947, p. 395.

16. ibid., no. 908, p. 377.

17. ibid., no. 909, p. 381.

18. ibid., VIII (1885), pp. 214–15.

19. ibid., VIII (1885), pp. 214–15.

20. *Cal. S.P. Span.*, V, pt ii (1888) no. 55, p. 122; *Letters and Papers*, X (1887), no. 901, p. 374.

21. *Cal. S.P. Span.*, IV, pt ii (1882), p. 638.

22. *Letters and Papers* X (1887), no. 901, p. 374.

23. John Strype, *Ecclesiastical Memorials*, Oxford, 1822, Vol. II, pp. 460–1.

24. Lacey Baldwin Smith, *A Tudor Tragedy: The Life and Times of Catherine Howard*, London, 1961.

25. *Letters and Papers*, XVI (1898), no. 712, p. 339.

26. ibid., no. 1332, p. 614.

27. ibid., no. 1426, pp. 665–6.

28. ibid., no. 589, p. 284.

29. ibid., XVII (1900), no. 178, p. 81.

30. ibid., XVIII, pt i (1901), no. 44, p. 29.

31. ibid., XII, pt i (1891) no. 1068, p. 486; *The Lisle Letters*, ed. M. St Clair Byrne, London and Chicago, 1981, Vol. IV, p. 288.

32. *Letters and Papers*, XII, pt ii (1891), no. 27.

33. ibid., XIII, pt ii (1893), no. 800, p. 313; ibid., pt i (1892), no. 995, p. 368.

34. ibid., pt ii, no. 800, p. 313.

35. ibid., XVI (1898), no. 589, p. 284.

36. *Cal. S.P. Span.*, VII, pp. 99, 100, 165; *Letters and Papers*, XIX, pt i (1903), nos 529, 530, pp. 326–7.

37. Chamberlain, *Private Life of Henry VIII*, pp. 208–10.

38. ibid., pp. 269ff; MacNalty, *Henry VIII*, pp. 159–65; Shrewsbury, Henry VIII, pp. 148–72.

39. S.M. Kybett, Henry VIII – A Malnourished King, *History Today* (Sept. 1989), pp. 19–25.

40. Shrewsbury, Henry VIII, 182–3.

41. Scarisbrick, *Henry VIII*, pp. 485; Elton, *Henry VIII*, p. 8.

42. Jasper Ridley, *Thomas Cranmer*, London, 1962, pp. 234–9.

43. *Cal. State Papers* (1834) II, p. 552.

44. Ralph Morice, *Anecdotes of Archbishop Cranmer* Camden Society, O.S. 77, p. 266.

45. *Letters and Papers* XVI (1898), no. 272.

46. ibid., no. 868, p. 411.

47. ibid., XIV, pt ii (1895) p. 64.

48. Erickson, *Great Harry*, p. 320.

49. *Letters and Papers*, XV (1896), p. 493. Only a short while previously Melanchthon writing to Henry had compared him to Alexander, Ptolemy Philadelphus and Augustus. He was now reacting to Henry's treatment of Cromwell.

50. ibid., XIV, pt i (1894), p. 53.

51. Lacey Baldwin Smith, *The Mask of Royalty*, London 1971 p. 234.

52. Foxe, *Acts and Monuments*, V, pp. 553 ff.

53. Baldwin Smith, *A Tudor Tragedy: The Life and Times of Catherine Howard*, pp. 132–3.

54. *Letters and Papers*, IV (1876), no. 5825, p. 2606.

55. There were five serious epidemics of the English Sweating Sickness (*Sudor Anglicus*), an illness distinct from the plague, first occurring in 1485, then in 1508, 1517, 1528 and finally in 1551. Conceivably a strain of influenza, it seems more likely to have been arbovirus in character. See Lorraine Attreed, Beggarly Breton and Faynte Harted Frenchmen. Age and Classic-specific mortality during London's sweating sickness of 1485, *Ricardian*, IV (1977) no. 59, pp. 2–16; J.A.H. Wylie and I.J. Linn, Observations upon the Distribution and Speed of the English Sweating Sickness in Devon in 1551, *Transactions of the Devon Society for the Advancement of Science,* CXII (1980), 101–15; J.A.H. Wylie and L.H. Collier, The English Sweating Sickness, A Reappraisal, *Journal of the History of Medicine* XXVI (1981), pp. 435–45.

In September 1528 the duchess of Norfolk wrote to Wolsey about the treatment of those suffering from the illness 'and if they be sick at heart I give them triacle and water imperial and divers both swell also their stomachs, to whom I give setwell to eat.' Wolsey, she advised him, should not let those who had the illness near him for a week. 'Vinegar, wormwood, rose water, and crumbs of brown bread is very good and comparable to put in a linen cloth to smell unto your nose, so that it touch not your visage.' The duke of Norfolk and some of his servants had had the complaint. 'My Lord, I never saw people so far out of the way in no disease as they be in this; and about 12 or 16 hours in the greatest danger. There be some that sweateth much, and some that sweateth very little . . . but the greatest surety is in any wise to keep your bed 24 hours' (*Letters and Papers*, IV, pt ii, no. 4710, pp. 2143–4).

Chapter 8 Swedish Saga

The principal source in English is Michael Roberts, *The Early Vasas*, Cambridge, 1968, pp. 199–241, with a full bibliography, pp. 482–5. See also a study of Eric's psychological problems in Viktor Wigert, *Erik XIV Historik-psykologisk studie*, 1920; Ingvar Andersson, *Erik XIV*, 1948.

1. Paul Reiter, *Christiern 2. Personlighed, Sjaeleliv og Livsdrama*, 2nd edn, Copenhagen, 1969.
2. Roberts, *The Early Vasas*, p. 201.
3. *Calendar of State Papers, Foreign 1559–60*, ed. J. Stevenson, London 1865, p. 86.
4. *C.S.P., Foreign 1558–9*, pp. 372–3.
5. ibid., p. 239.
6. ibid., pp. 404–5.
7. ibid., *1560–1*, p. 324.
8. R. Welford, *History of Newcastle and Gateshead*, London, 1884–7, II, 370.
9. *C.S.P. Foreign, 1562*, pp. 23, 71, 84, 132, 173, 190–1, 216–27, 298–9.
10. ibid., p. 412.
11. ibid., pp. 387–90.
12. Roberts, *The Early Vasas*, p. 241.

Chapter 9 Russian Bears

The sources for Ivan the Terrible's reign are unsatisfactory; see G.H. Bolsover, Ivan the Terrible in Russian HIstoriography, *Transactions of the Royal Historical Society*, 5th ser., VII (1957), 171–89. This is partly because of the bias of surviving contemporary accounts viz. *A.M. Kurbsky and Ivan IV, Correspondence, 1564–79*, trans. J.L.I. Fennell, Cambridge, 1955; and Prince A.M. Kurbsky's *History of Ivan IV*, ed. and trans. J.L.I. Fennell, Cambridge, 1965. In *The Kurbskii-Groznyi Apocrypha: The Seventeenth Century Genesis of the 'Correspondence' Attributed to Prince A.M. Kurbskii and Tsar Ivan IV* (Cambridge, Mass., 1971) Edward L. Keenan questioned the authenticity of the letters, which he attributed to the authority of a seventeenth-century writer Prince Semen Shakhovskoi. Whether genuine or not, the letters nonetheless convey well the flavour of the period.

Ivan has attracted biographers of which the very best may well remain K. Waliszewski, *Ivan the Terrible*, Paris, 1904, trans. Lady Mary Loyd, Hamden, Conn., 1966; other lives are by Stephen Graham (London, 1932), Jules Koslav (London, 1961), Ian Grey (London, 1964), Catherine Durand-Cheynet (Paris, 1981), and Henri Troyat [Lev Tatasov], trans. Joan Pinkham (London, 1985). Ruslan G. Skrynnikov, *Ivan the Terrible*, ed. and trans. Hugh Graham (1981), surveys the different interpretations placed on his reign.

For Peter the Great an important general survey is Nicholas V. Riasanovsky, *The Image of Peter the Great in Russian History and Thought*, Oxford, 1985; Vasily O. Kluchevsky, *Peter the Great*, trans. L. Archibald, New York, 1958; K. Waliskewski, *Peter the Great*, New York, 1897; Stephen Graham, *Peter the Great*, London, 1929; Ian Grey, *Peter the Great*, London, 1960; R. Wittram, *Peter I Tsar und Kaiser*, 2 vols, Göttingen, 1964; Alex de Jonge, *Fire and Water: A Life of Peter the Great*, London, 1977; The most recent authoritative biography is Robert K. Massie, *Peter the Great*, London, 1981; see also M.S. Anderson, *Peter the Great*, London, 1978.

A recent but not wholly convincing study is Hugh Ragsdale, *Tsar Paul and the Question of Madness. An Essay in the History of Psychology*, New York, 1988; see also Roderick E. McGrew, *Paul I of Russia*, Cambridge, 1993.

Chapter 10 The Bewitched King and His Legacy

There is no modern fully satisfactory study of Charles II. *Carlos the Bewitched* by J. Nada (John Langdon-Davies) (London, 1964), was largely based on the authoritative if conservative study by the duke of Maura, *Vida y reinado de Carlos II* (2 vols, 2 edn, Madrid, 1954), but there is an excellent study of Spain in Charles's reign, Henry Kamen, *Spain in the Later Seventeenth Century, 1665–1700* (London, 1980). A contemporary English source is Lord Mahon, *Spain under Charles II, extracts from the correspondence of Alexander Stanhope, 1690–99* (London, 1846).

For Philip V: William Coxe, *Memoirs of the Kings of Spain of the House of Bourbon*, 2nd edn, 5 vols, London, 1815; Alfred Baudrillart, *Philippe V et la cour de France*, 5 vols, Paris, 1890–1900; Edward Armstrong, *Elizabeth Farnese*, London, 1892; W.N. Hargreaves-Mawdsley, *Eighteenth-century Spain, 1700–1788*, London, 1979; J.L. Jacquet, *Les Bourbons d'Espagne*, Lausanne, 1968; John Lynch, *Bourbon Spain 1700–1808*, Oxford, 1989.

On Ferdinand VI: M. Dánvila y Collado, *Estudios españoles del siglo XVIII Fernando VI y Doña Bárbara de Braganza*, Madrid, 1905; A. Garcia Rives, *Fernando VI y Doña Bárbara de Braganza*, Madrid, 1917.

1. R.A. Stradling, *Philip IV and the Government of Spain 1621–65*, Cambridge, 1988.
2. C. Weiss, *L'Espagne depuis le règne de Philippe II*, Paris, 1844, Vol. II, p. 371, n.1, quoted in Kamen, *Spain in the Later Seventeenth Century*, p. 13.
3. ibid., pp. 67–105; H. Kamen, The decline of Spain; a historical myth? *Past and Present*, LXXXI (1978), pp. 24–50.
4. For a review of Charles II's health: Ramon Garcia Argüelles, Vida y figura de Carlos el Hechizado, *Actas II Congreso Español de la Medicina*, Salamanca, 1965, Vol. II, pp. 199–232.
5. L. Pfandl, *Carlos II*, Madrid, 1947, p. 386.
6. Sir William Godolphin, *Historia Illustrata or The Maxims of the Spanish Court 1667–8*, London, 1703, p. 148.
7. Mahon, *Spain under Charles II*, p. 42.
8. ibid., pp. 50, 99.
9. ibid., pp. 102–3.
10. Impotence was long believed to be a consequence of witchcraft as the Dominican inquisitors, Henry Kramer and James Sprenger concluded in their classic book, *Malleus Maleficarum* (1487), trans. Montague Summers, 2nd edn, London, 1948; see also Uta Ranke-Heinemann, *Eunuchs for Heaven, the Catholic Church and Sexuality*, trans. John Brownjohn, London, 1990, pp. 200–13, 'Witchcraft-Induced Impotence'.
11. Mahon, *Spain under Charles II*, pp. 126, 134.
12. ibid., p. 135.
13. ibid., pp. 136–7.

14. ibid., p. 191.

15. A. Girard, La Folie de Philippe V, *Feuilles d'histoire de XVIIIe siecle III, Revue Historique*, Paris, 1910.

16. *Historical Memoirs of the Duc de Saint-Simon*, ed. and trans. Lucy Norton, London, 1972, Vol. III, p. 357.

17. ibid. II, p. 319.

18. ibid. III, p. 353.

19. Alfonso Danvila, *El reinado relámpo: Luis I y Luisa Isabel de Orléans, reine d'espagne*, Madrid, 1952.

20. A. Pimodan, *Louise-Elizabeth d'Orléans, reine d'Espagne*, 2nd edn, Paris, 1923.

21. Keene to Newcastle, 17 October 1732, quoted in Armstrong, *Elizabeth Farnese*, p. 288.

22. Keene to Newcastle, 2 Aug. 1738; Armstrong, *Elizabeth Farnese*, p. 344.

23. Marquis d'Argenson, *Journal et Mémoires*, Paris, 1859–67, V, p. 16.; Armstrong, *Elizabeth Farnese*, p. 387n.

24. On Ferdinand's health an account by his physician, A. Piquer, Discurso sobre la enfermedad de Rey Fernando VI, *Colección de documentos inéditos XVIII*, pp. 156–7, and by his confessor, C. Pérez Bustamente, *Correspondencia privada e inédita de P. Rivago, confesor de Fernando VI*, Madrid, 1936. C. Stryienski, Fernand VI, roi d'Espagne, *Chronique Medicale*, XI, 15 November 1902.

25. W. Coxe, *Memoirs of the Kings of Spain of the House of Bourbon*, London, 1815.

26. John Lynch, *Bourbon Spain*, Oxford, 1989, p. 376.

Chapter 11 Florentine Frolics

The last stages of Medici rule in Florence have not been particularly well documented but most useful is Harold Acton, *The Last Medici*, London 1932, reprinted 1988; and his translation, with an introduction by Norman Douglas, of the *Life of Gian Gastone*, probably by Luca Ombrosi, privately printed, Florence, 1930. See also *Istoria del Granducato di Toscana* by R. Galluzzi, 1781 which Horace Walpole found 'mighty modest about the Caprean amours of John Gaston and his elder brother' (*Letters*, 25, 214). Also G. Robiny, *Ultime Medici*, 1905 and Gaetano Pieraccini, *La Stirpe de Medici di Cafaggiolo*, Florence, 1925. On the cultural background Erich Cochrane, *Florence in the Forgotten Centuries 1527–1800*, Chicago, 1973.

1. G. Burnet, *Travels*, Dublin, 1725, pp. 128–30; For comments by English travellers on the state of Florence see Edward Wright, *Some observations made in travelling through France, Italy etc in the years 1720, 1721 and 1722*, London, 1730, p. 429.

2. Wright, ibid., p. 429.

3. Acton, *The Last Medici*, p. 179.

4. ibid., p. 235.

5. *Life of Gian Gastone*, pp. 43–4.

6. Acton, *The Last Medici*, pp. 239–40.

7. Settimanni, *Storia Fiorentina, 1721*, quoted in Acton, *The Last Medici*, p. 276.

8. Horace Walpole, *Correspondence,* Yale edn., ed. W.S. Lewis, XVIII, pp. 39–40. Pieraccini suggested that they might have been the cardinal's bastards (II, pp. 705–12), but in view of his sexual inclinations this seems rather unlikely.

9. Michel Guyot de Merville, *Voyages historique et politique d'Italie*. The Hague, 1729, Vol. I, p. 617.

10. Montesquieu, *Voyages*, Bordeaux, 1894, Vol. I, p. 30.

11. *The Memoirs of Charles Lewis, Baron de Pollnitz*, London, 1737, Vol. II, pp. 130–2.

12. *Life of Gian Gastone*, p. 50.

13. ibid., p. 70.

14. *The Memoirs of Baron de Pollnitz*, II, p. 133.

15. *Life of Gian Gastone*, p. 73.

16. Mark Noble, *Memoirs of the House of Medici*, London, 1797. His account of Gian Gastone (pp. 432–56) is taken practically word for word from de Pollnitz's *Memoirs*.

17. Quoted in Acton, *The Last Medici*, p. 311.

18. *Memoirs of Baron de Pollnitz*, I, p. 428.

19. Walpole, *Correspondence*, XXIII, pp. 237–8.

20. ibid., XVIII, pp. 159–60.

Chapter 12 Mad George

M. Guttmacher, *America's Last King. An Interpretation of the Madness of George III* (New York, 1941), an interpretation of the king as a manic depressive; Charles Chenevix Trench, *The Royal Malady* (London, 1964), a scholarly and balanced account of the king's illness; Ida Macalpine and Richard Hunter, *George III and the Mad-Business* (London, 1969), a fresh, challenging and scholarly interpretation. For a contemporary account, *The Diaries of Robert Fulke Greville*, ed. F.M. Bladon, London, 1930, pp. 77–260.

1. Waldegrave, *Memoirs*, ed. Holland, 1829, p. 9.

2. H. Walpole, *Correspondence* ed. W.S. Lewis, Yale edn, New Haven 1937–74 Vol. XXII, pp. 23, 32.

3. ibid., p. 288.

4. Macalpine and Hunter, *George III and the Mad-Business*, pp. 14–16.

5. *Diaries and Letters of Madame d'Arblay*, ed. C.F. Barrett, 1904, Vol. IV, p. 131.

6. *The Journals and Correspondence of William, Lord Auckland*, ed. R.J. Eden, 1861, Vol. II, p. 244.

7. *Diaries of Robert Fulke Greville*, p. 133.

8. ibid., pp. 160–1.

9. ibid., p. 171.

10. L.G. Mitchell, *Charles James Fox and the Distintegration of the Whig Party, 1782–94*, Oxford, 1971, p. 126.

11. I. Macalpine and R. Hunter (eds), *Porphyria, A Royal Malady*, London, 1968, pp. 5–6.

12. *Memoirs of the Court and Cabinets of George III*, ed. duke of Buckingham, 1853, Vol. II, pp. 6–7.

13. Fred Reynolds, *Life and Times*, London, 1826, p. 164; quoted in R. Porter, *Mind's Forg'd Manacles*, London, 1987.

14. *Diaries of Robert Fulke Greville*, pp. 118–19.

15. ibid., p. 120.

16. Macalpine and Hunter, *George III and the Mad-Business*, p. 150.

17. *Diaries and Letters of Madame d'Arblay*, IV, p. 152.

18. J.W. Derry, *The Regency Crisis and the Whigs*, 1788–9.

19. *Diaries and Letters of Madame d'Arblay*, IV, 2 February 1789.

20. Macalpine and Hunter, *George III and the Mad-Business*, p. 119.

21. ibid., p. 125; *Historical Manuscripts Commission*, London, 1897, 15th Report Appendix, pt 6, pp. 733–4.

22. Macalpine and Hunter, *George III and the Mad-Business*, pp. 126–7.

23. ibid., p. 130.

24. ibid., p. 144; *Historical Manuscripts Commission*, Report on the manuscripts of J.B. Fortescue, Vol. X, London 1927, pp. 59–60.

25. Macalpine and Hunter, *George III and the Mad-Business*, pp. 160–1.

26. *The Letters of George IV 1812–30*, ed. A. Aspinall, Cambridge, 1938, Vol. II, pp. 298–9.

27. Walpole, *Correspondence*, XXXIV, p. 47.

28. Macalpine and Hunter, *Porphyria, A Royal Malady*, see subsequent correspondence in *British Medical Journal*, 3 February 1968, pp. 311–13; 17 February 1968, pp. 443–4; 24 February 1968, pp. 509–10; 16 March 1968, pp. 705–6. It has been suggested recently that George III's symptoms might be explained by lead-poisoning [plumbism] (McKinley Runyan, *Journal of Personality* Vol. lvi, 1988, pp. 295–326.

29. Geoffrey Dent, *The Porphyrias*, 2nd edn, London, 1971.

30. C. Rimington with Macalpine and Hunter in their *Porphyria*, 1968, pp. 21–2.

31. On Mary, Queen of Scots: Sir A. Macnalty, *Mary Queen of Scots*, London, 1960; The Maladies of Mary, Queen of Scots, *Medical History*, V (1961), 203–9; Macalpine and Hunter, *George III and the Mad-Business*, pp. 210–11. On James I: A.L. Goodall, The Health of James VI and I, *Medical History*, I (1957), 17–27; D.H. Willson, *James I*, London, 1956, pp. 336, 378–9, 404–5, 415–16; Macalpine and Hunter, *George III and the Mad-Business*, pp. 201–10.

32. John Brooke in *Porphyria*, pp. 58–65; *King George III*, London, 1972.

Chapter 13 Danish Charade

The principal study is Viggo Christiansen, *Christian Den VII's Sindssygdom*, Copenhagen, 1906, reprinted by Odense University Press in 1978 with a preface by Professor J. Schioldann-Nielsen and a postscript by Professor Niels Juel-Nielsen. There are two short and somewhat unhelpful contemporary reports: En Laegeberetning om Christian VII's Helbredstilstand, 1786, ed. Aa. Friis in *Historisk Tidsskrift*, Copenhagen 1907–8, 8R, 80–3 and Livlaege W. Guldbrand's Indberetning til Kronprins Frederik om Kong Christian VII's Sygdomsanfald ved Nytaar 1807, ed. Louis Bobé, *Personalhistorisk Tidsskrift*, Copenhagen, 1923, 8R (2B), 102–5. The most useful contemporary sources are E. Reverdil, *Struensée et la cour de Copenhague, 1760–72, Mémoires de Reverdil*, ed. A. Roger, Paris, 1858; and Struensee's own account of the king's state of mind compiled in 1772, in H. Hansen, *Inkvisitionskommissionen Af 20 Januar 1772*, Copenhagen, 1930, Vol. II, pp. 162–79.

See also: *Memoirs and Correspondence of Sir Robert Murray Keith*, ed. Mrs Gillespie Smyth, 2 vols, London, 1849, 2nd edn, *The Romance of Diplomacy*, 2 vols, 1862; Sir C.F.L. Wraxall, *Life and Times of Caroline Matilda*, 3 vols, London, 1864; W.H. Wilkins, *A Queen of Tears*, London 1904; P. Nors, *The Court of Christian VII of Denmark*, London, 1971; H. Chapman, *Caroline Matilda*, London, 1971; W.F. Reddaway, Struensee and the Fall of Bernstorff, *English Historical Review*, XXVII (1912), 274–86, and King Christian VII, *English Historical Review*, XXXI (1916), 59–84.

The most important book on Struensee is Stephen Winkle, *Johann Friedrich Struensee. Arzt. Aufklarer. Staasmann*, Stuttgart, 1982, 2nd revd edn, 1989. This contains two chapters on Christian's mental illness, 'Christian VII und seine verheimlichte Krankheit' (pp. 135–49) and 'Christian's fortschreitende geistige Umnachtung' (pp. 233–48). Winkle has also written Struensee, die Geisteskrankheiten und König Christians Leiden in *Hebel Jahrbuch* 1980, pp. 93–175.

I must express my grateful thanks for the help I have received, more especially on the bibliography, given to me by Dr J. Schioldann-Nielsen MD, Dr Med, who is writing on Christian VII, and by Dr Christine Stevenson of the Wellcome Institute for the History of Medicine who has contributed an essay on the treatment of lunacy in eighteenth-century Denmark, 'Madness and the picturesque in the kingdom of Denmark', to the *Anatomy of Madness*, ed. W.F. Bynum, Roy Porter and Michael Shepherd, Vol. III, London, 1988, pp. 13–47.

1. I. Macalpine and R. Hunter, *George III and the Mad-Business*, London, 1969, pp. 223–8.
2. Lady Mary Coke, *Letters and Journals 1754–1774*, 1970, Vol. II, p. 335.
3. Horace Walpole, *Correspondence* XXXV, ed. W.S. Lewis, Yale edn, New Haven, 1937–74, p. 327.
4. Reverdil, *Memoirs*, p. 10; 'Allons montrer ma poupée.'
5. ibid., pp. 2–5.
6. W.H. Sheldon, *The Varieties of Physique*, New York, 1940.
7. Roy Porter, *A Social History of Madness*, London, 1987, p. 53.
8. Wraxall, *Life and Times of Caroline Matilda*, I, p. 35.
9. Lady Mary Coke, *Letters and Journals*, I, p. 65.
10. N. Carter, *Letters*, Vol. III, p. 64.
11. Wraxall, *Life and Times of Caroline Matilda*, I, p. 87.
12. Nors, *The Court of Christian VII*, p. 71; e.g. *Kabinetsstyrelsen 1, Denmark, 1768–1772*, ed. Holger Hansen, Copenhagen, 1916–23, Vol. III, pp. 380, 397, 536, 537, 589.
13. Reverdil, *Memoirs*, pp. 129–32.
14. Walpole, *Correspondence*, XXXV pp. 325–6.
15. ibid., p. 326.
16. Lady Mary Coke, *Letters and Journals*, II, p. 341.
17. ibid., pp. 334–5.
18. Walpole, *Letters* VII, p. 57.
19. Lady Mary Coke, *Letters and Journals*, II, p. 336; Walpole, *Correspondence*, 7, pp. 42–3.
20. ibid., pp. 7, 57.
21. ibid., pp. 35, 323.
22. Lady Mary Coke, *Letters and Journals*, II, 349.
23. Reverdil, *Memoirs*, p. 154.
24. ibid., p. 301.
25. ibid., pp. 255–9.
26. ibid., p. 153.
27. Lady Mary Coke, *Letters and Journals*, III, p. 478.
28. *Memoirs and Correspondence . . . Keith*, I, pp. 234–6.
29. *A Faithful Narrative of the Conversion and Death of Count Struensee*, 1774.
30. H.B. Wheatley, 1884, Vol. IV, pp. 176–212; Vol. V, 397–421; Wraxall, *Life and Times of Caroline Matilda*, I, pp. 173–249; H. Chapman, *Caroline Matilda*, pp. 205–11; Macalpine and Hunter, *George III and the Mad-Business*, pp. 226–8.
31. Walpole, *Correspondence*, VII, p. 374.
32. Else Kai, *Sass, Lykkens tempel: et maleri af Nicolai Abildgaard*, Copenhagen, 1986, pp. 117, 119. The drawings are in the Danish State Archives (Rigsarkivet) in Copenhagen in the section 'Kongehusets arkivalilv A2 Christian VII's archive pk 5967.
33. *Memoirs and Correspondence . . . Keith*, I, p. 216.
34. *The Travel Diaries of Thomas Robert Malthus*, ed. P. James, Cambridge, 1966, pp. 62, 99.
35. E. Snorrason, King Christian VII's Death and Burial (in Danish with English abstract), *Nordisk Medicin-Historisk* Aabog, 1973, pp. 1–12.

Chapter 14 The Swan King

Henry Channon, *The Ludwigs of Bavaria*, London, 1933; Theodore Hierneis, *The Monarch Dines*, London, 1954; Desmond Chapman-Huston, *A Bavarian Fantasy*, London, 1955; Werner Richter, *The Mad Monarch*, Chicago, 1954. Wilfrid Blunt, *The Dream King*, London, 1970; Pierre Combescot, *Louis II de Baviere*, Paris, 1972; Christopher McIntosh, *The Swan King; Ludwig II of Bavaria* (London 1980), to whom I am indebted for translations of letters and documents from O. Strobel, *König Ludwig II und Richard Wagner*, Karlsruhe, 1936.

1. Ernest Newman, *The Life of Richard Wagner*, Vol. III, pp. 231–2.
2. Gottfried von Böhm, *Ludwig II*, Berlin, 1924, pp. 16–18.
3. Chapman-Huston, *Bavarian Fantasy*, pp. 133–7.
4. ibid., p. 104.
5. ibid., p. 173.
6. *Memoirs of Prince Chlodwig of Hohenlohe-Schillingfürst*, ed. F. Curtius, London, 1906, Vol. I, p. 354.
7. ibid., p. 150.
8. Otto Strobel, *König Ludwig II und Richard Wagner*, Vol. IV, p. 190; McIntosh, *The Swan King*, p. 100.
9. Otto Strobel, Introduction, *König Ludwig II und Richard Wagner*, Vol. I, p. xxxv, quoted in McIntosh, *The Swan King*, p. 39.
10. Strobel, *König Ludwig II und Wagner*, I, p. 105; McIntosh, *The Swan King*, p. 60.
11. Strobel, *König Ludwig II und Wagner*, I, p. 108; McIntosh, *The Swan King*, p. 61.
12. Strobel, *König Ludwig II und Wagner*, I, p. 161; McIntosh, *The Swan King*, p. 62.
13. Newman, *Life of Wagner*, III, p. 456.
14. Strobel, *König Ludwig II und Wagner*, III, p. 469; McIntosh, *The Swan King*, p. 68.
15. Newman, *Life of Wagner*, III, p. 471.
16. Strobel, *König Ludwig II und Wagner*, II, p. 192; McIntosh, *The Swan King*, p. 103.
17. Strobel, *König Ludwig II und Wagner*, III, p. 83; McIntosh, *The Swan King*, p. 163.
18. Newman, *Life of Wagner*, IV, p. 468.
19. Strobel, *König Ludwig II und Wagner*, II, pp. 224–5; McIntosh, *The Swan King*, p. 128.
20. Chapman-Huston, *Bavarian Fantasy*, p. 147.
21. ibid., pp. 166–7.
22. Arthur Ponsonby, *Sir Henry Ponsonby, Life and Letters*, London, 1942, p. 340.
23. Hohenlohe, *Memoirs*, I, p. 147.
24. R. Hacker, *Ludwig II*, Dusseldorf, 1966, p. 319; McIntosh, *The Swan King*, p. 179.
25. Hacker, *Ludwig II*, pp. 343–4; McIntosh, *The Swan King*, pp. 185–6.

Chapter 15 'An Infirmity' of Politicians

Hugh L'Etang, *The Pathology of Leadership*, London, 1969; and *Fit to Lead*, London, 1980; Bert Edward Park, *The Impact of Illness on World Leaders*, Philadelphia, 1986. A valuable examination of this problem, Jerrold M. Post and Robert S. Robins, *When Illness Strikes the Leader*, New Haven and London, 1993, was published after this book went to press.

1. Basil Williams, *William Pitt*, London, 1913, Vol. I, p. 220.
2. ibid., II, p. 241.
3. H. Montgomery Hyde, *The Strange Death of Lord Castlereagh*, London, 1959; Amphlett

Micklewright, The bishop of Clogher's case, *Notes and Queries*, CCXIV (1969).

4. L'Etang, *Pathology of Leadership*, p. 10.
5. David Marquand, *Ramsay Macdonald*, London, 1977.
6. ibid., p. 695.
7. ibid., p. 696.
8. ibid., p. 762.
9. Anthony Storr, *The Man in Churchill: Four Faces and the Man*, ed. A.J.P. Taylor, London, 1969, pp. 205–45, reprinted in Storr, *Churchill's Black Dog and other Phenomena of the Human mind*, London, 1989, pp. 3–51. On the younger Churchill, the Earl of Birkenhead, *Churchill 1874–1922*, London, 1989.
10. Sir Arthur Bryant, *The Turn of the Tide 1939–43*, London, 1957, p. 259.
11. Lord Moran, *Winston Churchill, The Struggle for Survival, 1940–65*, London, 1966.
12. R. Rhodes James, *Anthony Eden*, London, 1986, p. 370.
13. ibid., p. 11.
14. ibid., pp. 12–17.
15. ibid., pp. 362–6.
16. J.M. Post and Robert S. Robins, *When Illness Strikes the Leader*, pp. 68–9.
17. R.R. James, *Anthony Eden*, p. 594.
18. Alastair Horne, *Harold Macmillan*, Vol. II, 1989, pp. 540–66.
19. See e.g. Leo Abse, *Margaret, Daughter of Beatrice: a Politician's Psycho-biography of Margaret Thatcher*, London, 1989.
20. On the controversy over Wilson's illness, Edward A. Weinstein, *Woodrow Wilson: A Medical and Psychological Biography*, Princeton N.J., 1981; and subsequent articles in the *Journal of American History*, LXX (1984); Wilson's doctor, Cary Grayson wrote *Woodrow Wilson: An Intimate Memoir*, New York, 1980; and his wife, Edith Wilson, *My Memoir*, Indianapolis, 1939. For recent assessments B.E. Park, 'Prelude to Change' and 'Comments on the Medical Historiography of Woodrow Wilson' in *The Impact of Illness on World Leaders*, Philadelphia, pp. 3–76, 331–42.
21. ibid., p. 20.
22. ibid., p. 39.
23. H. Hoover, *The Ordeal of Woodrow Wilson*, New York, 1958, p. 293.
24. Edmund Starling, *Starling of the White House*, New York, 1946, p. 152.
25. Hoover, *Ordeal of Woodrow Wilson*, p. 237.
26. R. Scott Stevenson, *Famous Illnesses in History*, London, 1962, pp. 44–51; W.W. Keen, *The Surgical Operations on President Cleveland in 1893*, New York, 1928.
27. Park, *Impact of Illness*, pp. 231–94.
28. Ross McIntire later wrote a self-defensive book, *White House Physician*, New York, 1946.
29. J. Bishop, *FDR's Last Year 1 April 1944–April 1945*, New York, 1974.
30. Moran, *Churchill*, p. 226.
31. Russell D. Buhite, *Decisions at Yalta, An Appraisal of Summit Diplomacy*, 1986.
32. Harold L. Ickes, *The Secret Diaries*, London, 1955, Vol. II, pp. 30–1, 419. See also entries Vol. 1, 122, 151, 632, 637 ('he looks as if he might drop dead at any minute'); also Vol. II, pp. 609, 676.
33. L'Etang, *Fit to Lead*, p. 68; *The Pathology of Leadership*, pp. 106–8; Walter Millis, *The Forrestal Diaries*, London, 1952; L.L. Strauss, *Men and Decisions*, London, 1963, pp. 155–62; A.A. Rogon, *James Forrestal*, New York, 1964; Post and Robins, *When Illness Strikes the Leader*, pp. 105–14.
34. Ickes, *The Secret Diaries* Vol. III, p. 616.
35. Moran, *Churchill*, pp. 226–7, 'Physically he is only half in this world.'

36. See e.g. C. David Heymann, *A Woman Called Jackie*, London, 1989; Alastair Horne, *Macmillan*, London, 1989, Vol. II, p. 289.

37. On Kennedy's health, Theodore C. Sorenson, *Kennedy*, London, 1965, pp. 38–42, 568–9; H.S. Parmet, *The Struggle of John F. Kennedy*, New York, 1980, pp. 15–16, 45, 115–16, 121–2, 154, 165, 190–2, 238, 307–20; Peter Collier and David Horowitz, *The Kennedys*, London, 1984.

38. L'Etang, *Fit to Lead*, pp. 93–5.

39. H. Blair Neatby, *W.. Mackenzie King*, 2 vols, Toronto, 1965/76; C.P. Stacey, *A Very Double Life: The Private World of Mackenzie King*, Toronto, 1976. An edited version of King's diary was published as *The Mackenzie King Record*, ed. J.W. Pickersgill, Chicago, 1960.

40. Stacey, *A Very Double Life*, p. 139.

41. Neatby, *Mackenzie King* I, p. 203; Stacey, *A Very Double Life*, p. 163 ff.

42. ibid., p. 169.

43. ibid., p. 187.

44. ibid., p. 210.

45. ibid., pp. 198–9.

46. ibid., pp. 175–6.

47. Park, *Impact of Illness*, pp. 77–148.

Chapter 16 Madmen in Jackboots

1. Harold D. Lasswell, *Psychopathology and Politics*, introd. Fred Greenstein, Chicago 1977, p. 16.

2. H. L'Etang, *The Pathology of Leadership*, London 1969, p. 202; Alwyn Lishman, *Organic Psychiatry*, Oxford, 1980. Another minor illustration of the way in which the course of history is occasionally affected by mental ill-health had occurred when Kemal Atatürk was fighting the Greeks. His victory had been made in part possible by the neurotic behaviour of the Greek general who stayed in bed all day in the belief that as his legs were made of glass they would break if he got up.

3. Robert M. MacNeal, *Stalin Man and Ruler*, London, 1988, pp. 291ff.

4. Denis Mack Smith, *Mussolini*, London, 1981.

5. ibid., p. 151.

6. Among many works, Alan Bullock, *Hitler, A Study in Tyranny*, rev. edn, London, 1973; H. R. Trevor-Roper, *The Last Days of Hitler*, rev. edn, London, 1978; Robert G.L. Waite, *The Psychopathic God: Adolf Hitler*, New York, 1977; N. Bromberg and V. Small, *Hitler and Psychopathology*, New York, 1983; A.W.C. Langer, *The Mind of Adolf Hitler: the Secret Wartime Report*, New York, 1973; Alan Bullock, *Hitler and Stalin*, London, 1991.

7. Leonard Heston and Renate Heston, *The Medical Casebook of Adolf Hitler*, London, 1979.

8. David Irving, *The Secret Diaries of Hitler's Doctor*, New York, 1983;

9. B.E. Park, *The Impact of Illness on World Leaders*, Philadelphia, 1986, pp. 149–219, 343–53.

10. Robert Waite, *The Psychopathic God.*, p. 378.

11. Among many books, Robert Tucker, *Stalin as Revolutionary 1879–1929. A Study in History and Personality*, New York, 1973, esp. pp. 69–114 and 421–93; Alex de Jonge, *Stalin and the Shaping of the Soviet Union*, London, 1986; Robert M. Slusser, *Stalin in October: The Man Who Missed the Revolution*, Baltimore, Md, 1987; Robert H. McNeal, *Stalin Man and Ruler*, London, 1988; Daniel Rancour-Lafferiere, *The Mind of Stalin. A Psychoanalytic Study*, Ann Arbor, 1988.

12. De Jonge, *Stalin and the Shaping of the Soviet Union*, p. 304; Tucker, *Stalin as Revolutionary*.

13. McNeal, *Stalin*, p. 227.

14. ibid., p. 298.
15. ibid., p. 265.
16. L'Etang, *Pathology of Leadership*, p. 194.
17. McNeal, *Stalin*, p. 182.
18. De Jonge, *Stalin and the Shaping of the Soviet Union*, p. 378.
19. Tucker, *Stalin as Revolutionary*, p. 74.
20. De Jonge, *Stalin and the Shaping of the Soviet Union*, p. 11.
21. Rancour-Lafferiere, *The Mind of Stalin*, pp. 118–19. Lafferiere suggests that Stalin felt a homosexual attraction for Hitler, his 'favourite' aggressor and that he may have had a homosexual relationship with one of his bodyguards, but as one of his recent reviewers has intimated, the evidence for such charges is tenuous and the judgement highly speculative.
22. Tucker, *Stalin as Revolutionary*, pp. 424–5.
23. De Jonge, *Stalin and the Shaping of the Soviet Union*, p. 104.
24. McNeal, *Stalin*, p. 183.
25. De Jonge *Stalin and the Shaping of the Soviet Union*, p. 74.
26. R.E. Money-Kyrle, *Psychoanalysis and Politics*, London, 1951, p. 75.
27. John Sweeney, *The Life and Times of Nicolae Caeusescu*, London, 1992; Edward Behr, *Kiss the Hand you cannot Bite*, London, 1992.
28. R.E. Money-Kyrle, *Psychoanalysis and Politics*, p. 76.

Genealogical Tables

The Roman Emperors

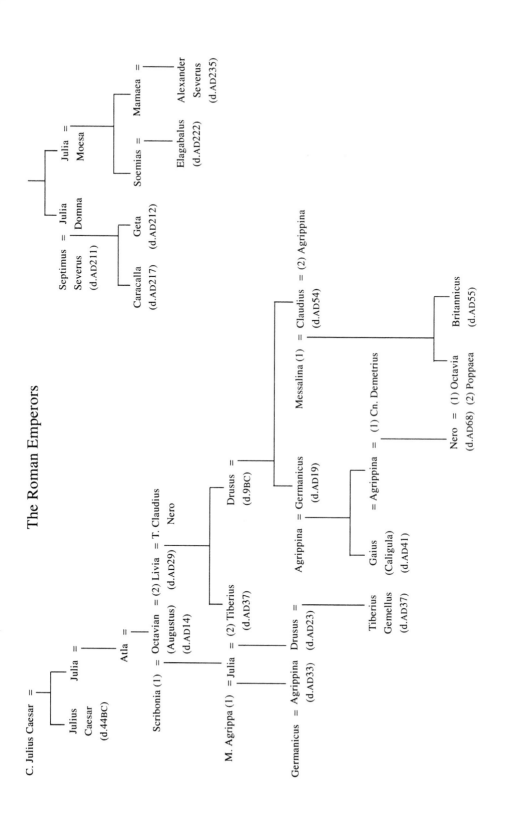

The English and French Medieval Kings

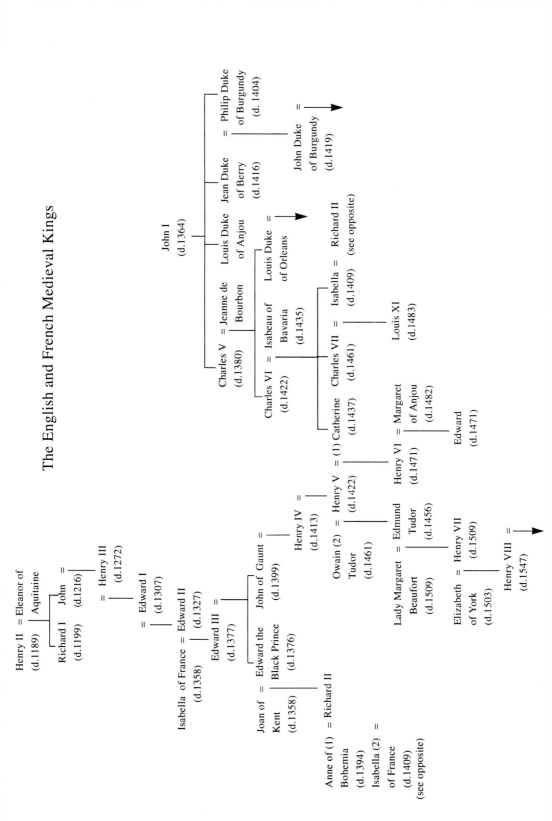

The Bourbons and Habsburgs

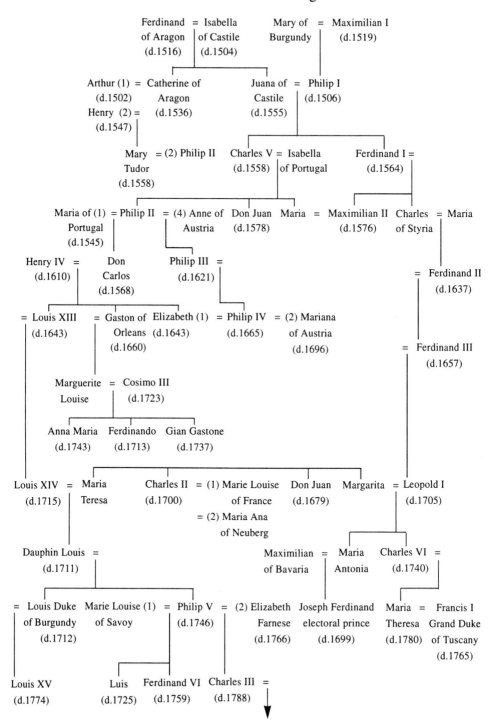

Index